INTEREST GROUP POLITICS

INTEREST GROUP POLITICS

Third Edition

edited by
Allan J. Cigler
Burdett A. Loomis

University of Kansas

A Division of Congressional Quarterly Inc.
Washington, D.C.

Cover design: Paula Anderson
Cover photo: R. Michael Jenkins

Copyright ©1991 Congressional Quarterly Inc.
1414 22nd Street, N.W., Washington, D.C. 20037

Printed in the United States of America

Second Printing

Library of Congress Cataloging-in-Publication Data

Interest group politics/edited by Allan J. Cigler, Burdett A.
    Loomis. -- 3rd ed.
        p.   cm.
    Includes bibliographical references and index.
    ISBN 0-87187-562-4
    1. Pressure groups--United States.   I. Cigler, Allan J., 1943-
    II. Loomis, Burdett A., 1945-
JK1118.1565   1990
322.4'0973--dc20   90-49519
                                                                         CIP

CONTENTS

PREFACE

The last ten years have witnessed both the proliferation of interest groups and the resurrection of an interest group subfield within political science. Drawing on the theoretical work of such scholars as E. E. Schattschneider, Mancur Olson, and Theodore Lowi, a generation of political scientists has returned to the basic questions that earlier confronted Arthur Bentley and David Truman: Why and how do groups form? How do they influence the governmental policy-making process? Through the work of Jeffrey Berry, Jack Walker, and Kay Schlozman and John Tierney, among others, we have learned a great deal about what interest groups do and how they organize themselves. The largely empirical projects of these scholars, along with the investigations of political scientist Robert Salisbury and his associates, provide an overview of how groups and their lobbyists operate within the inherently uncertain environment of American politics.

We hope that the earlier two editions of *Interest Group Politics* have played some modest role in the resurgence of academic interest in interest group politics, a trend that has paralleled the proliferation of interests within almost all parts of the political process. In our first edition (1983), we attempted to elucidate the initial stages of these phenomena, as we struggled to place the increasingly active groups within the broad context of American politics. The second edition (1986) of *Interest Group Politics* provided additional examples of group proliferation, as well as evidence that many interests were assuming new roles in such diverse areas as abortion and agriculture policy. In political action committees (PACs), we bore witness to powerful forces that had learned quickly to direct their funding in ways that benefited congressional incumbents. Indeed, PACs have helped solidify the congressional status quo over the past decade.

In this third edition of *Interest Group Politics,* we see interest groups continuing to evolve as they come to terms with organizational maintenance concerns (such as Mancur Olson's "free-rider" problem) stemming from the increasing competitiveness among groups for funds, members, and so-called policy niches, and with post-Reagan policy subsystems (in agriculture or the environment, for example). Still, we maintain our focus on three central elements of interest group politics: participation (Chapters 2-7), elections (Chapters 8-11), and policy making (Chapters 12-17). Likewise, there is great continuity among many of the issues addressed by the contributors to this edition. Abortion, agriculture, PACs, and the nature of the lobbying community all warrant renewed attention, but often in the context of adaptation rather than innovation.

As always, we have enjoyed our working relationship with CQ Press. Joanne Daniels and Margaret Seawell Benjaminson oversaw this project with the expertise to which we have grown accustomed. Sabra Bissette Ledent skillfully edited the manuscript, and Ann O'Malley served as our perceptive, energetic production editor. Our contributors provided stimulating essays that arrived, for the most part, on time, and we greatly appreciate their work and cooperation.

Finally, we dedicate this book to Jack Walker, who offered us many insights and who, absent his premature passing, would have offered many more. We and all interest group scholars stand in his debt.

Allan J. Cigler
Burdett A. Loomis

1. INTRODUCTION: THE CHANGING NATURE OF INTEREST GROUP POLITICS

Burdett A. Loomis and Allan J. Cigler

From James Madison to Madison Avenue, political interests have played a central role in American politics. But this great continuity in our political experience has been matched by the ambivalence with which citizens, politicians, and scholars have approached interest groups. James Madison's warnings on the dangers of faction echo in the rhetoric of reformers ranging from Populists and Progressives near the turn of the century to contemporary so-called public interest advocates.

If organized special interests are nothing new in American politics, can today's group politics be seen as having undergone some fundamental changes? Acknowledging that many important, continuing trends do exist, we seek to place in perspective a broad series of changes in the modern nature of interest group politics. Among the most substantial of these developments are:

1. a great proliferation of interest groups since the early 1960s;

2. a centralization of group headquarters in Washington, D.C., rather than in New York City or elsewhere;

3. major technological developments in information processing that promote more sophisticated, timelier, and more specialized grass-roots lobbying;

4. the rise of single-issue groups;

5. changes in campaign finance laws (1971, 1974) and the ensuing growth of political action committees (PACs);

6. the increased formal penetration of political and economic interests into the bureaucracy (advisory committees), the presidency (White House group representatives), and the Congress (caucuses of members);

7. the continuing decline of political parties' abilities to perform key electoral and policy-related activities;

8. the increased number, activity, and visibility of public interest groups, such as Common Cause, and the Ralph Nader-inspired public interest research organizations;

9. the growth of activity and impact by institutions, including

corporations, universities, state and local governments, and foreign interests; and

10. a continuing rise in the amount and sophistication of group activity in state capitals.

All these developments have their antecedents in previous eras of American political life; there is little genuinely new under the interest group sun. Political action committees have replaced (or complemented) other forms of special interest campaign financing. Group-generated mail directed at Congress has existed as a tactic since at least the early 1900s.[1] And many organizations have long been centered in Washington, members of Congress traditionally have represented local interests, and so on.

At the same time, however, the level of group activity, coupled with growing numbers of organized interests, distinguishes contemporary group politics from the politics of earlier eras. Current trends of group involvement lend credence to the fears of such scholars as political scientist Theodore Lowi and economist Mancur Olson, who view interest-based politics as contributing to governmental stalemate and reduced accountability.[2] If accurate, these analyses point to a fundamentally different role for interest groups than those suggested by Madison and later group theorists.

Several contemporary studies, such as those by Olson and political scientists Robert Salisbury and Terry Moe, illustrate the weakness of much interest group analysis that does not account adequately for the reasons groups form and persist.[3] Only during the last twenty-five years, in the wake of Olson's path-breaking research, have scholars begun to examine realistically why people join and become active in groups. It is by no means self-evident that citizens should naturally become group members—quite the contrary in most instances. We are faced, then, with the paradoxical and complex question of why groups have proliferated, as they certainly have, when usually it is economically unwise for individuals to join them.

Interest Groups in American Politics

Practical politicians and scholars alike generally have concurred that interest groups (also known as factions, pressure groups, and special interests) are natural phenomena in a democratic regime—that is, individuals will band together to protect their interests.[4] In Madison's words, "the causes of faction . . . are sown in the nature of man," but controversy continues as to whether groups and group politics are benign or malignant forces in American politics. "By a faction," Madison wrote, "I understand a number of citizens, whether amounting to a majority or minority of the whole, who are united and actuated by some common impulse of passion, or of interest, adverse to the rights of other citizens, or to the permanent and aggregate interests of the community." [5]

Although Madison rejected the remedy of direct controls over factions as "worse than the disease," he saw the need to limit their negative effects by promoting competition among them and by devising an elaborate system of procedural "checks and balances" to reduce the potential power of any single, strong group, whether representing a majority or minority position.

Hostility toward interest groups became more virulent in an industrialized America, where the great concentrations of power that developed far outstripped anything Madison might have imagined. After the turn of the century many Progressives railed at various monopolistic "trusts" and intimate connections between interests and corrupt politicians. Later, in 1935, Hugo Black, then a senator (and later a Supreme Court justice), painted a grim picture of group malevolence: "Contrary to tradition, against the public morals, and hostile to good government, the lobby has reached such a position of power that it threatens government itself. Its size, its power, its capacity for evil, its greed, trickery, deception and fraud condemn it to the death it deserves." [6]

Similar suspicions are expressed today, especially in light of the substantial growth of PACs since 1974. PAC contributions to congressional candidates rose from almost $23 million in 1976 to $148 million in 1988, which amounted to almost a third of all their funds. Still, the number of PACs has leveled off at just over 4,000, and only a fraction of these are major players in electoral politics. Reformers in and out of Congress have sought to limit purported PAC influence, but as of 1990 legislators could not agree on major changes in laws regulating campaign spending or group activity. PACs continue to be an attractive target for reformers. One typical expression of dismay came from Common Cause, the self-styled public interest lobby: "The Special Interest State is a system in which interest groups dominate the making of government policy. These interests legitimately concentrate on pursuing their own immediate—usually economic—agendas, but in so doing they pay little attention to the impact of their agendas on the nation as a whole." [7]

Despite the considerable popular distrust of interest group politics, political scientists and other observers often have viewed groups in a much more positive light. This perspective also draws upon Madison's *Federalist* writings, but it is tied more closely to the growth of the modern state. Political science scholars such as Arthur Bentley, circa 1910, and David Truman, forty years later, placed groups at the heart of politics and policy making in a complex, large, and increasingly specialized governmental system. The interest group becomes an element of continuity in a changing political world. Truman noted the "multiplicity of co-ordinate or nearly co-ordinate points of access to governmental decisions," and concluded that "the significance of these many points of access and of the complicated texture of relationships among them is great. This diversity assures various ways for interest groups to participate in the formation of policy, and this variety is a flexible, stabilizing element." [8]

Derived from Truman's work, and that of other group-oriented scholars, is the notion of the pluralist state in which competition among interests, in and out of government, will produce policies roughly responsive to public desires, and no single set of interests will dominate. As one student of group politics summarized,

> Pluralist theory assumes that within the public arena there will be countervailing centers of power within governmental institutions and among outsiders. Competition is implicit in the notion that groups, as surrogates for individuals, will produce products representing the diversity of opinions that might have been possible in the individual decision days of democratic Athens. [9]

In many ways the pluralist vision of American politics corresponds to the basic realities of policy making and the distribution of policy outcomes, but a host of scholars, politicians, and other observers have roundly criticized this perspective. Two broad (although sometimes contradictory) critiques have special merit.

The first critique argues that some interests systematically lose in the policy process; others habitually win. Without making any elite theory contentions that a small number of interests and individuals conspire together to dominate societal policies, one can make a strong case that those interests with more resources (money, access, information, and so forth) usually will obtain better results than those who possess fewer assets and employ them less effectively. The numerically small, cohesive, well-heeled tobacco industry, for example, does well year in and year out in the policy-making process; marginal farmers and the urban poor produce a much less successful track record. Based on the continuing unequal results, critics of the pluralist model argue that interests are still represented unevenly and unfairly.

A second important line of criticism generally agrees that inequality of results remains an important aspect of group politics. But this perspective, most forcefully set out by Theodore Lowi, sees interests as generally succeeding in their goals of influencing government—to the point that the government itself, in one form or another, provides a measure of protection to almost all societal interests. Everyone thus retains some vested interest in the ongoing structure of government and array of public policies. This does not mean that all interests obtain just what they desire from governmental policies; rather, all interests get at least some rewards. From this point of view the tobacco industry surely wishes to see its crop subsidies maintained, but the small farmer and the urban poor also have pet programs, such as guaranteed loans and food stamps, which they seek to protect.

Lowi labels the proliferation of groups and their growing access to government "interest-group liberalism," and he sees this phenomenon as pathological for a democratic government: "Interest-group liberal solutions to the problem of power [who will exercise it] provide the system with stability by spreading a *sense* of representation at the expense of genuine flexibility, at the expense of democratic forms, and ultimately at the expense of legitimacy." [10] Interest group liberalism is pluralism, but it is *sponsored* pluralism, and the government is the chief sponsor.

On the surface, it appears that the "unequal results" and "interest-group liberalism" critiques of pluralism are at odds. Reconciliation, however, is relatively straightforward. Lowi does not suggest that all interests are effectively represented. Rather, there exists in many instances only the appearance of representation. Political scientist Murray Edelman pointed out that a single set of policies can provide two related types of rewards: tangible benefits for the few and symbolic reassurances for the many.[11] Such a combination encourages groups to form, become active, and claim success.

Climate for Group Proliferation

Substantial cleavages among a society's citizens are essential for interest group development. American culture and the constitutional arrangements of the U.S. government have encouraged the emergence of multiple political interests. In the pre-Revolutionary period, sharp conflicts existed between commercial and landed interests, debtor and creditor classes, coastal residents and those in the hinterlands, and citizens with either Tory or Whig political preferences. As the new nation developed, its vastness, characterized by geographical regions varying in climate, economic potential, culture, and tradition, contributed to a great heterogeneity. Open immigration policies further led to a diverse cultural mix with a wide variety of racial, ethnic, and religious backgrounds represented among the populace. Symbolically, the notion of the United States as a "melting pot," emphasizing group assimilation, has received much attention, but a more appropriate image may be a "tossed salad." [12]

The Constitution also contributes to a favorable environment for group development. Guarantees of free speech, association, and the right to petition the government for redress of grievances are basic to group formation. Because political organization often parallels government structure, federalism and the separation of powers principles embodied in the Constitution have greatly influenced the existence of large numbers of interest groups in the United States.

The decentralized political power structure in the United States allows important decisions to be made at the national, state, or local levels. Even within governmental levels, there are multiple points of access. For example, business-related policies such as taxes are acted upon at each level, and interest groups may affect these policies in the legislative, executive, or judicial arenas. Because several organizations such as the U.S. Chamber of Commerce are federations, their state and local affiliates often act independently of the national organization. Numerous business organizations thus focus on the varied channels for access.

In addition, the decentralized political parties found in the United States are less unified and disciplined than parties in many other nations. The resulting power vacuum in the decision-making process offers great potential for alternative political organizations such as interest groups to influence policy.

Finally, American cultural values may well encourage group development. As Alexis de Tocqueville observed in the 1830s, values such as individualism and the need for personal achievement underlie the propensity of citizens to join groups. Moreover, the number of access points—local, state, and national—contributes to Americans' strong sense of political efficacy when compared to that expressed by citizens of other nations.[13] Not only do Americans see themselves as joiners, but they actually tend to belong to more political groups than do people of other countries.[14]

Theories of Group Development

A climate favorable to group proliferation does little to explain how interests are organized. Whatever interests are latent in society and however favorable the context for group development may be, groups do not arise spontaneously as a result. Farmers and a landed interest existed long before farm organizations first appeared; laborers and craftsmen were on the job before the formation of unions. In a simple society, even though distinct interests exist, there is little need for interest group formation. Farmers have no political or economic reason to organize when they work only for their families. In the early history of the country before the industrial revolution, workers were craftsmen, often laboring in small family enterprises. Broad-based political organizations were not needed, although local guilds often existed to train apprentices and to protect jobs.

David Truman has suggested that increasing societal complexity is fundamental to group proliferation, characterized by economic specialization and social differentiation.[15] In addition, technological changes and the increasing interdependence of economic sectors often create new interests and redefine old ones. Salisbury's discussion of American farming is instructive:

> The full scale commercialization of agriculture, beginning largely with the Civil War, led to the differentiation of farmers into specialized interests, each increasingly different from the next. . . . The interdependence which accompanied the specialization process meant potential conflicts of interests or values both across the bargaining encounter and among the competing farmers themselves as each struggled to secure his own position.[16]

Many political scientists assume that an expansion of the interest group universe is a natural consequence of growing societal complexity. According to Truman, however, group formation, "tends to occur in waves" and is greater in some periods than in others.[17] Groups organize politically when the existing order is disturbed and certain interests are, in turn, helped or hurt.

Not surprisingly, economic interests develop both to improve their position and to protect existing advantages. For example, the National Association of Manufacturers (NAM) originally was created to further the expansion of business opportunities in foreign trade, but it became a more powerful organization largely in response to the rise of organized labor.[18] Mobilization of business interests since the 1960s often has resulted from threats posed by consumer advocates and environmentalists.

Disturbances that act to trigger group formation need not be strictly economic or technological. Wars, for example, place extreme burdens on draft-age men. Thus, organized resistance to U.S. defense policy arose during the Vietnam era. Likewise, broad societal changes may disturb the status quo. The origin of the Ku Klux Klan, for example, was based on the fear that increased numbers of ethnic and racial minorities threatened white, Christian America.

Truman's theory of group proliferation suggests that the interest group universe is inherently unstable. Groups formed from an imbalance of interests in one area induce a subsequent disequilibrium, which acts as a catalyst for individuals to form groups as counterweights to the new perceptions of inequity. Group politics thus is characterized by successive waves of mobilization and countermobilization. The liberalism of one era may prompt the resurgence of conservative groups in the next. Similarly, periods of business domination often are followed by eras of reform group ascendancy. Entering the 1990s, a period of post-Reagan reform may well develop, with groups pushing environmental and family issues coming to the fore.

Personal Motivations and Group Formation

Central to theories of group proliferation are the pluralist notions that elements of society possess common needs and share a group identity or consciousness, and that these are sufficient conditions for the formation of effective political organizations. Although the perception of common needs may be necessary for political organization, whether it is sufficient for group formation and effectiveness is open to question. Historical evidence documents many instances in which groups do not emerge spontaneously even when circumstances such as poverty or discrimination would seem to require it.

Mancur Olson effectively challenged many pluralist tenets in *The Logic of Collective Action,* first published in 1965. Using a "rational economic man" model as the basis of his analysis, Olson posited that even individuals who have common interests are not inclined to join organizations that attempt to address their concerns. The major barrier to group participation is the "free-rider" problem: "rational" individuals choose not to bear the participation costs (time, membership) because they can enjoy the group benefits (such as favorable legislation) whether or not they join. Groups that pursue "collective" benefits, which accrue to all members of a class or segment of society regardless of membership status, will have great difficulty forming and surviving. According to Olson, it would be economically irrational for individual farmers to join a group seeking higher farm prices when benefits from price increases would be enjoyed by all farmers, even those who contribute nothing to the group. Similarly, it would be irrational for an individual consumer to become part of organized attempts to lower consumer prices, when all consumers, members or not, would reap the benefits. The free-rider problem is especially serious for large groups because the larger the group the less likely an individual will perceive his or her contribution as having any impact on group success.

For Olson, a key to group formation—and especially group survival—is the provision of "selective" benefits. These rewards, such as travel discounts, informative publications, and the like, go only to members. Organizations in the best positions to offer such benefits are those initially formed for some nonpolitical purpose and that ordinarily provide material benefits to their clientele. In the case of unions, for example, membership may be a condition of employment. For farmers, the American Farm Bureau Federation (AFBF) offers inexpensive insurance, which induces individuals to join, even if they disagree with AFBF goals. In professional societies, membership may be a prerequisite for occupational advancement and opportunity.

Olson's notions have sparked several extensions of the rational man model, and a reasonably coherent body of "incentive theory" literature now exists.[19] Incentive theorists view individuals as rational decision makers, interested in making the most of their time and money by choosing to participate in those groups that offer benefits greater than or equal to the costs they incur by participation.

Three types of benefits are available. As an economist, Olson was most concerned with *material* benefits—tangible rewards of participation, such as income or services that have monetary value. *Solidary* incentives—the socially derived, intangible rewards created by the act of association, such as fun, camaraderie, status, or prestige—also are significant. Finally, *expressive* (also known as *purposive*) rewards—those derived from advancing a particular cause or ideology—clearly are important in explaining individual actions.[20] Groups formed on both sides of such issues as abortion or the Equal Rights Amendment (ERA) illustrate the strength of such expressive incentives.

The examination of group members' motivations, and in particular the focus upon nonmaterial incentives, allows for some reconciliation between the traditional group theorists' expectations of group development and the recent rational actor studies, which emphasize the barriers to group formation. Nonmaterial incentives, such as fellowship and self-satisfaction, may encourage the proliferation of highly politicized groups and, according to Terry Moe, "have the potential for producing a more dynamic group context in which politics, political preferences, and group goals are more centrally determining factors than in material associations, linking political considerations more directly to associational size, structure, and internal processes." [21] Indeed, pure political benefits may attract potential members as well, and even collective benefits can prove decisive in inducing individuals to join large groups. Like elected officials, groups may find it possible to take credit for widely approved government actions, such as higher farm prices, stronger environmental regulations,[22] or the protection of Social Security.

Finally, several recent studies indicate that the free-rider problem may not be quite the obstacle to participation that it was once thought to be, especially within an affluent society. Albert Hirschman, for example, has argued that the costs and benefits of group activity are not always clear; in fact, some "costs" of participation for some individuals, such as time and effort expended, might be regarded as "benefits," in terms of personal satisfaction, by others.[23] Other researchers have questioned whether individuals even engage in rational, cost-benefit thinking as they make membership decisions. Michael McCann noted that "there seems to be a general threshold level of involvement below which free rider calculations pose few inhibitions for . . . commitment from moderately affluent citizen supporters." [24] In short, there is increasing evidence that in the modern era individuals may join and participate in groups for reasons beyond narrow economic self-interest or the availability of selective benefits.[25]

Contemporary Interest Group Politics

Several notable developments mark the modern age of interest group politics. Of primary importance is the large and growing number of active groups and other interests. The data here are sketchy, but one major study found that most current groups came into existence after World War II and that group formation has accelerated substantially since the early 1960s.[26] Also since the 1960s groups have increasingly directed their attention toward the center of power in Washington, D.C., as the scope of federal policy making has grown, and groups seeking influence have determined to "hunt where the ducks are." As a result, the 1960s and 1970s marked a veritable explosion in the number of groups lobbying in Washington.

A second key change is evident in the composition of the interest group universe. Beginning in the late 1950s political participation patterns underwent some significant transformations. Conventional activities such as voting declined, and political parties, the traditional aggregators and articulators of mass interests, became weaker. Yet at all levels of government, evidence of citizen involvement has been apparent, often in the form of new or revived groups. Particularly impressive has been the growth of citizens' groups—those organized around an idea or cause (at times a single issue) with no occupational basis for membership. Fully 30 percent of such groups have formed since 1975, and in 1980 they made up more than one-fifth of all groups represented in Washington.[27]

In fact, a participation revolution has occurred in the country as large numbers of citizens have become active in an ever-increasing number of protest groups, citizens' organizations, and special interest groups. These groups often comprise issue-oriented activists or individuals who seek collective material benefits. The free-rider problem has proven not to be an insurmountable barrier to group formation, and many new interest groups do not use selective material benefits to gain support.

Third, government itself has had a profound effect on the growth and activity of interest groups. Early in this century, workers found organizing difficult because business and industry used government-backed injunctions to prevent strikes. By the 1930s, however, with the prohibition of injunctions in private labor disputes and the rights of collective bargaining established, most governmental actions directly promoted labor union growth. In recent years changes in the campaign finance laws have led to an explosion in the number of political action committees, especially among business, industry, and issue-oriented groups. Laws facilitating group formation certainly have contributed to group proliferation, but government policy in a broader sense has been equally responsible.

Fourth, not only has the number of membership groups grown in recent decades, but a similar expansion has occurred in the political activity of many other interests such as individual corporations, universities, churches, governmental units, foundations, and think tanks.[28] Historically, most of these interests have been satisfied with representation by trade or professional associations. Since the mid-1960s, however, many of these institutions have chosen to employ their own Washington representatives. Between 1961 and 1982, for example, the number of corporations with Washington offices increased tenfold.[29] The chief beneficiaries of this trend are Washington-based lawyers, lobbyists, and public relations firms. The number of attorneys in the nation's capital, taken as a rough indicator of lobbyist strength, tripled between 1973 and 1983, and the growth of public relations firms was dramatic. The lobbying community of the 1990s is large, increasingly diverse, and part of the expansion of policy domain participation, whether in agriculture, the environment, or industrial development.

Governmental Growth

Since the 1930s the federal government has become an increasingly active and important spur to group formation. A major aim of the New Deal was to use government as an agent in balancing the relationship between contending forces in society, particularly industry and labor. One goal was to create greater equality of opportunity, including the "guarantee of identical liberties to all individuals, especially with regard to their pursuit of economic success."[30] For example, the Wagner Act, which established collective bargaining rights, attempted to equalize workers' rights with those of their employers. Some New Deal programs did have real redistributive qualities, but most, even Social Security, sought only to ensure minimum standards of citizen welfare. Workers were clearly better off, but "the kind of redistribution that took priority in the public philosophy of the New Deal was not of wealth, but a redistribution of power." [31]

The expansion of federal programs has accelerated since 1960. In what political scientist Hugh Heclo termed an "Age of Improvement," [32] the federal budget has grown rapidly (from nearly $100 billion in 1961 to well over a trillion dollars in 1991) and has widened the sweep of federal regulations. Lyndon Johnson's Great Society—a multitude of federal initiatives in education, welfare, health care, civil rights, housing, and urban affairs—created a new array of federal responsibilities and program beneficiaries. The growth of many of these programs has continued, although it was slowed markedly by the Reagan administration. In the 1970s the federal government further expanded its activities in the areas of consumer affairs, environmental protection, and energy regulation, as well as redefined some policies, such as affirmative action, to seek greater equality of results.

Many of the government policies adopted early in the Age of Improvement did not result from interest group activity by potential beneficiaries. Several targeted groups, such as the poor, were not effectively organized in the period of policy development. Initiatives typically came from elected officials responding to a variety of private and public sources, such as task forces composed of academics and policy professionals. [33]

The proliferation of government activities led to a mushrooming of groups around the affected policy areas. Newly enacted programs provided benefit packages that served to encourage interest group formation. Consider group activity in the field of policy toward the aging. The radical Townsend Movement, based on age grievances, received much attention during the 1930s, but organized political activity focused on age-based concerns had virtually no influence in national politics. Social Security legislation won approval without the involvement of age-based interest groups. Four decades later, by 1978, roughly $112 billion (approximately 24 percent of total federal expenditures) went to the elderly, and it is projected that in fifty years the outlay will be 40 percent of the total budget. [34] The development of such massive benefits has spawned a variety of special interest groups and has encouraged others (often those formed for nonpolitical reasons) to redirect their attention to the politics of the aging.

Across policy areas two types of groups develop in response to governmental policy initiatives: *recipients* and *service deliverers*. In the elderly policy sector, recipient groups are mass-based organizations concerned with protecting—and if possible expanding—old-age benefits. The largest of these groups—indeed, the largest voluntary association represented in Washington—is the American Association of Retired Persons (AARP).

The AARP is twice the size of the AFL-CIO and, after the Roman Catholic church, is the nation's largest organization. In 1988 the AARP counted 28 million members, up from 10 million a decade earlier. Almost half (48 percent) of all Americans over fifty, or one-fifth of all voters, belong to the group. Membership is quite inexpensive—$5 per year; much of the organization's revenues is derived from advertising in its bimonthly magazine, *Modern Maturity*. The organization's headquarters in Washington has its own ZIP Code, a legislative/policy staff of 125, and 18 registered lobbyists.[35] Charles Peters, *Washington Monthly* editor and certified curmudgeon, acidly observed that the "AARP is becoming the most dangerous lobby in America," given its vigorous defense of the elderly's interests.[36]

Federal program growth also has generated substantial growth among service delivery groups. In the health care sector, for example, these range from professional associations of doctors and nurses to hospital groups to the insurance industry to suppliers of drugs and medical equipment. Not only is there enhanced group activity, but many individual corporations (Johnson and Johnson, Prudential, Humana, among many others) have strengthened their lobbying capacities by opening Washington offices or hiring professional representatives from the capital's unending number of lobbying firms.

Federal government policy toward the aging is probably typical of the tendency to "greatly increase the incentives for groups to form around the differential effects of these policies, each refusing to allow any other group to speak in its name." [37] The complexity of government decision making increases under such conditions, and priorities are hard to set. Particularly troublesome for decision makers concerned with national policy is the role played by service delivery groups. In the area of the aging, some groups are largely organizational middlemen concerned with their status as vendors for the elderly. The trade associations, for example, are most interested in the conditions surrounding the payment of funds to the elderly. For example, the major concern of the Gerontological Society, an organization of professionals, is to obtain funds for research on problems of the aged. Middleman organizations do not usually evaluate government programs according to the criteria used by recipient groups; rather, what is important to them is the relationship between the program and the well-being of their organizations. Because many service delivery groups offer their members vitally important selective material incentives (financial advantages and job opportunities), they are usually far better organized than most recipient groups (the elderly in this case, the AARP not withstanding). As a result, they sometimes speak for the recipients. This is particularly true when recipient groups represent disadvantaged people, such as the poor or the mentally ill.

Middleman groups have accounted for a large share of total group growth since 1960, and many of them are state and local government organizations. Since the late 1950s the federal government has grown in expenditures and regulations, not in personnel and bureaucracy. Employment in the federal government has risen only 20 percent since 1955, while that of states and localities has climbed more than 250 percent. Contemporary federal activism largely involves overseeing and regulating state and local governmental units, which seek funding for a wide range of purposes. The intergovernmental lobby, composed of such groups as the National League of Cities, the International City Manager Association, the National Association of Counties, the National Governors' Association, and the U.S. Conference of Mayors, has grown to become one of the most important in Washington. In addition, many local officials such as transportation or public works directors are represented by groups, and even single cities and state boards of regents have established Washington offices.

Not only do public policies contribute to group proliferation, but government often directly intervenes in group creation. This is not an entirely new activity. In the early twentieth century, relevant governmental officials in the Agriculture and Commerce Departments encouraged the formation of the American Farm Bureau Federation and the U.S. Chamber of Commerce, respectively. Since the 1960s the federal government has been especially active in providing start-up funds and sponsoring groups. One study found that government agencies have concentrated on sponsoring organizations of public service professions:

> Federal agencies have an interest in encouraging coordination among the elements of these complex service delivery systems and in improving the diffusion of new ideas and techniques. Groups like the American Public Transit Association or the American Council on Education ... serve as centers of professional development and informal channels for administrative coordination in an otherwise unwieldy governmental system.[38]

Government sponsorship also helps explain the recent rise of citizens' groups. Most federal domestic legislation has included provisions requiring some citizen participation, which have spurred the development of various citizen action groups, including grass-roots neighborhood associations, environmental action councils, legal defense coalitions, health care organizations, and senior citizens' groups. Such group sponsorship evolved for two reasons:

First, there is the ever-present danger that administrative agencies may exceed or abuse their discretionary power. In this sense, the regulators need regulating. Although legislatures have responsibility for doing this . . . the administrative bureaucracy has grown too large for them to monitor. Therefore, citizen participation has developed as an alternative means of monitoring government agencies. Second, government agencies are not entirely comfortable with their discretionary power. . . . [T]o reduce the potential of unpopular or questionable decisions, agencies frequently use citizen participation as a means for improving, justifying, and developing support for their decisions.[39]

Citizen participation thus has two often inconsistent missions: to act as a watchdog over an agency and to act as an advocate for its programs.

Government funding of citizens' groups takes numerous forms. Several federal agencies—including the Federal Trade Commission (FTC), Food and Drug Administration (FDA), and Environmental Protection Agency (EPA)—have reimbursed groups for participation in agency proceedings.[40] At other times the government makes available seed money or outright grants. Interest group scholar Jack Walker found that nine citizens' groups in ten (89 percent) received outside funding in their initial stages of development.[41] Not all the money was from federal sources, but much did come from government grants or contracts. Government can take away as well as give, however, and the Reagan administration made a major effort to "defund" interests on the political Left, especially citizens' groups. But once established, groups have strong instincts for survival. Indeed, the Reagan administration provided an attractive target for many citizens' groups in their recruiting efforts.

Citizens' groups, numbering in the thousands, continually confront the free-rider problem since they are largely concerned with collective goods and rarely can offer the selective material incentives so important for expanding and maintaining membership. With government funding, however, the development of a stable group membership is not crucial. Increasingly, groups have appeared that are essentially staff organizations with little or no membership base.

Government policies contribute to group formation in many *unintended* ways as well. Policy failures can impel groups to form, as happened with the rise of the American Agriculture Movement in the wake of the Nixon administration's grain export policies. An important factor in the establishment of the Moral Majority was the perceived harassment of church-run schools by government officials. And, as for abortion, the 1973 Supreme Court *Roe v. Wade* decision played a major role in right-to-life group mobilization, as did the 1989 *Webster* decision in the creation of pro-choice groups.

Finally, the expansion of government activity itself often *inadvertently* contributes to group development and the resulting complexity of politics. Here a rather obscure example may prove most instructive: the development of the Bass Anglers Sportsman Society (yes, the acronym is BASS).

It all began with the Army Corps of Engineers, which dammed enough southern and midwestern streams to create a host of lakes, thereby providing an inviting habitat for largemouth bass. Anglers arrived in droves to catch their limits, and the fishing industry responded by creating expensive boats filled with specialized and esoteric equipment. The number and affluence of bass aficionados did not escape the attention of Ray Scott, an enterprising soul who began BASS in 1967. In 1990, with its membership approaching 1 million (up from 400,000 in 1982), BASS remained privately organized, offering its members selective benefits such as a slick magazine filled with tips on how to catch their favorite fish, packages of lures and line in return for joining or renewing their memberships, instant information about fishing hot spots, and boat owners' insurance. BASS also provided a number of solidary benefits, such as the camaraderie of fishing with fellow members in specially sanctioned fishing tournaments and the vicarious excitement of fishing with "BASS pros," whose financial livelihood revolved around competitive tournament fishing. The organization is an excellent example of Robert Salisbury's exchange theory approach to interest groups, as it provides benefits to both members and organizers in a "mutually satisfactory exchange." [42]

Although Scott *sold* the organization to a private corporation in 1986 (the ultimate expression of entrepreneurial success), he remains active in much of its work and writes a column for the monthly publication, *BassMaster.*

Like most groups, BASS did not originate as a political organization, and, for the most part, it remains a sportsman's group. Yet, BASS has entered politics. *BassMaster* has published political commentary and in both 1980 and 1988 endorsed George Bush for president. It also has called for easing travel restrictions to Cuba, where world-record catches may lurk.

Most groups claim that access is their major goal within the lobbying process, and here BASS has succeeded beyond its wildest dreams. President George Bush has been a life member of BASS since 1978 and has labeled *BassMaster* his favorite magazine. Scott has used his relationship with Bush to lobby for a number of concerns to the fishing community in general and BASS in particular. In March 1989 Scott visited the White House and, during a horseshoe match, indicated his concern about rumors that the Office of Management and Budget

(OMB) planned to limit the disbursement of $100 million in trust funds for various fisheries management projects. The next morning Bush informed Scott that "all of *our* monies are secure from OMB or anyone else." [43]

Scott and BASS have increased their political activities in other ways as well. The group now sponsors VOTE (Voice of the Environment), which lobbies on water quality issues, and the group has filed class-action lawsuits on behalf of fishermen against environmental polluters.

Regardless of the entrepreneurial skills of Ray Scott, however, there would probably be no BASS if it were not for the federal government and the Army Corps of Engineers. (Indeed, there would be far fewer largemouth bass.) Fifty years of dam building by the Corps has altered the nature of fish populations. Damming of rivers and streams has reduced the quality of fishing for coldwater species such as trout and pike and has enhanced the habitat for largemouth bass, a game fish that can tolerate the warmer waters and mud bottoms of man-made lakes. Finally, because many of these lakes are located close to cities, the government has made bass fishing accessible to a large number of anglers.

From angling to air traffic control, the federal government has affected, and sometimes dominated, group formation. Governmental activity does not, however, exist in a vacuum, and many other forces have contributed to group proliferation, often in concert with increased public sector involvement.

Decline of Political Parties

In a diverse political culture characterized by divided power, political parties emerged early in our history as instruments to structure conflict and facilitate mass participation. Parties function as intermediaries between the public and formal government institutions, as they reduce and combine citizen demands into a manageable number of issues, enabling the system to focus upon the society's most important problems.

The party performs its mediating function primarily through coalition building—"the process of constructing majorities from the broad sentiments and interests that can be found to bridge the narrower needs and hopes of separate individuals and communities." [44] The New Deal coalition, forged in the 1930s, illustrates how this works. Generally speaking, socioeconomic divisions dominated politics from the 1930s through the 1960s. Less affluent citizens tended to support government provisions for social and economic security and the regulation of private enterprise. Those better off economically usually took the opposite position. The Democratic coalition, by and large, represented disadvantaged urban workers, Catholics, Jews, Italians, eastern Europeans, and blacks. On a variety of issues, southerners joined the coalition along with smatterings of academics and urban liberals. The Republicans were concentrated in the rural and suburban areas outside the South; the party was made up of established ethnic groups, businessmen, and farmers, and was largely Protestant. Party organizations dominated electoral politics through the New Deal period, and interest group influence was felt primarily through the party apparatus.

Patterns of partisan conflict are never permanent, however, and since the 1940s various social forces have contributed to the creation of new interests and the redefinition of older ones. This has had the effect of destroying the New Deal coalition without putting a new partisan structure in its place and has provided opportunities for the creation of large numbers of political groups—many that are narrowly focused and opposed to the bargaining and compromise patterns of coalition politics.

Taken as a whole, the changes of recent decades reflect the societal transformation that scholars have labeled "postindustrial society," centering on

> several interrelated developments: affluence, advanced technological development, the central importance of knowledge, national com-munication processes, the growing prominence and independence of the culture, new occupational structures, and with them new life styles and expectations, which is to say new social classes and new centers of power.[45]

At the base is the role of affluence. Between 1947 and 1972 median family income doubled, even after controlling for the effects of inflation. During that same period the percentage of families earning $10,000 and more, in constant dollars, grew from 15 percent to 60 percent of the population.[46] A large proportion of the population thus enjoys substantial discretionary income and has moved beyond subsis-tence concerns.

The consequences of spreading abundance did not reduce conflict, as some observers had predicted.[47] Instead, conflict heightened, as affluence increased dissatisfaction by contributing to a "mentality of demand, a vastly expanded set of expectations concerning what is one's due, a diminished tolerance of conditions less than ideal." [48] By the 1960s the democratizing impact of affluence had become apparent, as an extraordinary number of people enrolled in institutions of higher education. Not surprisingly, the government was under tremendous pressure to satisfy expectations, and it too contributed to increasing demands both in rhetoric and through many of its own Age of Improvement initiatives.

With the rise in individual expectations, class divisions and conflicts did not disappear, but they were drastically transformed. Political parties scholar Walter Dean Burnham noted that the New Deal's class structure changed and that by the late 1960s the industrial class pattern of upper, middle, and working class had been "supplanted by one which is relevant to a system dominated by advanced postindustrial technology." [49] At the top of the new class structure was a "professional-managerial-technical elite . . . closely connected with the university and research centers and significant parts of it have been drawn—both out of ideology and interest—to the federal government's social activism." [50] This growing group tended to be cosmopolitan and more socially permissive than the rest of society. The spread of affluence in postindustrial society was uneven, however, and certain groups were disadvantaged by the changes. At the bottom of the new class structure were the victims of changes, those "whose economic functions had been undermined or terminated by the technical revolution of the past generation . . . people, black and white, who tend to be in hard core poverty areas." [51] The focus of the War on Poverty was to be on this class.

The traditional political party system found it difficult to deal effectively with citizens' high expectations and a changing class structure. The economic, ethnic, and ideological positions that had developed during the New Deal became less relevant to parties, elections, and voter preferences. The strains were particularly evident among working-class Democrats. New Deal policies had been particularly beneficial to the white working class, enabling that group to earn incomes and adopt lifestyles that resembled those of the middle class. And although Age of Improvement policies initiated by Democratic politicians often benefited minorities, many white workers viewed these policies as attempts to aid lower-class blacks at whites' expense. By the late 1960s the white working class had taken on trappings of the middle class and conservatism, both economically and culturally.

At the same time, such New Deal divisions as ethnicity also had lost their cutting edge because of social and geographic mobility. One analyst observed in 1973 that

> it does not seem inaccurate to portray the current situation as one in which the basic coalitions and many of the political symbols and relationships, which were developed around one set of political issues and problems, are confronted with new issues and new cleavages for which these traditional relationships and associations are not particularly relevant. Given these conditions, the widespread confusion, frustration, and mistrust are not surprising. [52]

Various conditions led to the party system's inability to adapt to the changing societal divisions by "realigning"—building coalitions of groups to address new concerns. For example, consider the difficulty of coalition building around the kinds of issues that have emerged over the past fifteen or twenty years.

"Valence" issues—general evaluations of the goodness or badness of the times—have become important, especially when related to the cost of living. Yet most such issues do not divide the country politically. Everyone is against inflation and crime. A second set of increasingly important issues are those that are highly emotional/cultural/moral in character such as abortion, the "right to die," AIDS, the death penalty, drug laws, and a nuclear freeze. These issues divide the electorate but elicit intense feelings from only a relatively few citizens. Opinion on such issues often is unrelated to traditional group identifications. Moreover, public opinion is generally disorganized or in disarray—that is, opinions often are unrelated or weakly related to one another on major issues, further retarding efforts to build coalitions.

There is some question about whether parties retain the capacity to shape political debate even on issues that lend themselves to coalition building. Although the decline of political parties began well before the 1960s, the weakening of the party organization has accelerated in the postindustrial age. The emergence of a highly educated electorate, less dependent upon party as an electoral cue, has produced a body of citizens that seeks out independent sources of information. Technological developments—such as television, computer-based direct mail, and political polling—have enabled candidates to virtually bypass political parties in their quest for public office. The rise of political consultants has reduced even further the need for party expertise in running for office. The recruitment function of parties also has been largely lost to the mass media, as journalists now "act out the part of talent scouts, conveying the judgment that some contenders are promising, while dismissing others as of no real talent." [53]

Evidence does suggest that parties are finally starting to adapt to this new political environment, but party organizations no longer dominate the electoral process. The weakness of political parties has helped to create a vacuum in electoral politics since 1960, and in recent years interest groups have moved aggressively to fill it.

Growth of Interest Groups

Although it may be premature to formulate a theory that accounts for spurts of growth, we can identify several factors fundamental to group proliferation in contemporary politics. Rapid social and economic changes, powerful catalysts for group formation, have produced both the development of new interests (for example, the recreation industry) and the redefinition of traditional interests (for example, higher education). The spread of affluence and education, coupled with advanced communication technologies, further contribute to the translation of interests into formal group organizations. Postindustrial changes have generated a large number of new interests, particularly among occupational and professional groups in the scientific and technological arenas. For instance, genetic engineering associations have sprung up in the wake of recent DNA discoveries.

Perhaps more important, postindustrial changes have altered the pattern of conflict in society and created an intensely emotional setting composed of several groups ascending or descending in status. Ascending groups, such as members of the new professional-managerial-technical elite, have both benefited from and supported government activism; they represent the new cultural liberalism, politically cosmopolitan and socially permissive. At the same time, rising expectations and feelings of entitlement have increased pressures on government by aspiring groups and the disadvantaged. The 1960s and early 1970s witnessed wave after wave of group mobilization based on causes ranging from civil rights to women's issues to the environment to consumer protection.

Abrupt changes and alterations in status, however, threaten many citizens. Middle America, perceiving itself as downwardly mobile, has grown alienated from the social, economic, and cultural dominance of the postindustrial elites, on one hand, and resentful toward government attempts to aid minorities and other aspiring groups, on the other. The conditions of a modern, technologically based culture also are disturbing to more traditional elements in society. Industrialization and urbanization can uproot people, cutting them loose from familiar life patterns and values and depriving them of meaningful personal associations. Fundamentalist elements feel threatened by various technological advances (such as test-tube babies) as well as by the more general secular liberalism and moral permissiveness of contemporary life. And the growth of bureaucracy, both in and out of government, antagonizes everyone at one time or another.

Postindustrial threats are felt by elites as well. The nuclear arms race and its potential for mass destruction fostered the revived peace movement of the 1980s and its goal of a freeze on nuclear weapons. In addition, the excesses and errors of technology, such as oil spills and toxic waste disposal, have led to group formation among some of the most advantaged and ascending elements of society.

Illustrating the possibilities here is the growth in the mid-1980s of the animal rights movement. Although traditional animal protection organizations such as the Humane Society have existed for decades, the last fifteen years have "spawned a colorful menagerie of pro-animal offspring" such as People for Ethical Treatment of Animals (PETA), Progressive Animal Welfare Society (PAWS), Committee to Abolish Sport Hunting (CASH), and the Animal Rights Network (ARN). Reminiscent of the 1960s, there is even the Animal Liberation Front, an extremist group.[54] Membership in the animal rights movement has increased rapidly and approached 2 million by 1990. PETA, founded in 1980, grew from 20,000 in 1984 to 250,000 in 1988.[55]

One major goal of these groups is to stop, or greatly retard, scientific experimentation on animals. Using a mix of protest, lobbying, and litigation, the movement has contributed to the closing of several animal labs, including the Defense Department's Wound Laboratory and a University of Pennsylvania facility involved in research on head injuries. In 1988 Trans-Species, a recent addition to the animal rights movement, forced the Cornell University Medical College to give up a $600,000 grant, which left unfinished a fourteen-year research project in which cats had to ingest barbituates.[56]

While postindustrial conflicts generate the issues for group development, the massive spread of affluence also systematically contributes to group formation and maintenance. In fact, affluence creates a large potential for "checkbook" membership. Issue-based groups have done especially well. Membership in such groups as PETA and Common Cause might once have been considered a luxury, but the growth in discretionary income has placed the cost of modest dues within the reach of most citizens. For a $15-$25 membership fee, people can make an "expressive" statement without incurring other organizational obligations. Increasing education also has been a factor in that "organizations become more numerous as ideas become more important." [57]

Reform groups and citizens' groups depend heavily upon the educated, white middle class for their membership and financial base. A 1982 Common Cause poll, for example, found that members' mean family income was $17,000 above the national average and that 43 percent of members had an advanced degree.[58] Other expressive groups, including those on the political Right, have been aided as well by the increased wealth of constituents and the community activism that result from education and occupational advancement.

Groups can overcome the free-rider problem by finding a sponsor who will support the organization and reduce its reliance upon membership contributions. During the 1960s and 1970s private sources (often foundations) backed various groups. Jeffrey Berry's 1977 study of eighty-three public interest organizations found that at least one-third received more than half of their funds from private foundations, while one in ten received more than 90 percent of its operating expenses from such sources.[59] Jack Walker's 1981 study of Washington-based interest groups confirmed many of Berry's earlier findings, indicating that foundation support and individual grants provide 30 percent of all citizens' group funding.[60] Such patterns produce many staff organizations with no members, raising major questions about the representativeness of the new interest group universe. Finally, groups themselves can sponsor other groups. The National Council of Senior Citizens (NCSC), for example, was founded by the AFL-CIO, which helped recruit members from the ranks of organized labor and still pays part of NCSC's expenses.

Patrons often are more than just passive sponsors who respond to group requests for funds. In many instances, group mobilization comes from the top down, rather than the reverse. The patron—whether an individual (Stewart Mott, Adolph Coors), institution, other group, or government entity—may serve as the initiator of group development, to the point of seeking entrepreneurs and providing a forum for group pronouncements.[61]

Postindustrial affluence and the spread of education also have contributed to group formation and maintenance through the development of a large pool of potential group organizers. This group tends to be young, well educated, and from the middle class, caught up in a movement for change and inspired by ideas or doctrine. The 1960s was a period of opportunity for entrepreneurs, as college enrollments skyrocketed and powerful forces such as civil rights and the antiwar movement contributed to an idea-orientation in both education and politics. Communications-based professions—from religion to law to university teaching—attracted social activists, many of whom became involved in the formation of groups. The government itself became a major source of what James Q. Wilson called "organizing cadres." Government employees of the local Community Action Agencies of the War on Poverty and numerous VISTA volunteers were active in the formation of voluntary associations, some created to oppose government actions.[62]

Compounding the effects of the growing number of increasingly active groups are changes in what organizations can do, largely as a result of contemporary technology. On a grand scale, technological change produces new interests, such as cable television and the silicon chip industry, which organize to protect themselves as interests historically have done. Beyond this, communications breakthroughs make group politics much more visible than in the past. Civil rights activists in the South understood this, as did many protesters against the

Vietnam War. Of equal importance, however, is the fact that much of what contemporary interest groups do derives directly from developments in information-related technology. Many group activities, whether fund-raising or grass-roots lobbying or sampling members' opinions, rely heavily on computer-based operations that can target and send messages and process the responses.

Although satellite television links and survey research are important tools, the technology of direct mail has had by far the greatest impact on interest group politics. With a minimum initial investment and a reasonably good list of potential contributors, any individual can become a group entrepreneur. These activists literally create organizations, often based on emotion-laden appeals about specific issues, from Sarah Brady's Handgun Control to Randall Terry's Operation Rescue.[63] To the extent that an entrepreneur can attract members and continue to pay the costs of direct mail, he or she can claim—with substantial legitimacy—to articulate the organization's positions on the issues, positions probably defined initially by the entrepreneur.

In addition to helping entrepreneurs develop organizations that require few (if any) active members, information technology also allows many organizations to exert considerable pressure on elected officials. The Washington-based interests increasingly are turning to grass-roots techniques to influence legislators. Indeed, by the mid-1980s these tactics had become the norm in many lobbying efforts.

Information-processing technology is widely available but expensive. Although the Chamber of Commerce can afford its costly investment in extensive television facilities, many groups simply cannot pay the cost of much technology, at least beyond their continuing efforts to stay afloat with direct mail solicitations. Money remains the mother's milk of politics. Indeed, one of the major impacts of technology may be to inflate the costs of political action, especially given group support for candidates engaged in increasingly expensive election campaigns.

Group Impact on Policy and Process

Assessing the policy impact of interest group actions has never been an easy task. We may, however, gain some insights by looking at two different levels of analysis: a broad, societal overview and a middle-range search for relatively specific patterns of influence (for example, the role of direct mail or PAC funding). Considering impact at the level of individual lobbying efforts is also possible, but even the best work relies heavily on nuance and individualistic explanations.

Although the public at large often views lobbying and special interest campaigning with distrust, political scientists have not produced much evidence to support this perspective. Academic studies of interest groups have demonstrated few conclusive links between campaign or lobbying efforts and actual patterns of influence. This does not mean, we emphasize, that such patterns or individual instances do not exist. Rather, the question of determining impact is exceedingly difficult to answer. The difficulty is, in fact, compounded by groups' claims of impact and decision makers' equally vociferous claims of freedom from any outside influence.

The major studies of lobbying in the 1960s generated a most benign view of this activity. Lester Milbrath, in his portrait of Washington lobbyists, painted a Boy Scout-like picture, depicting them as patient contributors to the policy-making process.[64] Rarely stepping over the limits of propriety, lobbyists' had only a marginal impact at best. Similarly, Raymond Bauer, Ithiel de Sola Pool, and Lewis Dexter's lengthy analysis of foreign trade policy, published in 1963, found the business community to be largely incapable of influencing Congress in its lobbying attempts.[65] Given the many internal divisions within the private sector over trade matters, this was not an ideal issue to illustrate business cooperation, but the research stood as the central work on lobbying for more than a decade—ironically, in the very period when groups proliferated and became more sophisticated in their tactics. Lewis Dexter, in his 1969 treatment of Washington representatives as an emerging professional group, suggested that lobbyists will play an increasingly important role in complex policy making, but he provided few details.[66]

The picture of benevolent lobbyists who seek to engender trust and convey information, although accurate in a limited way, does not provide a complete account of the options open to any interest group that seeks to exert influence. Lyndon Johnson's long-term relationship with the Texas-based construction firm of Brown & Root illustrates the depth of some ties between private interests and public officeholders. The Washington representative for Brown & Root claimed that he never went to Capitol Hill for any legislative help because "people would resent political influence."[67] But Johnson, first as a representative and later as a senator, systematically dealt directly with the top management (the Brown family) and aided the firm by passing along crucial information and watching over key government-sponsored construction projects.

> [The Johnson-Brown & Root link] was, indeed, a partnership, the campaign contributions, the congressional look-out, the contracts, the appropriations, the telegrams, the investment advice, the gifts and the hunts and the free airplane rides—it was an alliance of mutual reinforcement between a politician and a corporation. If Lyndon was Brown & Root's kept politician,

Brown & Root was Lyndon's kept corporation. Whether he concluded that they were public-spirited partners or corrupt ones, "political allies" or cooperating predators, in its dimensions and its implications for the structure of society, their arrangement was a new phenomenon on its way to becoming the new pattern for American society.[68]

Subsequent events, such as the savings and loan scandal, demonstrate that legislators can be easily approached with unethical and illegal propositions; such access is one price of an open system. More broadly, the growth of interest representation in the late 1980s has raised long-term questions about the ethics of ex-government officials acting as lobbyists.

Contemporary Practices

Modern lobbying emphasizes information, often on complex and difficult subjects. Determining actual influence is, as one lobbyist noted, "like finding a black cat in the coal bin at midnight," [69] but we can make some assessments about the overall impact of group proliferation and increased activity.

First, more groups are engaged in more forms of lobbying than ever before—both classic forms, such as offering legislative testimony, and newer forms, such as mounting computer-based direct mail campaigns to stir up grass-roots support.[70] As the number of new groups rises and existing groups become more active, the pressure on decision makers—especially legislators—mounts at a corresponding rate. Thus, a second general point can be made: congressional reforms that opened up the legislative process during the 1970s have provided a much larger number of access points for today's lobbyists. Most committee (and subcommittee) sessions, including the markups or writing of legislation, remain open to the public, as do many conference committee meetings. More roll-call votes are taken, and congressional floor action is televised. Thus, interests can monitor the performance of individual members of Congress as never before. This does nothing, however, to facilitate disinterested decision making or foster statesman-like compromises on most issues.

In fact, monitoring the legions of Washington policy actors has become the central activity of many groups. As Robert Salisbury recently observed, "Before [organized interests] can advocate a policy, they must determine what position they wish to embrace. Before they do this, they must find out not only what technical policy analysis can tell them but what relevant others, inside and outside the government, are thinking and planning." [71] Given the volume of policy making, just keeping up can represent a major undertaking.

The government itself has encouraged many interests to organize and articulate their demands. The rise of group activity thus leads us to another level of analysis: the impact of contemporary interest group politics on society. Harking back to Lowi's description of interest group liberalism, we see the eventual result to be an immobilized society, trapped by its willingness to allow interests to help fashion self-serving policies that embody no firm criteria of success or failure. For example, even in the midst of the savings and loan debacle, the government continues to offer guarantees to various sectors, based not on future promise but on past bargains and continuing pressures.

The notion advanced by Olson that some such group-related stagnation affects all stable democracies makes the prognosis all the more serious. In summary form, Olson argued, "The longer societies are politically stable, the more interest groups they develop; the more interest groups they develop, the worse they work economically." [72] The United Automobile Workers' protectionist leanings, the American Medical Association's fight against FTC intervention into physicians' business affairs, and the insurance industry's successful prevention of FTC investigations all illustrate the possible linkage between self-centered group action and poor economic performance—that is, higher automobile prices, doctors' fees, and insurance premiums for no better product or service.

Conclusion

The ultimate consequences of the growing number of groups, their expanding activities both in Washington and in state capitals, and the growth of citizens' groups remain unclear. From one perspective, such changes have made politics more representative than ever before. While most occupation-based groups traditionally have been well organized in American politics, many other interests have not. Population groupings such as blacks, Hispanics, and women have mobilized since the 1950s and 1960s; even animals and the unborn are well represented in the interest group arena, as is the broader "public interest," however defined.

Broadening the base of interest group participation may have truly opened up the political process, thus curbing the influence of special interests. For example, agricultural policy making in the postwar era was almost exclusively the prerogative of a tight "iron triangle" composed of congressional committee and subcommittee members from farm states, government officials representing the agriculture bureaucracy, and major agriculture groups such as the American Farm Bureau. Activity in the 1970s by consumer and environmental interest groups changed agricultural politics, making it more visible and lengthening the agenda to consider such questions as how farm subsidies affect consumer purchasing power and how various fertilizers, herbicides, and pesticides affect public health.

From another perspective, more interest groups and more openness do not necessarily mean better policies or ones that genuinely represent the national interest. "Sunshine" and more participants may generate greater complexity and too many demands for decision makers to process effectively. Moreover, the content of demands may be ambiguous and priorities difficult to set. Finally, elected leaders may find it practically impossible to build the kinds of political coalitions necessary to govern effectively, especially in an era of divided government.

This second perspective suggests that the American constitutional system is extraordinarily susceptible to the excesses of minority faction—in an ironic way a potential victim of the Madisonian solution of dealing with the tyranny of the majority. Decentralized government, especially one that wields considerable power, provides no adequate controls over the excessive demands of special interest politics. Decision makers feel obliged to respond to many of these demands, and "the cumulative effect of this pressure has been the relentless and extraordinary rise of government spending and inflationary deficits, as well as the frustration of efforts to enact effective national policies on most major issues." [73]

In sum, the problem of contemporary interest group politics is one of representation. For particular interests, especially those that are well defined and adequately funded, the government is responsive to the issues of their greatest concern. But representation is not just a matter of responding to specific interests or citizens; the government also must respond to the collective needs of a society, and here the success of individual interests reduces the possibility of overall responsiveness. The very vibrancy and success of contemporary groups help contribute to a society that finds it increasingly difficult to formulate solutions to complex policy questions.

Notes

1. Kay Lehman Schlozman and John T. Tierney, "More of the Same: Washington Pressure Group Activity in a Decade of Change," *Journal of Politics* 45 (May 1983): 351-377. For an earlier era, see Margaret S. Thompson, *The Spider's Web* (Ithaca: Cornell University Press, 1985).
2. Theodore J. Lowi, *The End of Liberalism,* 2d ed. (New York: Norton, 1979); and Mancur Olson, *The Rise and Decline of Nations* (New Haven,

Conn.: Yale University Press, 1982).

3. Mancur Olson, *The Logic of Collective Action* (Cambridge, Mass.: Harvard University Press, 1971); Robert Salisbury, "An Exchange Theory of Interest Groups," *Midwest Journal of Political Science* 13 (February 1969): 1-32; and Terry M. Moe, *The Organization of Interests* (Chicago: University of Chicago Press, 1980).

4. David Truman's widely used definition of interest groups is "any group that, on the basis of one or more shared attitudes, makes certain claims upon other groups in the society for the establishment, maintenance or enhancement of forms of behavior that are implied by the shared attitudes." Truman, *The Governmental Process,* 2d ed. (New York: Knopf, 1971).

5. James Madison, "Federalist 10," in *The Federalist Papers,* 2d ed., ed. Roy P. Fairfield (Baltimore: Johns Hopkins University Press, 1981), 16.

6. L. Harmon Ziegler and Wayne Peak, *Interest Groups in American Society,* 2d ed. (Englewood Cliffs, N.J.: Prentice-Hall, 1972), 35.

7. Common Cause, *The Government Subsidy Squeeze* (Washington, D.C.: Common Cause, 1980), 11.

8. Truman, *Governmental Process,* 519.

9. Carole Greenwald, *Group Power* (New York: Praeger, 1977), 305.

10. Lowi, *End of Liberalism,* 62.

11. Murray Edelman, *The Politics of Symbolic Action* (Chicago: Markham Press, 1971).

12. Theodore J. Lowi, *Incomplete Conquest: Governing America* (New York: Holt, Rinehart & Winston, 1976), 47.

13. Gabriel Almond and Sidney Verba, *The Civic Culture* (Boston: Little, Brown, 1963), chaps. 8 and 10.

14. Ibid., 246-247.

15. Truman, *Governmental Process,* 57.

16. Salisbury, "Exchange Theory of Interest Groups," 3-4.

17. Truman, *Governmental Process,* 59.

18. James Q. Wilson, *Political Organizations* (New York: Basic Books, 1973), 154.

19. Major works include: Olson, *Logic of Collective Action;* Peter Clark and James Q. Wilson, "Incentive Systems: A Theory of Organizations," *Administrative Science Quarterly* 6 (September 1961): 126-166; Wilson, *Political Organizations;* Terry Moe, "A Calculus of Group Membership," *American Journal of Political Science* 24 (November 1980): 593-632; and Moe, *Organization of Interests.* The notion of group organizers as political entrepreneurs is best represented by Salisbury, "Exchange Theory of Interest Groups," 1-15.

20. See Clark and Wilson, "Incentive Systems: A Theory of Organizations," 129-166; and Wilson, *Political Organizations,* 30-51. In recent years researchers have preferred the term *expressive* to *purposive,* since, as Salisbury notes, the term purposive includes what we call collective material benefits. Material, solidary, and expressive would seem to be

mutually exclusive conceptual categories. See Salisbury, "Exchange Theory of Interest Groups," 16-17.

21. Moe, *Organization of Interests,* 144.
22. John Mark Hansen, "The Political Economy of Group Membership," *American Political Science Review* 79 (March 1985): 79-96.
23. Albert O. Hirschman, *Shifting Involvements* (Princeton, N.J.: Princeton University Press, 1982).
24. Michael W. McCann, "Public Interest Liberalism and the Modern Regulatory State," *Polity* 21 (Winter 1988): 385.
25. See, for example, R. Kenneth Godwin and R. C. Mitchell, "Rational Models, Collective Goods, and Non-Electoral Political Behavior," *Western Political Quarterly* 35 (June 1982): 161-180; and Larry Rothenberg, "Choosing among Public Interest Groups: Membership, Activism and Retention in Political Organizations," *American Political Science Review* 82 (December 1988): 1129-1152.
26. Jack L. Walker, "The Origins and Maintenance of Interest Groups in America," *American Political Science Review* 77 (June 1983): 390-406; for a conservative critique of this trend, see James T. Bennett and Thomas Di Lorenzo, *Destroying Democracy* (Washington, D.C.: Cato Institute, 1986).
27. Walker, "Origins and Maintenance of Interest Groups," 16.
28. Robert H. Salisbury, "Interest Representation and the Dominance of Institutions," *American Political Science Review* 78 (March 1984): 64-77.
29. Gregory Colgate (ed.), *National Trade and Professional Associations of the United States 1982* (Washington, D.C.: Columbia Books, 1984).
30. Samuel H. Beer, "In Search of a New Public Philosophy," in *The New American Political System,* ed. Anthony King (Washington, D.C.: American Enterprise Institute, 1978), 12.
31. Ib d., 10.
32. Hugh Heclo, "Issue Networks and the Executive Establishment," in King, *New American Political System,* 89.
33. Beer, "In Search of a New Public Philosophy," 16.
34. Allan J. Cigler and Cheryl Swanson, "Politics and Older Americans," in *The Dynamics of Aging,* ed. Forrest J. Berghorn, Donna E. Schafer, and Associates (Boulder, Colo.: Westview Press, 1981), 171.
35. See John Tierney, "Old Money, New Power," *New York Times Magazine,* October 23, 1988; and "The Big Gray Money Machine," *Newsweek,* August 15, 1988.
36. Tierney, "Old Money, New Power."
37. Heclo, "Issue Networks and the Executive Establishment," 96.
38. Walker, "Origins and Maintenance of Interest Groups," 401.
39. Stuart Langton, "Citizen Participation in America: Current Reflections on the State of the Art," in *Citizen Participation in America,* ed. Stuart Langton (Lexington, Mass.: Lexington Books, 1978), 7.
40. Ibid., 4.
41. Walker, "Origins and Maintenance of Interest Groups," 398.

42. Salisbury, "Exchange Theory of Interest Groups," 25.
43. Ray Scott, "Presidential Promises," *BassMaster,* May 1989, 7 (emphasis added).
44. David S. Broder, "Introduction," in *Emerging Coalitions in American Politics,* ed. Seymour Martin Lipset (San Francisco: Institute for Contemporary Studies, 1978), 3.
45. Everett Carll Ladd, Jr., with Charles D. Hadley, *Transformations of the American Party System,* 2d ed. (New York: Norton, 1978), 182.
46. Ibid., 196.
47. See, for example, Daniel Bell, *The End of Ideology* (New York: Free Press, 1960).
48. Ladd and Hadley, *Transformations of the American Party System,* 203.
49. Walter Dean Burnham, *Critical Elections and the Mainsprings of American Politics* (New York: Norton, 1970), 139.
50. Ibid.
51. Ibid.
52. Richard E. Dawson, *Public Opinion and Contemporary Disarray* (New York: Harper and Row, 1973), 194.
53. Everett Carll Ladd, *Where Have All the Voters Gone?* 2d ed. (New York: Norton, 1982), 56.
54. Kevin Kasowski, "Showdown on the Hunting Ground," *Outdoor America,* 51 (Winter 1986): 9.
55. Sarah Lyall, "Scientist Gives Up Grant to Do Research on Cats," *New York Times,* November 21, 1988.
56. Ibid.
57. Wilson, *Political Organizations,* 201.
58. Andrew S. McFarland, *Common Cause* (Chatham, N.J.: Chatham House, 1984), 48-49.
59. Jeffrey M. Berry, *Lobbying for the People* (Princeton, N.J.: Princeton University Press, 1977), 72.
60. Walker, "Origins and Maintenance of Interest Groups," 400.
61. Ibid.
62. Wilson, *Political Organizations,* 203.
63. Sarah Brady, wife of former White House press secretary James Brady, organized Handgun Control after her husband was seriously wounded in John Hinckley's 1981 attack on Ronald Reagan. Randall Terry formed Operation Rescue, which seeks to shut down abortion clinics through direct action (for example, blocking entrances), after concluding that other pro-life groups were not effective in halting abortions.
64. Lester Milbrath, *The Washington Lobbyists* (Chicago: Rand-McNally, 1963).
65. Raymond Bauer, Ithiel de Sola Pool, and Lewis Dexter, *American Business and Public Policy* (New York: Atherton Press, 1963).
66. Lewis A. Dexter, *How Organizations Are Represented in Washington* (Indianapolis: Bobbs-Merrill, 1969), chap. 9.
67. See Ronnie Dugger, *The Politician* (New York: Norton, 1982), 273; and

Robert A. Caro, *The Years of Lyndon Johnson: The Path to Power* and *The Years of Lyndon Johnson: Means of Ascent* (New York: Knopf, 1982 and 1990, respectively).

68. Dugger, *Politician,* 286.
69. Quoted in "A New Era: Groups and the Grass Roots," by Burdett A. Loomis, in *Interest Group Politics,* ed. Allan J. Cigler and Burdett A. Loomis (Washington, D.C.: CQ Press, 1983), 184.
70. Schlozman and Tierney, "Washington Pressure Group Activity," 18.
71. Robert H. Salisbury, "The Paradox of Interest Groups in Washington— More Groups and Less Clout," in *The New American Political System,* 2d ed., ed. Anthony King (Washington, D.C.: American Enterprise Institute, 1990), 225-226.
72. Robert J. Samuelson's description in *National Journal,* September 25, 1982, 1642.
73. Everett Carll Ladd, "How to Tame the Special Interest Groups," *Fortune,* October 1980, 6.

2. ORGANIZED LABOR IN AN ERA OF BLUE-COLLAR DECLINE

Paul Edward Johnson

In the first half of the twentieth century organized labor became a major force in U.S. politics. Especially significant were those unions belonging to the American Federation of Labor (AFL) and the Congress of Industrial Organizations (CIO). Unions were a powerful force in support of the New Deal policy initiatives, and after the 1955 merger that created the AFL-CIO, organized labor continued to be a major supporter of policy issues on the liberal side of the political agenda. Its historic alignment with the Democratic party, including substantial aid to Democratic presidential and congressional candidates, has had a major effect on the nation's electoral politics as well.

In this chapter Paul Johnson argues that the high visibility of union political activity is deceptive. Unions have lost members in recent decades and continue to face organizational difficulties that threaten their political impact and, indeed, their very existence. He rejects the argument that the waning of the union movement is inevitable, given the decline of blue-collar industries and the rise of the service economy. Rather, for Johnson the most likely explanation for the decline in union membership is the inability of these organizations to convince workers that they will benefit from unionization, along with the tendencies for employers to make nonunion jobs satisfying or to convince workers that unionization would be undesirable.

Johnson suggests that unions can attract new members by improving the package of benefits they offer, such as free or discount legal services, supplemental life insurance, or attractive credit card programs. He finds that in the late 1980s unions expanded their recruiting efforts and benefit programs to overcome the "collective action" and "unraveling" problems, although it is too early to assess the success of such programs.

When Congress is in session, the legislative representatives of the national labor unions belonging to the American Federation of Labor-Congress of Industrial Organizations (AFL-CIO) meet weekly to discuss political strategy. These Monday morning meetings, which last an hour or two, are organized by the AFL-CIO's Legislative Department, which has twelve full-time professional staff employees (including the director) and eight support staff employees. The unions do not agree on all issues, of course, and the AFL-CIO staff has little power to enforce the group's decisions on unions that disagree.

In spite of their differences, the AFL-CIO unions wield considerable political influence. Union workers historically have preferred Democratic candidates, and thus unions play a significant role in Democratic party politics. In 1984 AFL-CIO unions provided early (and possibly decisive) support for Walter Mondale in the race for the Democratic presidential nomination. When a Democrat is elected president, labor expects to influence key appointments. To increase the chances that Congress will look favorably on labor, the AFL-CIO operates the Committee on Political Education (COPE), which raises money, recruits volunteers for campaigns, and educates voters about the candidates.

The high visibility of union political activity masks the real decline of labor unions, which has been underway for almost four decades. Many unions have lost members. The hardest hit have merged or simply ceased to exist. The decline was steepest in the 1980s, causing the outlook for labor to appear especially dreary.

From a longer-term perspective, however, one might be surprised that the AFL-CIO is able to maintain such a substantial operation. The early history of the organization was quite different. It began in 1881, when 107 representatives of labor organizations from thirteen states gathered in Pittsburgh. John Jarrett, president of the Amalgamated Association of Iron and Steel Workers was elected to preside over the convention, which created the Federation of Organized Trades and Labor Unions (FOTLU). The FOTLU constitution began with a policy platform favoring legalized unionism, compulsory state education for children, a national law limiting labor to eight hours per day, and tariffs to protect American businesses and their employees from foreign competition. The platform opposed convict labor, child labor, and immigration of Chinese laborers. The resolution calling for protective tariffs was adopted by a narrow margin;[1] some unions opposed it because their jobs depended on foreign trade.

Only nineteen delegates attended FOTLU's second annual meeting. Membership was low and funds were scarce, the dues rate adopted in 1881 was too high for most unions. The organization's executives, who served part time (dividing their work between their own unions and the federation), announced they could not even afford to have a report of their legal and legislative activities printed for the members. Thus, the delegates voted to reduce dues to attract new members and to drop the controversial call for tariffs, which they feared had alienated potential members.

Dropping the tariff issue did not attract new members, but it did alienate Jarrett and his union. After the 1882 meeting Jarrett wrote a letter explaining that he would rejoin FOTLU only if the tariff plank were reinserted. In response, the federation's secretary wrote Jarrett, asking him to accept the federation's neutrality,[2] but he did not respond and his union did not rejoin. The trials and tribulations of FOTLU continued along this line[3] until 1886, when its leaders met with other unions and combined to form the American Federation of Labor (AFL) that same year. AFL leaders began with the FOTLU constitution but took steps to firm up the federation.[4] The rest, as they say, is history.

The early FOTLU/AFL experience sheds some light on the fundamental difficulties that currently confront labor organizations, and helps illustrate the basic issues involved in the theory of organizational adaptation, which is the major focus of this chapter.

Theory of Organizations and Adaptation

Three fundamental problems confront the managers of voluntary organizations: the collective action problem, the unraveling problem, and the allocative dilemma. Until these problems are overcome, reform efforts will be frustrated.

The Collective Action Problem

A collective action problem exists when people could benefit from provision of a collective good (one from which no person may be excluded), but they—acting as self-interested individuals—prefer not to pitch in. If the political action succeeds, the benefits will be available to all workers whether or not they or their unions contributed to the political action. *Each individual is thus tempted to "free-ride" on the political efforts of others.*[5]

How do labor organizations overcome this collective action problem? Political economist Mancur Olson, whose research brought the collective action problem to the forefront in political science, argued that successful unions are those ones that find ways above and beyond the collective causes to make membership attractive. Unions thus have long lured new members by offering them "selective incentives"—that is, such benefits as health insurance, life insurance, or seniority perquisites. But they sometimes also coerced workers with economic or physical intimidation. Unions gained another important method of recruiting members in 1935, when the National Labor Relations Act (NLRA) was adopted. Congress created the National Labor Relations Board (NLRB) to oversee the union organization process and instructed employers to bargain "in good faith" with unions. A union became the bargaining representative of all the workers in a "bargaining unit" if it was chosen by a majority of them in a representation (or certification) election. Under the NLRA, the union membership of the AFL grew rapidly, as well as that of a breakaway group of industrial unions called the Congress of Industrial Organizations (CIO), which split from the AFL because of conflicts over jurisdiction—the right to organize workers. The AFL-CIO resulted from the merger of these groups in 1955.

The 1935 act allowed unions to sign "security agreements" with employers, stipulating that all employees had to pay union dues as a condition of employment. A business operating under such a contract was called a union or agency shop; a business that hired only union members was called a closed shop. Security agreements and closed shops were allowed in all states until 1947, when the federal law was amended by the Taft-Hartley Labor-Management Relations Act to ban closed shops and to allow states to adopt right-to-work (RTW) laws which forbid union or agency shops. Twenty-one states, mainly ones in which unions historically were weak, have adopted RTW laws, which make recruiting more costly for unions.

The major point here is that labor unions formed and grew because they were able to give workers selective incentives to join them. Early unions offered direct benefits, but later ones made workers choose between paying the union and finding a different job.

The federations faced a completely different collective action problem—convincing labor unions to donate their scarce dollars to a collective organization. In 1881 unions took little more than a look-see at FOTLU. The AFL attracted unions by coordinating the labor union efforts in a battle with a short-lived competing organization called the Knights of Labor. Unions that refused to join the AFL worried that they would be excluded from the AFL's protection against the Knights. The federation quickly developed other selective incentives to encourage unions to affiliate. In 1887 the AFL constitution was amended to forbid the city trade assemblies and state federations affiliated with the AFL from admitting local unions that had withdrawn from member national unions. Two leading labor historians, Selig Perlman and Philip Taft, observed that this provision was useful to the national unions in "protecting against the menace of 'dual' unions arisen as 'successions' from 'regular' unions or promoted from outside." They claimed that

> it is this function of the Federation, a function largely "invisible" to the outside world, which has built up the American labor movement. So long as the Federation is successful in discharging this "invisible" function, its failures in carrying out its more "visible" functions—lobbying for favorable legislation and related activities—are overlooked within the labor movement.[6]

As early as 1889 the AFL began to serve as a forum for the airing of jurisdictional conflicts among unions, but only its members could expect to have their complaints addressed. The Federation also coordinated union organizing campaigns. During the early years of the AFL, about 700 voluntary organizers served under AFL president Samuel Gompers. In the late 1890s a force of salaried organizers was employed by the AFL, and, "the Federation became the center for organizing." [7] The AFL's organizing activities not only served the national unions by adding to their membership roles, but also created what a skeptic might call a protection racket. National unions could not ignore the federation without fear that it would launch an effort to form a competing union. The AFL proved its willingness to carry out this threat in 1896, when the American Federation of Musicians was founded to compete with the National League of Musicians for members; the latter had refused to join the AFL.

The Unraveling Problem

After an organization has developed selective incentives to attract members, the possibility of collective action arises. The members may think to themselves, "As long as we are bound together by our desire to obtain the selective incentive, we might as well pay our leaders to represent our common interests." Russell Hardin showed that people with common interests will vote to fund collective projects as long as they receive selective benefits.[8]

When controversial issues arise at union conventions, they often are decided by majority rule. Decisions anger some members and cause them to quit, initiating a process called *unraveling*. For example, when a group is voting on the dues that all members will pay, majority rule will lead to a median dues rate, too high for some members. If these people withdraw, the next convention will be made up of richer people, willing to pay the existing rate and possibly more. If they are unaware of the possibility of further withdrawals, they will vote the dues rate up again and more withdrawals will follow. This unraveling process will continue until a chosen policy is both acceptable to all and able to defeat all other proposals in a head-on vote.[9]

Like the collective action problem, the unraveling problem is a roadblock to group organization, as shown by the early experience of FOTLU and the controversial tariff issue. The AFL changed its rules and procedures to prevent unraveling. A required two-thirds majority for constitutional amendments reduced the chance that controversial policies would be implemented, and some difficult issues, such as political partisanship, were ruled out of order. Dramatic steps to strengthen the federation's financial position, such as a national strike fund linking all unions, were considered but were rejected for fear of withdrawals by some important unions.

The AFL could not extract unlimited resources from its member unions, however. If it asked for more from unions than its selective incentives were worth to them, its membership would decline. One perennial issue in the AFL (and later, AFL-CIO) exemplifies how the collective action and unraveling problems fit together. State and local federations that belonged to the AFL periodically proposed a policy that would require national unions to discipline their locals that did not join city or state federations. But the national unions were reluctant to enforce these policies because they might alienate their local (dues-paying) affiliates. In 1894 the AFL constitution was amended to provide that nationals "instruct" their locals to join central labor bodies, and in 1901 the nationals were told to instruct their locals to join the state federations. These provisions were not enforced, however. The same convention found a proposal to withhold the benefits of the labor movement from these locals to be "inexpedient." The issue has arisen countless times since then. In 1950, for example, a delegate from Virginia called for a tougher AFL policy because more than 300 locals refused to affiliate with his state's federation. He proclaimed, "I say to you, if you please, those people are not doing their part . . . and it is up to the international unions to make them do their part." [10] A lengthy debate followed as the national unions and AFL leaders agreed in principle with the state federations, but they argued that it would be unwise to expel national unions from the AFL over the well-being of the state federations. In the late 1980s the AFL-CIO state federations began to offer discounts to unions when all locals affiliated, but the organization has been unwilling to risk unraveling by using stricter methods.

The unraveling problem causes organizations to lose members but also creates incentives for members to compromise by lowering dues or moderating political positions. In the case of funding, for example, no member will pay more than his or her total valuation of the selective incentives that led to membership in the first place. This condition acts as a tight lid on federation finances, and it sets an absolute limit on the nature of collective projects that the members are going to undertake. In particular, such collective projects as an all-out lobbying initiative for labor law reform are limited by the inability of the federation to make organizations pay more.

The Allocative Dilemma

Any interest group organization—including a labor union or federation—faces the task of allocating scarce dollars among administration (salaries, taxes, postage, stationery, legal fees, and so forth), new member recruitment, benefits, and political action. This fact is illustrated in Tables 2-1 to 2-3, which summarize the revenues and expenditures of the AFL-CIO, International Ladies' Garment Workers' Union (ILGWU), and National Rifle Association (NRA), respectively. Each invests heavily in administrative offices that provide selective and collective benefits. Political expenditures vary substantially among organizations. The NRA's political branch, the Institute for Legislative Action, consumes 15 percent of that organization's budget, about the same percentage as the combined COPE and Legislative Department expenditures of the AFL-CIO. Both dwarf the ILGWU's Political Department, which manages lobbying as well as the union's political action committee (PAC).

The tables present only a snapshot. The NRA's political expenditures more than doubled in 1988 during the fight over a law requiring a waiting period for handgun purchases (the Brady amendment). Many people might be surprised to see that the AFL-CIO spends only 2.5 percent of its resources on its Legislative Department, but this percentage is consistent with historical patterns. In fiscal years 1960, 1970, and 1980, for example, the federation spent, respectively, 2.3, 2.9, and 2.6 percent of its money on the Legislative Department. The expenditures on COPE, in contrast, reflect a sporadic upward trend in the committee's percentage of the total budget, from 7.9 percent in 1960, to 11.4 percent in 1970, to the 1983 level of 12.4 percent.

Political action is expensive and success is uncertain. Thus, even when political preferences are strong, money may be better spent on nonpolitical activities. The AFL-CIO's defeat on labor law reform in 1978, the centerpiece of its legislative agenda, prompted leaders to admit that resources would be better spent elsewhere.[11] AFL convention reports of the 1890s indicate that despite their strong political preferences, AFL leaders simply could not justify spending scarce money on politics.[12]

Sometimes leaders have searched for ways to channel into political programs money that members would prefer to spend elsewhere. The Taft-Hartley Act of 1947, for example, angered labor leaders and prompted them to push reluctant memberships into political action. The 1947 convention of the International Ladies' Garment Workers' Union, considered one of the most liberal, politically active unions in America, was rife with angry rhetoric against the act and the two-party system, but a proposal to create a permanent political department came to the floor with a negative recommendation by the Committee on the Officers Report. The reporting delegate said:

> Your committee feels that the President and the General Executive
> Board will fully discharge their duties along these lines; and while

Table 2-1   AFL-CIO Budget, 1983

Line item	Amount	%
Revenue		
Per capita taxes, assessments, contributions	$39,749,401	94.62
Rental income	915,609	2.18
Investment income	458,990	1.09
Sales of supplies and services	220,541	0.52
AFL-CIO News subscriptions	152,072	0.36
Other	512,771	1.22
Total	42,009,384	
Expenses		
Headquarters, administrative departments (salaries plus expenses)	$4,386,471	10.79
Headquarters, other departments and committees		
Committee on Political Education (COPE)	5,028,480	12.37
Information	3,117,274	7.77
Education	2,340,500	5.76
Legal	1,044,053	2.57
Legislative	1,016,609	2.50
Economic Research	950,963	2.34
Organization and Field Services	901,739	2.21
International Affairs	694,631	1.71
Social Insurance	410,107	1.00
Civil Rights	384,955	0.95
Community Services	346,333	0.85
Occupational Safety and Health	168,361	0.41
Headquarters, general other expenses (employee benefits, payroll taxes, travel, etc.)	13,227,604	32.55
Field operations		
Regional offices	6,554,884	16.13
Directly affiliated locals and central bodies	56,918	0.14
Total	40,629,882	

SOURCE: AFL-CIO, *Proceedings of the Fifteenth Constitutional Convention of the AFL-CIO* 1983, 12-31.

we do not see the need for establishment of a distinct Political Department, nevertheless we recommend that the incoming GEB consider the advisability of such action and that the establishment of such a department should be left entirely to its discretion.[13]

A few months later the General Executive Board created the Political Department and supported it with a $500,000 appropriation from the

Table 2-2   International Ladies' Garment Workers' Union Budget, 1983-1985

Line item	Amount	%
Revenue		
Dues	$38,429,500	64.47
Interest	20,928,639	35.11
Initiation tax	201,393	0.34
Miscellaneous	47,231	0.08
Total	59,606,763	
Expenses		
General officers (salary and expenses)	$1,221,157	1.57
Regional organizing expenses	26,823,312	34.39
Administrative expenses, excluding administrative departments	5,850,021	7.50
Administrative departments (salary and expenses)		
Benefit Funds	6,834,662	8.76
Welfare Funds Control	5,314,606	6.81
Auditing	3,571,436	4.58
Legal	1,404,615	1.80
Finance	1,364,216	1.75
General	1,090,759	1.40
Research	957,743	1.23
Political	910,454	1.17
Data Processing	843,300	1.08
Organizing and Field Services	781,225	1.00
Education	679,525	0.87
Management Engineering	629,202	0.81
Others (Mailing, Switchboard, and International Relations)	796,923	1.02
Master Agreements	397,476	0.51
Archives	340,220	0.44
Investment	164,386	0.21
Staff benefits and insurance	11,016,380	14.13
Publications expenses	2,967,602	3.81
Dues to affiliated organizations	2,457,304	3.15
Other	1,575,510	2.02
Total operating expenses	77,992,034	
Refunds from departments and other funds	21,742,615	
Net operating expenses	56,249,419	

SOURCE: *General Executive Board Report and Record of Proceedings, International Ladies' Garment Workers' Union, Thirty-ninth Convention* (New York: Astoria Press, 1986), 8-20.

Table 2-3 National Rifle Association Budget, 1987

Line item	Amount	%
Revenue		
Membership dues	$42,584,428	59.9
Advertising	7,586,201	10.7
Contributions	6,675,631	9.4
Dividends and interest	5,775,117	8.1
Other	8,473,397	11.9
Total	71,094,774	
Expenses		
Membership and promotions	$25,718,151	40.2
Publications	15,329,339	23.9
Institute for Legislative Action	9,611,399	15.0
Executive and administrative	6,700,305	10.5
General operations	6,683,637	10.4
Total	64,042,831	

SOURCE: National Rifle Association of America, *NRA 1988 Annual Report,* 19.

general purposes voluntary contribution fund. President David Dubinsky reported at the 1950 convention that "we were the first, and I believe the only international union, to establish a political department to promote on a national scale the union's program of political action." [14] To make the Political Department affordable on a permanent basis, the per capita tax was later raised thirteen cents per month.

The AFL Executive Council's major response to the Taft-Hartley Act was the creation of the Laborers' League for Political Education (a PAC since superseded by COPE, the Committee on Political Education). In 1948 the LLPE was endorsed by the AFL convention, and the unions were asked to pitch in ten cents per member for the LLPE's educational fund, which paid the expenses of administration and fundraising. In 1950 the convention voted another voluntary assessment of ten cents, but it brought in a bit less than ten cents per member. For the leaders, the next natural step was to make the payment mandatory. As secretary-treasurer (and future AFL-CIO president) George Meany later explained, at the May 1951 Executive Council meeting, "it was decided to abandon raising educational funds by means of these special voluntary assessments. The funds needed to carry on the year-round political education activities of the League will henceforth be taken over as a direct expense of the A. F. of L." [15] To cover the increased costs, the Executive Council requested that the next convention increase the dues rate one cent per member, effectively circumventing members' reluctance to pay for political action.

Nature of Union Decline

Union membership as a percentage of the nonagricultural workforce, (so-called union density), peaked at about one-third in the mid-1950s and has declined ever since. In the 1980s union density fell more rapidly and reached its lowest level since 1935. This decline stems from several sources. The number of certification elections doubled from 1954 to 1977, but because of a decline in success rates and the size of bargaining units organized, the total membership gain from certification elections was halved.[16] By 1987 the number of certification elections had fallen 60 percent from the 1977 peak.[17] In short, there were fewer elections, and unions won fewer of them. Economist Richard Freeman calculated that, during the 1950s, the unions organized between 1 and 2 percent of the work force per year. In contrast, during 1983 certification elections led to the unionization of just 91,000 workers—0.1 percent of a work force of 90 million.[18] Add to this the fact that a substantial number of elected unions—perhaps one-third—fail to negotiate a contract and disappear within a few years.[19] Finally, a small number of workers each year actually get rid of their unions in decertification elections.[20]

The onset of union decline reawakened academic interest in unions. The basic theory that guides current research is that membership trends reflect three forces: demand for representation by workers, supply of union services by unions, and the interference (or support) of employers. To oversimplify a complicated theory and a rich literature, the studies show that workers want unions when their nonunion jobs are unsatisfying and that they expect unions to do better for them.[21] Beyond this simple observation, there are about as many opinions as authors to explain why unions form and why they have declined. Four theories merit detailed attention, however.

Decline of Blue-Collar Industry

The idea that unions grow and saturate the unionizable part of the work force is known as the "saturation theory."[22] This theory argues that some workers—mainly male blue-collar—are more prone to unionization than white-collar and service workers. The postindustrial transition of the U.S. economy toward more employment in white-collar and service-oriented sectors is thus seen as a major threat to organized labor. Statistical analysis compiled since 1950 offers some support: states that lost blue-collar workers (and saw the increasing employment of women and young people) experienced declines in union density.[23]

The "blue-collar decline theory" has a number of flaws, however. First, union density has declined even in the blue-collar industries, leading to speculation that the antiunion factors are not confined to particular kinds of workers or businesses.[24] If occupational categories are defined more narrowly, a peculiar finding emerges. A comprehensive breakdown for the 1970s indicates a decline in unionization in "general building contracting, coal mining, automobiles, apparel, radio and television equipment, newspaper publishing and printing, and taxicab service,"[25] all blue-collar industries, while unionism rose among some categories of professionals (librarians, doctors and nurses, and teachers) thought to be antiunion.

Second, the blue-collar decline has been going on in other parts of the world as well. Leo Troy recently observed that unionism has stagnated or declined in some other Western countries, leading him to speculate that "the causes of union decline may be common to industrial economies making the transition to service dominated markets."[26] This claim has been disputed by Richard Freeman, who drew a larger sample of Western countries and found union density to be stable or rising in a majority of them. The industrial transition in the United States is not dissimilar to that of Canada, for example, and yet unionism in Canada doubled from 1970 to 1985, while the U.S. rate fell precipitously. Accordingly, the argument that unions are out of place in a service-oriented, postmodern economy does not hold much water.[27]

Changes in Worker and Public Opinion

A second explanation for the decline of unions has been offered by political scientist Seymour Martin Lipset, who argued that public opinion has turned against unions, and, in turn, unions have had more difficulty recruiting workers. According to Lipset, the decline in overall public approval of unions is "closely linked"[28] with the decline in union victory rates in NLRB elections. Peter Bruce refuted this thesis by examining Canada, where unions have grown in the recent decades, despite public views that are as negative as (if not more than) those in the United States. Bruce found that the variations in union growth among regions in Canada are more easily explained by differences in economic and political regimes than by differences in political culture and public opinion. Perhaps most troublesome, the public opinion theory does not explain why union growth up to 1970 was so similar in the United States and Canada and so different after that. Bruce settled on an explanation based on the differences in the political institutions and labor relations laws rather than on general political culture.[29]

Data on overall public opinion is not as illuminating as information about the reasons nonunion workers do not form unions. Labor economist Henry Farber's analysis of surveys of nonunion workers found that unions are losing support because today's nonunion workers are more satisfied with their pay and job security than in the past. Moreover, the fraction of nonunion workers who think that unions would improve wages and working conditions has declined. It is not totally clear why satisfaction rates have risen, but Farber hinted that it is a result of declining expectations. Stagnating income during the 1970s led people to expect less—and be happy with it! [30]

If the public opinion theory is correct, recent Roper polls offer unions some hope. Unions and their leaders are more popular today than ten or twenty years ago. That portion of the public having a good opinion of labor leaders has risen to 50 percent, up from 36 percent in 1982, and the overall approval of unions has risen to 61 percent. By a margin of thirty-three to twenty-eight—the reverse of survey findings in 1977—more people today say they instinctively side with the union against a company in a labor dispute. The upswing is particularly noticeable among young people.[31]

Business Adaptation

The business adaptation explanation for the decline of unions is based on microeconomic theory. Unionization causes wages to rise—by about 15 percent on the average[32]—which causes firms to lose money or reorganize. In the 1980s the popular media played up "concession bargaining" and union "givebacks," but these concessions have not reduced the union wage advantage. The figures indicate that, if anything, the union wage gap has widened during the last ten years, while union density has plummeted. Some authors link the wage rise to the union decline. The wage gap is a selling point in union recruiting, but the net effect of the premium is to force business adaptation that reduces the number of union jobs.[33] Businesses respond by opening nonunion plants and managing them with alternative human resource approaches, which keep workers happy and frustrate unionization efforts.[34] Indeed, union bargaining practices may disregard recruiting and membership maintenance, as the emphasis on increasing wages is pursued with the knowledge that union jobs will be lost.[35]

One of the primary examples of the shift to nonunion establishments occurred in the construction industry where some unique federal laws apply. In 1959 construction unions convinced Congress that, because of the seasonal and unpredictable nature of construction employment, they should be allowed to run hiring halls and that employers should be able to hire workers from a particular union, even if the existing workers have not chosen that union as their bargaining agent in a representation election. Though privileged by these rules, construction unions dropped to represent "22.2 percent of all construction workers, down from 40.1 percent in 1973." [36] In explanation, union employers opened nonunion subsidiaries (the unions call this double-breasting) and allowed unionized subsidiaries to wither. For a time, the superior skills and training of union workers gave union shops a productivity advantage and allowed them to keep up. As the nonunion sector grew and union employment declined, however, many union workers took nonunion jobs. This shift eroded the productivity advantage of union firms and eliminated their competitive advantage. [37] Employers found they could have their cake and eat it too—skilled union labor at nonunion prices.

There are some exceptions to this adaptation effect, however; industries that have "market power"—protection from domestic and foreign competition or legal monopolies—can afford to pay higher wages. Occasionally, by effectively threatening to strike or retaliate, a union will win the right to have a say in corporate investment decisions. [38] The United Automobile Workers (UAW), for example, fought plans by General Motors to open nonunion shops, and GM was forced to stay neutral in the organizing campaigns in new plants.

Perhaps the most important exception to the business adaptation argument occurs in the public sector (government). In 1962 President John Kennedy signed Executive Order 10988, which allowed federal employees to form unions to negotiate on *nonwage* and fringe benefit issues. Several states also passed laws allowing their employees to unionize. Public sector unionism grew dramatically until 1976 and then stabilized. [39] The government is subjected to some pressure to keep costs down, but many economists have argued that the pressure is not as intense as in the private sector. [40] Thus, public sector unions grew in the 1970s, while their private sector counterparts declined.

Union Busters versus Labor Organizers

Businesses now aggressively use "union avoidance" strategies. This "nice guy" alternative, also known as "progressive management" or "quality of life programs," is intended to make workers see unions as unnecessary. In fact, stories about businesses that rid themselves of unions by communicating openly with workers occasionally appear in the *Wall Street Journal*. [41] A study of these programs found that the progressive approach does significantly reduce support for unions. [42]

Many scholars argue, however, that progressive management is a rather small part of the management strategy. As an alternative, businesses can hire consultants to persuade workers to vote "no" in union elections. They also can break the law and commit "unfair labor practices." The same factors that push businesses to adapt and expand nonunion enterprises also inspire this kind of aggressive union avoidance. When President Ronald Reagan appointed avidly pro-business members to the National Labor Relations Board, breaking a pattern of balance in appointments, the NLRB was ready to allow an all-out business fight against unions.

Under the current system, it is perfectly legal for businesses to hire campaign specialists and lawyers to fight unions. Antiunion consulting firms are used much more frequently today than in the past, and one study found that these legal union avoidance strategies (mainly the use of consultants), have a negative impact on the overall chance of a union victory.[43]

In general, union election outcomes reflect the long-standing attitudes of the workers—feelings that insulate workers from the campaigns.[44] On the margins, however, campaign events can make a difference of several percentage points. The extent of union organizing efforts and the fact that smaller units are more prone to unionization also have a substantial impact.[45] Other variables, such as employer resistance and the length of the campaign, reduce union success, but their impact is dwarfed by union organizing effort and unit size.

Unfair labor practices include illegal threats against or firing of pro-union employees or making unduly pessimistic predictions about the effect of unionization on the firm. There is no way of knowing whether dirty tricks have increased, but complaints about them by labor unions have skyrocketed. According to one analysis, "In 1960 there was an average of 1.78 unfair labor practice claims of this type per election. This average had increased to 3.99 by 1977 and to 7.45 by 1982."[46] One of the most serious allegations is employment discrimination against union supporters. Harvard economist Richard Freeman, perhaps the most widely read proponent of the unfair labor practices thesis, argues that they account for about one-half of the drop in unionization in a state-by-state study.[47] Other scholars, however, have found little or no impact from unfair labor practices above and beyond the legal union avoidance strategies.[48]

The increased level of employer union avoidance activity has not been met by a similar increase in union organizing activity. One aspect of the allocative problem is that unions might reasonably spend less on organizing because the stiffer opposition reduces the value of organizing expenditures vis-à-vis other activities. National unions have spent a declining proportion of their money on organizing, although the absolute amount did increase from 1953 to 1977.[49] In addition, unless there is centralized leadership, organizing efforts may be wasted in costly raids as unions battle each other for the right to organize workers. In 1961 Solomon Barkin was one of the first to express disappointment about the organizing efforts of the recently merged AFL-CIO:

> One vision that inspired the AFL-CIO merger was the coordination of organizing efforts. The formation of an Organization Department with what appeared to be considerable status and support enthused many within the trade union movement. But the promise was short-lived. In its first five years the department helped individual unions in current organizing drives. But soon the staff was drastically cut in size and its activities sharply curtailed. The remaining crew of federation organizers has devoted itself primarily to building up organizations to compete with the expelled bakers' and laundry workers' unions and to assist unions in combating Teamsters' Union raids.[50]

A brief examination of AFL financial records bears this out. In 1947, for example, the AFL spent 39 percent of its money on organizers' salaries and expenses.[51] After the merger, a half year's budget indicated organizing expenditures amounting to 11.2 percent of all expenditures. In 1957 the figure fell to 4.9 percent, and two years later it fell to 2.4 percent. Organizing received just 0.8 percent of the 1974 expenditures, reflecting a decline in the absolute level of organizing expenditures. The Organization Department's mandate was broadened by the 1973 convention to include field services, and this led to a slight infusion of resources as the organizing and field services expenditures rose to 1.7 percent of the budget in 1975 and 2.1 percent in 1979.[52]

Union Adaptation and Response

What are some of the issues surrounding union adaptation to the modern economy? Will a major change in union structure and function occur?

A Major Reorientation of Labor Unions

The blue-collar/service economy explanation of union decline has led some prominent authors to argue that unions are unsuited to the modern economic realities. Economist Charles Heckscher has argued that workers do not want old-fashioned unions for collective bargaining. He called for

> the evolution of unionism toward a form that can effectively represent employees more flexibly than the present system—able

to embrace diverse types of members, including managerial and professional ranks; able to deal comfortably with both long-term strategic concerns and shopfloor participation bodies; able to engage in multilateral negotiations among several parties around complex issues; and able to use a range of tactics according to the situation.[53]

One first step toward this new unionism is occurring now in the form of labor-management cooperation programs. To preserve auto worker jobs, the UAW agreed to workplace reorganization. Some plants reorganized to include the Japanese team production approach. In 1989 the bricklayers' union announced it had cooperated with the International Council of Employers of Bricklayers and Allied Crafts-men to develop a standard contract form that would reduce the use of nonunion subcontractors. In return, the bricklayers agreed to greater flexibility in job assignments.[54] In the mid-1980s the well-publicized reports of the AFL-CIO Committee on the Evolution of Work called for more labor-management cooperation of this kind, as well as better union public relations work and more modern organizing tactics that minimize the belligerent aspects of unionization.[55]

It seems unlikely that there will be a full-scale shift in Heckscher's direction, however, in part because "workplace innovations so extensive as to require a truly radical departure on the part of labor are few, and where change is required it is not so massive as he suggests." [56] But even the comparatively minor workplace innovations that have been implemented are unpopular with union members. Dissidents within the UAW, for example, complain that the teamwork system allows worker input only when worker ideas result "in getting more work out of fewer workers," as one UAW member observed about team production in a U.S. Mazda plant.[57] Thus, labor-management cooperation can erode the union's support among the workers, and it also can create conflicts among workers.[58]

The call for major reorganization does not confront the basic organizational questions: Who will lead? Who will pay? What selective incentives will they be offered? It is ironic that unions are being asked to "reorganize for cooperation," while employers are staging widespread legal and illegal campaigns against labor unions. Unions—the victims—are now being asked to drop *their* conflictual stands and work cooperatively with management. This does not wash well with labor unions. As AFL-CIO president Lane Kirkland noted, "The persistence on a course of union avoidance (such as the National Association of Manufacturers' adventures with a Committee for a Union-Free Environment) can only engender continuing conflict." [59]

Figure 2-1 Memberships of AFL-CIO Unions and American
Association of Retired Persons (AARP), 1955-1987

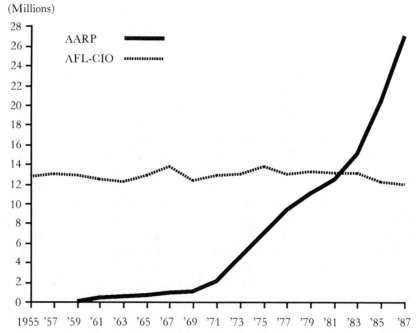

SOURCE: Paul E. Johnson et al., *American Government*, 2d ed. (Boston: Houghton Mifflin, 1990), 397. Compiled from AFL-CIO and AARP reports. Reprinted here with permission.

New Organizing Efforts and Selective Benefits

"I think we've survived about as bad as they can do to us and we're in pretty good shape," [60] observed Kirkland in 1990. This optimism reflects a new set of AFL-CIO programs to beef up organizing efforts. The first part of the AFL-CIO strategy, put crudely, is to copy the organizing concepts of the American Association of Retired Persons (AARP). Figure 2-1 above depicts the phenomenal growth of AARP and the stagnant membership of AFL-CIO unions. The AFL-CIO is trying to offer its members benefits similar to those offered by AARP.

The final report of the AFL-CIO's Committee on the Evolution of Work outlined a plan in which the AFL-CIO organizations would provide selective material benefits to former union members. [61] In 1986 a corporation was created to administer the Union Privilege Benefit Program (UPBP). Member unions may sign up, making their members eligible for benefits. It began with the Privilege MasterCard program, which offered a lower interest rate (by about 5 percentage points) than commercial bankcards. It now has added: free or discount legal services provided through contracts with 715 law firms; supplemental life insurance; travel services, including discounts on airfare, hotels, and car rentals; and a Health Needs Service, which provides prescription drugs and other medications at lower cost.

The UnionRATE service, a savings program, offers interest rates about 2.5 percent above the market ones. According to David Silberman, the president of the corporation that administers UPBP, these programs aim "to use the AFL-CIO's size and collective strength in a new way as consumers to develop benefits that will improve the quality of the lives of union members at home and on the job." [62] Although some unions, such as the Teamsters', do not participate, the programs are gaining momentum and popularity. Using the UnionRATE service, which was added in 1990, the AFL-CIO enrolled twenty-two unions and four million members in less than two months. The UPBP represents a return of the AFL-CIO unions to their selective benefit orientation before the Wagner Act. As Kirkland commented, "I think one of the arguments that perhaps convinced people that it was worth trying was that unions were formed when there were no collective agreements. . . . Many of our affiliates were formed and grew as benefit associations, nowhere near getting real collective bargaining with the employer." [63]

The UPBP originally was intended to encourage the member unions to create associate member programs. In this context, associate members are former union members, either retired or working in nonunion shops. Kirkland has estimated that currently there are about 300,000 of these associate members, although the figure is growing rapidly as the programs take effect.[64] Pilot programs are under way to broaden eligibility, but these are under the control of the individual unions and state federations. The AFL-CIO State Federation in Montana voted to create a division called the American Family Union, which opened its membership to the general public.[65] But this is considered a pilot program, and its effect remains to be seen. Since one of the cornerstones of the AFL in the 1880s was that only legitimate "workingman's" organizations could join the federation, these efforts represent a substantial break with tradition.

The benefit programs will probably have their major impact in making it easier for unions to win representation elections and gain members in right-to-work states. Unions can use these benefits as tangible evidence of the rewards of union membership.[66] "The major plea is 'What do I get for my money when I join the union?' . . . [U]sing the benefits has helped us a lot to get people in," said Linda Lampkin, director of research for the American Federation of State, County, and Municipal Employees union. "We're also using it to create members out of fee payers in states like New York. We use the benefits as another organizing tool." [67]

In addition to offering workers more tangible benefits, the AFL-CIO has structured its national offices to facilitate organizing. First, in 1987 a new office of Comprehensive Organizing Strategies and Tactics was created within the Department of Organization to help member unions plan "nonworkplace strategies in their campaigns to win recognition and first contracts from recalcitrant employers." [68] In 1989 the AFL-CIO created an Organizing Institute to reestablish the AFL-CIO's role in organizing. The institute "will be available at the request of affiliated unions for strategic advice, 'second opinions' on strategic options and postmortems on rights and wrongs." [69] The institute trains organizers, coordinates swaps of organizers among unions, and oversees campaigns. It already has played a role in educating organizers in the Teamsters' Union drive to organize fleet service workers at USAir[70] and helped the United Food and Commercial Workers launch a major southern organizing campaign among 6,000 workers in Harris-Teeter supermarkets.

Are these programs making a difference? The auto workers' defeat in the Nissan organizing drive in 1989, probably the most widely publicized organizing campaign in recent years, does not inspire much confidence. Lane Kirkland pointed out, however, that AFL-CIO unions won eight of the thirteen other representation elections in Tennessee in 1989.[71] On March 5, 1990, the Executive Council's Committee on Organizing reported that "the decline in [representation] election activity that began in 1982 has been reversed" [72] and claimed that unions are winning a majority of elections among low-paid workers, as well as white-collar and professionals in the service sector. Evidence of the organizing accomplishments include successful drives to organize employees of several universities: 3,500 at Harvard, 1,300 at the University of Massachusetts, and 1,200 at the University of Cincinnati.

One change in the concept of union jurisdiction is worth noting. The AFL unions emphasized strict separation of workers in different crafts to minimize conflict among unions. The AFL-CIO, however, has in place a system of arbitration and dispute resolution that renders such sharp delineations unnecessary. The philosophy, in essence, is: "There are lots of unorganized workers out there! Go find some and organize them. Don't worry about jurisdiction unless another union challenges you." This philosophy has always been present in the Teamsters'

Union, for example, but now the AFL-CIO unions are indeed branching out.

In the early 1970s the membership of the ILGWU peaked at around 400,000, but now it stands at half that level. After a series of failed efforts to expand membership in the core jurisdiction, the union's new president, Jay Mazur, appointed a Task Force on Organizing and New Directions in 1986. Their report led to an expansion of the organizing department and a branching out "beyond our traditional apparel base. The Metro Organizing Department and the new Water House Employees and the Professional and Clerical Employees divisions"[73] were established after the report. Currently, the ILGWU is organizing workers at K-Marts, auto scrapyards, and eyeglass manufacturers—without objections from the AFL-CIO.

Mergers and Economizing or Higher Dues

When times are tough—membership is declining and money is scarce—unions can reorganize to save money. Mergers of national unions, which have been much more common in the era of union decline,[74] economize on administrative expenses. National unions also may encourage their locals to merge for the same reason. Because of the shrinkage in membership, local ILGWU offices were asked to merge. The national ILGWU office also cut back, reducing staff from 1,242 in 1986 to 1,109 in 1989. Deep cutbacks were made in some offices, but the expansion of the organizing departments obscures them to some extent.

But it may not be enough to economize. At all three ILGWU conventions in the 1980s, the leadership felt compelled to request dues increases. The dues rate was increased in 1983, but efforts to economize and another increase in dues caused the union's president to report in 1986 that "declining membership has more than offset the dues increase voted by the last convention."[75] Many local delegates argued against the dues increase, but the argument grounded to a halt after this impassioned speech by President Sol Chaikin:

> We can cut out the Retiree Service Department. That's a choice. (Cries of "No") We have another choice: We can lay off all the organizers so that the non-union competition can be free and clear to eat up all the available work that's still left in the continental United States. (Cries of "No") We have another choice: We lay off half the business agents. (Cries of "No") Why not? We've got to make choices. We will close down some union offices. There's a choice.[76]

He concluded his speech with a discussion of the meaning of the word *delegate*, wondering aloud if the folks back home who instructed their delegates to vote against a dues increase were as well informed as the convention participants. "If you go back and if you have changed your position, you can tell them that for a good union member, there was no other way." [77] That increase passed, but the organization's financial woes continued. The 1989 convention passed another large dues increase to cover losses and expand organizing efforts. [78]

Increasing dues is a risky decision because the unraveling effect sets in. The union puts itself on a treadmill. Higher dues rates make new workers reluctant to join; existing locals may decertify. After the cheapskates withdraw, the remaining members can find a majority to raise dues yet again. Unless organizing efforts are stepped up several notches, total membership probably will not increase.

Turning toward Politics

Unions may spend some of their scarce resources on politics, but in strategies they differ. The ILGWU, which has one of the largest political departments, spends about 2 percent of its budget on politics. The ILGWU blames its current fate on imports and failed lobbying efforts for the Textile and Apparel acts of 1985 and 1987. These acts, which would have protected domestic manufacturers against foreign competition, were vetoed by President Reagan, and override attempts narrowly failed.

Other unions may press for legal changes that will assist them in labor relations. Most of the proposals that receive substantial lobbying effort are union-specific. The construction unions, for example, won special provisions to allow the use of hiring halls (in essence, closed-shop arrangements) in the 1959 Landrum-Griffin Act. In the late 1980s they pushed Congress to outlaw the practice of double-breasting by construction firms.

Some of the reforms demanded by labor would truly be collective goods among all unions. But these laws—which are widesweeping changes in labor relations policies pertaining to unionized workers only—seem the least likely to be enacted into law. Labor organizations probably will have trouble pushing through recently proposed policy changes that force businesses to rehire strikers after negotiations are finished, [79] enact tougher penalties for unfair labor practices by business, and eliminate employer participation in representation elections. The benefits of such laws would be shared collectively among all unions, and thus none of the unions are likely to be willing to expend the enormous amount of political energy and money that would be required for their passage.

The 1989 AFL-CIO convention adopted a resolution calling for a major change in labor law, but it did not call for major expenditures on lobbying activity. The delegates said they did not expect President George Bush to introduce such a bill or sign it, so they pledged to fight in the 1990 campaigns for "a Congress and . . . state officials committed to enacting fair labor legislation." [80] Whether or not this will translate into any substantial action remains to be seen. There has been an upward trend in AFL-CIO COPE expenditures, however.

The AFL-CIO's political victories do not benefit primarily labor. The union calls itself the "People's Lobby" and expends a great deal of time pushing for laws to benefit the poor or working people, even if they do not benefit union members in particular. The sixty-day plant closing notification law passed in 1988, for example, had labor's support, but it benefits a much broader category of workers. Because the unions do not have the political clout to win on unionized labor issues, they end up appealing for broad social programs. The AFL-CIO emphasis on these social issues can be seen as good public relations more than anything else.[81]

Conclusion

American labor unions have not withered and died. Total membership has been stable, but the unionized percentage of the work force has been steadily declining. Many explanations have been offered for this effect, but perhaps the most widely accepted by the general public and the media is the notion that the transition to a service economy has rendered unions obsolete. The academic literature rejects this "blue-collar decline" theory quite solidly, however. Instead, the decline is explained by changes in the opinions of workers about their jobs and unions, business adaptation to union-related wage costs, and the increasingly sophisticated use of union avoidance tactics by business.

More distressing to union advocates than a simple decline in blue-collar industry is the fact that unionization has declined among blue-collar workers. Although there is support for unions among many groups of workers that were thought to be antiunion—such as women, minorities, and some service and professional workers—the labor unions, at least until the mid-1980s, had not found a way to organize them quickly enough to compensate for declines in membership. Recent AFL-CIO efforts to attract workers with new selective incentives, in combination with additional organizing efforts, may reverse the trend, but it is too soon to say whether these programs will undo the adverse effects of business adaptation, union avoidance, and changes in workers' opinions toward unions.

Labor organizations, at least in the AFL-CIO, are aiming to attract members with better selective benefits. Massive reorientation of unions, as Heckscher has called for, is not in the cards for American labor organizations because the alternative schemes lack the internal coherence that successful voluntary organization requires. These organizations must fashion institutions to overcome the collective action and unraveling problems. A new system might be attractive to contemplate, but labor is not headed in this alternative direction. If anything, American labor organizations are going in the opposite direction, returning to the organizational methods of the pre-Wagner Act era, which emphasize selective incentives.

Notes

An earlier version of this chapter was presented at the 1990 annual meeting of the Midwest Political Science Association, held in Chicago. The author thanks the panel participants for their comments. He also is grateful to Professors Allan Cigler, Carolyn Porto Johnson, and Burdett Loomis of the University of Kansas and Professor Jack Fiorito of the University of Iowa's College of Business Administration for their helpful observations.

1. Platform item 11 resolved "that we recommend to the Congress of the United States the adoption of such laws as shall give to every American industry full protection from the cheap labor of foreign competition." *Report of the First Annual Session of the Federation of Organized Trades and Labor Unions of the United States and Canada,* November 15-18, 1881 (Cincinnati: Press of Robert Clarke, 1982), 4 (hereafter cited as *FOTLU Proceedings).*
2. *FOTLU Proceedings,* 1883, 19.
3. For example, FOTLU continually lost money on the printing of its annual reports. In fact, things became so bad that in 1885 the federation was forced to pay $18 return freight on 1,500 copies of the annual convention reports that the New Orleans Trade Assembly ordered but refused to pay for. As for other problems, funds were insufficient to pay full-time officers, and plans to create a united strike fund to assist members were considered but not adopted.
4. The AFL created an Executive Council and a full-time position of president (to which it elected Samuel Gompers) and took some measures to increase collection of funds. Affiliates paid a flat charter fee on joining, thus generating seed money. Other adaptations are discussed later in this chapter.
5. Mancur Olson, *The Logic of Collective Action* (Cambridge, Mass.: Harvard University Press, 1965). For an overview of more recent literature, see Russell Hardin, *Collective Action* (Baltimore: Johns Hopkins University Press, 1982).
6. Selig Perlman and Philip Taft, *History of Labor in the United States, 1896-1932* (New York: MacMillan, 1935), 354.

7. Philip Taft and John Sessions, "Introduction," in *Samuel Gompers, Seventy Years of Life and Labor* (New York: Dutton, 1957), 19.
8. Russell Hardin, "Collective Action as an Agreeable n-Prisoner's Dilemma," *Behavioral Science* 15 (1971): 472-479.
9. See Paul Edward Johnson, "Unraveling in Democratically Governed Groups," *Rationality and Society* 2 (January 1990): 4-34.
10. American Federation of Labor, *Report of the Proceedings of the Sixty-Ninth Convention of the American Federation of Labor,* 1950 (hereafter cited as *AFL Proceedings*).
11. The 1977 labor law initiative died on the Senate floor on June 22, 1978, after a five-week filibuster. *AFL-CIO Proceedings of the Thirteenth Constitutional Convention of the AFL-CIO,* 1979, 132.
12. It sometimes is incorrectly argued that the AFL was apolitical. Gary Marks, for example, has claimed that in 1890 the AFL convention rejected the creation of a legislative committee—see Marks, *Unions in Politics: Britain, Germany, and the United States in the Nineteenth and Early Twentieth Centuries* (Princeton, N.J.: Princeton University Press, 1989), 71. This resolution was not rejected. It was referred without qualification to the Executive Council *(AFL Proceedings,* 1890, 30). Throughout the early years of the federation, Gompers lobbied Congress on a variety of issues. In 1896, as Marks noted, a permanent legislative department was established by the convention. He did not mention, however, that the primary constraint faced by the department was finances, not a philosophical opposition to lobbying. Gompers was in favor of the new legislative department. Supporters proposed a tax of five cents per member to start the department, but it, together with a three cents tax, was defeated. Only a one cent tax was approved, *(AFL Proceedings,* 1896, 78). In its final stages the 1896 convention voted to reduce the size of the legislative department from two staff members to one, *(AFL Proceedings,* 1896, 106). This activity is completely inconsistent with the picture painted by Marks, who hinted that the members favored politics but Gompers preached "pure and simple" unionism.
13. *Record of Proceedings, International Ladies' Garment Workers' Union,* 26th Convention, 1947, 600 (hereafter cited as *ILGWU Proceedings*).
14. *ILGWU Proceedings,* 1950, 305.
15. George Meany, "Report of George Meany to the National Committee Meeting of Labor's League for Political Education," reprinted in *AFL Proceedings,* 1951, 447.
16. Joseph Krislov, "Decertification Elections Increase But Remain No Major Burden to Unions," *Monthly Labor Review,* 102 (November 1979): 147-161.
17. Gary N. Chaison and Dileep G. Dhavale, "A Note on the Severity of the Decline in Union Organizing Activity," *Industrial and Labor Relations Review* 43 (April 1990): 369.
18. Richard B. Freeman, "Contraction and Expansion: The Divergence of Private Sector and Public Sector Unionism in the United States," *Journal*

of Economic Perspectives (Spring 1988): 74.

19. See William N. Cooke, "The Failure to Negotiate First Contracts: Determinants and Policy Implications," *Industrial and Labor Relations Review* 38 (January 1985): 163; and William T. Dickens and Jonathan S. Leonard, "Accounting for the Decline in Union Membership, 1950-1980," *Industrial and Labor Relations Review* 38 (April 1985): 328.

20. Dickens and Leonard, "Accounting for the Decline," 327. After their study of decertification rates, the authors observed that "it would take over 15 years for decertification to cause a one percent drop in the percentage of the labor force organized—all other factors held constant."

21. Henry S. Farber, "Trends in Worker Demand for Union Representation," *American Economic Review* 79 (May 1989): 166-171; and Farber, "The Extent of Unionization in the United States," in *Challenges and Choices Facing American Labor,* ed. Thomas A. Kochan (Cambridge, Mass.: MIT Press, 1986).

22. Daniel Bell, "The Next American Labor Movement," *Fortune,* April 1953, 204. Also see Bell, *The Coming of the Post-Industrial Society* (New York: Basic Books, 1973); and Charles Sabel and Michael Piore, *The Second Industrial Divide* (New York: Basic Books, 1984).

23. William J. Moore and Robert J. Newman, "A Cross-Section Analysis of the Postwar Decline in American Trade Union Membership," *Journal of Labor Research* 9 (Spring 1988): 123.

24. Freeman, "Contraction and Expansion," 65. Also see Michael Goldfield, *The Decline of Organized Labor in the United States* (Chicago: University of Chicago Press, 1987).

25. Edward C. Kokkelenberg and Donna R. Sockell, "Union Membership in the United States, 1973-1981," *Industrial and Labor Relations Review* 38 (July 1985): 500. Also see Henry S. Farber, "The Recent Decline of Unionization in the United States," *Science,* November 13, 1987, 917.

26. Leo Troy, "The Rise and Fall of American Trade Unions: The Labor Movement from FDR to RR," in *Unions in Transition: Entering the Second Century,* ed. Seymour M. Lipset (San Francisco: ICS Press, 1986), 76-77.

27. Freeman, "Contraction and Expansion," 69. Freeman wrote: "Even read cautiously, [the figures] clearly contradict the notion that the decline in union density in the United States is part of a general collapse of unions in the developed world."

28. Seymour Martin Lipset, "North American Labor Movements: A Comparative Perspective," in Lipset, *Unions in Transition,* 438.

29. Peter G. Bruce, "Political Parties and Labor Legislation in Canada and the U.S.," *Industrial Relations* 28 (Spring 1989): 115-141.

30. See Farber, "Trends in Worker Demand," 170; and Farber, "Recent Decline," 919.

31. "Labor's Image on the Upswing, Roper Concludes," *AFL-CIO News,* March 5, 1990, 5; and "Outpouring of Support Bolsters Strikers," *AFL-CIO News,* November 27, 1989, 3.

32. For a recent review of more than 200 studies, see H. Gregg Lewis, *Union Relative Wage Effects: A Survey* (Chicago: University of Chicago Press, 1985).

33. See Richard Edwards and Paul Swaim, "Union-Nonunion Earnings Differentials and the Decline of Private-Sector Unionism," *American Economic Review* 76 (May 1986): 99; Peter Linneman and Michael L. Wachter, "Rising Union Premiums and the Declining Boundaries among Noncompeting Groups," *American Economic Review* 76 (May 1986): 99; Richard B. Freeman, "The Effect of the Union Wage Differential on Management Opposition and Union Organizing Success," *American Economic Review* 76 (May 1986): 92-96.

34. John T. Addison and Barry T. Hirsch, "Union Effects on Productivity, Profits, and Growth: Has the Long Run Arrived?" *Journal of Labor Economics* 7 (January 1989): 101. Also see Anil Verma, "Relative Flow of Capital to Union and Nonunion Plants within a Firm," *Industrial Relations* 24 (Fall 1985): 396.

35. Edwards and Swaim, "Union-Nonunion Earnings Differentials," 99. The authors claim that "unions assign a lower priority to maintaining membership levels than is commonly believed." Also see Michael Wallerstein, "Union Organization in Advanced Industrial Democracies," *American Political Science Review* 83 (June 1989): 481-502.

36. Herbert R. Northrup, "Construction Doublebreasted Operations and Pre-Hire Agreements: Assessing the Issues," *Journal of Labor Research* 10 (Spring 1989): 217.

37. Steven G. Allen, "Productivity Levels and Productivity Change under Unionism," *Industrial Relations* 27 (Winter 1988): 94-113; and Allen, "Declining Unionization in Construction: The Facts and the Reasons," *Industrial and Labor Relations Review* 41 (April 1988): 343-359.

38. Verma, "Relative Flow," 403, fn. 6.

39. Linda N. Edwards, "The Future of Public Sector Unions: Stagnation or Growth?" *American Economic Review* 79 (May 1989): 161-165.

40. For an illustration of this difference, see Steven G. Allen, "Further Evidence on Union Efficiency in Construction," *Industrial Relations* 27 (Spring 1988): 239.

41. Marj Charlier, "How a Mine in Arizona Wooed Workers Away from Union Loyalties," *Wall Street Journal* August 8, 1989, A1.

42. Jack Fiorito, Christopher Lowman, and Forrest D. Nelson, "The Impact of Human Resource Policies on Union Organizing," *Industrial Relations* 26 (Spring 1987): 113-126.

43. John J. Lawler and Robin West, "Impact of Union-Avoidance Strategy in Representation Elections," *Industrial Relations* 24 (Fall 1985): 406-419.

44. See J. G. Getman, B. Goldberg, and J. B. Herman, *Union Representation Elections: Law and Reality* (New York: Russell Sage Foundation, 1976).

45. William T. Dickens, Douglas R. Wholey, and James C. Robinson, "Correlates of Union Support in NLRB Elections," *Industrial Relations*

26 (Fall 1987): 245.

46. Farber, "Recent Decline," 919.

47. Freeman, "Effect of the Union Wage Differential," 95. For similar results, see William N. Cooke, "The Rising Toll of Discrimination against Union Activists," *Industrial Relations* 24 (Fall 1985): 436.

48. Lawler and West, "Impact of Union-Avoidance Strategy," 418. Also see Moore and Newman, "Cross-Section Analysis," 123. For a response to these arguments, see Richard B. Freeman and Morris M. Kleiner, "Employer Behavior in the Face of Union Organizing Drives," *Industrial and Labor Relations Review* 43 (April 1990): 351-365.

49. Paula B. Voos, "Trends in Union Organizing Expenditures, 1953-1977," *Industrial and Labor Relations Review* 38 (October 1984): 52-63. Also see Richard B. Freeman and James L. Medoff, *What Do Unions Do?* (New York: Basic Books, 1984): 228-230.

50. Solomon Barkin, *The Decline of the Labor Movement and What Can Be Done about It* (Santa Barbara, Calif.: Center for the Study of Democratic Institutions, 1961), 54.

51. *AFL Proceedings,* 1947, 145.

52. These figures are calculated from the Executive Council Financial Reports presented in various years in the *Proceedings of the Constitutional Convention of the AFL-CIO.* Accounting procedures changed after the merger, so this comparison is not precise. Postmerger organizing expenditures were measured generously by including the AFL-CIO's national Department of Organization along with expenses paid to the national unions.

53. Charles C. Heckscher, *The New Unionism: Employee Involvement in the Changing Corporation* (New York: Basic Books, 1988), 254.

54. "Bricklayers Develop Contract Form to Counteract 'Double-breasting,'" *AFL-CIO News,* December 11, 1989, 6.

55. AFL-CIO Committee on the Evolution of Work, *The Future of Work and The Changing Situation of Workers and Their Unions* (Washington, D.C.: AFL-CIO, August 1983 and February 1985, respectively).

56. Adrienne E. Eaton and Paula B. Voos, "The Ability of Unions to Adapt to Innovative Workplace Arrangements," *American Economic Review* 79 (May 1989): 175.

57. Kirk Victor, "Tensions over Teamwork," *National Journal,* May 20, 1989, 1228.

58. See, for example, Donald M. Wells, *Empty Promises: Quality of Working Life Programs and the Labor Movement* (New York: Monthly Review Press, 1987).

59. Lane Kirkland, "It Has All Been Said Before ..." in Lipset, *Unions in Transition,* 404.

60. "Bad-News 1980s End on Upswing," *AFL-CIO News,* January 8, 1990, 1.

61. AFL-CIO Committee on the Evolution of Work, *The Changing Situation of Workers and Their Unions.*

62. "Union Privilege: Using Quality to Serve Members," *AFL-CIO News,* August 19, 1989, 6-7.
63. "UnionRATE Savings Takes Off, Boosting UPBP," *AFL-CIO News,* March 5, 1990, 10.
64. "Unions Find Ways to Aid Associate Members," *AFL-CIO News,* September 2, 1989, 10.
65. *AFL-CIO News,* November 13, 1989, 5.
66. See Paul Jarley and Jack Fiorito, "Associate Membership: Unionism or Consumerism?" *Industrial and Labor Relations Review* 43 (January 1990): 209-224.
67. "Union Privilege: Using Quality to Serve Members," *AFL-CIO News,* August 19, 1989, 7.
68. Kirkland, "It Has All Been Said Before . . . ," 402.
69. This is a paraphrase of John Sweeny, service employees president who chaired the Executive Council's organizing committee. "New Institute to Study, Bolster Organizing," *AFL-CIO News,* May 13, 1989, 2.
70. "Teamsters Map Campaign at USAir," *AFL-CIO News,* October 14, 1989, 9.
71. *AFL-CIO News,* September 2, 1989, 1.
72. "Solidarity, New Approaches Boost Organizing," *AFL-CIO News,* March 5, 1990, 12.
73. *General Executive Board Report to the 40th Convention of the International Ladies' Garment Workers' Union,* June 1989, 7.
74. Gary N. Chaison, "A Note on Union Merger Trends, 1900-1978," *Industrial and Labor Relations Review* 34 (October 1980): 114-120; and Chaison, *When Unions Merge* (Lexington, Mass.: D.C. Heath, 1986).
75. Israel Mechlowicz, Finance Committee Secretary, *ILGWU Proceedings,* 1986, 314.
76. *ILGWU Proceedings,* 1986, 323.
77. Ibid, 324.
78. *AFL-CIO News,* June 24, 1989, 2.
79. Sen. Howard Metzenbaum, D-Ohio, introduced S. 2112 and Rep. William Clay, D-Mo., introduced H.R. 3936. See "Bill Seeks to Restore Strike Rights after Permanent Replacement Rulings," *AFL-CIO News,* March 5, 1990, 3.
80. "Labor Law Overhaul Is Urged to Protect Rights of Workers," *AFL-CIO News,* November 27, 1989, 1.
81. This question does not receive much attention. See Vernon Coleman, "Labor Power and Social Equality: Union Politics in a Changing Economy," *Political Science Quarterly* 103 (1988): 687-705.

3. NATIONALIZATION OF INTEREST GROUPS AND LOBBYING IN THE STATES

Clive S. Thomas and Ronald J. Hrebenar

In this chapter political scientists Clive Thomas and Ronald Hrebenar argue that there has been a nationalization of interest group politics at the state level. Observers familiar with lobbying in the nation's capital would be struck by the similarities in techniques, strategies, and tactics used by statehouse interests to those employed by groups at the national level. Particularly noteworthy at the state level has been the proliferation of organized interests, due largely to the enormous expansion of state government activities and expenditures. Correspondingly, professionalism among state lobbyists has increased, as exemplified by the greater number of full-time "specialist" lobbyists and the emergence of full-service lobbying firms that represent a host of clients.

In one area, the regulation and control of special interests, many states appear to be ahead of the federal government, as they seek to cope with some of the negative consequences of special interest influence in the policy process. The authors suggest that a number of states have a valuable body of experience with lobbying registration, reporting, and disclosure provisions that can be models for possible future federal-level reforms.

The authors believe that while singular, context-based styles of lobbying will continue to characterize group politics in many state capitals, state-level lobbying will continue to absorb the successful techniques and styles from Washington. As the stakes increase in statehouses in the post-Reagan era, states may well inherit many of the problems that continue to bedevil group-based politics in Washington. This will test the strength of their lobbying and ethics laws, as the states become the battlegrounds for key policy battles ranging from abortion to social services to taxation.

As interest group politics has become increasingly sophisticated and professionalized in the nation's capital during the last three decades, similar changes have occurred in the various state capitals around the nation. In Sacramento, Springfield, and Albany, as well as in Salt Lake City, Richmond, and Des Moines, the nature and style of lobbying more closely mirror that found in Washington than in those same state capitals just a few decades ago. Thus, to modify the first sentence of the introduction to this book: "From James Madison to

Madison Avenue *and to Madison, Wisconsin,* political interests have played a central role in American politics *at both the national and state levels."*

Interest groups at the state level have long played a significant and often dominant role in policy making. Despite the extensive coverage given interest groups at the national level, they probably have been more powerful in the states.[1] In state after state, powerful interests once dominated the institutions of state government to a degree not found at the national level. In Montana, Anaconda dominated state politics, just as the sugar industry and the "Big Five" companies once dominated Hawaii.[2] Likewise, West Virginia and Kentucky were once nearly the private property of the coal industry. In almost all states at one time or another in the late 1800s, railroads had enormous influence in state legislatures. Around 1900 the Southern Pacific Railroad was the power manipulator in the California state government. The Republicans ran the California government, and the Southern Pacific controlled the Republican party.[3] In Texas and Pennsylvania, oil interests exercised great influence: "It was said that Standard Oil did everything to the Pennsylvania legislature except refine it." [4] This type of powerful single-interest domination of given state governments did not occur on the federal level because of the diversity of interests found in Washington, D.C.

According to Cigler and Loomis, the major changes in the nature of interest group politics at the national level are: (1) their great proliferation; (2) centralization of their headquarters in the nation's capital; (3) more sophisticated lobbying techniques; (4) the rise of single-interest groups; (5) the growth of political action committees (PACs); (6) the spread of interest group politics into more political arenas; (7) the rise of so-called public interest groups; and (8) the recognition of governments and other institutions as major lobbying actors.[5] In our study of interest group politics in the fifty states, we identified all eight of these changes at the state level as well. In this chapter we explore the significance of this nationalization of interest group politics.[6]

State Laws to Control Lobbying

One other change at the state level can be added to the eight national trends also evident in state politics: the adoption of various lobbying registration and reporting laws.

In the areas of lobby and lobbyist registration and the reporting of lobbying expenditures, the states are significantly more advanced than the federal government. In the 1880s, long before ineffectual federal laws were devised in this century, attempts were made to regulate interest group activities at the state level. The major impetus was the often-flagrant abuses of America's first major lobby, the railroads.

By the 1950s thirty-eight states and the territory of Alaska had enacted lobby regulation laws of one type or another. Laws that required lobbyists to register were found in only twenty-nine states and Alaska, and only nineteen states required the reporting of lobbying expenditures.[7] Since the 1950s there has been a frenzy of activity across the states directed toward passage of public disclosure and lobby laws. California's famous Proposition 9, or the Political Reform Act of 1974, for example, provided for the detailed regulation of lobbying, campaign spending, and standards of conduct for public officials. Despite being significantly weakened by interest group court challenges, Proposition 9 is still more effective than any laws found at the national level.

The lobby laws now found in all fifty states require the registration of lobbyists and their employers and, in most cases, the reporting of lobbying expenditures. Rather than prohibit certain types of lobbying activities, reformers decided to require their disclosure in the hope that the public would consider this information before making collective political decisions. Indeed, because of the provisions relating to the right to "petition government" in the First Amendment to the Constitution and similar provisions in many state constitutions, attempts to restrict lobbying would run into serious constitutional problems.

A survey of state lobby laws, however, would reveal great variations among states in their reporting requirements and enforcement. Some progressive states have fairly stringent laws and require even government personnel to register if they engage in lobbying. At the other end of the continuum are the states that traditionally have had extremely narrow and laxly enforced laws.[8] States with the most stringent lobby laws tend to be those with weaker interest group systems.[9] The weakest laws are found in the South, where some of the major abuses have taken place, and the strongest laws are found in those states that traditionally have had relatively little corrupt lobbying.

All states now have laws relating to the activities of political action committees, but the effectiveness of these laws at the state level varies enormously from state to state. The last two states to adopt such laws, Utah and Nevada, did so reluctantly in the late 1980s.

Another category of laws related to lobbying deals with possible financial conflicts of interest of public officials. These laws require disclosure of the financial connections that public officials have with individuals, groups, organizations, and businesses. And in yet another attempt to reduce corruption of administration officials, several states have passed public ethics laws that prohibit certain officials from being employed by an interest group within a specified period of time after their involvement in government decisions that directly affected that interest.

Although this latter provision is similar to the 1978 federal Ethics in Government Act—which proved to be largely ineffective during the Reagan administration's Nofziger and Deaver influence-peddling cases—by and large the other loophole-plagued federal lobbying regulation laws are but pale reflections of the more effective laws found in several states such as California and Wisconsin.[10] With the federal lobby laws generally acknowledged to be nearly complete failures, it is at the state level that a valuable body of experience with various lobbying registration, reporting, and disclosure provisions has been built over the past two decades. This experience should contain lessons for possible future federal-level reforms.

Expansion of the Interest Group Universe in the States

Throughout the fifty states the numbers and types of interest groups and their lobbying activities have greatly proliferated since 1960. Part of the reason for this is an enormous expansion in state government activities. As state governments do more, spend more, and affect more segments of the economy and society, more interest group activity is generated. Clearly, all state governments do more now than they did in the 1950s and 1960s and spend much more money to perform their traditional and newly acquired functions. In the postwar period, education has come to account for up to 40 percent of the budgets in some states, and new and powerful education lobbies have risen to the top of many state interest group systems.

Beginning with the Carter administration and intensifying throughout the Reagan presidency, the federal government sought to shift to the states the financial obligation for many of its programs. A longer-term trend has been the vast expansion of state government programs since the 1930s. These shifts are reflected in a multiplication in state government budgets. Overall state government expenditures tripled during the 1970s, from $85 billion to nearly $260 billion. Just one state, California, had a state government budget of more than $36 billion in 1989. The stakes involved in state government decision making have clearly reached magnitudes, attracting the attention of more and more interests.

There also has been an explosion in the already covered types of interest groups active at the state level, as new interests—such as social issue, public interest, and single-issue groups—have entered the political arena and traditional interests have fragmented. Fragmentation has been particularly evident within the business and local government lobbies. Individual corporations and businesses and individual cities and special districts (especially school districts) have increasingly lobbied on their own.

Other researchers have grouped the various state-level interests into five major categories: business, labor, education, agriculture, and local government groups.[11] Our study of interest groups in the fifty states used a broader focus and more specific categories of interests to give a clearer picture of the range and types of groups active at the state level.[12]

Of the traditional interest group categories, business is the vaguest. To say that the majority of groups lobbying in state capitals are business groups may obscure more than it enlightens. Business groups range from individual corporations to banks and utilities and usually include professional and trade associations. Use of the term *business lobby* frequently masks the often-bitter competition among business interests and thus creates the false impression of a powerful, cohesive business lobby. The other four categories of traditional interests—labor, education, agriculture, and local government—suffer from the same problems.[13] Thus, it is more helpful to identify specific types of interests as opposed to broad categories.

Table 3-1 lists the most continually active interests in the fifty states in the order of the estimated intensity of their lobbying efforts. From this we can conclude that a very broad range of interests, both public and private, operate in the states today. We estimate that in terms of time and money as much as 75 percent of the state-level lobbying effort is attributable to these sixteen interests.

Some significant changes have affected the types of interests most active at the state level. First, government lobbies have become an important force in the states. These include lobbyists for individual cities, counties, special local government districts, and various state agencies. The most prominent state agencies in all states are the departments of education or public instruction, transportation, and welfare, as well as state universities and colleges.

Second, associated with this rise in government lobbying has been the increased prominence of public sector unions, particularly state and local employees' and teachers' unions. In state after state, teachers' unions and public employees' unions are now among the most influential interests.

Third, ideological groups, which often focus on a single issue such as abortion, also have become quite active in recent years. Public interest organizations—particularly good government, senior citizens, and, most of all, environmental groups—are other forces that now have a significant presence in almost all state capitals. Interests with an

Table 3-1 Rankings of the Sixteen Most Influential and Active Interests in the Fifty States

Ranking	Interest	Number[a]
1	School teachers' organizations	43
2	General business organizations	31
3	Bankers' associations	28
4	Manufacturers	23
5	Traditional labor organizations (AFL-CIO)	23
6	Utility companies	20
7	Individual banks and financial institutions	20
8	State and local government employee associations	16
9	Lawyer associations	15
10	Local government associations	15
11	Doctors	14
12	Insurance companies and associations	13
13	Individual traditional labor unions (Teamsters', autoworkers)	13
14	Realtors' associations	12
15	General farm organizations (farm bureaus)	11
16	K-12 educational interests (other than teachers)	10

SOURCE: Based on data published in Clive S. Thomas and Ronald J. Hrebenar, "Interest Groups in the States," in *Politics in the American States,* 5th ed., ed. Virginia Gray, Herbert Jacob, and Robert B. Albritton (Glenview, Ill.: Scott, Foresman/Little, Brown, 1990), 123-158.

[a] Number of states in which the interest was ranked in the "most effective interest" category.

intermittent or less consistent presence tend to be newly formed groups, such as consumer and animal rights, or those representing an interest concentrated in certain states, such as Native Americans and Hispanics.

Thus, Table 3-1 above reveals that interest group politics at the state level is very diverse. It is important to remember, however, that the exact dimensions of the state group systems vary from state to state and that one cannot directly equate presence with power. Just because a group or interest is active in state politics does not by itself ensure its success in achieving its goals. In fact, some of the interests listed in Table 3-1 are often effective, while others have very little influence at all.

Professionalization of State-Level Lobbyists

Lobbyists receive little respect from the general public at either the state or federal levels of American politics. Perhaps the only occupations held in lower regard by the general public are those of member of Congress or used-car dealer. Although the negative images remain, the reality has changed drastically. Significant changes in American government and politics over the last twenty-five years have had a major impact on the kinds of people who make up the lobbying community, the skills required of them, and their styles and methods of doing business. The developments in the state capital lobbying community probably have been even more dramatic than those in Washington simply because, until recently, state lobbyists operated in a much less-sophisticated, less-demanding, and less-scrutinized political environment than their counterparts in the nation's capital. With state capitals in major states more and more resembling the U.S. capital in terms of style and nature of lobbying, one of the major changes has been the decline of the "good old boy" style of lobbyist and the rise of the professional lawyer-lobbyist.[14]

Today at the state level as well as in the nation's capital, we can identify four types of lobbyists. These lobbyists have different assets and liabilities, hail from different backgrounds and experiences, and represent different types of interest groups. Thus, they are perceived differently by public officials. Each lobbyist's power base is determined by public officials' perceptions of the lobbyist and the group he or she represents. Consequently, each lobbyist plans his or her strategies and tactics based on the specific characteristics and assets they possess.

Contract lobbyists get the big headlines when exposés on lobbying are run in local newspapers, in part because some of these big-name lobbyists earn the biggest incomes. The other explanation is that many contract lobbyists represent business and professional interests with big money and political clout. Approximately 10 percent of state-level lobbyists are contract lobbyists. This figure reflects the sharp increase in their numbers at the state level since they began to appear in the 1930s. These lobbyists are sometimes called "pros" or "hired guns."

In-house lobbyists are regular employees of the interests they represent. Many also are executive directors, presidents, executives, staff members, or government affairs specialists. These are and always have been the largest group of lobbyists since they first made their appearance in the mid-1800s when business saw the need to have more regular contacts with government decision makers. Seeking to neutralize the negative image of lobbyists, in-house lobbyists often call themselves government relations or legislative liaisons.

Legislative liaisons are the lobbying corps for state and local governments. Because of the negative connotation of the term *lobbyist,* most states do not officially refer to those engaged in lobbying for government agencies as lobbyists. Yet there is no doubt that governmental legislative liaisons are very much lobbyists.

Citizen or volunteer lobbyists are often an unknown and unpredictable element in a state's lobbying system. They tend to represent local ad hoc groups or small nonprofit organizations. Volunteer lobbyists are not well-paid and are driven by their commitment to a cause, not by monetary rewards. The private "hobbyists" or self-styled lobbyists tend to carry the banners of their causes year after year in the legislature and are always ready to fill in some time on the local evening news.

All lobbyists, regardless of type, seek to maintain a reputation for honesty, trust, and credibility by providing useful and honest information. Beyond this common denominator, each of the major categories of lobbyists tends to focus on different strategies and methods of influence.

Most contract lobbyists do not rely mainly on subject matter information and expertise for their success. As political insiders, they are hired primarily for their knowledge of the political system and their close contacts with public officials. Most tend to be specialists in a specific part or parts of the governmental process. Just as Michael Deaver had special knowledge of and access to the Reagan White House, so too do former legislators or former state party chairs at the state level. Two of the most successful lobbyists in Alaska, for example, are Kent Dawson and Wes Coyner, both former chiefs of staff to Alaskan governors. Contract lobbyists also may have a great influence on their clients' disbursement of campaign funds. Moreover, many contract lobbyists organize fund-raisers for candidates and work to help them get elected or reelected. By representing clients who are important economically at the state level, these lobbyists are among the most important political forces in each state.

Subject-matter expertise is the primary asset of many in-house lobbyists. Additional resources available to them include in-cash and in-kind campaign contributions and an ability to mobilize grass-roots campaigns. In contrast, government lobbyists have only one major weapon—information, although they can, and often do, surreptitiously utilize their client groups to their advantage. Volunteer lobbyists usually rely on moral arguments to sell their causes to public officials. They also may provide political perspectives or insight not available elsewhere, but they usually lack the status of political insiders or access to big campaign contributions and sophisticated organizations. Self-styled lobbyists have the fewest political assets of all, unless they have been major campaign contributors.

During the last two decades, the state lobbying community in general has become much more pluralistic and professional. Contract lobbyists and in-house lobbyists, particularly those representing associations, have made the greatest advances in professionalism, although the levels of professionalism vary from state to state and even from region to region. Despite these variations, signs of this increased professionalism are evident in three trends: (1) an increase in the number of full-time lobbyists; (2) the emergence of lobbying firms that provide a variety of services and represent multiple clients; and (3) the increased specialization of many contract lobbyists in response to the growing complexity of government. Just as a Washington lobbyist may specialize by representing the diet food industry, for example, lobbyists in the states are now specializing in representation of agricultural interests, educational groups, or various unions.

The new lobbyist at the state level is likely to be a well-educated, well-trained employee of an interest group, and increasingly, a female member of what was once a nearly all-male club. In replacing the old-style wheeler-dealer lobbyists who have largely disappeared from the lobbying scene in state capitals, the new, sophisticated model of wheeler-dealers uses a much more multifaceted approach to establishing access to and influence with public officials. For modern lobbyists, information is their most useful commodity and because technical information has gained importance, they are perceived as being increasingly professional.

The professionalization of lobbyists at the state level has proceeded hand in hand with the general professionalization of state government and its major actors. Conventional wisdom argues that group influence is greater in those states with less-professionalized legislatures and bureaucracies,[15] which then are forced to rely more heavily on groups for information. In contrast, states having more professionalized legislatures and bureaucracies possess their own research resources, giving groups less control over information, a key ingredient in any policy-making situation.[16]

Adoption of Modern Interest Group Tactics at the State Level

During the last twenty years lobbyists at the state level have widely adopted the lobbying strategies and tactics successfully tested at the national level. Contemporary interest groups and lobbyists employ a much wider range of methods than their predecessors did just a few years ago. Interest group leaders have had to match their resources to the nature of their group, its available resources, the way it is perceived by policy makers, the issue it is pursuing, and its political circumstances.

By far the most common and still the most effective of interest group tactics in the states is the use of one or more lobbyists. In fact, until very recently it was the only tactical device used by the vast majority of groups, and it remains the sole approach used by many today. But increased competition among the expanding number of groups has forced some interests to update their strategies and to adopt the successful tactics developed by national groups, often after testing at the state level in grass-roots campaigns. These include mobilizing grass-roots support through networking (sophisticated member contact systems), undertaking public relations and media campaigns, building coalitions with other groups, and contributing workers and especially money to election campaigns, particularly by establishing a PAC.[17] These tactics are employed to enhance the ability of the group's lobbyist or lobbyists to have access to and influence public officials. Because the new tactics are often expensive, interests tend to use the newer techniques only if traditional lobbying activities prove to be insufficient. Such multifaceted lobbying campaigns also are difficult to coordinate and administer, yet increasingly they are being used in almost all the state capitals.

Political Action Committees

State-level groups participate in state and local elections usually by recruiting or endorsing candidates, providing campaign support in the form of workers and services, and contributing money. Many groups use one or more of these techniques. There also has been an explosion in the formation and use of political action committees, the primary way to channel money to candidates. In Washington State, for example, the number of PACs almost doubled (from 114 to 200) over the period 1978-1980. And Larry Sabato reported an increase in Illinois PACs from 54 in 1974 to 372 in 1982.[18] In Connecticut 307 PACs were operating in 1987; seven of the top ten lobbies had established such groups.[19] Finally, in the West, PACs in Oregon proliferated—from 57 to 410 during the 1970s.[20]

Although campaign contributions have long been important for the establishment of group access to key politicians, changes in the nature of campaigns in the states have made PACs one of the most significant resources for many interests.[21] The most important change has been the tremendous increase in the cost of getting elected.[22] The cost of gubernatorial races in some states is approaching $20 million, and in California, state assembly campaigns with a price tag of more than $1 million are becoming rather commonplace. Even in rural states the cost of running for state offices has been rising steadily, and with state and local political parties unable or unwilling to provide significant funding, interest groups stand ready to meet politicians' funding needs.

Generally, the increased demand for campaign funds has been met by interest groups. Even in such states as Connecticut, Massachusetts, and New York, where political parties are seen as strong and historically have made major contributions to their candidates' campaigns, candidates are relying increasingly on interest group money and PAC contributions, as are the parties themselves.

By 1980 PACs provided 45 percent of all contributions over $100 to California state legislative candidates.[23] Also by the early 1980s Arizona PACs were providing over half the campaign funding for legislative races. PACs in New York State contributed almost $20 million to senate and assembly campaigns during the five-year period ending in January 1988 and accounted for 60 percent of the contributions to the legislative campaign committees of both major parties.[24]

Data from our study of interest group politics in the fifty states strongly suggests that those groups and organizations making the biggest contributions to politicians' campaign chests wield more relative influence on the state level than on the federal level.[25] There also appears to be a strong relationship at the state level between the percentage of campaign contributions originating from interest groups and the overall impact of these groups on the political system. This is not the only reason for their success, but it does appear to be an important contributing factor. Consequently, regardless of the strength of a political party in a state, the power triangle of elected official, lobbyist, and PAC is becoming ever more apparent.[26]

Multi-Institutional Approaches

Although in state campaigns most interest groups still tend to spend the majority of their time and resources in dealing with legislators and their staffs, some groups increasingly are directing their efforts toward the executive branch—the governor's office and state agencies. Few lobbyists concentrate solely on the legislature because a successful lobbying campaign, especially one that seeks to promote something, requires the cooperation and often the active support of one or more executive agencies. Without this support, the chances of even partial victory are considerably reduced. All but the most politically naive lobbyists have known this for decades and have acted accordingly. Thus today, as in the past, a focus solely on the legislative aspect provides only a partial understanding of group tactics.

Interests also have expanded their activities to the judicial branch and increasingly to such popular democracy arenas as initiatives and referenda. In California and Oregon, for example, many of the most controversial issues are battled among large interest group coalitions that spend millions of dollars and often turn to the courts to fine-tune the resulting laws. The average initiative in California costs $1 million to qualify by gathering approximately 372,000 signatures. At perhaps the extreme was the 1988 set of initiatives sponsored by California's insurance industry, aimed at defeating several other initiatives that would have lowered insurance costs to consumers. Estimates placed the cost of qualifying and promoting the insurance industry initiatives at more than $70 million. Even with this expensive effort, the objectives of consumer groups were not sidetracked until the industry won a key decision in the California Supreme Court.[27]

Cooperative Lobbying

Not only are interest groups using coalitional tactics more often at the state level, but they also are engaging in frequent cooperative lobbying with their national organizations. Many state groups have national affiliates. The extensive and sophisticated national organizations of a number of environmentalist and labor groups, for example, provide all sorts of aid and advice to their state affiliates. The state affiliates in turn are often activated to assist their Washington offices in lobbying campaigns. Major national corporations with factories and offices in many parts of the country coordinate the political actions initiated by the state offices of these organizations. According to L. Harmon Zeigler, there also is an increase in interstate cooperation and funding of groups,[28] particularly for ballot propositions involving social issues.

Changing Nature of Interest Group Influence
in the States

Historically, when states were dominated by a single interest, or a few interests, that dominant interest was usually business. Those days are gone, however; the Anacondas and Southern Pacific Railroads have largely relinquished their one-time dominance. To be sure, many states still have a single *prominent* interest such as gaming in Nevada; oil in Texas, Louisiana, and New Mexico; the Mormon church in Utah; and agriculture in many farm states. But now the politics in these states is characterized by a pluralism and a sharing of power. Given the growing diversity in even the most rural states, it is unlikely that any state will be dominated by a single interest as some were before the 1950s.

Business remains the most widespread and powerful interest active at both the national and state levels, despite its fragmentation into specialized groups. And, as must be expected in a dynamic system, at any given moment some business interests are in decline while others are in ascent. For example, coal has declined in West Virginia and agricultural interests have declined in most midwestern states, but high-tech industries have risen in prominence in California, Oregon, Massachusetts, and Colorado.

Organized labor has declined in power at the national level, but its pattern of power change is less clear at the state level. The national decline of the American Federation of Labor-Congress of Industrial Organizations (AFL-CIO) was most visible late in the Carter administration and early in the Reagan presidency, when labor's political agenda lost its clout in Washington. For labor's lobbyists, the 1980s were largely a period of desperately trying to hold on to previously secured gains. At the state level some once-powerful unions such as the United Mine Workers and United Automobile Workers have declined in power (in Michigan, for example) as their memberships have plummeted. The extractive and basic manufacturing industry unions have lost tremendous numbers of members and political influence in recent decades. Yet the overall picture for organized labor at the state level is mixed because of the rise of the service industry and government employee unions.

Organized labor's new political strength is based on teachers' associations and state and local public employees' associations. This metamorphosis of labor is one of the most significant developments in the changing configuration of group power in state capitals. With the growth of state government in the postwar era, the seeds were sown for the revival of labor in the form of public employees' and teachers' unions—both organizations with memberships much more political than those of the older types of unions. Overall in the fifty states the most prevalent, active, and influential interest is education, especially in its most frequent manifestation—the state-level education association. Public employee unions and associations rank as the twelfth most influential interest.

In the late 1980s labor and business began to engage in a new series of political conflicts. Largely set aside were the traditional business regulation and labor protection issues of past years; the new conflicts revolved around the service programs of state government, the environment, and budgetary, educational, and political reform issues. The new labor organizations have adopted grass-roots organization campaign tactics, PACs, computers, voting record analyses, and media campaigns to gain influence in state legislatures. Business has been forced to react to this new threat to its secured position of access by adopting many of these same tactics. These trends mirror patterns occurring in the nation's capital.

Rise of State-Level Public Interest Groups

Another significant change in state-level interest group systems has been the proliferation of public interest groups. In numbers and influence, public interest groups have become an important, if not overwhelming, force in most states. Particularly prominent are the hundreds of environmentalist groups that have formed at the state and local levels since the 1960s. Part of the growth in public interest groups has been in response to a wide variety of state and local issues. It is true, however, that many of the most significant state-level public interest groups are the state affiliates of such national groups as Common Cause and Planned Parenthood, established to meet the grass-roots demands by their membership.

Because many of the more liberal public interest groups found national politics less than favorable as a site for political action during the 1980s, they shifted their agenda implementation to the states. Scenic America, for example, a lobbying group seeking to regulate billboards along our nation's highways, shifted its focus to the states while continuing to maintain a national lobbying effort. In 1990 Scenic America noted that a bill in Congress to prohibit new billboards on federal highways was being strongly opposed by the billboard industry's lobby, the Outdoor Advertising Association of America. But it also pointed out that five states and more than 500 cities had banned or restricted billboards.[29] The public interest lobby Common Cause initially had no plans to establish state affiliates, but eventually it relented because of demands by its local and state activists for the introduction of Common Cause-supported reforms in state and local government. During the 1980s many of Common Causes' most significant victories occurred in the states (from, for example, such reform programs as OUTS—Open Up The System), as the zeal for political reform evaporated in Washington.

Although public interest groups are still relatively lightweight forces when compared to the traditional powers of business, labor, agriculture, education, and government in general, they have overall made some progress in gaining access and influence in state politics. Steady yet small gains have been made by environmentalists and senior citizens. And some single-issue groups—antiabortionists in Missouri, taxpayers' groups in California and Massachusetts, Mothers Against Drunk Driving (MADD) in several states—have had their successes, but many of these groups are now inactive or declining in influence. During the latter 1980s the issue of tort reform, as it was played out in the various states, particularly the desire by many to place a cap on awards in damage suits, brought three of the most well-financed and well-organized interests—doctors, lawyers, and insurance companies— into the ranks of the most effective interests.

The successes of interests outside the traditional five major ones, including social issue and minority groups, do not appear to have been significant enough across states to emerge as a trend. Indeed, the changes in the configuration of group power across the states has been far less dramatic over the last twenty-five years than the major expansion in group activity might lead us to assume. The players in the game may have changed by the addition of new groups, but the rules of success remain virtually unchanged.

Conclusion

One of the most interesting questions regarding the similarities in the patterns of changes in interest group politics in Washington and in the states is: What forces helped drive the changes at the state level? Were the changes the result of the dissemination of information and ideas from the national level, or were they the result of such state-level factors as increased competition for resources and budgetary allocations? Part of the changes, of course, are explained by the development of lobbying techniques, strategies, and tactics at the federal level and their utilization as appropriate at the state level. Grass-roots lobbying, for example, which is used so frequently in attempts to influence policy making in Washington, has been used increasingly at the state level, especially by single-interest groups. One interesting development has been the augmentation and enhancement of state-level affiliates by their national organizations to facilitate such grass-roots lobbying campaigns. This development allows the state-level organizations to pursue their own agendas as well.

Despite some evidence to support the dissemination explanation, it seems that state-level political phenomena better account for the increased sophistication and complexity of state-level interest group activities. One phenomenon was the transfer of many significant functions and obligations to the states during the Reagan and Carter administrations and the consequent enhancement of state politics as a worthy arena for interest group politics. During the 1970s and 1980s state government budgets multiplied in heavily populated states such as California and New York and even in rural states such as Utah and Idaho. These budget increases were partially the result of inflation, increased demands for services, and reduced federal program funding for which the states stepped in to fill the gap.

Whatever the causes, it is clear that interest group politics at the state level has moved in the direction of the style and substance found at the national level. Observers familiar with lobbying in Washington would be struck by the similarities in techniques, strategies, and tactics used in Sacramento, Springfield, and Albany, as well as by the wide range of organizations represented in the state interest group systems. Even in the smallest states, the essential features of national-level interest group politics can be identified. What appears to be happening is the nationalization of interest groups and lobbying in the states.

Finally, we must ask: "Will a total nationalization of interest groups and lobbying occur at the state level?" Clearly, national styles of lobbying have had differing impacts on the various states. But, overall, state-level lobbying will continue to absorb the successful techniques and styles from Washington, while maintaining the unique traditions that continue to make the states different from each other and from the nation's capital.

Notes

1. James Madison predicted this in his *Federalist* No. 10 where he argued that while the impact of interest groups would certainly be significant at the federal level, the size of the nation and the diversity of the *factions* (his term for interests) would work to prevent any one interest from gaining a stranglehold on national politics. He also suggested that the lack of economic and social diversity in most states would lead to their domination by a few interests or a single all-powerful interest. See Clinton Rossiter, ed., *The Federalist Papers* (New York: New American Library, 1961), 62-70.
2. During the first half of the twentieth century, the sugar industry and five other companies dominated Hawaii's social and political institutions. These companies, known as the "Big Five," were Castle Cook, C. Brewer, AMFAC, Alexander and Baldwin, and Theo H. Davis.
3. John R. Owens, Edmond Costantini, and Louis Weschler, *California Politics and Parties* (New York: Macmillan, 1970), 32-33.
4. Ruth K. Scott and Ronald J. Hrebenar, *Parties in Crisis* (New York: Wiley, 1984), 236.
5. Burdett A. Loomis and Allan J. Cigler, "Introduction: The Changing Nature of Interest Group Politics," in *Interest Group Politics*, 2d ed., ed Cigler and Loomis (Washington, D.C.: CQ Press, 1986), 1-26.
6. Clive S. Thomas and Ronald J. Hrebenar, "Interest Groups in the States," in *Politics in the American States,* 5th ed., ed. Virginia Gray, Herbert Jacob, and Robert B. Albritton (Glenview, Ill.: Scott, Foresman/Little, Brown, 1990), 123-158.
7. Belle Zeller, *American State Legislatures* (New York: Crowell, 1954), 220-221.
8. COGEL (Council of State Governments), *Campaign Finance, Ethics, and Lobby Laws* (Lexington, Ky.: Council of State Governments, 1988).
9. Sarah McCally Morehouse, *State Politics, Parties and Policy* (New York: Holt, Rinehart, and Winston, 1981), 130-131.
10. Ronald J. Hrebenar and Ruth K. Scott, *Interest Group Politics in America,* 2d ed. (Englewood Cliffs, N.J.: Prentice-Hall, 1990), chap. 9.
11. L. Harmon Zeigler, "Interest Groups in the States," in *Politics in the*

American States: A Comparative Analysis, 4th ed., ed. Virginia Gray, Herbert Jacob, and Kenneth N. Vines (Boston: Little, Brown, 1983), 99.

12. Almost all informed observers agree that an expansion in group activity has occurred during the past twenty years or so. They disagree, however, over the extent of these changes. We believe that this expansion has been extensive, particularly the range of groups active in the states. To try to better measure this expansion of the state interest group system, we took three paths. First, we tried to identify the so-called hidden lobbies such as those maintained by governments. Second, we focused on interest activity not just in the state legislature but in state government as a whole, including all branches of government and such processes as initiatives and referenda. Third, in contrast to many previous studies and obtain an accurate picture of the range of groups operating in a state, we studied not just one but several legislative sessions. For a more detailed explanation, see Thomas and Hrebenar, "Interest Groups in the States."

13. William Browne's study of agricultural interests illuminates the wide variety of farm interest groups and their divisions. See Browne, *Private Interests, Public Policy, and American Agriculture* (Lawrence: University Press of Kansas, 1988).

14. Our definition of a lobbyist is *a person designated by an interest group to represent it to government for the purpose of influencing public policy in that group's favor.*

15. Morehouse, *State Politics,* 132-133; and Zeigler, "Interest Groups in the States," 120-121.

16. Increased professionalism on state policy-making process participants, is only one of several variables that affect overall group power. Findings from our study suggest that the relationship between overall group power in a state and the level of professionalism is much weaker than previously believed. More important factors such as campaign contributions, which cause public officials to remain dependent on groups, have worked to negate any changes caused by increased professionalism. The groups themselves have become more sophisticated and professional in gathering and presenting information. The net effect of all these factors is that today increased professionalism of public officials is often accompanied by increased group power. California is a prime example, as are such diverse states as Alaska, Colorado, and Georgia.

17. Clive S. Thomas, "Understanding Interest Group Activity in the American States," in *Studies in American Politics,* ed. D. K. Adams (Manchester, England: University of Manchester Press, 1989), 203.

18. Larry Sabato, *PAC Power* (New York: Norton, 1985), 117.

19. Sarah McCally Morehouse, "Connecticut," in *Interest Group Politics in the Northeast,* ed. Ronald J. Hrebenar and Clive S. Thomas (forthcoming).

20. William H. Hedrick and L. Harmon Zeigler, "Oregon," in *Interest Group Politics in the American West,* ed. Ronald J. Hrebenar and Clive S. Thomas (Salt Lake City: University of Utah Press, 1987), 109.

21. L. Harmon Zeigler and Michael Baer, *Lobbying: Interaction and Influence in American State Legislatures* (Belmont, Calif.: Wadsworth, 1969), 176-177; and Zeigler and Hendrik van Dalen, "Interest Groups in the States," in *Politics in the American States: A Comparative Analysis,* 3d ed., ed. Herbert Jacob and Kenneth N. Vines (Boston: Little, Brown, 1976), 121-123.
22. Malcolm E. Jewell and David M. Olson, *Political Parties and Elections in American States* (Chicago: Dorsey Press, 1988), 154-157; and Frank J. Sorauf, *Money in American Politics* (Glenview, Ill.: Scott, Foresman, 1988), 260-274.
23. Sabato, *PAC Power,* 117.
24. "The Albany Money Machine" (Report of the New York State Government Integrity Commission), *New York Times,* March 18, 1989.
25. Diana M. Evans, "PAC Contributions and Roll-Call Voting: Conditional Power," in *Interest Group Politics,* ed. Allan J. Cigler and Burdett A. Loomis (Washington, D.C.: CQ Press, 1986), 114-132.
26. Morehouse, "Connecticut."
27. John Garamendi, "California's Ballot Industry," *New York Times,* May 7, 1990.
28. Zeigler, "Interest Groups in the States," 117-118.
29. "Billboard Opponents Want Signs Restricted," *USA Today,* April 25, 1990.

4. ORGANIZATIONAL MAINTENANCE AND POLITICAL ACTIVITY ON THE "CHEAP": THE AMERICAN AGRICULTURE MOVEMENT

Allan J. Cigler

The questions of why groups arise and why they have proliferated have drawn the lion's share of scholarly attention in recent years. Less consideration has been accorded to the issues of group evolution and survival, particularly how organizations attempt to adapt to and survive in a changing political world. The universe of interest groups is highly unstable, and organizational survival is often precarious, especially for those groups that attempt to mobilize and represent large numbers of citizens rather than form around narrow occupations or economic interests.

In this chapter Allan Cigler investigates the continuing organizational evolution of the American Agriculture Movement (AAM), thereby extending his research and analyses expounded in the two earlier editions of this book. The AAM was founded in the late 1970s as an ad hoc, system-challenging protest group seeking to improve the financial fortunes of family farmers. More recently, it became a permanent Washington, D.C.-based lobby, complete with a professional lobbyist and a political action committee.

The AAM has attained an impressive level of activity in the policy and electoral processes, despite its limited resources and an inability to expand its membership significantly. In fact, the group has developed a niche in the Washington agriculture policy community as a watchdog for family farm interests. Structurally, the AAM has become a staff organization with a small membership base but with a cadre of leaders who have become highly skilled in extracting resources from group supporters and outside patrons. Cigler suggests that the long-term survival of the group is still problematic, however, unless new activists are recruited and the group stabilizes its flow of financial resources.

The proliferation of organized interests in the postwar era has been one of the most significant trends in American political life. But many groups do not survive, particularly those that initially are organized for primarily political reasons. The group universe is an unstable one, characterized by group demise, group absorption by other groups, and group transformation to serve new goals. It is one thing to mobilize individuals in the short run for political action, but it is quite another to build a stable, permanent organizational structure and acquire the resources necessary to be influential in the policy and electoral processes on an ongoing basis.

This chapter focuses on the organizational development and activities of the American Agriculture Movement. The group was founded in the southern Great Plains in 1977 with the purpose of raising the income of family farmers through direct action protest activities.[1] The group attracted national attention in 1978 and 1979 when large numbers of the nation's farmers journeyed to Washington, D.C., many on their tractors, in an attempt to influence policy makers. Over the past decade the AAM has undergone a difficult transformation from a protest movement to a formally organized interest group with a permanent Washington presence. It has sought to create a niche for itself in an agriculture policy sector already occupied by four general farm associations and a number of occupational and other associational interests.[2]

The AAM illustrates the organizational difficulties faced by groups whose formation was sparked by a chaotic political and economic environment. Many fail to achieve permanence. Some groups survive, however, especially those not wedded to the idea of remaining or becoming mass membership organizations. Operating resources are perhaps the single most crucial element of group survival, and a small cadre of clever organizational entrepreneurs can, at times, acquire such resources with little help from a mass of followers or group supporters. Group survival may depend less on attracting and keeping large numbers of members than on maintaining a cadre of highly motivated and committed individuals who, in political scientist Jack Nagel's words, "care about the rightness of their actions regardless of what others do and regardless of individual and collective practical effect." [3]

An Incentive Theory of Group Formation and Maintenance: The Case of the American Agriculture Movement

For groups originally founded for political purposes, achievement of organizational stability is difficult and requires two interrelated phases. In the initial mobilization phase a number of individuals identify a common problem and agree that collective action is needed. In this stage it is important that a cadre of leaders or group entrepreneurs arise to secure the resources necessary for collective action, develop strategies for accomplishing collective goals, and incite the rest of the group to support or engage in actions directed toward achieving group goals.

The second phase, institutionalization and group maintenance, occurs after the group has developed an identity as a political collectivity to its adherents, its opponents, and other relevant political actors. The group becomes concerned with its permanence and turns its attention to such matters as organizational stability, leadership recruitment and continuity, development of a reliable membership base, and establishment of an enduring role in the political influence process.

"Incentive theory" provides a useful framework for studying stages of group development. Its central proposition is that individuals are rational actors interested in participating in groups that offer benefits greater than the costs they incur.[4] Three basic types of benefits are available: (1) material benefits—the tangible rewards of participation such as income or services that usually have monetary value; (2) solidary benefits—the socially derived, intangible rewards created by the act of association, such as fun, camaraderie, status, or prestige; and (3) purposive or expressive rewards—those derived from advocating a particular cause or ideological orientation.

Some incentives are collective and others selective. Collective benefits cannot be made available to members without also making them available to nonmembers. If, for example, a farm protest group succeeds in winning higher support prices, its members receive those benefits but so do all other farmers. Selective benefits, in contrast, go only to members; examples are discount insurance or publications provided by the group. Because groups originally organized for political purposes typically seek to provide collective benefits, they often face severe "free-rider" problems. Rational individuals will choose not to bear the participation costs (time, dues, and so forth) because they can enjoy the benefits without joining.

Theoretically, group mobilization can be viewed as an exchange process in which group leaders offer a package of incentives to potential members with distinct needs, wants, and preferences, in return for their support.[5] During the mobilization stage, conditions or events make such incentives particularly attractive and potential members are likely to have the capacity and willingness to bear the costs.

In the case of the AAM, a skillful group of entrepreneurs, using collective material incentives (the promise of higher farm prices) and expressive incentives (standing up for the family farm and the "rural way of life"), were able to mobilize a large group of farmers angry about low farm prices in 1977-1978. Rhetoric, symbolism, and emotionalism also were put to clever use, and open, democratic organizational arrangements that provided solidary benefits were utilized as well.[6] While there is no way to know exactly how many farmers participated in AAM's early activities, one survey estimated that 9 percent of the nation's farmers were involved.[7]

The AAM's 1979 tractorcade was a public relations disaster, however, as protesters were responsible for an estimated $1.2 million in well-publicized property damage in the nation's capital. Most observers then concluded that the group would vanish like most of the agrarian protest groups of the past. The AAM had not been successful in gaining its promised collective material benefits, and many participants became disillusioned with its reputation as unruly and radical. The expressive and solidary benefits offered paled in comparison to the costs of participation for many financially squeezed farmers.

From an incentive theory perspective, because the demand for benefits and the willingness to bear costs among group populations may change in response to varying conditions and circumstances, a group's survival ultimately depends on the skill with which its leaders tailor and adapt group incentives to the changing environment. Both improving and declining contextual conditions may be a barrier to group evolution. Conditions such as farm incomes may improve, making collective material benefits less attractive, or they may worsen, making material costs such as dues prohibitive. Furthermore, if group participants realize that their initial optimism about the group's likely success was unrealistic, they can no longer be mobilized by such "cheap" resources as political rhetoric from group leaders. The groups that tend to be most successful at the institutionalization and group maintenance stage are those that can, for their members and potential members, replace collective incentives with stable, tangible selective material benefits such as travel discounts, informative publications, and the like. Such benefits can be withheld from nonmembers, however.

For the AAM the move from a protest group to an institutionalized entity with a permanent Washington presence has proved difficult. In the early 1980s the group endured a factional dispute in response to the national leadership's attempt to change the group's incentive mix. A number among the group's leadership felt that the group could expand its membership and succeed politically only by moderating its appeal (reducing its expressive costs to potential members) and participating in aspects of mainstream politics, from having a permanent Washington office headed by a professional lobbyist to becoming involved in federal elections through the vehicle of a political action committee. But the attempt to moderate the group's orientation imposed high expressive costs upon many of the original protest activists who were suspicious of mainstream politics, and objections to the new direction caused the rapid demobilization of many AAM activists in 1982-1983. Many observers felt the group would fold shortly.

Organizational Maintenance on the "Cheap"

The AAM originally was designed to avoid what many farmers did not like about agriculture groups: a typically bureaucratic, top-dominated style of operation, that was unresponsive to producers' needs and overly responsive to corporate and agribusiness interests. The original AAM had no leaders, only "spokesmen," and no members, only "participants." It was a loosely structured grass-roots organization, with little internal discipline or control over its participants and no stable funding base.

After the factional dispute the national leadership attempted the difficult task of designing an organization that could be centrally directed and managed (to control the disruptive grass-roots elements that handicapped the Washington-based leadership efforts), yet could continue to draw on the AAM's grass-roots protest tradition as an alternative to traditional farm organizations. The aim was to keep the political agenda true to AAM's original policy purpose (with its expressive and collective material appeal) and retain much of the sense of camaraderie and friendship and other solidary benefits of AAM grass-roots participation, while appealing more to both moderate farmers and Washington policy makers, groups that were offended by the radical tactics of the original AAM.

The result was a compromise that took into consideration both the elements of a centralized national organization and those of the loosely organized state groups. "Membership" was to be on both an individual and a state basis. Individuals contributing $50 (currently $100) to AAM were sustaining members, and states were paid-up members, according to a formula based on state individual membership figures ($50 contributed to national AAM for each state member). State chapters could operate as they wished, but the national leadership had the power to expel any state groups that proved embarrassing to AAM's Washington efforts.

Policy for the organization was to be determined by a national delegate body, composed of representatives chosen by affiliated state organizations. The national delegate group was to meet quarterly. A national president and four other officials were to be elected at an annual convention. An executive committee (composed of the five elected officers and six members selected by the national delegate body) was empowered to carry out the functions of the delegate body when it was not in session.

Initially, the leadership was optimistic that the AAM could become a membership organization speaking for the nation's family farmers. But they underestimated political realities. The bulk of the original participants in AAM activities could not be wooed back since the notion of a centrally directed membership group itself was incompatible with AAM's original purpose and spirit. In fact, only about 300 farmers attended the first national convention after the split, held in January 1984, although the group claimed that nationwide participation was 150,000. The outgoing AAM president reluctantly admitted, "It doesn't matter how many don't come. The leaders are here, and we have the moral support of thousands back home." [8] Clearly, the AAM leadership was going to operate without a mass base if necessary.

Without the basic resources to develop selective incentives (such as insurance) to attract members, and with an inability to point to policy successes, AAM was greatly handicapped in any attempt to expand its membership. Moreover, the realities of the mid-1980s farm crisis proved to be a major recruiting barrier for a membership group. The crisis had moved from the southern Great Plains to the northern Corn Belt states such as Iowa. In this region even the original AAM had never had strong support from which to construct a membership base, and a number of existing groups in the region (such as the National Farmers Organization and the Farmers Union) seemed to have cornered the market for membership group challenges to mainstream agriculture policy. New group development in the nation's midsection in the mid-1980s was again grass-roots in nature but tended to take the form of local constituent service groups designed to help farmers deal with emotional and financial distress. In Iowa, for example, rural churchmen as well as farm activists played prominent roles in such new organizations as Prairiefire Rural Action and the Iowa Farm Unity Coalition.[9] Few of the new groups were based on individual memberships.

It became clear by mid-1984 that AAM had evolved largely into a staff organization, with organizational decisions decided by a relatively few. The national director, David Senter, had emerged as the chief policy initiator in the organization aided by the elected national officers, ex-officers, and the key elected delegates from a number of the state organizations. Most of the leadership cadre had been involved since the group's inception, had enjoyed strong friendships, and were in agreement on the group's goals.

Like a number of other organized interests in the modern era, AAM continued to exist despite its inability to expand its membership. Organizational resources do not always have to come from a mass membership. Groups sometimes can overcome the free-rider problem by finding sponsors who will support the organization, thereby reducing its reliance on membership dues. As political scientist Jack Walker has noted, "Patrons of political action play a crucial role in initiation and maintenance of groups, particularly foundations and wealthy individuals." [10]

Today, AAM operates as a national voice for family farmers on a remarkably small budget, which in the mid- to late 1980s ranged from $250,000 to $350,000. AAM National Director Senter, who is the only full-time paid professional lobbyist, is assisted by two full-time paid assistants. Volunteers who come to Washington to lobby, as well as the national delegates, pay a good portion of their own expenses (sometimes, however, the state affiliates help with costs). The expenses of national officials who travel around the country are paid, but they often receive food and lodging from sympathetic farmers and help with other expenses (at times, passing the hat at a picnic or a rally). The AAM rents, at low cost, a modest office close to Capitol Hill and is always happy to have the aid of unpaid interns.

Although AAM membership figures are not made public, an estimated 1,500-2,000 dues-paying members (representatives of thirteen states and Canada were present at the 1989 national convention) provide a partial financial base. The group also has a 100% Parity Fund made up of $1,000 contributions by various AAM participants. The interest from the fund goes toward the operating expenses of the organization. The AAM-sponsored American Family Farm Foundation, a 501(c)(3) organization, accepts tax-deductible contributions. Foundation activities are managed by AAM's national office for "educational" purposes.

For such a group with relatively few dues-paying members and an ambitious political agenda, "money is the most overwhelming obstacle to [its] success," one national delegate volunteered in 1989, complaining that "too many meetings are limited by discussions of payments on the fax machine." Employees are considered dedicated but underpaid. Senter, considered by many in the organization to be so indispensable that the AAM might fold if he were to leave, has no group-funded pension plan, for example.

Fortunately, some AAM members have been willing to make substantial contributions to the group in addition to their membership dues. A number of individuals who are part of or close to the national leadership regularly send checks to the Washington office as the need arises, or they make large "bids" at the auction the group holds at its national convention (the proceeds of which go to the national office). Even for the rank and file, membership dues institute only part of their financial contributions, many being quite responsive to emergency requests for funds.

The AAM also has "farmed" a number of corporate patrons who underwrite some of the group's activities, but AAM leaders do not like to talk about such matters given the group's essentially anticorporate, populist orientation. In both 1983 and 1988, for example, the group worked closely with the railroads to defeat a coal slurry pipeline bill, which the AAM viewed as not only increasing grain-hauling costs if the railroads suffered from the lack of coal-hauling business but also infringing on farmers' control over their land and potentially influencing water availability. Railroads such as the CSX Corporation, Norfolk-Southern, and Burlington-Northern became big fans of the group as a consequence, and they often pay substantial fees to advertise in the *AAM Reporter,* the group's official newspaper. Burlington-Northern, in particular, has been financially helpful to the group, including paying, at times, for the group's entertainment and hospitality night at its national convention. Corporate sponsors also help underwrite the AAM's "Congressional Fish Fry," held each February for members of Congress and their staffs and one of AAM's most visible Washington events.

Money from noncorporate, outside patrons is more problematic. One noteworthy exception is the money AAM and its affiliated organizations have received from singer Willie Nelson's Farm Aid Foundation. Since 1985 the AAM has received $113,500 from the foundation, while the group's American Family Farm Foundation has received $98,000 since 1986 (or about one-third of the American Family Farm Foundation budget). The Tennessee state affiliate of AAM has received $16,000 from Farm Aid as well.

The precarious funding situation of the organization has led to a number of creative internal efforts to raise funds. The group enjoys a financially rewarding rebate relationship with American Hybrids, marketers of hybrid corn, grain sorghum, and forage sorghum seeds. In fact, a number of AAM members serve as sales managers or dealers for the company. Not only does the group profit from the sale of each bag of grain, but some members benefit financially as well (clearly a selective material benefit). Sales of AAM memorabilia (such as the AAM cap) bring funds to the group's coffers, as do subscriptions to the group's newspaper, *AAM Reporter,* which is circulated beyond the immediate membership. At least one member of the group regularly leases hunting privileges on his Texas ranch, and he noted at the 1989 annual meeting that he had sent $2,000 of the proceeds to the Washington office.

Although the AAM does not have an expanding membership and has continuing financial difficulties, it has retained both a core leadership cadre and a number of loyal rank and file members. The reasons tend to be both solidary and expressive. According to one member, "this group [AAM] is the most important thing I have been associated with in my life," and, although the group is only thirteen years old, members share what another member called a "unique history," connected to the farm protest movements of the past. Group leaders have become very skilled at using the group's protest past to maintain organizational *esprit de corps*. At past national conventions, for example, ribbons have been given to registrants to commemorate their past activities (the various tractorcades or various protest incidents), as well as to indicate the level of their current involvement in the group (for example, contributor to the 100% Parity Fund or AAM's political action committee—AAMPAC). In 1988 the national office collected contributions to purchase the original lead tractor from the 1979 Washington tractorcade and donated it to the Smithsonian. A couple of hundred AAM members from across the country attended the formal ceremonies at the Smithsonian (the group's desire to drive the tractor in Washington was quashed by government officials).

Both the leadership and rank and file have come to enjoy their status as participants in a political influence process, particularly the sense that they are both "rebels" and "insiders." Stylistic symbolism is crucial. Members, including the national director and other group leaders, are almost never without their AAM baseball caps, even in relatively formal settings such as in testimony before Congress. The title of the group's in-house history, *Gentle Rebels,* aptly captures the self-image of many in the group.[11] Members represent an unusual blend of cynicism and optimism, a sense that they are fighting injustice against terrific odds but that in the end they will prevail. In spite of policy and electoral failures, they continue because, in the words of their national director, "it is the right thing to do."

Although it is probably true that a mass membership group cannot be sustained by such organizational incentives, an organized interest in contemporary Washington politics might survive on such a basis. The AAM has evolved into a staff organization with central direction, yet it has enough of a membership or activist base to give it legitimacy as a representative of the nation's family farmers. The membership, although small, is diverse and represents a broad range of farming interests, from rice and citrus growers in the South to wheat, corn, and livestock producers in the Plains, to almond and grape growers in California. On almost any issue or commodity of concern, the AAM can present to Congress an AAM farmer who is directly affected. The membership is important to the AAM and its operation in Washington and has the sense that it is valued.

AAM and Public Policy: A "Pest" Organization

The AAM has played a role in the agriculture policy process far in excess of its size and resource base. Its original political strategy emphasized massive demonstrations and tractorcades to call attention to farm problems and to pressure decision makers to change policy, leading to higher farm prices. The demands were controversial, but they were in keeping with the group's ideological foundation, especially the demand for 100 percent parity and the creation of a board of agriculture producers within the U.S. Department of Agriculture to formulate policy and administer programs. The policy demands were considered radical, as was the group's explanation for its lack of policy successes, which revolved around a conspiratorial theory related to the Trilateral Commission.[12]

Even after the factional dispute in 1982-1983, parity remained the long-term goal of the group, and at AAM gatherings parity is still treated, in the eyes of one longtime group observer, "as if it were another word for Heaven." But by the early 1980s parity pricing had become a negative buzzword for national legislators, conveying the impression that its advocates thought only of themselves and had no conception of the public interest. Parity pricing originally was established in 1933 to ensure that farmers' incomes would remain on a par with those of the 1910-1914 period, an era of both stability and prosperity for farmers. Because farm productivity has nearly tripled since that period, guaranteed parity would provide farmers with a price more than three times the cost of production.[13] In the short run, according to Sen. Alan Simpson, R-Wyo., parity pricing for farmers "is a lot like the best Christmas you ever had." [14] In the long run, parity pricing is viewed by many legislators as a cause of excessive inflation, leading to the overproduction of farm products and the demise of the U.S. grain export business.

Although AAM members still give lip service to parity as a long-term goal, by 1984 the group's goals had become more short term (such as keeping farmers on their land), as many farmers faced serious debt crises. During 1984 and early 1985, the AAM national office and group leaders worked closely with Texas Department of Agriculture Commissioner Jim Hightower, an unabashed populist and personal friend of a number of AAMers. Hightower set up meetings in the nation's midsection to solicit farmer input in anticipation of putting forth a proposal during the 1985 farm bill deliberations. Although many of the participants in the meetings represented the newer farm crisis groups, AAM state organizations and the Washington office played a key role in the activities.

The result was a proposal for the 1985 farm bill that stood in stark contrast to the mainstream proposal supported by almost all other elements of the agriculture lobby.[15] In fact, the proposal became AAM's political agenda. Dubbed the Farm Policy Reform Act, the proposal sought mandatory production controls on acreage and bushel allotments, the setting of loan rates at not less than 70 percent parity (eventually rising to 90 percent parity), the establishment of a national food reserve, the labeling of agriculture imports as to country of origin, subsidies for U.S. grain exports, the closing of farm tax loopholes for nonfarmer investors, a moratorium on farm foreclosures, and a program of debt restructuring and the rescheduling of farm credit.

By virtue of its Washington presence and its experience in coordinating grass-roots activity to pressure legislators, AAM quickly emerged, in the view of a leader of one of the grass-roots crisis organizations, as the "focal point of grass-roots political efforts" on the farm bill. This included coordinating visits to Washington by its members and representatives of the local crisis groups. The alternative policy proposal became part of the congressional agenda and received serious consideration, with AAM's national director playing a key role in trying to forge a coalition to pass the legislation. But few of its provisions were part of the eventual new farm bill.

Still, AAM seemed to benefit organizationally from the farm bill experience. The group apparently had made major strides in creating a niche for itself as the Washington presence for coordinating grass-roots political input. But too many people outside the AAM were uneasy with the "excess baggage" that AAM brought to policy debates, particularly its radical past, and AAM membership rolls did not expand as a result of the experience. Rather, the failure of the alternative proposal, coupled with the recognition by many of the grass-roots groups that a Washington presence was indeed in their interest (but not as part of AAM), quickly led to the formation of a new grass-roots presence in Washington—the National Save the Family Farm Coalition.[16]

The coalition is made up of and funded by a hodgepodge of rural interests, ranging from self-help and advocacy groups such as the Illinois South Project, to political action committees (PACs) such as the Rural Caucus, to elements of the so-called hunger lobby such as Interfaith Action for Economic Justice. AAM itself is a dues-paying member of the coalition, which has a Washington office and a paid lobbyist, just like AAM. Even though the policy agenda of AAM is virtually identical to that of the coalition and the two groups have developed a symbiotic relationship (particularly in jointly carrying out various protest and grass-roots lobbying activities), the reality is that AAM must now share its niche with another grass-roots presence in Washington.

Since the experience with the 1985 farm bill, and a modified version introduced two years later by Sen. Tom Harkin, D-Iowa, and Rep. Richard Gephardt, D-Mo., AAM has refocused its policy activities and is actively fighting against virtually anything that would raise farm producer costs and advocating anything that would raise farm prices. This has led one AAM opponent to refer to the group admiringly as "the number one pest group in Washington." The group can point to a number of successes, including easier farmer access to credit through the Agricultural Credit Act of 1987. This act began largely as a bailout for farm lenders but soon had important borrowers' rights provisions, thanks in part to AAM persistence.

The group also has been involved in the biotechnology debates—for example, it has opposed the patenting of live animals. Particularly worrisome is the possibility that patenting new, superior breeds of animals would lead to higher costs for small farmers who would be competitively disadvantaged.[17] Excise taxes on such consumer products as liquor and tobacco are opposed as well, as they would lead to decreased consumption of farm products (and thus lower farm prices). An excise tax on gasoline draws AAM opposition as well because it would drive up the cost of production.[18]

But the AAM's special niche among agriculture interests is still its role as a vehicle for dramatizing the plight of the farmer. The free media remains the group's primary political resource. For example, some of the leaders of the group were instrumental in planning and directing Willie Nelson's Farm Aid concerts to raise money for financially stressed family farmers, which received nationwide coverage in the mid- and late 1980s.[19] AAM leaders argued that a substantial portion of the funds raised should be used for national legislative lobbying, but they were not successful. The celebrity participants in Farm Aid, however, came to be associated with the political views of such groups as AAM and those who supported the Family Farm Reform Act. Willie Nelson, for example, testified before Congress on the nation's farm policy, using testimony prepared by AAM's Washington office. Other celebrities, including John Cougar Mellencamp, attended and sang at a number of local political protests organized by AAM activists.

Although AAM has toned down its Washington protest activity, it has participated selectively in a number of direct protest actions across the country, ranging from efforts led by the California AAM chapter to close the port of Stockton when Cargill, a grain importer and exporter, attempted to bring into port a shipment of barley priced below the cost of production to American farmers, to demonstrations at the Chicago Board of Trade (CBOT) protesting CBOT's alleged rigging of soybean futures contracts to the disadvantage of soybean growers. Conspiracy theories focusing on rigged grain markets by agribusiness interests have replaced the Trilateralist interpretations of the early AAM as the explanation for failed U.S. farm policy.

The group's dislike of grain futures speculation has received special attention, and AAM activists have picketed CBOT offices on a number of occasions. In November 1989 the AAM filed a class action lawsuit on behalf of farmers against CBOT for a July 11 order that caused soybean prices to drop 20 percent.[20] With U.S. supplies of soybeans declining in the summer of 1989 because of the 1988 drought, a number of the bigger merchants and traders who were short in the futures market and who could expect big losses allegedly convinced officials of CBOT to force holders of long futures contracts to sell. Short sellers were then relieved of their obligation to deliver, and soybean prices fell dramatically.[21]

CBOT's action confirmed the group's conspiratorial view of how agribusiness interests keep prices low to benefit the large grain merchants at the expense of family farmers. AAM's president noted that "CBOT snatched America's harvest from farmers and gave it to the big grain merchants and speculators in the futures market . . . in a self-serving action initiated by CBOT's dominant members to create profits for their accounts and for their clients." [22] After a press conference to announce the class action suit, roughly thirty members of the AAM carried a bushel of soybeans to the front of the CBOT building, where they confronted CBOT officials by handing them a copy of the lawsuit and the bushel of soybeans, noting that "we [the AAM] understand you folks have a problem delivering on soybeans." [23]

Because of its fundamental distrust of government decision makers and the motives of other agriculture interests, the AAM increasingly has paid attention to international trade issues, at times to the dismay of government officials. Worried that the United States, "in the name of 'free trade,' seems hell-bent to dismantle a system of agricultural support," [24] the AAM sent a representative to the General Agreement on Tariffs and Trade (GATT) talks in Geneva and opposed Reagan and Bush administration efforts to make the Japanese lower trade barriers to permit importation of rice from the United States (they see this as an attempt by the Rice Millers Association to lower domestic rice prices). In 1987 the vice president of AAM traveled to Cuba (sponsored by a philanthropic group) as part of a contingent interested in improved trade with Cuba, including possible exports of U.S. agricultural commodities (currently, exports to Cuba are forbidden by an embargo). And in 1988 two AAM officials traveled to Japan as the guests of Zenchu (Central Union of Agricultural Cooperatives of Japan) to "develop cooperation with family farm groups; and, to work together for the survival of family farms world-wide." [25] The trip was criticized by the U.S. secretary of agriculture, who felt the AAM was interfering in delicate trade discussions.

Thus, to fill its special niche in Washington the AAM serves as a watchdog for grass-roots farm interests and those opposed to the "politics as usual" in agriculture policy making.

Tilting at Windmills: AAM and Electoral Politics

The factional dispute in 1982-1983 that led to the demobilization of many AAM participants was caused in no small part by the desire of the national leadership to get involved in PAC politics. But such politics were seen by some as corrupt and as a symbol of AAM becoming like other political interests. After the dispute, the leadership, committed to PAC politics, attempted to cultivate an image of being nonpartisan and evenhanded in its dealing with both parties, not wanting to further divide the remaining group members whose partisan identification varied. The AAM did not formally endorse candidates and followed a conservative PAC strategy. Democratic representatives open to the group's ideas—such as Dan Glickman of Kansas and Glenn English of Oklahoma—received campaign contributions, but so too did Republican senators Robert Dole of Kansas and Jesse Helms of North Carolina, both strong supporters of what the AAM believed to be a farm policy that created difficulties for family farmers.

The AAM's experiences in lobbying for the 1985 farm bill drastically altered the group's electoral perspective. The leadership felt they had been misled by a number of political leaders, including some who previously had received AAMPAC funds. They believed the lines were clearly drawn between those in Congress who felt the answer to the farm problem lay in maximizing the international competitiveness of American farm products (with the potential for even lower domestic prices), and those who agreed with the AAM that the answer lay in increasing domestic farm prices through a program of government-enforced curbs on supplies to prevent overproduction. From the group's perspective, there were too few members of Congress in the latter camp, and conversion of the former seemed remote.

"To get the system working for farmers, we have to get farmers inside the system," was the view of Senter, and the organization decided to field a slate of candidates in the 1986 elections.[26] During that year, the national office actively recruited candidates, targeting seated members of the House Agriculture Committee who had been unresponsive to AAM's lobbying efforts.

Six former or current AAM activists ran for House or Senate seats in 1986, and four survived to face incumbent House members in the general election.[27] Among the four were two bona fide AAM folk heroes: Gerald McCathern, the "wagonmaster" or lead driver in the 1979 Washington tractorcade, who was opposing Republican representative Larry Combest in the Nineteenth District in Texas, and Wayne Cryts, farm activist from southeastern Missouri, who in 1981 had "liberated" his soybeans from a bankrupt grain storage elevator in Ristine, Missouri. Cryts decided to challenge incumbent Republican representative William Emerson in Missouri's Eighth District.

The AAM and its candidates were well aware of the difficulties inherent in raising sufficient funds to challenge legislative incumbents. Moreover, they knew that the meager financial resources of the AAM would not be enough. The group also was aware that federal law limited group contributions and that the candidates would have to broaden their support bases. Along these lines, the AAM believed that the Democratic Congressional Campaign Committee was ready to target a number of Republican incumbents in rural districts and would be willing to support farm activist candidates in order to call attention to the inadequacies of the Reagan administration's farm policy. Political parties can be group patrons too.

Cryts for Congress

The candidate who appeared to have the best chance of winning was Cryts. His candidacy illustrated the difficulties faced by an "outsider group" in the electoral process and how the AAM's image held over from its early days remained a barrier to its involvement in mainstream political activity.

Cryts had long been active in the AAM, including participation in the 1979 Washington tractorcade. He also had served as a national officer of the organization and as president of the group's Missouri chapter. But his appeal to rural voters was potentially much broader. Cryts was a genuine rural folk hero in some quarters, with ballads written about his exploits, thanks to a widely publicized episode in 1981 in which he defied federal marshalls and took soybeans he claimed were his from a bankrupt grain elevator in southern Missouri.[28]

With a charismatic media presence and an effective stump speech, Cryts became an instant hero fighting injustice in the farm community after the soybean incident. The fact that he was put in jail for thirty-four days by the bankruptcy judge for refusing to name his accomplices (ironically, his congressional opponent had arranged for his release) only added to his Robin Hood image. Cryts emerged as one of the most popular speakers on the rural speakers circuit, and, during the mid-1980s farm crisis, he was much in demand by the national media as a spokesman for disadvantaged farmers. The soybean incident also was the impetus for later federal legislation that gave farmers somewhat more preferential treatment in bankruptcy proceedings involving grain elevators, and Cryts received much of the credit. To some in the AAM he was viewed as our "best political resource," the "soul of our organization." Even to outside observers he entered the congressional race in 1986 with a very good chance against Republican incumbent Emerson.[29] And, unlike many congressional challengers, he would not need money to purchase basic name recognition.

At first glance, Missouri's Eighth District, located in the southeast quadrant of the state, seemed ideal for a populist candidate running under the Democratic banner, even though a three-term Republican was the incumbent. Although there were strong Republican parts of the district, the district had a strong Democratic base, as well as the highest percentage of blue-collar workers in the state (especially in the northern part of the district populated largely by St. Louis commuters). The southern part of the district, in the Missouri Bootheel, initially was settled by Deep South cotton farmers, although soybeans increasingly were the crop of choice. This region had a strong southern Democratic heritage, but it had been carried by social conservative Ronald Reagan in both 1980 and 1984 (American Independent presidential candidate George Wallace had won the region in 1968). The western part of the district had a farming, forestry, and lead mining base, and was one of the more depressed areas in the state.[30]

Although Cryts had never been actively involved in Democratic party affairs in the district, his name familiarity discouraged serious primary opposition; the national Democratic party helped him even before the primary issue was settled. Some longtime workers in the party were uneasy with that "upstart" Cryts, but the local Democratic party seemed relatively united for the fall campaign. As a social conservative who opposed abortion, believed in permitting organized school prayer, and paid dues to the National Rifle Association, Cryts appeared capable of winning over the conservative Democrats in the district who previously had supported Emerson.

Realizing that he had to both raise funds and recruit campaign workers beyond his AAM base, Cryts worked hard to develop a strong farm-labor coalition. The coalition seemed like a natural one because farmers not only shared a number of economic concerns with labor because of jobs leaving the country but also had a similar notion of what the problem was—U.S. trade policy. In Cryts's view, U.S. trade policy both supported the importation of cheap manufactured goods to the detriment of blue-collar workers and held down domestic commodity prices for American farmers by allowing the importation of cheap foreign grain.

While the national AAM vowed to do "everything possible" to see that Cryts was elected, federal PAC laws constrained the group's efforts financially.[31] A number of small contributions from farmers proved useful, but Cryts was forced to rely heavily on sources from outside the district. Unions became his patrons. Maximum PAC contributions were received from such groups as the International Brotherhood of Teamsters, the International Association of Machinists and Aerospace Workers, the National Association of Letter Carriers, and the United Automobile Workers. The National Education Association contributed the maximum of $10,000, and healthy contributions were received from a number of Democratic party committees. Noticeably absent were contributions from agriculture groups.

Being singled out by national Democratic party organizations for special attention also was financially helpful. Stewart Mott, noted Democratic party contributor and a supporter of many liberal causes, held a fund-raiser for Cryts at his home in Washington. And House majority leader Jim Wright, D-Texas, was the speaker at a $25-a-plate fund-raiser attended by 300 people in Cape Girardeau, Missouri. Although they probably were unaware of some of Cryts's cultural conservative views, a variety of nonunion, liberal groups contributed to the Cryts campaign as well, including SANE and a number of other peace groups. Prominent media celebrities also made appearances in the district, one of whom was Mike Farrell of M.A.S.H. fame.

Despite strong union support, Cryts campaigned as a farm activist, and his "denim clothes and 'American Agriculture' cap symbolize[d] not only his campaign but opposition to it as well," wrote the *St. Louis Globe Democrat*.[32] To many, he simply did not appear "congressional," and a number of party regulars were turned off by his style. "He wears that damn cap indoors. He wears it through dinner. He doesn't even have the courtesy to remove it in the presence of ladies," a Democratic state representative was heard to complain privately.[33] The campaign soon became not only an election, but also a referendum on the AAM.

The campaign had a strong grass-roots flavor, as Missouri AAMers, farm activists from surrounding states, and even union workers went to Missouri to aid Cryts. Pictures of an abandoned shoe factory in the district that once employed 400 workers and was now used to store surplus raw grain served as a symbol of the campaign, aptly reflecting Cryts's coalition. Cryts portrayed the incumbent Emerson as a lackey for corporate America, a supporter of agribusiness at the expense of the family farmer, and a supporter of Reagan's free-market farm policy. He advocated the AAM policy agenda, calling for a referendum among farmers on mandatory acreage reductions coupled with price supports, noting that "the government has got to be in agriculture. The only way for us to survive is to put a floor under prices and put in supply management." [34] Cryts also proudly proclaimed the populist message: "It's time we elected some people that got callouses on their hands." [35]

Support for Emerson was predictable. His commercials alluded to support from the American Farm Bureau Federation, and he received large financial contributions from a number of agribusiness corporations and farm commodity groups, outspending Cryts two to one. The incumbent charged that Cryts's support for production controls "will shut down one-third of rural America and cost more than two million farm-related jobs." [36]

Unlike many congressional elections in which the incumbent points with pride and the challenger views with alarm, this campaign—and some of the others involving AAM activists—tended to focus on the challenger and his association with "radical" elements in American society, including the AAM itself. Cryts's opposition to right-to-work laws was viewed as support for the unionization of farm workers, and his courtship of a farm-labor coalition and union funds from outside the district suggested to some in the 'Emerson campaign that he was "the boy of the Democratic party's left wing." The association of Cryts and the AAM with black political leader Jesse Jackson during the farm crisis came back to haunt the candidate (in 1986 Jackson was enlisting farmers in his Rainbow Coalition and had appeared at a number of farm rallies, "Save the Family Farm Breakfasts," and AAM meetings). Thus, Emerson supporters made quick use of a statement by an ex-Farm Bureau official at an Emerson rally: "I'd rather have a congressman who wears a suit and takes advice from farmers than someone who wears jeans and takes advice from Jesse Jackson." [37]

In the final analysis, however, it was the 1981 Ristine soybean incident that set the tone for the election, and even Cryts admitted he was viewed as either a hero or a lawbreaker. On August 22, 1986, the *St. Louis Post-Dispatch* broke the story that Cryts had collected twice on the soybeans that he had recovered from the bankrupt grain elevator in Ristine.[38] Not only had he not repaid the $4.54-a-bushel government loan (a total of nearly $143,000), but he had received another $5.66 a bushel from his friends who had sold the soybeans for him (for a total of $10.20 per bushel). Furthermore, the other eleven farmers who had had grain in the Ristine elevator had gotten only $3.61 a bushel for their grain, or only about 55 percent of the bankruptcy settlement given to farmers who had beans in the other elevators owned by the bankrupt elevator operators. It thus appeared that not only had Cryts gained financially from his raid, but also he had cost other farmers money by his actions, suggesting to some in the opposition that "Robin Hood cared only about himself." The Emerson campaign ran commercials charging Cryts with accepting payments from the government and then selling the crop again. By mid-October Emerson had a comfortable lead in the polls.

Late in the campaign Cryts was subpoenaed by the attorney representing the trustee of the bankrupt grain elevator to give a deposition about his personal finances, including turning over his tax returns. The attorney just happened to be an Emerson supporter, who in previous elections had contributed to the incumbent's campaign. It then was revealed that the grain elevator company had been awarded a $465,000 judgment against Cryts in April 1985 and that Cryts had not responded to previous requests for information on his assets.

Cryts's Robin Hood image got a boost from the episode, and his enraged supporters stepped up their campaign efforts, including picketing the attorney's office. As one Emerson campaign operative offered, "Lawyers are even less popular than radical farmers in this part of the world." Thus, the election tightened up considerably during the final days.

The final election tally was close. Emerson, after trailing in the early returns, won with 52.5 percent of the vote compared with Cryts's 47.5 percent. The other three AAM congressional candidates lost by much bigger margins.

Another Lesson in Electoral Politics

The 1986 election results did not deter, but rather encouraged, the AAM, and it became even more active in the electoral process, again unofficially. Because of Democratic representative Richard Gephardt's cosponsorship of the Harkin-Gephardt farm bill (which was totally compatible with the AAM's policy orientation) and his tough positions on international trade, many AAMers were active in his 1988 presidential nomination efforts, especially in Iowa (Cryts was on his campaign staff).

Six AAM members (known affectionately to the group as the AAM Six-PAC) ran in the 1988 congressional elections, including the four defeated in the November 1986 contests. Individual members of the group became involved in all six elections. The president of the California chapter, for example, pursued his interest in publicizing the cause of the family farmer by investing a reputed $30,000 and 1,500 hours of labor in renovating a Southern Pacific caboose (dubbed the Parity Train) for use by AAM congressional candidates. Powered by a truck provided by two AAM members, the caboose played a prominent role in a number of the campaigns, especially that of former AAM president Corkey Jones in Nebraska.[39]

But special effort was devoted to the Cryts's campaign in Missouri against Emerson, who looked especially vulnerable because of personal problems. Two days after the filing date Emerson announced that he had voluntarily undergone treatment for alcohol dependency. (Republican presidential candidate George Bush also seemed to have little appeal to voters compared with Reagan, and he barely won Missouri in the spring primary.) Cryts raised more than $100,000 in both individual and PAC contributions before the general election. And he had the clear support of the national Democratic party, although some "regular" Democrats in the district had come to regard Cryts as a "loose cannon."

This time Cryts toned down the populist, anticorporate rhetoric that in the previous campaign had made many of the more conservative farmers in the district uneasy. He exchanged his denims and AAM cap for a suit and a tie (although he still wore his knee-high boots), and he concentrated on more specific issues of rural and urban decay, including health care for the elderly and education. Gephardt made a number of appearances in Cryts's behalf in the general election. Even Democratic presidential candidate Michael Dukakis, who differed with Cryts on such cultural issues as abortion and the death penalty, made an appearance in the district with Cryts.

Both candidates promised an issue-oriented campaign, but it quickly degenerated into a nasty contest, one newspaper noting that Cryts versus Emerson made "George Bush and Michael Dukakis look like Boy Scout buddies." [40] AAM again became the central issue, as Emerson, who personally was rather passive in the 1986 campaign, decided to pursue the AAM-Cryts linkage. The incumbent charged that Cryts had profited from Farm Aid funds through his connection with the American Family Farm Foundation, the nonprofit arm of the AAM.

After his 1986 campaign, Cryts had been forced to leave farming because of his bankruptcy problems. He then had worked part time for the American Family Farm Foundation's speakers bureau. Noting that Willie Nelson's Farm Aid Foundation had made large contributions to the American Family Farm Foundation, Emerson alleged that Cryts had received money from Farm Aid—money that should have gone to economically depressed farmers. The AAM countered that Cryts had been paid $25,000 in "per diem" expenses and $5,000 in salary for his 1987 work and that none of Farm Aid's money had gone to support the foundation's speakers bureau. [41] Willie Nelson himself was forced to come to Cryts' defense, noting that "Mr. Cryts received no Farm Aid money" and that documentation to that effect had been "filed with the IRS." [42] Cryts contended that he had received the money in 1987 before formally announcing his candidacy and that he had performed all the work for the foundation outside of the Eighth District. Furthermore, he countercharged that Emerson had been on the payroll of defense contractor TRW in 1980 while he was running in his first congressional race.

Then, Rep. Edward Madigan, an Illinois Republican serving on the House Agriculture Committee and also running against an AAM candidate in 1988, filed a complaint with the Federal Election Commission (FEC) charging that Cryts had received illegal campaign contributions from the AAM and its foundation (a similar complaint was filed against California congressional candidate Wayne Meyer, who also had worked for the American Family Farm Foundation in 1987). The complaint charged that the AAM had made unreported, "in-kind" contributions to the Cryts campaign by sponsoring a whistle-stop tour of Missouri, using the restored caboose also known as the Parity Train.[43]

The attacks on Cryts and the AAM increased after the FEC episode. In the first debate between the candidates, Emerson accused Cryts of hiring a man known as "the prime minister of pot" to be general counsel of the American Family Farm Foundation.[44] The attorney, Keith Stroup, was one of the original founders of the National Organization for the Reform of Marijuana Laws (NORML), who evidently had been hired by the executive director of the foundation without any knowledge of his connection to the drug reform group. Cryts did not answer the charge during the debate, but afterward he indicated that he did not even know Stroup.

On election day the results were even more decisive than in 1986. Emerson, who in 1986 had won by 7,610 votes, this time won by more than 32,000 votes, or by a 58 percent to 42 percent margin. All the other AAM candidates went down to defeat by large margins as well. The group had learned about American electoral politics the hard way.

Can the AAM Continue to Survive?

The AAM has survived for nearly thirteen years, a lot longer than most observers thought possible when it began as a rather unruly protest movement. Given its resource base, the group has had a level of involvement in both the national agriculture policy process and in federal elections that is quite extraordinary. Group leaders have become quite skilled at using free resources such as the media, at obtaining financial support from outside sources, and at building coalitions in the policy process to challenge groups far larger and with much greater resources. The AAM's Washington presence acts as a focal point for grass-roots opposition to many of the mainstream groups in the agriculture policy process, although AAM has had to share this presence with the National Family Farm Coalition, a group untarnished by the negative image that has hounded the AAM.

Still, the long-run survival of AAM is in doubt. The group has not developed a stable funding base, and too much effort is being expended by its leadership on raising the funds needed just to keep the organization viable. The group recently undertook a major effort to "sell memberships," but its success has been rather modest.[45] According to one group official, the biggest current barrier to an expanded membership is not the AAM's image as a radical group but rather its image as a "loser group"—a group of farmers who, by emphasizing farm problems, create the impression that the group represents unsuccessful farmers. The group desperately needs some wins in the policy process, for which they would receive widely publicized credit, to create the impression of a successful group. In the electoral process the group is likely to reduce its role. According to AAM leaders, they "now understand the power of incumbency," which they claim to have previously underestimated.

In large measure the group has survived because of the dedication of a cadre of national leaders who have contributed both time and money out of their belief in the group and its goals. Whether the organization could survive the exit of its national director, in particular, is a special concern.

Survival of the AAM also has stemmed largely from what it represents to a number of farmers (almost all original participants in the movement) and from the social and expressive benefits that come with like-minded people working and interacting socially together. The AAM has come to represent to a core element—largely the original activists—part of their own identity. The history and symbolism of the AAM are its major strengths, but they also will act as major weaknesses if the group wishes to expand; simply put, it is very difficult to attract new blood on this basis. Attrition, without a corresponding increase in the number of new activists, may eventually cause the group's demise.

Few among the leadership cadre were not involved in the group before the 1982-1983 factional dispute. The organizational danger in an expressive and solidary group such as the AAM is that the group relies on the leaders they know and trust and makes little effort to involve others. It is not that others would not be welcome (they surely would be), but the precarious state of organizational survival and the economic crisis atmosphere that pervades the group's political perspective appears to mitigate against any long-range thinking about future leadership needs. The need is still real, however.

The AAM may face its biggest challenge in the 1990s. U.S. budgetary constraints and the movement among western democracies to reduce trade barriers and phase out government subsidies in various policy sectors could create great pressure to reduce the role of government in propping up farm incomes by decreasing or eliminating government subsidies and various other floors on agriculture commodities. Small and medium-sized farmers may be threatened with their basic survival as a consequence. Under such conditions, it would not be surprising to see the AAM return to its original militancy.

Notes

1. The material presented in this chapter represents some of the most recent findings in a long-term project on the evolution of the AAM. Material on the initial phase of the project, focusing on the group's mobilization in 1977, is found in Allan J. Cigler and John M. Hansen, "Group Formation through Protest: The American Agriculture Movement," in Cigler and Burdett A. Loomis eds., *Interest Group Politics* (Washington, D.C.: CQ Press, 1983), 84-109. The transition phase of the group is covered in Allan J. Cigler, "From Protest Group to Interest Group: The Making of American Agriculture Movement, Inc.," in Cigler and Loomis, *Interest Group Politics,* 2d. ed. (Washington, D.C.: CQ Press, 1986), 46-69. Some material at the beginning of this chapter is drawn directly from these two articles to familiarize the reader with the early history of the group as well with the theory underlying the research.

    Included in this chapter is material gathered from personal and telephone interviews with AAM activists, members of Congress and their staff members, officials of groups that deal with the AAM (including those in opposition), and, in one case, a member of the press. Interviewees, in most cases, were promised anonymity. The interviews were conducted on an irregular basis from the winter of 1986 through the spring of 1990, mostly by the author (a student conducted a number of interviews related to the electoral campaigns covered). Quoted but uncited material in this chapter was taken from personal interviews.
2. The American Farm Bureau Federation, the National Farmers Union, the National Farmers Organization (NFO), and the National Grange are considered the "Big Four" farm membership groups.
3. Jack H. Nagel, *Participation* (Englewood Cliffs, N.J.: Prentice Hall, 1987), 33.
4. The starting point for this theoretical literature was the publication in 1965 of Mancur Olson's *The Logic of Collective Action* (Cambridge, Mass.: Harvard University Press). The bulk of the research is theoretical rather than empirical. A list of the most important literature in this area would include: James Q. Wilson, *Political Organizations* (New York:

Basic Books, 1973); Terry Moe, *The Organization of Interests* (Chicago: University of Chicago Press, 1980); Moe, "A Calculus of Group Membership," *American Journal of Political Science* 24 (November 1980): 593-623; Robert Salisbury, "An Exchange Theory of Interest Groups," *Midwest Journal of Political Science* 13 (February 1969): 1-32; and John Mark Hansen, "The Political Economy of Group Membership," *American Political Science Review* 79 (March 1985): 79-96. For a review of this literature, see Allan J. Cigler, "Interest Groups: A Subfield in Search of an Identity," in William Crotty ed., *Political Science: Looking to the Future* (Evanston, Ill.: Northwestern University Press, forthcoming).

5. Salisbury, "An Exchange Theory."

6. See, William P. Browne, "Mobilizing and Activating Group Demands: The American Agriculture Movement," *Social Science Quarterly* 64 (March 1964): 19-35; and Cigler and Hansen, "Group Formation through Protest."

7. *Doane's Agriculture Report,* December 1977.

8. Charles Johnson, "AAM Attacks Reagan and Calls for Action in 1984," *Farm Journal* (Mid-February 1984): 22-D.

9. William P. Browne, *Private Interests, Public Policy, and American Agriculture* (Lawrence: University Press of Kansas, 1988), 64-88; and Browne and Mark H. Lundgren, "Farmers Helping Farmers: Constituent Services and the Development of a Grassroots Farm Lobby," *Agriculture and Human Values* 4 (Spring/Summer 1987): 11-28.

10. Jack L. Walker, "The Origins and Maintenance of Interest Groups in America," *American Political Science Review* 77 (June 1983): 402.

11. Gerald McCathern, *Gentle Rebels* (Hereford, Texas: Food for Thought Publications, 1982).

12. Because many important industrial, financial, government, and media leaders are members of the Trilateral Commission, the Council on Foreign Relations, and the Council on Economic Development, these groups are said to control government policy by monopolizing economic and political resources. According to J. C. Lewis, a prominent speaker at early AAM rallies, these groups, dominated by the Rockefeller family, were "scheming to submerge the United States politically and economically in a one-world socialistic government."

13. Jonathan Rauch, "What if Congress Won't Act," *National Journal,* March 23, 1985, 637. Technically, parity is a Department of Agriculture index of the purchasing power of one unit of a farm commodity based on 1910-1914 prices. When commodity prices are at full parity, a bushel of grain will buy the same quantity of nonfarm products that it did during the base period.

14. Ibid.

15. Browne, *Private Interests,* particularly 213-236.

16. Browne and Lundgren, "Farmers Helping Farmers." The group later changed its name to the National Family Farm Coalition.

17. Although farm groups generally do not have good reputations among environmentalists, the AAM, more than most groups, has worked closely with them on a number of issues of mutual concern. The AAM has become increasingly interested in so-called sustainable agriculture (a pet subject of Texas Agriculture Commissioner Jim Hightower) because chemical usage increases farmer costs and poses health threats to farmers. On the coal slurry pipeline bill noted earlier, the AAM cooperated with the unlikely combination of the railroads and the environmentalists. One legislative director of an environmental group, however, suggested in an interview that AAM has a reputation of being an environmentalist only when it serves its narrow interests and becomes involved in a number of environmental issues because "they want an exemption for family farmers."

18. "AAM Fights Excise Tax Increase," *AAM Reporter,* September 8, 1987.

19. Ann Toner and Mike Weatherford, "Day of Music to Ease Plight of Farmers," *Kansas City Star,* September 20, 1987.

20. "CBOT—AAM Sues Board of Trade," *AAM Reporter,* December 5, 1989.

21. Ibid. Individuals who sell short have sold a commodity they do not possess in anticipation of a fall in prices. If prices rise, they would experience a loss because they would be obligated to deliver the product, which they would have to purchase at higher prices.

22. Ibid.

23. Ibid. The class action lawsuit filed by AAM has been a major drain on AAM finances, and the group has appealed to a number of other farm groups for assistance. The National Farmers Organization has been especially responsive, and in the spring of 1990 it contributed $36,000 in funds collected by NFO growers and promised to contribute another $35,000 pending approval from contributing Minnesota farmers. See "American Ag Receives Support to Continue Lawsuit," *AAM Reporter,* June 5, 1990.

24. "Congress Should Respond to GATT," *AAM Reporter,* May 2, 1989.

25. Marlon Garland, "International Ties," *AAM Reporter,* November 1, 1988.

26. Ward Sinclair, "Farmers Seeking Crop of Votes," *Washington Post,* August 31, 1986.

27. One of those defeated was Darrell Ringer of Kansas, a participant in AAM prior to its factional dispute in 1982-1983. Ringer ran in the Democratic primary for senator, seeking the nomination to oppose Republican senator Robert Dole in the general election. Even though he was endorsed by a number of Democratic party state officials, he lost the primary to an unknown candidate who spent no money and did not campaign.

28. For a detailed discussion of Cryts and the soybean incident, see Micki Nellis, *One Man with Courage. . .* (Iradell, Texas: American Agriculture News, 1981).

Cryts, thirty-five years old at the time of the incident, was a soybean farmer in southern Missouri who rented space at a Ristine, Missouri, grain elevator in 1979 to store more than 31,000 bushels of beans, for which he received a receipt, paid storage fees, and got a loan of $4.54 for each bushel from the U.S. Department of Agriculture's Commodity Credit Corporation. When the grain elevator corporation went bankrupt, Cryts and other farmers were unable under federal law to take custody of their soybeans. In the late summer and fall of 1980 Cryts and other AAM participants surrounded the grain elevator with their tractors and stood guard to prevent removal of the soybeans. In early 1981 Cryts, financially strapped by lack of access to his soybeans, (which then were selling at high prices and projected to go lower) physically removed his soybeans from the elevator with the help of other AAM participants and had his friends sell them for him. He was, of course, breaking federal law, but the law was viewed as unjust by many farmers, who sympathized with him.

29. *Congressional Quarterly Weekly Report,* October 11, 1986, 2449.
30. Dan Gilmour, "Farmer vs. Congressman," *Kansas City Times,* August 23, 1986. Of all the districts in Missouri, the Eighth had the highest percentage of the over-65 population, the lowest median family income, the highest percentage of non-high school educated, and the lowest percentage of college attendees.
31. Clay Haterorin, "Conflicting Views of Emerson, Cryts Split Allegiance of Missouri Farmers," *Commercial Appeal,* September 22, 1986.
32. James F. Wolfe, "Race Provides Farm-Issue Battleground," *St. Louis Globe-Democrat,* June 26, 1986.
33. Ibid.
34. Ibid.
35. Steve Lillenthal, "Missouri: On Guard," *Political Report,* vol. 10, August 28, 1986, 3.
36. Ibid.
37. "Emerson Gets Strong Farm Backing," *St. Louis Globe-Democrat,* August 25, 1988.
38. Fred Lindecke, "Cryts Collected Twice on Crops," *St. Louis Post-Dispatch,* August 22, 1986.
39. *AAM Reporter,* August 2, 1988.
40. Terry Lemons, "Cryts, Emerson Slug Way through Dirty Campaign," *Springfield News-Leader* (Missouri), October 30, 1988.
41. Ibid.
42. Ibid.
43. The complaint was not formally resolved until after the election. The FEC, in a 6-0 vote announced in June 1989, concluded that Cryts had not violated any federal election laws in his relationship with the American Family Farm Foundation. The commission also found that AAM did not violate campaign laws in the caboose incident, ruling that the caboose was owned and operated by a private individual. The Cryts campaign committee, however, was cited for its failure to report $195 in "ear-

marked" funds given through AAMPAC but designated for Cryts. See "Financial Allegations Rejected," *Kansas City Times,* June 7, 1989.

44. Lemons, "Cryts, Emerson Slug Way through Dirty Campaign."
45. The group seems to be targeting sponsors as well as members in its drive, directing its attention toward businesses that serve farmers such as local grain companies and farm implement dealers. Cryts has been rehired by the organization to concentrate on increasing the number of sustaining members and appears to have had at least limited success, especially in California and Texas.

5. MORE BANG FOR THE BUCK: THE NEW ERA OF FULL-SERVICE PUBLIC INTEREST ORGANIZATIONS

Ronald G. Shaiko

The growth of public interest representation has been one of the most significant features of the changing group universe over the past few decades. More than 2,500 public interest organizations existed as of 1990, representing a vast range of political perspectives, each seeking to advocate its own particular version of the public interest. More than 40 million citizens support these organizations through contributions of over $4 billion annually, in addition to the financial backing received from private foundations, corporations, and government agencies.

In this chapter Ronald Shaiko explores some of the more politically salient changes within the public interest sector. He finds not only that there has been a significant growth in the number of organizations and their members, budgets, and staffs but also that contemporary public interest organizations are "qualitatively different" from their predecessors. No longer are such groups staffed by the untrained social reformers typifying the "era of flannel-shirted, "Flower Power," antiestablishmentarianism [which] has virtually vanished"; more common is staffing based on professional merit. Public interest organizations are hiring attorneys, management consultants, direct-mail specialists, and communications directors.

Still, individual public interest organizations "remain constrained by government regulations," and many have been forced to reorganize to comply with tax laws that limit direct policy advocacy. The author concludes that most of these groups are not effectively managed, professionally organized, or politically effective and that their contributors deserve "more bang for the buck" in direct policy advocacy.

Public interest representation has become a big business in the United States. During the past two decades public interest movements have developed into major political industries. Today, the public interest sector includes more than 2,500 national organizations that "represent almost every conceivable viewpoint." [1] Beyond the mobilization of interests at the national level, tens of thousands of regional, state, and local organizations are now providing public interest representation in many political arenas previously unchecked. Together, these organizations are supported through the memberships and contributions of more than 40 million individuals, whose giving totals more than

$4 billion annually. In addition to the support of individual citizens, private foundations and corporations, as well as government agencies, provide significant financial support for public interest advocacy.[2]

In just two decades the public interest movement has been transformed into a collection of autonomous, often competing, organizations, each seeking to represent its own particular version of the public interest. Kay Schlozman and John Tierney concluded that the most accurate description of the changes in the entire interest group sector is "more of the same,"[3] but the changes that have taken place in the public interest sector are not simply quantitative in nature. The transformation in the organization and maintenance of public interest organizations has resulted in a qualitative change.

Public Interest Organizations: Then and Now

Several authors have chronicled the development of the public interest movement since the turn of the century. Throughout the 1950s and 1960s it was thought that mobilizations of the citizenry were in response to "disturbances" in society, including the general increase in the complexity of working relationships and the more specific imbalances caused by wars, fluctuations in business activity, and the increased role of government in everyday life.[4] David Truman's "disturbance theory," which stood as conventional wisdom for twenty years, was later challenged by Robert Salisbury's "exchange theory" of interest group development. Rather than stressing market disturbances as catalytic forces in the formation of groups, Salisbury focused more broadly on the origins and maintenance of organized interest groups. By doing so he was able to identify the role of the leader or political "entrepreneur" as an important factor in determining the success or failure of such groups.[5] In his important work *Lobbying for the People* (referred to in greater detail later in this chapter), Jeffery Berry tested these two theories. He found that two-thirds of the eighty-three public interest groups in his study "were begun by entrepreneurs working without significant disturbances as additional stimuli."[6]

More recently, Andrew McFarland offered a "civic balance theory" of public interest representation, which incorporates some aspects of both the disturbance and exchange theories but also refers to the civic reform tradition and beliefs in America.[7] McFarland presents seven factors influential in the development of the public interest sector:

> (1) the increase in middle-class participation in American politics in the 1960s and 1970s; (2) the corresponding increase in the politics of issues and systems of beliefs are opposed to the politics of party identification, personality or patronage; (3) the growth of

"civic skepticism"—the disbelief in the utility of existing politics and public administrative practices in solving important social problems; (4) skillful leadership of public interest groups; (5) technical advances in communications; (6) economic prosperity; and (7) initial success bringing more success.[8]

McFarland's theory of representation in which civic values (even if limited to the middle class) are balanced against special interest (economically driven) values that pervade the "scope of conflict" is an accurate casting of the roles that public interest organizations have sought to play.[9] The author traces the civic balance theme to "the reform tradition of the Progressives and . . . local government reform groups" and argues that Common Cause, the focus of his recent research, is simply "a recent manifestation of the mobilization of elements of the American middle class who attempt to enhance democracy and effective government through the adoption of procedural reforms supported for reasons other than clear-cut economic gain." [10]

Given the civic reform tradition as well as the unique spirit of voluntarism in American society, the presence of public interest organizations as possible balancing forces is not surprising, economic research on group formation notwithstanding.[11] What is not as easily explained by earlier patterns of social activation, however, is the dramatic transformation in the organization and maintenance of public interest groups during the past two decades. According to Douglas J. Bergner, executive director of the Foundation for Public Affairs, a public interest/public policy clearinghouse, "Public interest and public policy groups in the 1970s often served as the drivers for social or corporate change, or they were established in order to counteract activism in different policy areas. Today, the activities and agendas of the public interest organizations are considerably more diverse." [12] The transformation in the size, organization, and management of public interest enterprises is the focus of this chapter.

To assess the changes that have taken place over the past twenty years in the public interest sector, two data sources will be compared. The first data set ($N = 83$) was collected by Jeffrey Berry in 1972 and his findings presented in *Lobbying for the People*. More recent data on public interest organizations ($N = 221$) were collected by the Foundation for Public Affairs (FPA) in 1985.[13] From their files of more than 2,500 organizations, the foundation staff selected 250 organizations on the basis of the following criteria:

- the extent of the group's influence on national policy,
- the number of requests received for information on the group,

Table 5-1 Year of Origin

	Berry (1972)		FPA (1985)	
	%	No.	%	No.
1983-1985			6.8	15
1978-1982			16.7	37
1973-1977			22.6	50
1968-1972	49.4	39	22.2	49
1960-1967	16.5	13	9.0	20
1940-1959	17.7	14	10.4	23
1920-1939	10.1	8	6.3	14
Before 1920	6.3	5	5.9	13
Total		79		221

- the range and quantity of news coverage generated by the group, and
- the representative nature of the group in its field of interest.[14]

Growing Size of the Public Interest Sector

One of the most obvious changes in the public interest sector over the past twenty years has been the exponential increase in the number of groups. Of the more than 2,500 public interest organizations in existence today, less than a third of these groups, by various accounts, were organized two decades ago. Table 5-1 compares the years of origin of the organizations studied by Berry with those of the organizations presented in the Foundation for Public Affairs study (henceforth referred to as the Berry sample and the FPA sample, respectively).

While almost half of the organizations in the Berry sample were founded between 1968 and 1972, fully two-thirds of the FPA groups had been organized since 1968. Moreover, almost half of the FPA groups did not exist when Berry conducted his analysis. While the growth in the public interest sector has been dramatic, a core of organizations with histories spanning several decades remains. The Berry data offers evidence of the ability of organizations to adapt to changes in the public interest agenda as more than 80 percent of the groups he studied remain in operation. Of the organizations that no longer exist, many were directed at efforts to end the war in Southeast Asia, clearly an issue of major consequence at the time of Berry's study. Yet that war, despite its injudicious resolution, no longer garners the same citizen interest that it did twenty years ago.[15]

The increase in the number of public interest organizations active today has been paralleled by increases in the budgets and memberships of these groups. By converting the Berry data on organizational budgets to 1985 constant dollars, an accurate comparison of organization budgets from the two samples is possible (see Table 5-2).[16] The samples are quite similar in the middle range—$500,000-$1,249,999—but they differ at the lower and upper ends of the scale. The FPA sample has 20 percent fewer organizations with budgets under $500,000 (25 percent versus 45 percent for the Berry sample) and 20 percent more organizations with budgets exceeding $1,250,000 (48 percent versus 28 percent for the Berry sample). Organizations in the FPA sample are simply not receiving greater support from private foundations. In fact, the general level of foundation support for public interest organizations, as reported by the major donor foundations, has declined during recent years. According to Table 5-3, fewer FPA organizations receive almost total support from foundations, yet more of them receive some level of foundation support. Overall, foundation support of FPA organizations constitutes approximately 20 percent of each group's budget. Almost half of the budgets of the FPA organizations are derived from direct contributions from members or member organizations. Corporate donations, income from publications, seminars, and investments account for much of the remaining support.

Related to the growth in budgets among public interest organizations in recent years has been a growth in membership size. While the percentage of nonmember or federated organizations has remained fairly constant, more organizations with large memberships exist now than two decades ago. Of those groups with memberships, almost half of the FPA groups have 100,000 or more members, whereas just over 20 percent of the Berry groups have similarly large memberships (see Table 5-4). Since 1972 numerous organizations have come into being, several of which have experienced dramatic growth in recent years. The National Right to Life Committee, for example, was not yet organized at the national level in 1972 but now claims a membership of more than 13 million with fifty state chapters and more than 7,000 local organizations.

Organizations founded before the 1960s also have experienced dramatic increases in membership since Berry's analysis. The National Wildlife Federation, for example, has almost doubled its associate membership since 1972 to just under 1 million. The Sierra Club has more than quadrupled its membership during this time, with a current membership of more than a half million. Perhaps one of the most effective mobilizations in the public interest sector, however, has been

Table 5-2   Organization Budgets (1985 constant dollars)

	Berry (1972)		FPA (1985)	
	%	No.	%	No.
Less than $125,000	14.9	11	6.6	13
125,000-249,999	13.5	10	7.1	14
250,000-499,999	16.2	12	11.2	22
500,000-1,249,999	27.0	20	27.0	53
1,250,000-2,499,999	6.8	5	16.3	32
2,500,000 +	21.6	16	31.6	62
Total		74		196

Table 5-3   Foundation Support

	Berry (1972)		FPA (1985)	
	%	No.	%	No.
None	55.7	44	42.6	69
Less than 10%	10.1	8	8.0	13
10-49%	13.9	11	30.9	50
50-89%	8.9	7	16.7	27
90% and above	11.4	9	1.9	3
Total		79		162

Table 5-4   Membership

	Berry (1972)		FPA (1985)	
	%	No.	%	No.
No members or members are organizations	40.5	32	38.6	59
Less than 1,000	10.1	8	0.7	1
1,000-24,999	17.7	14	16.3	25
25,000-99,999	18.9	15	15.0	22
100,000-199,999	5.1	4	9.2	14
200,000+	7.6	6	20.9	32
Total		79		153

achieved by senior citizens groups. The American Association of Retired Persons (AARP), for example, reported just over 1 million members in 1968; today AARP has more than 27 million members. More than 12 percent of the FPA groups reported memberships in excess of a half million members. Excluding the national church organizations in the Berry study (United Methodist Church, United Church of Christ, United Presbyterian Church), only one organization, the National Wildlife Federation, had more than a half million members.

As memberships have grown, many organizations have expanded their operations by establishing chapters or branch offices. Berry reported that more than two-thirds of the organizations in his study had no chapters or branch offices. Almost half of the FPA organizations, however, have offices or chapters beyond their national headquarters. In many cases the recent increase in chapters and branch offices has included the establishment of an office in Washington, D.C., or its immediate environs. While the bias toward having one's national headquarters in the capital area remains high (65 percent of the FPA sample are headquartered in Washington), several major public interest organizations (stubbornly) have avoided moving their operations to the capital: Sierra Club, San Francisco; National Audubon Society, New York; National Association for the Advancement of Colored People, Baltimore; and Union of Concerned Scientists, Cambridge, Massachusetts. Yet, as these examples illustrate, most organizations not headquartered in Washington remain a short commuter flight or Amtrak ride away. Fully 85 percent of the FPA groups are headquartered in the Northeast corridor from Boston to Washington. This is not altogether surprising as the Eastern establishment, both its liberal and conservative wings, has remained an important source of financial and intellectual support for many public interest enterprises.

The general pattern of expanding operations through chapters and branch offices is even more pronounced in the growth of staffs of public interest organizations. Clearly, the operation of public interest organizations has become much more labor-intensive over the past decade and a half (see Table 5-5). The percentage of organizations with more than ten employees has tripled since 1972 (23 percent of the Berry sample versus 69 percent of the FPA sample). And when only full-time professional staff members are considered, there has been a fivefold increase in the percentage of groups with ten or more professionals (9 percent of the Berry sample versus 45 percent of the FPA sample). In addition, more than 15 percent of the FPA organizations report having more than 100 employees on their payrolls.

Table 5-5   Organization Staffing

	Overall Staff (Professional and Support)				Professional Staff			
	Berry (1972)		FPA (1985)		Berry (1972)		FPA (1985)	
	%	No.	%	No.	%	No.	%	No.
0ᵃ					4.9	4	0.7	1
1	6.1	5	0.5	1	21.0	17	1.3	2
2-3	28.0	23	2.7	6	29.6	24	7.3	11
4-6	23.2	19	12.8	28	19.8	16	24.5	37
7-10	19.5	16	15.1	33	16.0	13	20.4	31
11-20	12.2	10	24.2	53	4.9	4	18.5	28
21-40	6.1	5	18.3	40	1.2	1	12.6	19
41 and above	4.9	4	26.5	58	2.5	2	14.6	22
Total		82		219		81		151

ᵃ There were four Berry groups with no paid professional staffers, but with at least one support staff.

Transformations in Organization and Management

With their significant growth in memberships, budgets, and staffs, today's public interest organizations are quite distinct from their predecessors. The transformations in organization and management within the public interest sector have resulted in a more professional and increasingly competitive political industry, which has adapted to the increasingly complex political environment.

A final comparison of the Berry and FPA samples offers additional evidence of a pattern of organizational adaptation to government regulation of organization activities. Berry identified four alternatives available to public interest organizations for compliance with Internal Revenue Service (IRS) requirements for tax-exemption of nonprofit organizations:

> First, they may be committed to lobbying or participating in political campaigns and eschew tax deductible dollars [501(c)(4)]. The second, and most advantageous alternative, is to have a lobbying unit [501(c)(4)] and a 501(c)(3) affiliated public foundation. Third, organizations may take their 501(c)(3) exemption seriously and restrict their advocacy to administrative agencies or the courts. Fourth, 501(c)(3) groups may try to influence Congress, consciously or unconsciously violate the law, and run the serious risk of getting into trouble with the IRS.[17]

Public interest organizations obviously do not operate in a political vacuum. They are a small but significant part of the ever-growing nonprofit sector of the economy. As such they are "interdependent with the governmental and for-profit sectors." Through its regulation and support, the federal government "simultaneously encourages and discourages nonprofits—subsidizing them and restricting them, proclaiming their virtues and distrusting them." [18] The larger nonprofit sector has been a catalytic force in American society at least since the turn of the twentieth century. The federal government's role in directing this sector, however, has been less than coherent. Nevertheless, it is agreed that, in principle, nonprofit organizations, through their provision of services or representation, offer societal benefits that warrant special consideration from the government. [19]

Tax Status of Public Interest Organizations

Public interest organizations, by virtue of their inclusion in the nonprofit sector, receive the benefits attributed to such organizations, but they also must bear the regulatory costs as well. The public interest sector today contains the basic types of organizations defined by Berry: (1) 501(c)(3) organizations, (2) 501(c)(4) organizations, and (3) 501(c)(4) organizations with affiliated 501(c)(3) foundations. [20] All types of nonprofits are exempt from corporate income taxes, and supporters (individuals as well as corporations) of 501(c)(3) organizations are allowed to deduct their contributions on their income tax returns. Moreover, 501(c)(3) groups may receive bequests, which are deductible for estate and gift taxes, as well as grants from foundations; 501(c)(4) organizations receive none of the selective benefits. But for an organization such as a 501(c)(3) to receive tax-exemption, it must refrain from devoting "a substantial part of its activities" to "carrying on propaganda or otherwise attempting to influence legislation." In its original form as a part of the Revenue Act of 1934 (the Code was revised in 1954), this statute made no effort to define "propaganda," "legislation," or "substantial part." [21]

Since the inception of this regulation, Congress and the courts have managed to give it some concrete meaning. In the Tax Reform Act of 1976 Congress provided alternative tests for public charities in order to bypass the original "substantial part" guidelines and denied absolutely the right of organizations to "participate in, or intervene in, any political campaign on behalf of any candidate for public office." And in *Haswell v. United States,* 500 F.2d 1133 (1974), the federal courts provided some focus to the issue by defining which activities did *not* constitute lobbying activities. The courts ruled that "technical advice or assistance" and "nonpartisan analysis, study, or research" do *not* constitute lobbying only when the organization receives a "specific written request" for such information. Other legitimate political activities included presentation of information to Congress (without request) when the information is also available to the general public and nonpartisan voter registration activities (carried on in five or more states).[22]

Organizations falling into the 501(c)(4) category need not meet these requirements; they can lobby Congress on a full-time basis. Their members may not deduct their contributions, however. As Berry noted, the "most advantageous alternative" is what more recently has been called "piggybacking" or structuring the organization such that there are two distinct entities: a lobbying-influence enterprise—501(c)(4)— and an education-research wing—501(c)(3). As one specialist in the area of exempt organizations explained, "The (c)(3) is the idea chamber, and the (c)(4) is the money chamber that puts the idea on the street." [23]

In addition to tax-deductibility, 501(c)(3) organizations receive lower mail rates and hence become the "prospecting wings" of the macro-organizational structures. When 501(c)(3) foundations are affiliated with 501(c)(4) groups, the foundations also may become depositories for organizational costs. Overhead expenses, salaries, rent payments, and the like are easily shuffled from one organization to the other. In fact, in some instances direct transfers of 501(c)(3) funds are made to the 501(c)(4) parent organization. For example, according to the financial reports the 501(c)(4) organization Environmental Action, Inc. (EA) and its affiliate 501(c)(3) organization, Environmental Action Foundation (EAF), 15 percent of EAF's total expenses ($52,300 of $333,541) appear in the form of a grant to EA, Inc.—tax-deductible funds transferred to a non-tax-exempt organization.[24]

Financial information on all public interest organizations is, at least theoretically, available through the Internal Revenue Service. Nonprofit organizations are required by law to file annual reports with the IRS, providing full financial disclosure of organizational activities (known as 990 forms). A 1983 General Accounting Office study of approximately 11,000 501(c)(3) organizations revealed, however, that 94 percent "did not completely respond to certain public information reporting requirements." [25] Unfortunately, the IRS does not have the capacity to address these reporting discrepancies, as today there are approximately 900,000 tax-exempt organizations reporting income of at least one-quarter *trillion* dollars. In 1986 the IRS division responsible for regulating 501(c)(3) organizations employed less than 800 workers.[26] While there are instances in which tax-exempt organizations have relinquished their 501(c)(3) status because of excessive

Table 5-6   Tax Status of Public Interest Organizations

	Berry (1972)		FPA (1985)	
	%	No.	%	No.
501(c)(3) tax-exempt	53.0	44	67.6	144
501(c)(4) non-tax-exempt	36.1	30	10.8	23
501(c)(4) organization with affiliated 501(c)(3) foundation	10.8	9	21.6	46
Total		83		213

political activity (the Sierra Club in the mid-1960s, for example), many organizations have managed to escape the wrath of the IRS while lobbying Congress beyond allowable limits.

Regardless of whether or not contemporary public interest organizations are consciously violating IRS requirements, most of these groups currently operate as 501(c)(3) organizations. Table 5-6 compares the tax status of the Berry and FPA samples. It reveals that more than two-thirds of the FPA groups are tax-exempt and, among 501(c)(4) organizations, it points out an interesting development. In the Berry sample fewer than one-quarter of 501(c)(4) groups had affiliated 501(c)(3) foundations; two-thirds of the FPA groups with 501(c)(4) status, however, are linked with 501(c)(3) foundations.

The trend toward linking a 501(c)(4) organization with a 501(c)(3) foundation demonstrates the ability of public interest organizations to adapt to the current political rules of the game. This is not to say that 501(c)(3) organizations will purposely forfeit their tax-exempt status to follow this pattern. But this "most advantageous" organizational structure has proved to be the most effective in influencing the federal policy-making process. Organizations are free to lobby Congress without the restrictions imposed by 501(c)(3) requirements. At the same time, large individual contributors as well as major corporate donors, conscious of the tax-deductible nature of their giving, still have an outlet for their monetary generosity. After the Sierra Club lost its 501(c)(3) status because of its perceived excessive (direct and indirect) lobbying efforts, the parent 501(c)(4) Sierra Club leaders, with their 501(c)(3) Sierra Club Legal Defense Fund and Sierra Club Foundation, had no intention of requalifying for tax-exempt status. The club has shown no appreciable difference in membership contributions without tax-deductibility as an incentive, although its larger donors do tend to give to the Sierra Club Foundation. But, like the

Environmental Action example provided earlier, more than 90 percent of Sierra Club Foundation income is legally funneled into the 501(c)(4) parent organization (for "educational purposes" only, of course).[27]

Organizational Activities of Public Interest Organizations

Recognizing the legal limits of public interest influence, these "full-service" public interest organizations provide more "bang for the buck." With their 501(c)(3) foundation linkage, such organizations are able to receive the benefits shared by all 501(c)(3) groups. With their 501(c)(4) structures, however, these groups bear few of the organizational costs. Table 5-7 reveals the breadth of activity undertaken by 501(c)(4)/501(c)(3) organizations compared with the more common 501(c)(3) tax-exempt groups. Note that for 501(c)(3) organizations the tasks presented earlier as acceptable activities appear prominently: congressional testimony, 60 percent; research, 59 percent; and technical assistance, 49 percent. These groups tend to couch their activities in legally accepted terms—for example, more than 80 percent include public education as an important group activity. Litigation (39 percent) and federal government agency monitoring (50 percent) are also allowable activities for 501(c)(3) groups. Conferences and seminars and group publications are utilized by most groups as well.[28] Grass-roots organizing (33 percent) is not considered to be an activity directed at influencing the legislative process, but, grass-roots lobbying (22 percent)—which includes letter-writing campaigns and phone mobilizations—is a restricted activity. Given the emotional and purposive appeals utilized by group leaders in direct mail campaigns to expand the memberships of these 501(c)(3) organizations, it is ironic that the majority of the money raised by these groups is spent not on influencing legislation but rather on organizational maintenance.

In contrast, the full-service 501(c)(4)/501(c)(3) organizations attempt to influence the policy-making process in a large variety of ways. In addition to direct and indirect means of influencing specific policy issues—congressional testimony (80 percent), federal lobbying (76 percent), grass-roots lobbying (65 percent), federal government agency monitoring (61 percent), and litigation (41 percent)—these organizations seek to influence the electoral process as well. As 501(c)(3) groups are explicitly forbidden to participate in political campaigns, 501(c)(4)/501(c)(3) groups are distinctly at an advantage in this political forum. Fifty-seven percent of 501(c)(4)/501(c)(3) organizations provide congressional ratings based on member roll-call voting. Almost half of these groups maintain political action committees for the purpose of supporting or opposing congressional candidates, and almost 30 percent become involved directly in campaigning for congres-

Table 5-7 Organizational Activities by Tax Status (percent)

	501(c)(3) Orgs.	501(c)(4) Orgs. with 501(c)(3) Foundations	501(c)(4) Orgs.
Congressional testimony	60.4	80.4	50.0
Coalition formation	52.8	82.6	64.3
Conferences/seminars	75.7	76.1	50.0
Electoral politics	3.5	28.3	39.3
Congressional voting analysis	9.0	56.5	46.4
Campaign contributions (PAC)	0.7	43.4	43.4
Demonstrations	9.0	23.9	25.0
Federal government agency monitoring	50.0	60.9	35.7
State government agency monitoring	22.6	34.8	14.3
Grass-roots organizing	32.6	80.4	64.3
Initiative/referendum	4.2	23.9	21.4
Litigation	38.9	41.3	25.0
Federal lobbying	30.6	76.1	67.9
State lobbying	14.6	45.7	32.1
Grass-roots lobbying	21.5	65.2	60.7
Local/municipal affairs	8.3	21.7	14.3
Participation in federal regulatory proceedings	18.8	32.6	11.1
Participation in state regulatory proceedings	10.4	28.3	10.7
Public education	84.0	84.0	78.6
Publications	91.0	95.7	82.1
Research	58.7	26.8	42.9
Technical assistance	48.6	41.3	53.6
	(N = 144)	(N = 46)	(N = 23)

SOURCE: Foundation for Public Affairs sample, 1985.

Table 5-8   Tax Status by Organizational Classification (percent of groups)

	501(c)(3) Orgs.	501(c)(4) Orgs. with 501(c)(3) Foundations	501(c)(4) Orgs.
Civil/constitutional	53.1	34.4	12.5
Community/grass-roots	47.6	23.8	28.6
Consumer/health	72.2	22.2	5.6
Corporate accountability	100.0	0.0	0.0
Environmental	69.2	30.8	0.0
International affairs	70.0	15.0	15.0
Media	100.0	0.0	0.0
Political/governmental process	52.0	32.0	16.0
Public interest law	100.0	0.0	0.0
Religious	100.0	0.0	0.0

SOURCE: Foundation for Public Affairs sample, 1985.

sional candidates (electoral politics). In addition, an overwhelming percentage of these organizations mobilize their members at the grass-roots level (80 percent), and social protest serves as a political resource for almost one-quarter of the groups.

Aside from "technical assistance" and "research," the full-service organizations outperform their 501(c)(3) public interest partners in all other dimensions of organizational activity. Similarly, when one compares the 501(c)(4)/501(c)(3) organizations with the 501(c)(4) groups, one finds the groups of the former organizational type to be more active in virtually all dimensions.

Amounting to less than one-quarter of the FPA sample groups, the 501(c)(4)/501(c)(3) organizations are represented disproportionately in the civil/constitutional rights, environmental, and political/governmental process classifications (see Table 5-8). Another distinguishing characteristic of these organizations is their identifiable ideological predisposition. An effort was made to identify the political orientation of each of the organizations in the FPA sample. Although the results of this effort were hampered by missing data, a discernible pattern emerged nonetheless.

Table 5-9 offers evidence of the more obvious liberal and, to a lesser degree, conservative orientations of 501(c)(4)/501(c)(3) organizations and 501(c)(4) groups. By virtue of the political restrictions placed upon them, 501(c)(3) groups are less likely to be identified with any particular ideological perspective. Thus, a plurality of these groups fall into the moderate category. Regardless of any foundation affiliation,

Table 5-9 Political Orientations by Tax Status

	All Orgs.	501(c)(3) Orgs.	501(c)(4) Orgs. with 501(c)(3) Foundations	501(c)(4) Orgs.
Liberal	41.3	35.9	58.6	53.3
Moderate	32.3	45.7	10.3	13.3
Conservative	26.5	18.5	31.0	33.3
	(N = 155)	(N = 92)	(N = 29)	(N = 15)

SOURCE: Foundation for Public Affairs sample, 1985.

501(c)(4) organizations exhibit two interesting patterns. First, they have a point of view, as only a fraction are considered middle-of-the-road ideologically. Second, these groups have a liberal bias. Surely this comes as no surprise to those familiar with the public interest sector. What may be surprising, however, is the rather significant minority of conservative organizations active in public interest advocacy, considering that just over a decade ago Andrew McFarland concluded that "no conservatively oriented public interest group is now influential at the national level." [29]

The 501(c)(4)/501(c)(3) organizations include several of the prominent public interest organizations active in Washington today. Those representing liberal causes include: American Civil Liberties Union, Americans for Democratic Action, Ralph Nader's Public Citizen, Consumer Federation of America, TransAfrica/TransAfrica Forum, National Abortion Rights Action League, National Council of Senior Citizens, Sierra Club, and Friends of the Earth. The League of Women Voters, a bipartisan organization, also utilizes this organizational structure. Conservative groups have organized themselves in this manner as well. They include the American Conservative Union, Phyllis Schlafly's Eagle Forum, and the Conservative Caucus. Given the benefits of dispersed costs and increased organizational activities, these organizations are better equipped to provide political representation for their causes (and their members).

Public Interest Organizations for the 1990s

Public interest organizations are institutionalized in order to represent various public interests more effectively. Over the last two decades the memberships in these organizations have increased significantly, their budgets have grown dramatically, their staffs have expanded and become more professional, and new technologies have aided in efforts at organizational maintenance. Yet the majority of public interest organizations face the same constraints imposed by IRS regulations.

Interestingly, many of the recent transformations in structure and group maintenance have been possible through compliance with 501(c)(3) requirements. More specifically, with increased revenues yet consistent constraints on political activities, public interest organizations must find ways of spending member contributions in a manner not related to influencing policy outcomes. Thus, organizations have become computerized, and membership development has become an increasingly important aspect of organizational maintenance. Direct mail is used by virtually all public interest organizations. The techniques of Madison Avenue have reached K Street and Dupont Circle inhabitants in a significant way. The quality of leadership communications also has improved (at least on the entertainment front). In fact, many 501(c)(3) organizations have become quite comfortable with the restrictions placed on them by the IRS. While the proselytizing letters filling the mail boxes of white, liberal, middle-class Americans "stress fear and threat, and portray issues in extreme black-and-white alternatives," [30] the leaders receiving the emotionally charged contributions are spending less than one-third of their budgets on direct political influence.

The public interest sector today is qualitatively different from the organizations of two decades ago. No longer do these organizations provide refuge to untrained social reformers seeking a couch on which to sleep in return for in-kind services rendered. The era of flannel-shirted, "Flower Power," antiestablishmentarianism has virtually vanished. Today, jobs are awarded on merit, and public interest organizations are hiring economists, Ivy League lawyers, management consultants, direct mail specialists, and communications directors. Although these new breeds of staffers may not have marched on Washington or actively protested "the War," they are trained either to conduct research, to litigate, to administer, to mobilize, or to market.

Scott Sklar, member of several public interest governing boards, including those of the Environmental Action Foundation and the League of Conservation Voters, and government relations director of the Solar Energy Industry Association, has been active in the public interest movement for more than twenty years. He has participated, in fact, in the significant transformation in the public interest community. According to Sklar,

> Over the last ten years the role of public interest groups has very much changed. In the late sixties and early seventies when a good

portion of these groups came about, the goal was really to show your collective mass to the system and by its sheer weight develop a movement. Now that there has been a decade, almost two decades, of real proactive public interest representation in Washington, it's taken on very much like corporate offices have in Washington, and you find you have a much more professional leadership. . . . We all wear suits and ties, tend to be more educated, with Hill experience. In some ways, I see it going too far to the professional side.[31]

Yet, with all the growth and the resulting professionalism in the public interest sector, individual organizations remain constrained by government regulations. Existing tax laws limit the amount of time and money organizations may spend on direct policy advocacy—lobbying. This particular organizational dilemma is one of the more difficult problems to resolve; nonetheless, it reaches to the core of public interest representation. Public interest organizations attract members by stressing the eminent dangers arising from government or industry decisions or nondecisions. Yet the leaders of 501(c)(3) organizations, which constitute roughly two-thirds of the public interest sector, may spend only a small portion of their organizational resources on congressional lobbying. A growing number of organizations have managed to find some resolution to the lobbying constraint problem by reorganizing as full-service public interest organizations, and this may be the organizational structure for the 1990s. Public interest contributors deserve "more bang for the buck" in direct policy advocacy.

Organizational diversification allows political influence in all aspects of the public policy-making process. Public interest enterprises structured to include a 501(c)(4) parent organization, a 501(c)(3) foundation, a litigation arm, and a political action committee offer public interest contributors numerous opportunities to support direct policy advocacy without legal constraints. These full-service organizations, if managed by effective leaders, provide the multiple mechanisms necessary to influence the policy-making process at all possible access points. This is not to say, however, that 501(c)(3) organizations are uniformly inferior to full-service organizations. On the contrary, some of the most influential public interest organizations have retained their 501(c)(3) status. Likewise, some full-service enterprises play only minor roles in the advocacy process. Nonetheless, given the limited information available to potential supporters through direct mail solicitations, organizational diversification should be viewed as a positive attribute, *ceteris paribus*, when selecting an organization to support. Not all public interest organizations are effectively managed, professionally organized, and politically effective. In fact, most are not. Without the assistance of the organizations themselves or the IRS in providing organizational information on budgets, size, structure, and leadership, the advice for potential public interest supporters (members) is *donator emptor,* let the donor beware.

Notes

1. Haynes Johnson, "Turning Government Jobs into Gold," *Washington Post National Weekly Edition,* May 12, 1986, 7. The Foundation for Public Affairs monitors approximately 2,500 public interest organizations.
2. The Urban Institute has identified more than 124,000 nonprofit organizations that serve or provide benefits to the public, cited in Pablo Eisenberg, "Community/Grassroots Organizations," in *Public Interest Profiles,* ed. Douglas J. Bergner (Washington, D.C.: Foundation for Public Affairs, 1986), 22.

    Charles T. Clotfelter has estimated that more than $60 billion is donated to nonprofit organizations annually. The bulk of these charitable contributions is received by religious organizations ($35 billion), but more than $4 billion in donations reach so-called social welfare organizations. According to tax return data, more than 60 million Americans donate to nonprofit organizations. See Clotfelter, "Charitable Giving and Tax Legislation in the Reagan Era," *Law and Contemporary Problems* 48 (1985): 197-212. And according to polls conducted by the Gallup Organization, "as many as 20 million Americans are members of [public interest] organizations, and another 20 million have given money to these groups during the past year." See, "Participation in Interest Groups High," *Gallup Report,* 191 (August 1981): 45-57.
3. Kay L. Schlozman and John T. Tierney, *Organized Interests and American Democracy* (New York: Harper and Row, 1985), 388.
4. David B. Truman, *The Governmental Process,* 2d ed. (New York: Knopf, 1971).
5. Robert H. Salisbury, "An Exchange Theory of Interest Groups," *Midwest Journal of Political Science* 13 (February 1969): 1-32. See also, Norman Frolich, Joe Oppenheimer, and Oran Young, *Political Leadership and Collective Goods* (Princeton, N.J.: Princeton University Press, 1971).
6. Jeffrey M. Berry, *Lobbying for the People: The Political Behavior of Public Interest Groups* (Princeton, N.J.: Princeton University Press, 1977), 24. Also see, Berry, "On the Origins of Public Interest Groups: A Test of Two Theories," *Polity* 10 (1978): 379-397.
7. Andrew S. McFarland, *Public Interest Lobbies: Decision Making on Energy* (Washington, D.C.: American Enterprise Institute, 1976), 1-24; and McFarland, *Common Cause: Lobbying in the Public Interest* (Chatham, N.J.: Chatham House, 1984), chap. 2.
8. McFarland, *Public Interest Lobbies,* 4-5.
9. E. E. Schattschneider, *The Semi-Sovereign People* (New York: Holt,

Rinehart, and Winston, 1960); see also Andrew S. McFarland, "Public Interest Lobbies versus Minority Faction," in *Interest Group Politics,* ed. Allan J. Cigler and Burdett A. Loomis (Washington, D.C.: CQ Press, 1983), 324-353.

10. McFarland, *Common Cause,* 23.
11. See Robert H. Wiebe, *The Search for Order, 1877-1920* (New York: Hill and Wang, 1967); Richard Hofstadter, *The Age of Reform* (New York: Vintage Books, 1955); Alexis De Tocqueville, *Democracy in America* (New York: Mentor Books, 1956). Also see, Mancur Olson, *The Logic of Collective Action* (Cambridge, Mass.: Harvard University Press, 1965, 1971).
12. Bergner, *Public Interest Profiles,* iii.
13. The Berry data presented in this chapter were drawn from Chapters 2 and 3 of *Lobbying for the People.* The Foundation for Public Affairs data (N = 250) was drawn from the foundation's publication edited by Bergner, *Public Interest Profiles.* Only 221 groups are included in the following tables, however, as "Think Tanks" (N = 21) and several "Business/Economic" groups (N = 8) were eliminated because of their 501(c)(6) tax status as "Business Organizations." For each public interest group that is presented, seventy-eight variables were coded by the author from the raw data presented in each profile.

    To enhance the comparability of the two data sources, the author analyzed those organizations included in both data sets (N = 35) and pieced together data for an additional fourteen organizations not found in the Foundation for Public Affairs publication. The tables presented in this chapter were replicated using the data from the 49 groups available for both data sources as well as from additional data gathering. Aside from the findings in Table 5-1 on year of origin, the patterns uncovered in the full analysis of all Berry groups and FPA groups are comparable to those in the smaller "panel" study. Any variation in the two data sources reflects changes made in the public interest sector during the thirteen years intervening between the two studies. Sample sizes reported in the following tables differ due to missing values in the data sets.
14. Bergner, *Public Interest Profiles,* iii.
15. Interestingly, the Vietnam issue, recast by Vietnam veterans and their supporters in the late 1970s and early 1980s, has managed to reclaim a position on the public agenda and has resulted in the (re)mobilization and organization of citizens concerned with the plight of those who survived the war. If antiwar groups are eliminated from the sample, more than 90 percent of Berry's groups are still functioning.
16. The budget figures presented by Berry were converted to 1985 dollars by multiplying by a factor equal to the 1985 Consumer Price Index (318.5) divided by the 1972 Consumer Price Index (125.3), or roughly multiplying by 2.5 (actual conversion factor is 2.54). Thus, a budget of $50,000 in 1972 is roughly equal to $125,000 in 1985. In both data sets the number of observations vary because of missing data.

17. Berry, *Lobbying for the People*, 58-59.
18. Burton A. Weisbrod, *The Nonprofit Economy* (Cambridge, Mass.: Harvard University Press, 1988), 7. According to Weisbrod, the number of nonprofit organizations in the United States is approaching 900,000. The largest class (about 40 percent of the total) includes educational, health, welfare, scientific, and cultural organizations. Nearly half of the growth of the nonprofit sector between 1969 and 1985 occurred within this class, which grew by nearly 170 percent. Public interest organizations are included in this category.
19. I. Richard Gershon, "Tax-Exempt Entities: Achieving and Maintaining Special Status under the Watchful Eye of the IRS," *Cumberland Law Review* 16(2): 301-327; and Peter Dobkin Hall, "A Historical Overview of the Private Nonprofit Sector," in *The Nonprofit Sector*, ed. Walter W. Powell (New Haven, Conn.: Yale University Press, 1987).
20. Most public interest organizations are classified as either 501(c)(3) tax-exempt organizations or 501(c)(4) social welfare organizations. Other organizations included in the interest group community, however, fall into several other IRS categories—for example, veterans' organizations, 501(c)(19); labor and agricultural organizations, 501(c)(5); business organizations, 501(c)(6); and employees' associations, 501(c)(4), (9), and (17). See Internal Revenue Service, "Tax-Exempt Status for Your Organization," Publication 557 (Washington, D.C.: Department of the Treasury, July 1985).
21. The first federal legislation recognizing the importance of granting tax-exempt status to certain sectors of the economy was the Revenue Act of 1894. While this original legislation was ruled unconstitutional by the Supreme Court in *Pollock v. Farmers' Loan and Trust,* 157 U.S. 429 (1895), passage of the Sixteenth Amendment paved the way for future federal regulatory action. See Gershon, "Tax-Exempt Entities."
22. Paul E. Treusch and Norman A. Sugarman, "Initial Qualification of a Charitable Organization: Limitations on 'Action' Organizations," in *Tax-Exempt Charitable Organizations* (Philadelphia: ALI-ABA, 1983). The alternative test provided in the 1976 Tax Reform Act allows for a sliding scale that permits an organization to spend 20 percent of its first $500,000 on direct lobbying efforts, 15 percent of its next $500,000, and 5 percent of its remaining budget. Twenty-five percent of these expenditures may be used on indirect lobbying efforts (citizen mobilization, grass-roots lobbying). See Bruce R. Hopkins, *The Law of Tax Exempt Organizations,* 2d ed. (Washington, D.C.: Lerner Law Book Company, 1977), 149; and Weisbrod, *Nonprofit Economy,* 120.
23. William J. Lehrfeld, quoted in John Riley, "Tax-Exempt Foundations: What Is Legal?" *National Law Journal* 9 (February 1987): 8.
24. Environmental Action, *1985 Annual Report: Environmental Action/Environmental Action Foundation* (Washington, D.C.: Environmental Action, 1985).
25. John Wark and Gary Marx, "Faith, Hope and Chicanery," *Washington*

Monthly 19 (January 1987): 29.

26. Ibid., 29.

27. Michael McCloskey, chairman, Board of Directors, Sierra Club, interview with the author, Sierra Club National Headquarters, San Francisco, Calif., December 19, 1985.

28. Organizational publications are also subject to "substantial part" restrictions governing 501(c)(3) groups. Articles addressing specific policy issues facing Congress are included as activities attempting to influence legislation.

29. McFarland, *Public Interest Lobbies,* 37.

30. R. Kenneth Godwin, *One Billion Dollars of Influence* (Chatham, N.J.: Chatham House, 1988), 33.

31. Scott Sklar, Solar Energy Industry Association, interview with the author, Washington, D.C., October 24, 1985.

6. AGENDA SETTING AT COMMON CAUSE

Lawrence S. Rothenberg

Who determines organizational goals is a central issue for students of interest group politics. In this chapter Lawrence Rothenberg provides a theoretical outline of who should make such decisions and then applies this perspective to the public interest group Common Cause. He particularly emphasizes the dramatic shift in the group's political agenda during the early 1980s, when it moved away from its traditional progressive, good government concerns and focused on military issues, most notably the production and deployment of the MX missile.

Rothenberg's analysis lends credence to his theoretical construct, which predicts that organizational leaders will pay the greatest attention to those members who contribute the most to the group and whose participation depends most heavily on a group's political goals. Common Cause activists derived their greatest leverage from their agenda-setting authority, which directed the group toward the peace movement. These activists fit precisely the profile of those who wield the greatest influence. The rank and file exercised veto authority, as group leaders made sure that redirecting objectives would not unduly alienate their contributor base. The leaders themselves possessed discretionary authority, which stemmed from their room to maneuver in implementing their broad mandate. Thus, as an organization Common Cause can be termed democratic but in a less egalitarian way than the classic "one person, one vote" sense.

For most students of politics, the major value of a theory of interest groups derives from what it can say about group goals and, in particular, how they are formulated as a function of member goals.
— Terry M. Moe, *The Organization of Interests*

Terry Moe's commentary pinpoints an issue that lies at the heart of why scholars ought to study organizations.[1] They should want to understand how group goals are specified and to what extent an association's objectives emerge as a product of the will of organizational leaders, the desires of members as a collectivity, or the preferences of a subset of contributors.[2] Put another way, how do directives embodying specific objectives get placed successfully on a group's political agenda?

Why is this such a crucial issue? This question can be answered from one of two perspectives: that of the positivist who aspires to comprehend how interest groups actually function or that of the normativist who wishes to evaluate whether organizations are a desirable or a pernicious force in the political world. For the former, it is critical to assess just how significant, if at all, contributors are in governing how a group operates and who among the ranks of the membership actually wields influence. For the latter, who wishes to evaluate whether organizations are to be viewed as augmenting, rather than hindering, the process of democratic representation, it is essential to determine whether they are run in a democratic fashion, rather than as the exclusive domains of insulated, unresponsive leaderships.

Thus, a strong prima facie case can be made for addressing the issue of how associational goals are formulated. The logical inference—that a voluminous, detailed literature exists that analyzes the importance of the internal operations of interest groups in goal formation—is incorrect, however, for reasons to be discussed later in this analysis. On the contrary, there is a dearth of empirical investigations, and only a modicum of theoretical work, inquiring into the crucial linkage that underlies the relationship between member and group goals. The following inquiry is aimed at partially filling this vacuum.

Outline of Research

Two principal empirical research designs might be employed to study which preferences of individuals are reflected in a group's goals. One method is to define a sample of organizations, assess the ends that they pursue, and explain the cross-sectional differences between these objectives as a function of each association's internal politics. The other method is to single out a specific association and explain how its goals vary over time in accordance with changes in the organization and its environment. The latter approach is employed here both because there are fewer difficult-to-measure factors that must be controlled to draw inferences about group goals and because it is easier to conduct a comprehensive study of just one organization.[3]

The subject of this investigation is the public interest group Common Cause.[4] Common Cause was founded in 1970 as a "People's Lobby" by John Gardner, former secretary of health, education, and welfare in the Lyndon Johnson administration. It is undoubtedly the best known of all public interest groups, with a membership that generally fluctuates between 200,000 and 300,000. The association's high profile is one reason for selecting it as the focus of this study. The principal motivation for its selection as a case study for investigating internal politics and organizational goals is that in the early 1980s it experienced a sudden—and in retrospect temporary—redirection of its political agenda.[5]

The remainder of this investigation proceeds in six stages. The first stage provides an overview of how Common Cause dramatically shifted its political objectives in the first half of the 1980s. The next two stages survey two theoretical perspectives that one might apply to understanding the internal politics of organizations. Both are traditional approaches that include work completed through the mid-1960s and revisionist alternatives that have been proposed in the quarter century since then. The fourth stage recounts in more depth the internal politics occurring at Common Cause as it changed its political agenda, while the next stage assesses these events in light of the theoretical understanding of organizations advanced earlier. This is followed by some brief conclusions about the implications of the findings of this analysis.

Common Cause's Issue Agenda

"It was my notion that the chief mission of Common Cause should be to hold government accountable," recounted founding father John Gardner.[6] At its inception Common Cause had some roots in the anti-Vietnam War movement, but in the aftermath of the Watergate scandal it firmly established a focus and a reputation that emphasized classic progressive concerns. Around Common Cause these came to be known as structure and process issues. Such matters, each of which were high-profile concerns for periods in the 1970s, included ethics laws, lobby disclosure, "sunshine" legislation (laws providing for public access to federal meetings), and, especially, campaign finance reform.

To fight its political battles Common Cause developed a distinctive lobbying technique, what its leaders called an insider-outsider approach. This involves coordinating Washington-style direct lobbying of congressional decision makers with constituent pressure via grass-roots mobilization of members back in the legislators' home districts. In Washington, the association's professional staff works to bring its expertise—particularly its special knowledge about the technical details of the issues—to bear on the relevant decision makers. An activist core of volunteers who are organized at the congressional district level periodically turn up the electoral heat by seeing to it that the necessary phone calls are made, letters written, and meetings attended.

From the group's formation, Common Cause received widespread recognition for its efforts in behalf of this variety of progressive causes. In particular, the organization garnered a great deal of publicity about its involvement in the events surrounding the passage of the Federal Election Campaign Act (FECA) of 1974, which set up much of the present campaign finance system.[7] From these events and through much hard work during the following years, Common Cause has achieved a reputation as the unchallenged authority on campaign finance in the public interest group community. As an example of the lengths to which the organization will go, its staff regularly take on the arduous task of sifting through the reams of candidate and political action committee (PAC) reports filed with the Federal Election Commission and aggregating and interpreting these data for public consumption. The hope is that the generation of easy-to-digest documents will foster media publicity about what, according to Common Cause, is the inherently corrupt nature of the current electoral system.

Structure and process issues remained the principal draw on the group's attention throughout the 1970s. Although in the late 1970s Common Cause did become involved in several substantive debates (compared to the procedural issues that were the organization's bread and butter) such as the B-1 bomber and trucking deregulation, their efforts were limited. Indeed, even staff members who were interviewed admitted that many potential allies had become skeptical about the organization's commitment to substantive causes. There is little dispute that the organization's principal *raison d'être* and its public identity continued to revolve around its traditional concerns.

The 1970s may have been kind to Common Cause in terms of keeping structure and process issues in the public eye, but the 1980s found the group's issue agenda diametrically opposed in emphasis to that adopted by the Reagan administration. Campaign finance reform suddenly faded from political view in the early 1980s, despite an increase in the level of campaign spending and a proliferation of political action committees. The late 1970s had witnessed a series of unsuccessful efforts, despite support from President Jimmy Carter, to break a partisan deadlock over electoral reform.[8] With no obvious means of arranging a legislative accord, and a lack of presidential encouragement once Ronald Reagan came to office, campaign finance was placed on the back burner. Other core issues of Common Cause met similar fates and fell from public view as well.

While the group initially held firm to its basic issue agenda, it did not stake out daring new policy initiatives. The organization could have elected, for example, to concentrate on concerns related to its traditional interests, such as battles over congressional redistricting in the wake of the 1980 census or efforts to facilitate voter registration, including the fight over the renewal in the early 1980s of the Voting Rights Act of 1965. Common Cause was somewhat involved in each of these issues, but the organization did not make a major commitment of organizational resources in either instance.

Instead, in late 1982 the group chose to deal with a qualitatively different type of issue and veer away from its established structure and process focus. The official turning point occurred in November when the group's governing board met and decided that the association would center its energies and resources on preventing the production and deployment of the Air Force's MX missile.[9] The MX, which stands for Missile Experimental (the missile project is officially known within the military as the Peacekeeper), is a land-based intercontinental ballistic missile designed to replace the Minuteman II and III as they allegedly approach technological obsolescence.

The MX initially had risen to prominence in the 1970s, especially with the Carter administration's decision in early 1979 to commence full-scale engineering development for 200 missiles. During the first term of the Reagan administration, the missile emerged as the most controversial element of the president's "strategic modernization program."[10] By late 1982 the entire program seemed in jeopardy. Not only were the nascent peace and nuclear freeze movements sweeping the nation, but also the search for a basing mode for the missile that was both strategically viable and politically acceptable (citizens even in conservative states did not appreciate the idea of MX missiles being transported by truck near where they lived) had proven embarrassing. The Reagan administration, however, was absolutely committed to the program for both symbolic and strategic reasons, and it made the missile a top priority.

Intuitively, the decision of Common Cause to focus on the MX seems a strange choice for two reasons that, in a sense, emanate from the same source: the organization's investment in progressive concerns such as campaign financing. First, Common Cause would find it difficult to get much popular recognition for its efforts on MX policy; on defense issues the nation's popular media would likely turn to others for their views. Such expectations certainly were borne out. An analysis of both the *New York Times* and the nightly network news broadcasts revealed that the group was a virtual nonentity when it came to the MX. At the same time the more specialized media products directed at Washington insiders, such as the *Congressional Quarterly Weekly Report* or the *National Journal*, demonstrated that the organization stood at the forefront of an extensive effort to defeat the missile.

Second, for reasons roughly analogous to why popular news organizations would ignore Common Cause on defense issues, the group would seem to have no obvious comparative political advantage either. Consider both elements of the organization's insider-outsider lobbying strategy—the application of staff expertise in Washington and the mobilization of grass-roots pressure—when it came to the procurement and deployment of missile systems. On the one hand, Common Cause appeared to be disadvantaged when lobbying in Washington because it lacked any particular credibility on the subject of military hardware procurement. On the other hand, the association seemed to face an equivalent challenge in utilizing its grass-roots organizations, which consisted of members who presumably joined, to the extent that they signed up for political reasons at all (to be discussed later in this analysis), because of the group's efforts on structure and process issues.[11] This would be a clear handicap in terms of both energizing this constituency and achieving credibility for any mobilization effort that did occur.

Arguing that Common Cause had no obvious comparative advantage, however, is not tantamount to saying that the organization had nothing to offer the anti-MX coalition. What the association could, and did, provide its often-inexperienced allies was its general expertise on how to lobby in Washington and its knowledge about grass-roots mobilization. Common Cause could also combine those in its congressional district organizations with other activists caught up in the groundswell of the arms control movement. By filling this niche of a generalist organization with political savvy, Common Cause found itself for once, at the center of a coalition rather than the lone wolf acting with few committed allies. Ultimately, the organizational network that coalesced had a moderate effect in influencing the key votes that members of Congress were forced to cast over the next few years.[12]

For two and a half years Common Cause was at the forefront of the anti-MX coalition led by its former president David Cohen (the other lead organization was the peace group SANE). The MX was the organization's principal issue for this entire period. The small inner circle around Cohen plotted the allies' strategies and worked at keeping a unified front—especially in light of the tendencies of some of the more extreme members (including some in SANE) to oppose anything in the way of compromise.

In its newly found role as an arms control organization, Common Cause quickly embroiled itself in a series of highly visible, bruising congressional fights, with both the president and the Pentagon strongly mobilized in opposition. Eventually, after a number of dramatic twists and turns, a compromise was hammered out in 1985 which stipulated that fifty MX missiles would be deployed in existing silos. This accord furnished the Air Force with considerably fewer missiles than it wanted but nonetheless represented a concession by program opponents who wanted the MX scrapped altogether. With this, the Peacekeeper faded from the congressional agenda until the end of the Reagan administration, when the matter of building additional missiles to be placed on railroad cars brought the program back into public view.

Almost as soon as the MX faded from the nation's political consciousness in 1985, the Common Cause issue agenda swung back to its traditional focus, electoral reform. In late 1985 Sen. David Boren, D-Okla., began a frontal assault on the campaign finance system, the idea of enacting more restrictive regulation consequently regained some prominence, and Common Cause began mobilizing its forces. In addition, the nation's attention was redirected toward ethical issues as the Iran-contra scandal began to unravel. Although it maintained a modest interest in military matters, Common Cause reverted its attentions back to where they might have belonged more naturally in the first place.

What accounts for these fascinating changes in the group's political agenda? Why would an organization such as Common Cause, so firmly identified with such issues as campaign finance, dramatically switch gears? To answer these questions adequately, it is necessary first to investigate in greater depth the available theoretical perspectives on the internal politics of organizations.

Theoretical Perspectives on the Internal Politics of Organizations: Traditional Approaches

Scholars traditionally have given short shrift to the internal politics of organizations compared with studies of why members join and how groups try to exercise influence. This absence of attention stems in a logical fashion—with some caveats that will be evident shortly—from the traditional theoretical approaches that scholars have developed on member decision making.[13] In particular, two conceptual outlooks on organizations—essentially the flip sides of the same coin—might be cited for the neglect of internal politics: one might be called the residual of pluralism and the other the aftermath of Olsonian logic.

Pluralist scholars, dating from Arthur Bentley, David Truman, and Earl Latham, typically believed that interest groups exist because members share a common interest.[14] If this is a valid assumption, it is logical to deduce that the internal politics of organizations are immaterial because member opinions' do not vary. Thus, members, ranging from the rank and file through the leadership, will advocate identical objectives. Put another way, there is no reason to presume that any subgroup will advance its own interests at another's expense. Although pluralism's popularity as a means of understanding collectivities has waned considerably in the past quarter of a century, the residual effect may be to discourage work on intraorganizational politics.

The pluralist lesson that it is acceptable to ignore internal group politics may have been reinforced by the principal theoretical alternative that followed it: the economically based rationale developed most prominently by Mancur Olson in his seminal book, *The Logic of Collective Action*.[15] Olson's "by-product theory" almost completely severed the linkage between member preferences and group goals by arguing that an organization's political objectives play no role in the decisions of most members to join the organization (and presumably in their continued contributions to the group).

Specifically, Olson proposed a model in which individuals are assumed (1) to be interested only in the economic returns of participation, (2) to possess perfect information about what a group has to offer, and (3) to maximize the returns on their group activities without error. For the vast majority of contributors who furnish so little organizational support that it has no discernible impact on the amount of collective, nondivisible goods (such as electoral reform by Common Cause) produced by the organization—so-called small members—an association's stated political goals have little relevance. Members are interested only in the divisible, selective rewards that the group offers. Political action is merely the by-product of private decision making.

If Olson is correct, internal politics will reflect the will of the association's leaders or of the few large members who can influence the amount of collective goods the group can produce. For an organization such as Common Cause, which lacks large members for whom politics matters, this dictates that its leaders ordain what political goals the association pursues, if they elect to concentrate on achieving any political objectives whatsoever.[16] In other words, entrepreneurs who assemble a package of private benefits for potential members can then decide whether or not to put any of their profits into having a political impact.

The Olsonian logic implies, by definition, that those at the helm of an organization satisfied the economic desires of perfectly informed contributors if they were successful at getting the contributors to sign up in the first place. The implication is that, under most conditions, once a contributor always a contributor, and even if members leave, it will be because they are dissatisfied with the private package of benefits that an association offers. The key to understanding group goals is nothing more than evaluating the idiosyncrasies of the successful entrepreneur; more complex conceptualizations of internal politics should not prove illuminating.

Although this is a neat dichotomy between pluralism and the Olsonian approach, the actual history of thought about group goals unfortunately has been more muddled—presumably because scholars have too infrequently made the systematic linkage between the contribution decision and the objectives an organization pursues. Specifically, when pluralism was the conventional wisdom, a separate orthodoxy developed about the role of leadership in organizations, the so-called iron law of oligarchy.[17] In his classic work Robert Michels argued that leaders directing Western European socialist parties quickly lost their zest for transforming the political landscape and became interested exclusively in employing their specialized knowledge and abilities to control the organization and ensure their own self-perpetuation. Scholars quickly transported this perspective to the analysis of organizations, arguing that interest groups also are run by an insulated oligarchy which loses sight of the association's larger goals and disregards the interests of those whose contributions sustain them.

It must be clear that the ideas of an iron law of oligarchy and of membership based on shared interests are contradictory; the Michelian view of the world is much more consistent with the Olsonian viewpoint. Yet, as Moe has pointed out, beliefs in pluralism and the iron law coexisted for a long time.[18] To reiterate, the only explanation for this combination is that theorists who reflected on why groups existed did not attempt to link in logical fashion this conceptualization to a perspective on internal politics. Now that most scholars accept some version of an economic theory of organizations, the belief in the iron law, which by and large continues to be held, makes more sense.

Despite these inconsistencies, the basic lesson to be taken away from the above discussion remains the same. Whether the scholar's view of the world has been characterized by a pluralist harmony created by absolute agreement among the rank and file and leaders alike or an oligarchic/Olsonian dictatorship by those at the top of the association's hierarchy, the dominant theoretical perspectives of the past century undoubtedly have discouraged serious investigation of internal organizational politics. In either instance, group goals were self-evident and required no particular study.

Theoretical Perspectives on the Internal Politics of Organizations: Revisionist Approaches

In the last quarter century since the publication of *The Logic of Collective Action,* a number of works have been written that have challenged, in one way or another, the fundamental tenets of Olson's path-breaking analysis.[19,20] When taken jointly, this research can provide the analyst with a theoretical perspective from which to assess Common Cause's selection of organizational goals.

Interestingly, with some rare exceptions few examinations have focused on the relationship between the contribution decision and the internal politics of organizations. In particular, there have been few efforts to link empirical applications to theoretical approaches in this tradition.[21]

For associational goals to be an intellectually appealing subject for analysis, there must be reason to believe that member donations are contingent on the political objectives the group pursues. Yet, in Olson's by-product theory perfectly informed individuals are concerned exclusively with private economic returns; the organization's political objectives consequently possess no allure except to large contributors. Put another way, it is necessary to establish that Olson's logic is flawed in a manner that makes studying group goals a worthwhile endeavor.

In operational terms this dictates the establishment of either of two, not mutually exclusive, propositions. One is that members are interested in noneconomic rewards, which provides leaders with an incentive to pay attention to contributor preferences on political issues. Another is that those belonging to the organization are incompletely informed and, consequently, believe that they should be concerned about political matters—even if they are devoted solely to maximizing their own economic returns. Members thus (falsely) think that their contributions are having a noticeable impact. To one extent or another scholars have devised persuasive arguments supporting both assertions.

Thus, one compelling proposition that has been advanced is that individuals are sometimes motivated by so-called purposive rewards, intangible returns that stem from contributing to a worthwhile endeavor.[22] This implies that, at a minimum, what a group stands for will be relevant to contribution choices even in a world where members know that their individual donations have no perceptible impact on the level of collective goods produced.[23] Indeed, when asked why they joined Common Cause, almost every member surveyed for this study cited broad, purposive motivations as the principal reasons.[24]

Another point that has been maintained effectively is that it is almost certainly correct to assume that organization members are incompletely informed. Several variations of this theme more or less give credence to the proposition that this incomplete information leads members to believe that they have an impact on the level of collective goods produced. Moe makes the strongest argument in this respect.[25] I suggest that members might harbor such misperceptions early on in their group tenure but that contributors have the capacity to learn over time. Certainly, veteran Common Cause members are far more likely than relative newcomers to know how the organization functions and to have opinions about group positions on relevant issues. It is probably more reasonable to believe that contributions are contingent on organizational goals because individuals fuse assessments of their own donations to collective goods with their evaluations of purposive returns.[26]

The bottom line is that associational goals should matter for at least some members of an organization when it comes to their decision to contribute. This should be especially likely in the case of public interest groups, since they tend to offer what appear to be insufficient levels of selective rewards to precipitate membership. Even if they do provide sufficiently attractive private incentives, they rarely provide extra selective benefits for those contributing more than the minimal dues. Thus, group objectives might matter for at least this subset of members.

The implications of the above discussion for leadership behavior—assuming that those in charge wish, at a minimum, to maintain their organization—are straightforward. Leaders are motivated to identify the "relevant members," to find out what they are thinking, and to integrate this information into their deliberations about what goals the association should pursue. In turn, relevant members are defined by two criteria: (1) their value to the association as measured by contribution levels and (2) the probability that they will exit if they are dissatisfied with group goals.[27]

At Common Cause these dual criteria position the spotlight squarely on the activist cadre on whom the group depends for grass-roots mobilization. Intuitively, it makes sense that contributors who care the most about the group's purposive and collective returns select themselves to join the activist cohort, particularly since few exclusive private benefits are offered to these volunteers. Therefore, they must be activists either because of the sheer joy of being involved—the so-called solidary rewards—or because of the purposive/collective returns. Each of these factors is demonstrated to be germane when members' decisions to be or not to be activists are systematically analyzed.[28] By definition, activists contribute far more to the organization in both money and especially time than do those in the rank and file. Thus, they satisfy both of the key prerequisites elaborated above for exercising intraorganizational influence.

Common Cause leaders, however, possess an incentive not to ignore the rank and file completely, despite their focus on activists' concerns. Members generally are interested in purposive and collective returns when, for example, they decide whether to stay in the group. This makes focusing exclusively on activists a risky strategy, since they may differ from the bulk of the membership in their preferences concerning the organization's political activities. The rank and file must be accorded a significant, even if a secondary, role.

In short, when activists talk the leadership should listen. Since other members make their (albeit lesser) contributions partially contingent on their assessments of the group's adopted goals, they should be expected to play a role in the formation of associational objectives as well.

This perspective reflects a different view of goal formation than that derived from the pluralist nirvana of shared interests, the oligarchic/Olsonian portrayal of the leadership dominance, or the standard "one person, one vote" conception of direct democracy. Instead, in the organizational world depicted, the unequal distribution in members' willingness to make large contributions and differences in how contingent their activities are on political matters accord each stratum in the group differing levels of influence.

How does this portrayal of how goals are formed compare to how Common Cause actually operates? The ultimate test is ascertaining which model of goal formation is consistent with the empirical evidence.

Common Cause and Goal Formation

At first blush, the answer to the question just posed might be "poorly." Common Cause is often trumpeted as being unique among public interest groups because it is formally democratic. Not only do members have the option of voting for the governing board (20-25 percent actually do), but they also may fill out an annual poll that probes members' opinions on issues and asks what priorities the organization should adopt. But, given the previous discussion, strict adherence to formal democratic processes would not be sensible from the perspective of organizational maintenance.

The explanation for this contrast between theory and apparent reality is that, in practice, the group's formal structure for member participation is far less efficacious than it might seem. As Andrew McFarland has pointed out, voters in governing board elections have low levels of information and the vast majority of those elected are from the pool of candidates chosen from above—such elections are hardly a very effective method of control.[29] In addition, any careful examination of the annual poll will reveal that it is relatively unilluminating, since the wording of questions produces little distribution in the way members respond. Indeed, when I mentioned to Common Cause staffers that according to their published poll, the MX was less popular with the membership than other issues, they were quick to point out how little the level of support varies from one issue to another.

As would be expected from the prior theoretical discussion, member input flows through more informal means that reflect the disproportionate attention that some members are given as compared to others. For example, the organization's staff members routinely travel from Washington around the country to maintain contact with their activists (who, according to the association, constitute roughly 4 percent of all contributors). Not only do such interactions with the folks from the home office help coordinate grass-roots operations and make activists feel that their efforts are appreciated, but these trips also provide the staff with a means of sampling the feelings of their most valued members. Most of the time the feedback is positive since contributors are rather homogeneous and the group's monitoring of opinion is fairly continual. When responses are negative, however, a red flag is raised for the leadership. Just such a warning went up in the early 1980s when staffers noted during their grass-roots travels a flurry of unsolicited pleas that Common Cause participate in the blossoming peace movement.

Why choose defense politics and why at that point in history? Although Common Cause was a good government organization rather than an arms control group—the activists, more than anybody else in the membership, should have understood this—the supply of structure and process issues had run low in the early 1980s. On the demand side, issues of war and peace had gained an intensity that harkened back to the height of the cold war. U.S. politics was consumed with the implications of Ronald Reagan's military buildup. The backlash to this massive escalation in defense spending and its associated tensions was the almost overnight development of a widespread peace movement, much of it tied to the idea of implementing a nuclear freeze. In this context Common Cause included a large grass-roots contingent that was predisposed to being mobilized but was being kept on the political sidelines.

Although these contributors could have fallen on either side of the nuclear freeze debate, virtually every signal that the leadership received was that they were opposed to increased military budgets. If the direction of activist opinion had been split, the defense issue would have been dropped with little fanfare. Even though Common Cause is avowedly nonpartisan—for example, the group petitioned for the investigation of Democratic Speaker Jim Wright in 1988—the association's activists were nearly all opposed to the Reagan buildup. They were clearly troubled by the images of a nuclear holocaust that escalating arms expenditures conjured up.

Thus, staff members uncovered a profound concern in the activist cadre through their normal temperature taking. Especially given the larger context—that the supply of structure and process issues was low—the leadership had an incentive to take these opinions seriously. But this did not mean that the organization proceeded full steam ahead. Another question required consideration: How would the rank and file react to a change in course? Because this was a dramatically new initiative, the group commissioned a private poll of 4,000 members to assess whether the preferences of the activist cadre were in lock step with those of the bulk of contributors. The poll confirmed that there was considerable accord throughout the membership over defense issues.

Finally, the governing board was confronted with the evidence that Common Cause should make a commitment to the peace movement. This was a fairly simple task in that a large number of the board's members were anxious to see the group move in a more substantive direction. As Gardner put it, Common Cause's structure and process focus had always proven to be "a somewhat austere approach for a lively, politically sensitive board." [30] Although some board members, including Gardner, were opposed to the departure from the organization's bread-and-butter issues, the initiative was endorsed easily.

Political scientist Thomas Cronin, who served on the Common Cause governing board and opposed the move to the MX, summed up the events that transpired as follows:

> I felt, as I believe he [Gardner] did, that the organization would weaken its focus or its mission if it got involved in a variety of other issues outside the explicitly structure and process issues the organization was formed to address. It was very hard, however, to contain or dissuade the anti-war activists on this set of issues. I believe that to some extent here is an example of where the citizen activists and constituents "led" the leadership in the organization. [31]

Activists, with the blessing of the rank and file, did not simply take hold of the organization with the leadership going along sheepishly. Rather, the top echelon at Common Cause had considerable room to maneuver. In specifying the details of where it would take the organization's antiwar activities, the leadership felt the MX was a logical choice. It was an issue that was amenable to the insider-outsider strategy, that was high on the congressional agenda, that was potentially winnable, and that was evocative of strong feelings from both members and nonmembers at the grass-roots level. It was also one to which the group could make an obvious contribution. It fit the organization's needs and abilities much more than an idealistic concern such as the nuclear freeze, which seemed to have little hope of long-term success. Thus, the organization went from the previously discussed general declaration in mid-July to the specific announcement that it would concentrate on the MX in November. It remained the province of the Common Cause staff, under the direction of the organization's president, Fred Wertheimer, to determine how the group would construct the roadblocks required to stop the MX.

Discussion: The Politics of Organizational Goals

This recitation of the events of the early 1980s at Common Cause meshes nicely with the general theoretical propositions outlined previously. Thus, the activists, rank and file members, and the leadership of Common Cause might be characterized as possessing three types of authority: agenda setting, veto, and discretionary.

By exercising their agenda-setting authority, Common Cause activists can define the general issues that the organization considers. Instances in which activists feel compelled to try to open new fronts will not occur very frequently in a group such as Common Cause, where there is considerable harmony among contributors about what organizational objectives should look like and where the leadership should be able to anticipate what its more valued participants desire. As anyone who has studied congressional decision making knows, agenda-setting authority can have considerable influence associated with it. The ability to advance a proposal that, at least in broad terms, can be either accepted or rejected yields considerable influence.

Similarly, the rank and file might be seen as playing a role comparable to that of Congress when it considers proposed legislation. Organizational contributors, like members of Congress, have the authority to reject the proposition and retain the status quo or to accept it and see the group's policy change. This veto authority, it should be stressed, is a function of the contingent nature of member contributions to group goals. When it came to the MX, the rank and file was in accord, but in other instances tests of member opinion have dealt the deathblow to initiatives.

Much like the bureaucracy that is delegated authority after a vague piece of legislation is passed, the organizational leadership, once a broad initiative has been agreed upon, has the discretionary authority to decide upon its implementation. Just as the bureaucracy is limited by the possibility of congressional oversight, the leadership's latitude is constrained by the potential reaction of its rank and file, and especially its activists, as well as by the need to attract new members. This delegation of authority is significant nonetheless; it allows leaders to winnow out some issues, to narrow broad objectives into specific goals, and to decide upon the means to realize these ends.[32]

Conclusion: Organizational Democracy and Goal Formation

The formation of organizational goals at Common Cause corresponds to none of the classic conceptions of associational democracy or oligarchy. Deciding upon group objectives—and the positive and normative evaluations of intraorganizational politics that follow—is a more subtle process.

In an organizational context such as that found at Common Cause, members' rights are not equivalent, and there is considerable slack between contributors' sentiments and the leadership's execution. Whether this is thought of as democracy in action, an aberration of democratic principles, or something in between is contingent upon one's normative viewpoint.

Although the empirical analysis in this paper is specific to Common Cause, the lessons are more general. Organizational goals are fundamentally important to our understanding of groups, and the presence or absence of formal democratic processes should be far less important than the nature and extent of member contributions. Only an approach that links the contribution process to goal formation is likely to provide a very illuminating perspective on associational objectives and organizational democracy.

Notes

The results of this research are derived from a larger, ongoing project. As a consequence, a number of the findings are somewhat tentative. The author thanks all those who agreed to be interviewed and replied to his written queries, the University of Rochester for funds made available through a faculty research grant, and Bruce Jacobs, Burdett Loomis, Jonathan Nagler, and Barbara Rothenberg.

1. Terry M. Moe, *The Organization of Interests* (Chicago: University of Chicago Press, 1980), 73.
2. Goals can be defined as *conceptions of desired ends*—conditions that participants attempt to effect through their performance of task activities. W. Richard Scott, *Organizations* (Englewood Cliffs, N.J.: Prentice-Hall, 1981), 16 (italics in original).
3. Nevertheless, an important long-term ambition should be to supplement the essentially temporal design of the present inquiry with cross-sectional studies.
4. On public interest groups generally, see Andrew S. McFarland, *Public Interest Lobbies* (Washington, D.C.: American Enterprise Institute, 1976); Jeffrey M. Berry, *Lobbying for the People* (Princeton, N.J.: Princeton University Press, 1977); David Vogel, "The Public Interest Movement and the American Reform Tradition," *Political Science Quarterly* 95 (Winter 1980-1981): 607-627; and Michael W. McCann, *Taking Reform Seriously* (Ithaca, N.Y.: Cornell University Press, 1986). On Common Cause specifically, see Andrew S. McFarland, *Common Cause* (Chatham, N.J.: Chatham House, 1984); and Lawrence S.

Rothenberg, "Organizational Maintenance and the Retention Decision in Groups," *American Political Science Review* 82 (December 1988): 1129-1152.

5. As Common Cause is a single case study, the usual caveats about generalizing to the larger universe apply.

6. John Gardner, personal communication with author, 1990.

7. As McFarland noted, no detailed analysis of the legislative battle that was fought has ever been done, so it is inappropriate to equate evidence that Common Cause was active with confirmation of the group's influence. McFarland, *Common Cause,* 156.

8. The Federal Election Campaign Act amendments of 1979 enacted only noncontroversial reforms after efforts by Common Cause and its legislative allies to achieve more dramatic changes were stalemated. Pledges that more far-reaching campaign finance reforms would be taken up in the next legislative session(s) went unfulfilled.

9. The governing board comprises sixty people elected by the membership to three-year terms (after two terms one must rotate off), as well as the chairman and the president of Common Cause (in 1982 John Gardner and Fred Wertheimer, respectively). In July 1982 the board committed the organization to joining the battle to end the nuclear arms race. In November the board further committed the association to opposing congressional appropriation and authorization of funds for the MX missile.

    The decision to lead the anti-MX juggernaut did not mean that a traditional Common Cause issue such as campaign finance reform would be ignored, if it came to the fore, people would, at least in the short term, perform double duty. Rather, the group's commitment meant that, barring unexpected exogenous events such as the reemergence of campaign finance on the congressional agenda, the organization's energies would be devoted to fighting what everybody understood would be a major legislative battle to stop the missile.

10. See, for example, William D. Hartung, *The Economic Consequences of a Nuclear Freeze* (New York: Council on Economic Priorities, 1984).

11. The caveat to this point is that compared to virtually any other potential Common Cause issue, the MX was a concern that people at the grassroots level generally cared about. Legislators faced the prospect that their vote on the MX could have electoral consequences.

12. This assessment derives from my own analysis. See Lawrence S. Rothenberg, "Interest Group Influence and Public Policy" (Paper presented at the annual meeting of the American Political Science Association, Atlanta, Ga., September 1989). For a more glowing review of the anti-MX coalition's activities, see Michael Pertschuk, *Giant Killers* (New York: Norton, 1986), 181-228.

13. Another explanation for this lack of research might center on the reality that the study of interest groups constitutes what Allan Cigler has called "a 'catch all' subfield." Scholars are frequently experts in other substan-

tive areas—the Congress, the bureaucracy, elections, political participation, and so on—and discuss organizations only when they overlap with their area of concern. Goal formation is ignored because the process by which groups actually arrive at their objectives seems irrelevant to scholars whose principal focus is not political organizations. Allan J. Cigler, "Interest Groups: A Subfield in Search of an Identity" (Paper presented at the annual meeting of the Midwest Political Science Association, Chicago, Ill., April 1989).

14. Arthur F. Bentley, *The Process of Government* (Chicago: University of Chicago Press, 1908); David B. Truman, *The Governmental Process* 2d ed., (New York: Knopf, 1971); and Earl Latham, *The Group Basis of Politics* (Ithaca, N.Y.: Cornell University Press, 1952).

15. Mancur Olson, *The Logic of Collective Action* (Cambridge, Mass.: Harvard University Press, 1965).

16. Olson's model is about economic interest groups and not public interest groups such as Common Cause. The point, however, that many scholars may ignore internal politics because Olson's model implies they are generally irrelevant still holds. In addition, although one might assume that people join Common Cause exclusively for political reasons, both it and other public interest groups do offer selective benefits to members. Indeed, one critique of public interest groups (and also voiced about Common Cause) is that they are exclusively mail-order operations that exist to perpetuate themselves very much in the Olsonian tradition—that is, for aggrandizement rather than the pursuit of political goals. See, for example, Michael T. Hayes, "Interest Groups: Pluralism or Mass Society?" in *Interest Group Politics,* ed. Allan J. Cigler and Burdett A. Loomis (Washington, D.C.: CQ Press, 1983), 110-125.

17. See Robert Michels, *Political Parties,* trans. Eden and Cedar Paul (New York: Free Press, 1958). Originally published in 1915.

18. Moe, *Organization of Interests,* 259. To the knowledge of this author, this insight has not been picked up by anyone else.

19. As mentioned earlier, pluralism, largely because of the work of Olson, has been virtually discredited. Thus, the following discussion centers on work written in the Olsonian tradition that nonetheless represents alternative conceptualizations.

20. James Q. Wilson, *Political Organizations* (New York: Basic Books, 1973); and Moe, *Organization of Interests.*

21. McFarland's analysis of Common Cause represents one of the few attempts to develop such a linkage, although his theoretical approach is somewhat different than that employed here and his empirical work was completed before Common Cause made the dramatic break from its traditional agenda by getting involved in the MX debate. McFarland, *Common Cause,* 93-107.

22. Peter B. Clark and James Q. Wilson, "Incentive Systems: A Theory of Organizations," *Administrative Science Quarterly* 6 (September 1961): 126-166.

23. Other scholars who have elaborated on the role of purposive rewards include Robert H. Salisbury, "An Exchange Theory of Interest Groups," *Midwest Journal of Political Science* 13 (February 1969): 1-32; and John Mark Hansen, "The Political Economy of Group Membership," *American Political Science Review* 79 (March 1985): 79-96.

24. Rothenberg, "Organizational Maintenance," 1136-1138. Note that these descriptive findings should not be construed as definitive evidence of *why* people joined; they are just members' personal assessments.

25. Moe, *Organization of Interests,* 22-35.

26. Rothenberg, "Organizational Maintenance." Also see, Russell Hardin, *Collective Action* (Baltimore: Johns Hopkins University Press, 1982), 101-124.

27. The model of internal politics outlined here owes a debt to two previous theoretical works: Moe, *Organization of Interests,* 73-112; and Albert O. Hirschman, *Exit, Voice, and Loyalty* (Cambridge, Mass.: Harvard University Press, 1970).

28. Lawrence S. Rothenberg, "The Route to Activism Is through Experience" (Paper presented at the annual meeting of the Western Political Science Association, San Francisco, Calif. March 1988).

29. McFarland, *Common Cause,* 96.

30. Gardner, personal communication.

31. Thomas Cronin, personal communication with author, 1990.

32. The leadership also might have agenda-setting authority in that it can propose an initiative that it then will have to present to the activists and rank and file, paying particular attention to the reactions of the former.

7. ADAPTATION AND CHANGE IN THE ENVIRONMENTAL MOVEMENT

Christopher J. Bosso

An inherent instability characterizes movement politics. The energy and emotion needed to sustain any major movement are unlikely to be sustained long, especially in a pluralist setting in which negotiation and compromise are required. Since the first Earth Day in 1970, the environmental movement has changed a great deal. New groups have been established, the membership of the movement has grown, and in some ways the movement elements of environmentalism have metamorphosed into a set of "Green" interests, standing to the left of the major organizations.

In this chapter Christopher Bosso details the evolution of environmental politics from 1970 to 1990, and notes a universe of groups that differs substantially from that of the mid-1970s. Not only have more radical groups split off from the major or "Big Ten" organizations, but a third set of groups has become an important force in environmental politics: narrow or local interests that emphasize specific projects or issues rather than broad objectives.

Bosso argues that "the environmental movement has 'matured' to the point that even calling it a movement obscures the real vibrancy and diversity that lies within." Environmentalism may be more difficult to pin down in 1990 than it was in 1970, as almost every interest—from McDonald's to plastic manufacturers—portrays itself as environmentally sensitive.

Indeed, one of the great problems facing environmentalists in the 1990s is that although they have won the war, they must continue to fight myriad battles on an unending series of specific issues, ranging from protection of ancient forests to offshore drilling to ozone depletion. If we are all environmentalists, then groups must continually redefine particular environmental interests in specific situations.

The evolution of the contemporary environmental movement can be marked by two Earth Days. The first, held on April 22, 1970, was the brainchild of Sen. Gaylord Nelson, D-Wisc., whose idea to convene campus "teach-ins" on the environment was stimulated by the disastrous Santa Barbara, California, oil spill. Nelson's educational venture mushroomed unexpectedly into a day of national environmental awareness, with an estimated 20 million Americans taking part in demonstrations, seminars, and community cleanups.[1] Coordinating it all was the Environmental Action Coalition, a loosely organized group of student activists supported by a small Conservation Foundation grant.[2]

The values underlying this first Earth Day were noticeably outside the American mainstream, for they directly confronted the social norms prevailing in an era still dominated by the post-World War II industrial economy. In many ways the emerging environmental movement was a successor to the civil rights and antiwar movements of the 1960s, and Earth Day was to be the capstone of a decade marked by the beginnings of a tectonic shift in public attitudes about the political system and the culture at large. Indeed, environmental activists echoed these earlier movements in their harsh critiques of big business, indifferent government, and an apparently rapacious consumer culture.[3] Yet, despite its attachment to countercultural norms, Earth Day raised issues that resonated powerfully within a public increasingly concerned about the quality of American life and was a critical threshold for the "environmental decade" to come.[4]

Years of government regulation and uncounted policy battles later, the twentieth anniversary of Earth Day commenced under eerily similar conditions. Just as the Santa Barbara oil spill helped to transform traditional conservation values into a more aggressive environmental ethos, the 1989 *Exxon Valdez* oil spill off Alaska was the grand finale in a series of "eco-shocks" that seemed to reawaken mass awareness after years in which such issues had drifted to the periphery of the nation's agenda.[5] Despite the disturbing parallels, the twentieth anniversary of Earth Day differed markedly from the original. Whereas the first event was confined primarily to the United States, the twentieth observance was truly global, with an estimated 200 million people in 140 nations taking part in what many called the largest grassroots demonstration in history.[6] This Earth Day also was rooted more firmly in the American mainstream, for societal values themselves had shifted markedly since the late 1960s, as revealed by the broad range of people who took part in Earth Day events, by the ways that corporations (especially those with low public credibility) used the day to wave their ecological credentials, and by the enthusiasm with which political elites across the board joined in the activities. Participation for some no doubt was motivated by political self-preservation, but no elected official in 1990 wanted to be seen as on the "wrong" side of the environment.[7]

The 1990 Earth Day also was a more structured and sophisticated affair, led by competing organizations that took sharply diverging approaches to the observance. Early efforts to merge the groups in fact foundered over leadership struggles and incompatible organizational ideologies. One group, Earth Day 1990, was headed by Denis Hayes, a key organizer of the original event, and supported more than two dozen paid professionals on a $3 million budget.[8] The organization included business and labor leaders on its board (a far cry from the days when corporations and unions regarded environmentalists as scruffy malcontents) and used computers donated by Apple and Hewlett-Packard, pollsters to gauge the effects of various themes, advertising to raise public awareness, and extensive direct-mail fund-raising to tap the wallets of potential supporters. Products linked to Earth Day were licensed and the royalties used to support the organization's activities. It was, in short, a campaign like that in any recent presidential election or, perhaps, the selling of any major entertainment spectacle. "I want Earth Day to be as well known on April 22 as 'Batman' was the day it opened," declared publicist Josh Baran months before the event. "Environmental groups haven't used public relations and advertising in a very professional way until very recently." [9] Indeed, the publicity surrounding Earth Day was extensive, with virtually every media outlet in the nation running environmental stories in the weeks before the event.[10]

The second major organization, Earth Day 20, focused less on utilizing the mass media and more on mobilizing college students and the thousands of local activist groups that had sprung up nationally during the late 1980s. "We are building at the grassroots, while Hayes is building from the Big 10 environmental groups and their mailing lists," declared board member John O'Connor, director of a coalition of more than one thousand groups fighting toxic waste dumps. "We don't like it that they have Hewlett Packard on their board, since they are the second biggest emitter of chlorofluorocarbons in Silicon Valley...." [11] Among the activities promoted by Earth Day 20 were protests outside chemical plants, campus rallies, and a global television transmission of Earth Week environmental symposia.

Juxtaposed, the two Earth Days are apt metaphors for what has happened to the place of the environment in the American value system and, more to the point, to the environmental movement itself as ecological values have become more rooted in society. Indeed, the diverging paths to planning the twentieth observance of Earth Day underscore the growing diversity of organizational ideologies and political styles among activists. The movement always was far more multidimensional and fractious than was perceived publicly, but today that fragmentation and open competition are more acute. The major environmental organizations now command resources and use a range of tactics similar to anything deployed by the traditional economic interests on which most theories of interest group politics are based.

Advocacy groups hostile to the moderate directions taken by the centrist organizations are splitting off and pursuing more radical paths. As a result, the environmental movement as an entity has matured into a heterogeneous community of actors, ideologies, and approaches.

This chapter examines the evolution of the environmental movement since the late 1960s and asks where it may be heading through the 1990s. The literature on social movements in American politics is vast, but common throughout is the view that broad social movements usually fail in the short run, thwarted by prevailing mainstream values and by a constitutional structure of bias favoring the status quo.[12] The environmental movement has been no exception, judging by the pessimism about its achievements voiced by many longtime activists. Yet, like the civil rights and feminist movements, the environmental movement may in fact succeed over the long run because it will help to alter the values of society at large. As this occurs, the nature of and roles played by the movement itself are changed.

Environmentalism Institutionalized

The art of politics is not practiced in a vacuum: those seeking to make public policy are affected powerfully by broad social, economic, and political conditions.[13] The nature of the times, the intrinsic qualities of the issue at hand, the prevailing public values, and the avenues for access and representation made available to outside interests by the system of governance all shape an advocacy group's very existence, its capacity to attract and mobilize adherents, and the roles it plays in and impacts it has on policy making. The foundations of the American constitutional system (for example, separation of powers) may remain constant, but most of these contextual factors are fluid, changeable, and prone to ever-greater complexity. The very rules of the game themselves shift and mutate endlessly—at times imperceptibly— and those who seek to participate must adapt to each new bundle of conditions if they are to remain relevant. As for the environmental movement, these conditions have shifted palpably since the 1960s, generally in directions that have institutionalized ecological values in the political debate.

The Public Agenda

The nineties may well be the Decade of the Earth. The environment is again atop the agenda of mass attention at an intensity not experienced since the early 1970s. Sharpening public anxieties about global warming, polluted coastal waters, waste disposal, and depletion of natural resources led *Time* in 1989 to declare the earth "Planet of the Year." [14] Citizens groups sprouted almost spontaneously across the nation in the late 1980s, mobilized to battle landfills, incinerators, or other local disturbances.[15] McDonald's is seeking to recycle Big Mac containers to quell criticism over the fast-food industry's abundant use of nonbiodegradable polystyrene, while corporations generally are more sensitive to public demands for more environmentally benign consumer goods. Congress is debating reauthorization of major environmental programs with an urgency felt rarely in the 1980s, while President George Bush, in conscious contrast to his predecessor, is espousing mainstream environmental values and has announced his intention to elevate the Environmental Protection Agency to cabinet department status.[16]

The place of the environment in the debate over national priorities is a critical question since societies can address but a few of the innumerable public problems "out there" in any given instance. Only the most salient issues—those about which the mass public evinces the greatest passions—tend to rise to the top of the government's agenda, at least until public concern wanes.[17] In practical terms, public attention to issues creates an atmosphere conducive to open policy debate, enhances the capacity of relevant advocacy groups to mobilize members and generate new resources, and provides more "windows of opportunity" for substantial policy change.[18] Issues that fade from mass public attention migrate to the backburner; the issues are still important intrinsically, but policy debates are far less public, advocacy groups find it more difficult to energize members, and opportunities for major policy changes become fewer. If politics is the art of the possible, the nation's agenda is critical to shaping what is possible.

Twice in the past three decades environmental issues have enjoyed an intensity of public saliency conducive to major policy change. The first such wave, lasting from 1969 through 1973, was marked by the first Earth Day, the creation of the Environmental Protection Agency, and the passage of most of the environmental statutes in force today. As was inevitable, however, public awareness of environmental issues eventually waned, to be replaced atop the nation's agenda by the energy crisis of the mid-1970s.[19] By the late 1970s environmental and energy issues competed actively for space on the federal government's agenda and in the budget, and both took a back seat to the nation's economic woes into the early 1980s.[20]

The second great environmental wave has come since the late 1980s but under a much different set of conditions. What changed in the interim was the *strength* of public support for environmental protection. According to Robert Cameron Mitchell, there has been a "quiet revolution" in the American value system, an incremental but measurable migration of environmental norms toward the mainstream.[21] These trends not only show up among the young and educated but also are reflected among sectors of the population— particularly the working class—not viewed traditionally as environmentally conscious. One early 1990 Gallup poll showed that 76 percent of Americans consider themselves environmentalists.[22] Because few respondents would admit openly to opposing environmental protection, a much more valid measure of attitudinal strength is found in the public's response to a *New York Times*/CBS poll statement, "Protecting the environment is so important that requirements and standards cannot be too high, and continuing environmental improvements must be made regardless of cost." In April 1990, 74 percent of those surveyed agreed with a view regarded as zealous even by many environmentalists, while in 1981 only 45 percent agreed with the statement.[23] Moreover, citizens are willing to pay higher taxes to support higher spending on environmental protection.[24]

This permeation of environmental values throughout society has stemmed largely from a shift in the environmental debate to focus primarily on human health rather than on nature preservation.[25] Anxieties about the purity of food and water, the safety of the home, and the degradation of local habitats pervade public discourse across lines of class and occupation. In 1990 one out of five Americans said that they knew someone whose health had been damaged by pollution, and the public generally believes that environmental decay actually has worsened despite two decades of government regulation.[26] This apparent public concern buttresses an emerging perception that environmental activism will be in the vanguard of profound social and political change in next decade. From the White House to town halls across the country officials are confronted both by public anger about a broad array of hazards and by pervasive skepticism about the capacity or will of representative government to address these threats. Citizens want more stringent environmental protection, yet they saw little federal government action from Congress or the Reagan administration in the 1980s.[27] Even in more recent times President Bush's high personal popularity has not masked public perception that much of his agenda has been more talk than action.[28]

Such skepticism surfaces in how citizens have chosen to become involved. Voter turnout for elections has eroded badly since the early 1960s, but more direct forms of action have flourished.[29] In many cases residents are bypassing state legislatures, long regarded as defenders of industry interests, to rely instead on referenda to impose their will directly. To cite just one example, in 1988 Californians discounted dire warnings by corporate interests and overwhelmingly passed Proposition 65, which contained some of the nation's strictest and most extensive

standards for informing the public about the use of possibly carcino-
genic chemicals in manufacturing and on food.[30] More telling, throughout the country citizens groups have mobilized to fight new power
plants, landfills, and incinerators, while supporting waste recycling
plans with more equanimity than one might have presumed from
Americans' renowned individualistic ethos.

This mass support for environmental protection also has made it
easier for activists to gain receptive audiences for their views. In fact,
citizens tend to give greater credibility to environmentalists than to
corporate and government representatives, whose capacity to provide
"balanced" views is not helped by such highly publicized episodes of
malfeasance or insensitivity as the *Exxon Valdez* disaster or the long-
hidden problems at federal nuclear weapons plants.[31] Buttressed by a
traditional populist hostility to large institutions generally, the public
unsurprisingly tends to agree with environmentalists' definition of
salient issues. Because, as E. E. Schattschneider put it cogently, "the
definition of alternatives is the supreme instrument of power," the
superior credibility of one side in the environmental debate is a
considerable asset.[32]

Environmental values are not yet as deeply ingrained as environmentalists might like, however. Society is still marked by a throw-away
consumer culture and a (poorly challenged) perception that there is a
clear trade-off between a clean environment and a healthy economy.
But Americans today seem readier to address the ecological ramifica-
tions of their actions.[33] Questions of values and priorities are important
when one asks why at any one time some groups thrive and others do
not, or why some tactics are pursued and others are neglected. Societal
values are screening devices, sorting legitimate viewpoints from those
deemed antithetical to the mainstream ethos. Supportive public values
at a minimum can improve the ability of activists to recruit new
members and to overcome the "free-rider" problem endemic to public
interest groups.[34] The environmental movement survived the ups and
downs of the previous decades less on the innate strengths of its
component organizations—although their resiliency helped when times
got tough in the late 1970s and early 1980s—and more because
environmental values took root and spread throughout society. As a
result, environmental advocates no longer are on the outside looking in;
they are legitimate, long-term players in the game.

Loosening the Structure of Bias

The societal values that endow issues and interests with legitimacy
are but part of the total equation. After all, those who do gain access to
policy making find themselves competing within arenas in which

formal processes and informal norms are hardly neutral. There is no such thing as an unbiased decision-making process; the "rules of the game" significantly affect opportunities for success or failure, or even getting a fair chance to compete.[35]

The most fundamental structural bias is the American constitutional system itself; according to James Madison, it was designed to "cure" the "mischiefs of faction." [36] It is a system of divided institutional power and fractionated interest representation directed ultimately at dissipating momentary spasms of mass issue saliency before they produce rapid and potentially destabilizing change. The system itself, not some flaw in the American psyche, produces weak political parties and divided partisan control.[37] Societal majorities are fragmented rather easily into narrower and more parochial interests by the geographical basis of congressional representation. It is, in sum, a system in which policy making typically produces incremental change and in which intense narrow interests can easily thwart broad yet inchoate majorities.

In addition, policy advocates compete within institutional arenas in which positions of incredible policy leverage are occupied not by inert drones but by political actors with their own values, policy biases, and ideological beliefs. Members of Congress sympathetic to environmental issues are valuable "patrons" who will sponsor legislation, lobby colleagues, and use their committee positions to push new policies or oversee the implementation of existing ones.[38] On the flip side, administrators hostile to allegedly excessive regulation have ways of delaying, underfunding, or otherwise softening the execution of laws already on the books. The overall picture is a far cry from the image painted by pluralist theorists during the 1950s of government as the "neutral referee" [39]

Beneath the constants set in place by the Constitution, however, the particular rules and processes found in governing institutions are hardly set in stone. In fact, the entire structure of bias embedded in the American system has undergone profound change since the 1960s. The federal government today is arguably more open and more permeable to broad outside interests, despite oscillations in access produced by whomever occupies the Oval Office or by whichever party dominates a chamber of Congress.[40] This expansion in the opportunities for access and influence has been relentless, if not quite smooth, and the cumulative effect has been to make it easier for those promoting public interests to become legitimate players.

The changes are evident throughout the federal establishment. Prior to the 1970s Congress was an institution in which policy-making arrangements tended to nurture constituent interests in ways that gave life to a whole literature on "subgovernments."[41] Much of this bias was inherent in a constitutional system in which representation was based on geography, but longtime institutional dynamics—such as an almost feudal committee system and strict rules of seniority—coalesced to make Congress relatively closed to those promoting broader public goods.[42] This structural bias was one major reason why during the 1960s environmental groups tended to seek policy change through the federal courts.[43] But the story today is substantially different. The tremors of institutional and behavioral change to hit Congress since the 1960s may not have enhanced legislative speed or thoroughness, but there seems little doubt that the congressional policy process today is far more democratic.[44] Such reforms as a more open committee system, televised floor debate, electronic roll-call voting, and a modified House seniority system also have served to expand networks of policy influence and allow the previously excluded to at least have their say.

Members of Congress also have become more sensitive to environmental concerns, particularly those of interest to voters back home. The infusion since the early 1970s of more independent and environmentally aware legislators has had a lagged effect on the current structure of congressional decision making; those members now occupy positions of leverage in the parties and atop the committee structure.[45] Sensitivity to environmental issues may not be sufficient for pushing through new programs or promoting more spending, however—witness the capacity of Rep. John Dingell, D-Mich., and Sen. Robert Byrd, D-W.V., to slow the 1990 reauthorization of the Clean Air Act until their constituent needs were addressed. But it certainly has proved critical when environmentalists needed allies in Congress to defend existing programs against attacks by the Reagan White House.[46]

In the executive branch the story is more complicated, given traditional tensions among agencies, between political appointees and career civil servants, and between the departments and the White House. Individual presidents obviously dictate access to the highest circles, yet the existence of the Environmental Protection Agency (EPA) at least gives environmental advocates a point of access and appeal that must be kept open if the agency is to maintain its very legitimacy.[47] Regardless of efforts by the White House to soften or cut the funding of specific programs, the EPA by law must implement a wide range of existing programs, subject always to the perils of congressional oversight. In this regard, the judiciary remains an instrument for keeping policy makers honest. The federal court system was the avenue of first resort for many environmentalists through the early 1970s, with the trailblazing judicial decisions of the late 1960s taking place within rather undefined policy and procedural contexts.

Two decades and a host of statutes later, goals and standards are set in place, and administrators have learned well the at least symbolic virtues of established rules and procedures. Such processes do not entirely deter cozy relations between the regulators and the regulated—judges are willing to defer to the expertise of agency professionals as long as administrative procedures are known and rules are followed—but procedural due process never did guarantee substantive policy victory.[48]

The 1980s also produced a shift in much of the environmental debate away from the federal government and toward the states, which during that decade became highly fertile arenas for policy innovation.[49] This shift largely resulted from the federal government's abdication of much of its traditional leadership on environment protection, forcing the states to pick up the slack, but it also came about simply because the states began to reflect the greater transformation in public values. Whatever the precise reasons, the states today often are way ahead of the federal government in regulating the environment. In fact, many of the current policy debates in Congress stem from a perceived need to reimpose a degree of national uniformity on what threatens to be a patchwork of laws and standards. The calls for renewed national standards come particularly from the regulated, a far cry from the days when "states' rights" meant defending local industries against federal regulation. Political reforms, environmentally conscious state officials, and, perhaps most important, the mobilization of powerful grass-roots forces have made states into dynamic engines for policy experimentation. Not surprisingly, both environmentalists and industry groups have become highly active at the local and state levels.

The overall story of the past two decades is of tremendous ferment and change, the spread of new values, and the reshaping of formal and informal policy-making processes. Examined broadly, the environment has become *institutionalized* on the governmental agenda. Its relative place in a president's priorities or on the congressional agenda may wax and wane, but it will not go away as long as there are laws on the books requiring government to clean the air and water, regulate chemicals, and safeguard the health of all citizens. By extension, the story also is of an advocacy community itself, for those who promote environmental protection too have changed. They have had to alter their outlooks, tactics, and perceptions about their roles so that they could capitalize on their opportunities and thus remain relevant to the ever-shifting policy contexts. Moreover, they have had to operate in a much subtler and more complex decision-making milieu in which access is more easily established but victory on any specific policy is as difficult to achieve as ever.

One virtue of the American constitutional system has been its provision for multiple avenues for access, and this truth seems reaffirmed. Should any single avenue be closed at any moment, there usually are others in which access and potential influence remain open. Such adaptation does not come automatically or without conflict, and in the process the environmental movement as a whole has become more multifaceted and internally fragmented. Paradoxically, this greater complexity may have made it stronger and more resilient than it was that first Earth Day.

The Environmental Movement in Transition

If the two Earth Days provide convenient markers for studying the evolution of environmental politics in the United States, three episodes in 1985 nicely exemplify the transitions characterizing the environmental movement itself. First, the leadership of half of the nation's "Big Ten" environmental organizations changed hands.[50] The clustering of these successions was somewhat coincidental, but most of the departing leaders had delayed their retirements to fight the Reagan administration's early efforts to dismantle the framework of environmental regulation put in place during the 1970s. In all cases the organizations appointed new executives whose managerial expertise and pragmatism contrasted profoundly with the missionary zeal of their predecessors.[51] Second, David Brower, one of the movement's great activists, broke acrimoniously with Friends of the Earth (FOE), which he founded in 1969 after leaving as head of the Sierra Club. The split between Brower and the FOE board centered on organizational philosophies, tactics, and the board's decision to move FOE from San Francisco to Washington, D.C., a step Brower stridently opposed. And, third, the Big Ten issued *An Environmental Agenda for the Future,* their effort to forge consensus on the movement's overall goals and tactics.[52] Just the act of putting together the report sparked sharp intramural debate, and the final product was criticized sharply by grass-roots activists as being a dilution of basic values, accommodative, too much centered on mainstream institutional solutions, and more concerned with global issues than those closer to the concerns of average Americans.[53]

In different ways these episodes encapsulate the transitions that took place in the environmental movement during the 1980s, changes that undoubtedly will accelerate through the 1990s. These episodes also highlight the fragmentation of the broader movement into three rather distinct types of groups: the mainstream, the so-called Greens, and the grass-roots. The leadership changes of 1985 manifested the efforts by the major national groups to adapt their outlooks and organizational styles to changes in broader policy-making contexts. Examined more closely, the divorce between Brower and the FOE board reflected the apparent incompatability between the tactics of the mainstream groups and the values of the burgeoning "Green" wing of the movement. The friction between the national groups and grass-roots activists over the Big Ten consensus report reflected fractures that are likely to widen as those at the grass-roots level become increasingly vocal about setting the movement's future agenda. What was reflected cumulatively was a fundamental transition within the movement, one inevitable (and probably necessary) if environmental activists are to remain in the vanguard of a social force that has expanded beyond the ability of any single group to shape or direct.

The Mainstream

The most surprising thing about the major environmental groups is how well they have survived. Given the relative fragility of public interests and the always centrifugal nature of social movements, one might reasonably have expected a sizable percentage of the groups formed since the late 1960s to have gone out of business in short order. That most did survive despite tremendous financial and organizational obstacles underscores the sheer strength of the movement's values and, just as important, the capacities of these organizations to adapt successfully to new wrinkles in the political climate.

In statistical terms the national organizations are relatively healthy. As Table 7-1 shows, the 1980s were years of strong membership growth, with notable expansion early in the decade as environmental groups fought against the Reagan deregulatory agenda. Expanding membership rolls might be construed as proof of public alarm over the early Reagan agenda, but growth also came because these groups had to work harder to survive financially. Several of the national groups were long content to depend on private foundation grants and affluent donors, shying away from mass memberships to avoid maintaining an elaborate fund-raising apparatus and the pressures that might come from balancing members' demands with aggressive lobbying tactics. But as foundations altered their own priorities (for example, in the late 1970s the Ford Foundation shifted its giving away from public interest litigation to social welfare and economic development programs) and as competition for resources intensified, the major organizations almost uniformly geared fund-raising toward the public. The Natural Resources Defense Council (NRDC) and the Environmental Defense Fund (EDF), for example, both begun purely as environmental law firms, by the late 1970s were actively recruiting dues-paying members and diversifying their resource bases. The NRDC, once dependent on foundation grants, by the late 1980s relied

Table 7-1 Membership of Selected National Environmental
Organizations, 1970-1990 (selected years)

	1970	1975	1980	1985	1990
National Audubon Society	75,000	275,000	400,000	550,000	575,000
Environmental Defense Fund	a	30,000	45,000	50,000	150,000
Natural Resources Defense Council	a	55,000	42,000	50,000	130,000
Sierra Club	80,000	140,000	183,000	360,000	553,200

SOURCES: *The Encyclopedia of Associations* (Detroit: Gale, various editions); "1990 Directory of Environmental Organizations," *Buzzworm: The Environmental Journal* 2 (May/June 1990): 65-77; George Hager, "For Industry and Opponents, a Showdown Is in the Air," *Congressional Quarterly Weekly Report,* January 20, 1990, 144; Robert Cameron Mitchell, "Public Opinion and the Green Lobby: Poised for the 1990s?" in *Environmental Policy in the 1990s,* ed. Norman J. Vig and Michael E. Kraft (Washington, D.C.: CQ Press, 1990), 92.

a Until the mid-1970s neither the Environmental Defense Fund nor the National Resources Defense Council had mass memberships.

on membership dues (its greatest single source of funds) for almost 45 percent of its budget.[54]

A dramatic growth in operating budgets magnified these pressures. The Sierra Club, for example, saw its budget more than triple during the 1980s (from about $9 million to $30 million), with similar growth seen at the NRDC (from about $3.5 million to $10 million) and EDF (from $2.5 million to about $7 million).[55] Bigger budgets did not make the groups flush, however. New monies were poured into more sophisticated and expensive scientific and legal talent to monitor existing programs and pursue lawsuits, more experienced lobbyists to carry the fight to Congress, and additional professional staff to maintain the organizational apparatus and keep funds coming in. Just defending previous gains against the Reagan agenda cost the national groups dearly, and it was small wonder that many of them skated on the edge of fiscal disaster until prospects brightened later in the decade.[56]

As a result of these pressures, by the mid-1980s the major national environmental lobbies were transformed into almost corporate entities. They may have tried to avoid the constraints that come from maintaining large organizations, but competition for funding and the resources needed to maintain a permanent presence in the Washington lobbying community eventually forced them to succumb to such pressures.

Moreover, the institutionalization of the environment on the federal agenda and the shift in emphasis from policy initiation to program oversight required greater professionalism, more sophisticated lobbying and managerial skills, and, most important, a less zealous approach to working with policy actors both in government and in the regulated industries.[57]

These trends help explain the leadership shifts of the mid-1980s. Organizational growth, the need to expand professional and technical expertise, and the range of tactics and services increasingly required to remain credible players compelled the major environmental groups to adopt a host of organizational capacities and outlooks far removed from days when they were small, loosely configured collections of young activists. Today the mainstream organizations occupy large offices in Washington, carry out a broad array of functions, and engage in the full menu of tactics typical of any conventional lobby group. As William Browne argued, "policy entrepreneurs become more conventional as they move from a situation in which they are organizing to one in which they seek to keep the interest together...." [58] Given the pressures to maintain a permanent presence in the policy arena, these groups simply had no choice.

As part of this strategy and to maximize the movement's resources, the mainstream organizations consciously occupy more or less well-defined niches in the overall policy agenda, with one organization typically taking the lead on any particular problem.[59] The NRDC, for example, focuses heavily on the public health impacts of air- and water-borne toxins; the Sierra Club leads the fight against the oil industry over pollution of coastal waters; the EDF was highly visible in the 1990 reauthorization of the Clean Air Act; and the National Audubon Society maintains its long primacy over wildlife issues, including agricultural pesticide use and groundwater contamination. This search for distinctive niches even played a major role in the merger of the Friends of the Earth and the Environmental Policy Institute and the Oceanic Institute, with the new organization (still called Friends of the Earth) dedicating itself to environmental issues in developing nations.[60]

The mainstream organizations also have adapted their tactics to meet changing policy contexts, and in most cases have become full-service providers. The changes are most pronounced in the movement's two "law firms." The NRDC still engages in substantial litigation, but today it is just as likely to lobby Congress, negotiate directly with regulated industries, produce extensive scientific studies, and offer technical support to other groups.[61] The EDF for its part is well known for its innovative cost-benefit analyses, which it uses to talk to regulated industries in their own language. In sum, the national organizations have become pragmatists, inside players oriented to obtaining acceptable compromises. These groups have not sold out their values, as some of their critics suggest, but they certainly have adapted their perspectives and tactics to seek greater acceptance among policy makers and to meet the changing nature of the policy game itself.

Just as important, the organizational needs and approaches of the major groups have been affected by the demographics of their constituencies. The youthful volunteers of the past are today middle-aged with jobs and families. Their support for environmental values remains strong, but their activism is more in the form of a check than a placard on the street. Although such checkbook participation is passive and provides organizational leaders with a great deal of flexibility in pursuing goals and tactics,[62] it is fickle in other respects. Even the most dedicated of checkwriters must be convinced continually that their contributions are having real impacts, and, given the heightened competition for the environmental dollar, fund-raisers face constant pressures to stir the public and keep the money flowing.

This dynamic produces its share of costs for the organizations themselves. There is probably an inherent contradiction between the need of citizens groups to play a credible "Washington game" and the need to use the kinds of emotional and symbolic appeals that they usually find necessary if they are to keep supporters loyal and generate additional funds.[63] All the major environmental organizations engage in a significant array of conventional interest group activities, ranging from providing Congress with technical assistance to negotiating directly with industry representatives. Such activities are sold to subscribers as proof of the sophistication and clout of these groups, yet at the same time the groups must continue to portray themselves as unswerving defenders of core values. But touting "moderate" tactics and "successful compromises" hardly is the stuff that stirs the blood of the true believers, who, after all, joined out of their faith in the cause.[64] The result for the organizations themselves can be a bit schizophrenic: Dr. Jekyll in government affairs negotiates directly with industry lobbyists even as Mr. Hyde in fund-raising paints these same industries in the darkest of terms and warns gloomily of the Apocalypse should members not pay their dues. This dynamic is rather common within the broader lobbying community—all interest groups play pretty much the same game—which probably is of little solace to critics who see the national groups as so constrained by organizational maintenance pressures that they have lost their lead in espousing environmental values.

The Greens

Movements revolve inherently around some cause, and all inevitably are riven by ideological schisms that produce new factions and, over time, greater heterogeneity of organizational types and tactics. This dynamic affected the civil rights movement in the late 1960s—the split between the National Association for the Advancement of Colored People (NAACP) and the Black Panthers being the most dramatic—as it did the pro-Equal Rights Amendment (ERA) forces in the 1970s.[65] It is no less true of the environmental movement, whether pictured as the early clashes between Gifford Pinchot and John Muir over conservation versus preservation or as the emergence of newer, more aggressive environmental groups at the end of the 1960s.[66]

The split between David Brower and the board of Friends of the Earth and the growth in the memberships of Greenpeace and other "direct action" groups (or the so-called Greens), underline this disputatious matter of values and tactics. Brower, ousted in the late-1960s as head of the Sierra Club after his unswerving attacks on southwestern water projects undermined the group's tax-exempt status, this time battled openly with the FOE board over the future of the fiscally troubled organization. Brower had always been opposed ideologically to maintaining large organizations, once arguing only half facetiously that any group should be abolished after ten years to prevent bureaucratization.[67] He was even more adamant against becoming "just another D.C. lobbying group," but his board was more concerned about FOE's finances and its niche within the broader environmental movement.[68] FOE eventually moved to Washington and merged with two other financially pressed groups, a move that probably presages trends to come. Indeed, in 1988, Environmental Action, which also struggled financially during the decade, merged with the Environmental Task Force.[69] Brower began yet another organization, this time unconstrained, he hoped, by mass memberships and their administrative headaches—precisely the same reason he had founded FOE in 1969, only to see that organization forced to recruit members to stay afloat.

In the same vein as David Brower's split with Friends of the Earth, many new and longtime environmental activists have judged the major groups too bureaucratic, conservative, and accommodative. Defectors charge that the national organizations have "sold out" their values for the sake of respectability inside the Washington Beltway, a grave indictment in a movement in which shaking up the Establishment was always a rallying cry. The critics also charge the mainstream groups with shutting off access to their leadership, and they maintain that, save for writing checks, group members play little role in setting organizational priorities or directions.[70] Indeed, among the Big Ten, the Sierra Club stands apart for its bottom-up agenda-setting process, with the organization's priorities set through votes taken by members at the grass-roots.

To the Greens, the major environmental groups have become just another set of lobbyists, and those holding "deep ecology" values are just as unlikely to find common ground with their more mainstream brethren as they are to have any trust in corporate or government leaders. The difference is one of values: mainstream environmentalists see their roles as ones of competitors in interest group politics; Greens shun institutional approaches for a fundamental reconfiguration of social values and behavior. For the mainstream groups the issues are political; for the Greens the issues revolve around lifestyle, and the tactics pursued by the mainstream activists are futile in the face of overwhelming corporate and government power. The only legitimate path is the long-run promotion of a "Green cultural revolution" that "rebuilds communities around economic institutions more compatible with the environment." [71]

For any movement this matter of vision is critical. As Sierra Club chair Michael McCloskey suggested, "Increasingly, the radical groups embody the passion over the issues and articulate the visions of what the future should hold, while the mainstream groups have more of the resources and the steady management sense." [72] Those committed to Green values, however, do not respond well to mainstream tactics, and the organizations that have grown the fastest since the late 1980s are those that distinguished themselves as the most zealous defenders of the cause. Greenpeace, which made a name for itself through well-publicized acts of nonviolent civil disobedience, has grown the most spectacularly—in the United States from about 240,000 members in 1980 to more than 1.5 million members ten years later. This is a rate of about 50,000 new members per month since the late 1980s. Even more radical groups such as Earth First! and the Sea Shepherds, both of which pursue dramatic and usually illegal forms of "ecotage" (for example, scuttling whaling ships), grew from a relative handful in 1980 to more than 11,000 each at decade's end.[73] These trends are ironic insofar as today's more mainstream groups were regarded once as mavericks compared to such old-line conservation groups as the National Wildlife Federation, but this dynamic also is typical within any movement that endures beyond a few years.

Even as they grow in numbers, the Greens themselves are split over tactics. Most focus on grass-roots activism, education, and alternative lifestyles, but many of the more radical among them have taken to direct action against their perceived villains. The "eco-commandos" of

Earth First! have obstructed logging of old-growth forests by destroying equipment and spiking trees, have felled billboards on scenic highways, and, as alleged by the federal government, had planned to down high-voltage power lines in Arizona. This last action landed group cofounder David Foreman and three others in jail on federal charges of terrorism.[74] Such highly public episodes of "monkeywrenching" have generated new members but also have many in the mainstream organizations worrying about a backlash should someone get hurt. More important, those in the mainstream groups worry that the radicals might besmirch the hard-won image of environmental activists as something more than a fringe element.

As with all movements, however, mainstream environmental organizations need the radicals. Groups such as Greenpeace and Earth First! provide the spark needed to reenergize the movement after more than a decade of fighting rearguard actions. Perhaps more critically, the zeal of the direct action groups makes the mainstream organizations look all the more respectable in the eyes of industry and government policy makers. After all, utility executives probably would rather work with the Environmental Defense Fund to improve energy conservation than face the possibility that a proposed generating plant might be on some Earth First! hit list. For their part, the Greens need the diverse resources and expertise that in many cases only the major groups can provide. "The dilemma is how to get these two needed ingredients into a productive relationship," said the Sierra Club's McCloskey. "The radical groups may spend their energies with little tangible to show for it, and the mainstream groups may lose their way with no lodestar to pursue." [75] Few may acknowledge it publicly, but the mainstream groups and the Greens, even the most radical among them, need one another.

The Grass-roots

The third category of environmental groups may be the most problematic sector in the current environmental movement, for its groups typically focus on narrow, localized issues. The late 1980s witnessed an explosive growth in environmental activism at the grass-roots level, with about 25 million Americans involved in some way in specific local and regional issues.[76] One umbrella organization of local groups, the Clean Water Action Project, has a low national profile but more than 500,000 members; another, the Citizens Clearing House for Hazardous Waste, claims some 9,000 member groups and is doubling its base annually.[77] Most of these groups did not exist until the late 1980s.

While many who belong to these local groups also are members of the mainstream national organizations, the majority are not.[78] They are instead average citizens and homeowners mobilized to oppose a specific facility (for example, a waste dump) out of concern about the health of their children and the value of their property. They also are, in many ways, the greatest single manifestation of how the movement's values have permeated the mass culture. The average citizen is simply no longer sanguine about assurances given by corporate or government officials that some facility is relatively benign, and likeminded citizens today are more likely to band together to voice their concerns, block construction, or do whatever is necessary to ward off a perceived threat.[79] Their uncompromising resistance leads many observers to complain that this surge in local activism is a manifestation of the "Not in My Backyard Syndrome" (NIMBY) at its worst, but it also is, in the words of Barry Commoner, "environmental democracy" in action.[80]

More important to the movement as a whole, these local activists have little formal interaction with or need for the major national environmental organizations beyond contracting for their technical and legal expertise. To many of these activists the national groups are almost as remote and submersed in their cost-benefit analyses as are corporate and government representatives, a charge that must grate against those engaged in the daily tedium of monitoring federal regulatory programs and fighting industry lawyers in court. Those in the major organizations, aware of the real trade-offs inherent in any complex policy decision, often simply find the grass-roots activists difficult to work with. As the Sierra Club's Doug Scott observed, "The grass-roots reality is very big, damn close to lawless, and inherently frustrating to deal with if you have a neat mind and want everything well organized." [81]

In many ways the explosion in environmentalism at the grass-roots level is another resurgence in the always potent populist strain that runs through the American psyche: decentralized, parochial, and inherently hostile to government and large institutions in general. It also is a class issue. As Gary Cohen of the National Toxics Campaign argued, "The people at these dump sites tend to be lower-income and, especially in the South, tend to be minorities. These people are increasingly having a voice, and they are seeing that the Washington groups, by focusing on lowering permissible levels of benzene, for example, are not addressing basic issues of production."[82] This issue of priorities lies at the heart of the tensions between the local activists and the national organizations. For grass-roots activists the priorities are clear: protect local habitats, prevent threats to health, and avoid unpleasant or dangerous facilities such as incinerators and trash dumps. These agendas are narrow and fragmented into any number of particular local battles. For the Big Ten environmental organizations, however, the question of the issue agenda is not so simple because these groups tend to look at environmental questions from a more global perspective. If answers to the greenhouse effect, acid rain, and the depletion of natural resources can be obtained only on a global scale, it is not surprising that such groups as the NRDC and Friends of the Earth are becoming ever more active in international environmental issues. In their view, what happens anywhere has a cumulative impact on the health of Mother Earth.

To the national groups this global perspective not only makes sense analytically but also presents opportunities to work with environmentalists in Eastern Europe or with governments in developing countries, which is surely more rewarding than working with outraged homeowners to fight against yet another waste dump or incinerator. The grass-roots groups are driven primarily by a fear of cancer—that is, by a sense of moral outrage about being victimized that makes them far less amenable to compromise. They also feel abandoned by the national groups for whom global environmental issues are the "hot buttons" that excite those who write out the checks. These trends bother the grass-roots activists, who tend to think that there are plenty of problems left to address at home and who see in global environmental questions few opportunities for direct involvement by average citizens.

The criticisms aimed by grass-roots activists at *An Environmental Agenda for the Future* reflect their views that the mainstream organizations are more willing to think globally than to act locally. This is overblown, however, because many of the national groups expend a great deal of time and resources at the local and state levels. Still, the current situation is a far cry from years past when the national organizations set the agenda and mobilized action at the local levels. The grass-roots activists today have their own distinct agendas, which may or may not coincide with those of the mainstream groups.

Into the Nineties: The Third Environmental Era

The environmental movement has changed fundamentally over the past two decades. At one level it is characterized by an array of established national organizations whose talents and resources make them legitimate inside players in Washington and, increasingly, around the world. At another level it is characterized by an ever more potent grass-roots activism powered by average citizens seeking to resist threats to their health and their homes. It is across the board a movement of great heterogeneity where ideological and tactical differences stand out vividly and where one often finds sharp competition and conflict among those ostensibly on the same side. In short, the environmental movement has "matured" to the point that even calling it a movement obscures the real vibrancy and diversity that lies within.

Perhaps this is one reason why there is at present a pervasive and, for the outsider, somewhat odd sense of gloom among environmental activists. Many long in the movement strongly believe that they have failed, that the movement did not capitalize as it should have on its past opportunities.[83] Yet if one looks back at other movements in American history, this disquiet among the truest of the believers is understandable. If the trends discussed above accelerate through the 1990s, the activists will not necessarily be in the vanguard of a movement that once was theirs. No longer will it be the relatively cozy network of idealists who battled the longest odds to seek a better environment for all; the institutionalization of environmentalism into law and everyday behavior has transformed a movement into something else. Activists are not sure what it is, but they are very sure about what it is not.

Despite the gloom of the activists, the greatest success of the environmental movement may well be that its values now are part of the everyday language of behavior and political debate. If this is so, it is unlikely that the environment will lose its place on the agenda for action as readily as it did after the wave of the early 1970s. Middle America in many ways has been radicalized to the threats to a clean environment and a healthy life, and the grass-roots activism that emerged in the late 1980s is likely to be the big story domestically through the upcoming decade. This, of course, poses tremendous problems for industry officials, government policy makers, and those in the mainstream environmental organizations, since the local groups typically are largely motivated by their rigid opposition to anything in their backyards. One suspects that the American system of representative government—which has never been very good at overcoming entrenched parochial interests—will be hard pressed to forge national or even regional answers to many of the most daunting domestic problems to come (for example, waste disposal, groundwater protection). If events in California are precursors of the future, frequent citizen referenda and more localized policy responses are the likely trends.

For the major environmental groups the 1990s may well be years of even greater intramural competition over policy niches and resources. In fact, it might not be surprising to see a wave of mergers as like-minded organizations match up to maximize their expertise and clout on the national and, increasingly, international scenes. Indeed, they might find that big is not all that bad because their future policy roles probably will be oriented primarily toward providing technical and legal expertise to both foreign governments and to activists at the American grass-roots level, functions for which organizational capacities are critical. This trend will leave the field open to whatever successors to Earth First! come along to rally the faithful and keep the professionals honest, which in turn will generate new groups. The entire landscape of environmental advocacy is likely to become even more variegated as we near the end of the millenium.

The first environmental era sought to preserve wilderness tracts and to use natural resources in a more rational manner, and the second was characterized by efforts to clean up the detritus of the industrial age. The third environmental era may well be marked by the fundamental penetration of environmental values into virtually every aspect of the postindustrial economy and culture. This dynamic will produce a plethora of new domestic and international cleavages, for the environmental debate increasingly is one that includes such questions as the equitable distribution of resources and the very worth of economic growth.[84] If this is so—and it will be a long time before we really know for sure—new ideas and activists will emerge to set the agenda for debate, while the roles played by the established organizations will be altered dramatically. In many ways the environmental movement has outstripped its parents, as it must if its values are to pervade the American culture into the next century.

Notes

1. Philip Shabicoff, "Veteran of Earth Day 1970 Looks to a New World, *New York Times,* April 16, 1990, B8.
2. John Mitchell, "A Perfect Day for the Earth," *Audubon,* March 1990, 118.
3. See Samuel P. Hays, *Beauty, Health and Permanence: Environmental Politics in the United States, 1955-1985* (New York: Oxford University Press, 1987); and Robert Paehlke, *Environmentalism and the Future of Progressive Politics* (New Haven, Conn.: Yale University Press, 1989).
4. For a good review of the legislation enacted in the 1970s, see Norman J. Vig and Michael E. Kraft, "Environmental Politics from the Seventies to the Eighties," in *Environmental Policy in the 1980s: Reagan's New Agenda,* ed. Vig and Kraft (Washington, D.C.: CQ Press, 1984), 3-26.
5. See Norman J. Vig and Michael E. Kraft, "Environmental Policy from the Seventies to the Nineties: Continuity and Change," in *Environmental Policy in the 1990s,* ed. Vig and Kraft (Washington, D.C.: CQ Press, 1990), 3-33.
6. Robert D. McFadden, "Millions Join Battle for a Beloved Planet," *New York Times,* April 23, 1990, 1.
7. David Kirkpatrick, "Environmentalism: The New Crusade," *Fortune,*

February 12, 1990, 47.

8. Barnaby Feder, "The Business of Earth Day," *New York Times,* November 12, 1989, E4.

9. Ibid.

10. McFadden, "Millions Join Battle," 1. So great was the media saturation that its sharp dropoff after Earth Day could not have gone unnoticed.

11. Feder, "Business of Earth Day," E4.

12. See, for example, Jane Mansbridge, *Why We Lost the ERA* (Chicago: University of Chicago Press, 1986).

13. For an in-depth discussion on the impact of contexts on policy activists, see Christopher J. Bosso, *Pesticides and Politics: The Life Cycle of a Public Issue* (Pittsburgh, Pa.: University of Pittsburgh Press, 1987); and Charles O. Jones, *An Introduction to the Study of Public Policy,* 3d ed. (Monterey, Calif.: Brooks-Cole, 1984).

14. *Time,* January 2, 1989.

15. The classic discussion of the "disturbance theory" of interest group mobilization can be found in David B. Truman, *The Governmental Process* (New York: Knopf, 1951).

16. See David Rapp, "Power of the Earth," and George Hager, "Clean Air: The 'White House Effect' Opens a Long-Locked Political Door," *Congressional Quarterly Weekly Report,* January 20, 1990, 128 and 142, respectively.

17. On the importance of issue agendas, see E. E. Schattschneider, *The Semi-Sovereign People* (Hinsdale, Ill.: Dryden Press, 1960); Roger W. Cobb and Charles D. Elder, *Participation in American Politics: The Dynamics of Agenda Building* (Boston: Allyn and Bacon, 1972); and Anthony Downs, "Up and Down with Ecology: The 'Issue-Attention Cycle,'" *Public Interest* 28 (Summer 1973): 38-50.

18. On "windows of opportunity," see John Kingdon, *Agendas, Alternatives, and Public Policy* (Boston: Little, Brown, 1984).

19. See Downs, "Up and Down with Ecology"; and Christopher J. Bosso, "Setting the Agenda: Mass Media and the Discovery of Famine in Ethiopia," in *Manipulating Public Opinion: Essays on Public Opinion as a Dependent Variable,* ed. Michael Margolis and Gary Mauser (Monterey, Calif.: Brooks-Cole, 1989), 153-174.

20. See Robert Cameron Mitchell, "Public Opinion and the Green Lobby: Poised for the 1990s?" in Vig and Kraft, *Environmental Policy in the 1990s,* 81-99. Also see Bosso, *Pesticides and Politics,* chaps. 7-9.

21. Mitchell, "Public Opinion and the Green Lobby," 84-87.

22. Matthew Wald, "Guarding Environment: A World of Challenges," *New York Times,* April 22, 1990, 24.

23. Ibid.

24. See Richard L. Berke, "Oratory of Environmentalism Becomes the Sound of Politics," *New York Times,* February 17, 1990, B10; John Robinson, "Poll Says 54% Willing to Pay More Taxes for Environment," *Boston Globe,* April 19, 1990, 22; Mitchell, "Public Opinion and the Green

Lobby," 84-87.

25. See Hays, *Beauty, Health and Permanence.*

26. Berke, "Oratory of Environmentalism," B10; and Rapp, "Power of the Earth," 128.

27. See Michael E. Kraft, "Environmental Gridlock: Searching for Consensus in Congress," in Vig and Kraft, *Environmental Policy in the 1990s,* 103-124.

28. Berke, "Oratory of Environmentalism," B10.

29. See Richard Brody, "The Puzzle of Participation in America," in *The New American Political System,* ed. Anthony King (Washington, D.C.: American Enterprise Institute, 1979), 316.

30. Bob Benenson, "California: In the Cradle of Environmentalism, the Political Fight is Hot," *Congressional Quarterly Weekly Report,* January 20, 1990, 189-191.

31. See Berke,"Oratory of Environmentalism," B10; and George Hager, "For Industry and Opponents, a Showdown Is in the Air," *Congressional Quarterly Weekly Report,* January 20, 1990, 145-147.

32. Schattschneider, *Semi-Sovereign People,* 65.

33. On the debate about the relationship between environmentalism and economic growth, see Paehlke, *Environmentalism.*

34. On the incentives to join groups that do not offer tangible incentives, see Allan J. Cigler, "From Protest Group to Interest Group: The Making of American Agriculture Movement, Inc.," in *Interest Group Politics,* 2d ed., ed. Cigler and Burdett A. Loomis (Washington, D.C.: CQ Press, 1986), 46-69.

35. Schattschneider calls this the "mobilization of bias," see *Semi-Sovereign People.* Also see discussions in Bosso, *Pesticides and Politics;* and in Jones, *Introduction to the Study of Public Policy.*

36. Alexander Hamilton, James Madison, and John Jay, *The Federalist Papers,* ed. Clinton Rossiter (New York: Mentor Books, 1961), 77-84.

37. See James Sundquist, *Constitutional Reform and Effective Government* (Washington, D.C.: Brookings Institution, 1986).

38. This notion of "patrons" is discussed nicely in Jack Walker, "The Origins and Maintenance of Interest Groups in America," *American Political Science Review* 77 (June 1983): 390-406.

39. See in particular Earl Latham, *The Group Basis of Politics* (Ithaca, N.Y.: Cornell University Press, 1952).

40. See, among many examinations of these changes, Richard A. Harris and Sidney M. Milkis, eds., *Remaking American Politics* (Boulder, Colo.: Westview Press, 1989); John E. Chubb and Paul E. Peterson, eds., *New Directions in American Politics* (Washington, D.C.: Brookings Institution, 1985); and King, *New American Political System.*

41. On "subgovernments" see such classics as J. Leiper Freeman, *The Political Process* (New York: Random House, 1955); Douglass Cater, *Power in Washington* (New York: Random House, 1964); and A. Grant McConnell, *Private Power and American Democracy* (New York: Knopf, 1966).

42. The House Appropriations Committee epitomized this reality, as is discussed in Richard F. Fenno, Jr., *Power of the Purse: Appropriations Politics in Congress* (Boston: Little, Brown, 1965).

43. Bosso, *Pesticides and Politics,* chap. 6.

44. See Leroy Reiselbach, *Congressional Reform* (Washington, D.C.: CQ Press, 1986).

45. On the lagged impacts of new blood in Congress, see Burdett A. Loomis, *The New American Politician* (New York: Random House, 1988).

46. On the roles played by Dingell and Byrd, see George Hager, "Clean Air: War about Over in Both House and Senate," *Congressional Quarterly Weekly Report,* April 7, 1990, 1057-1063.

47. Bosso, *Pesticides and Politics,* chap. 10.

48. See R. Shep Melnick, *Regulation and the Courts: The Case of the Clean Air Act* (Washington, D.C.: Brookings Institution, 1983); Lettie M. Wenner, *The Environmental Decade in Court* (Bloomington: Indiana University Press, 1982); and Wenner, "Environmental Policy in the Courts," in Vig and Kraft, *Environmental Policy in the 1990s,* 189-210.

49. See James P. Lester, "A New Federalism? Environmental Policy in the States," in Vig and Kraft, *Environmental Policy in the 1990s,* 59-80; and Ann O'M. Bowman and Richard C. Kearney, *The Resurgence of the States* (Englewood Cliffs, N.J.: Prentice-Hall, 1986).

50. These leadership changes occurred at the National Audubon Society, Sierra Club, Wilderness Society, Friends of the Earth, and Environmental Defense Fund, which, along with the National Parks and Conservation Association, Natural Resources Defense Council, National Wildlife Federation, Izaac Walton League, and the Environmental Policy Institute, composed the so-called Big Ten or Group of Ten. This configuration has changed recently with the merger of the Friends of the Earth and the Environmental Policy Institute and the Oceanic Institute.

51. Rochelle L. Stanfield, "Environmental Lobby's Changing of the Guard Is Part of Movement's Transition," *National Journal,* June 8, 1985, 1350-1353.

52. Robert Cahn, ed., *An Environmental Agenda for the Future* (Washington, D.C.: Island Press, 1985).

53. See Peter Borelli, "Environmentalism at the Crossroads," *Amicus Journal* (Summer 1987): 31; and Rochelle L. Stanfield, "The Green Blueprint," *National Journal,* July 2, 1988, 1735-1737.

54. H. R. Mahood, *Interest Groups in America: A New Intensity* (Englewood Cliffs, N.J.: Prentice-Hall, 1989), 175.

55. Brandon Mitchener, "Out on a Limb for Mother Earth," *E: The Environmental Magazine,* January-February 1990, 44.

56. Borelli, "Environmentalism at the Crossroads," 36.

57. See, for example, Christopher J. Bosso, "Transforming Adversaries into Collaborators: Interest Groups and the Regulation of Chemical Pesticides in the United States," *Policy Sciences* 21 (1989): 3-21.

58. William P. Browne, *Private Interests, Public Policy, and American*

Agriculture (Lawrence: University Press of Kansas, 1988), 245.

59. On this notion of "niches," see ibid.

60. Mitchener, "Out on a Limb for Mother Earth," 45.

61. Mahood, *Interest Groups in America,* 173.

62. On "checkbook participation," see Michael T. Hayes, "The New Group Universe," in Cigler and Loomis, *Interest Group Politics,* 133-145; and Borelli, "Environmentalism at the Crossroads," 36.

63. Hayes, "New Group Universe."

64. Mansbridge makes this point nicely when discussing the tensions within the pro-ERA movement, see *Why We Lost the ERA.*

65. See ibid.

66. On the value dimensions of the movement, see Geoffrey Wandesforde-Smith, "Moral Outrage and the Progress of Environmental Policy: What Do We Tell the Next Generation about How to Care for the Earth?" in Vig and Kraft, *Environmental Policy in the 1990s,* 325-347.

67. Brower interview in *E: The Environmental Magazine,* January-February 1990, 12.

68. Mitchener, "Out on a Limb for Mother Earth," 45.

69. Mitchell, "Public Opinion and the Green Lobby," 93.

70. James L. Franklin, "Earth Day Message: Get Tough," *Boston Globe,* April 15, 1990, 15.

71. Peter Steinhart, "Bridging the Gap: Can Earth Day 1990 Bring Together Greens and Mainline Conservationists?" *Audubon,* January 1990, 22.

72. Franklin, "Earth Day Message," 15.

73. Borelli, "Environmentalism at the Crossroads," 26; and Mitchener, "Out on a Limb for Mother Earth," 44.

74. See Dick Russell, "The Monkeywrenchers," *Amicus Journal* 9 (Fall 1987): 28-42; and Jim Robbins, "Attack, Counterattack in 'Eco-war,' " *Boston Globe,* April 16, 1990, 3.

75. Franklin, "Earth Day Message, 15.

76. Borelli, "Environmentalism at the Crossroads," 29.

77. Steinhart, "Bridging the Gap, 20.

78. Borelli, "Environmentalism at the Crossroads," 29. Also see Norman Boucher, "Earth Love," *Boston Globe Sunday Magazine,* April 22, 1990, 23-38.

79. See Daniel Mazmanian and David Morell, "The "NIMBY" Syndrome: Facility Siting and the Failure of Democratic Discourse," in Vig and Kraft, *Environmental Policy in the 1990s,* 125-144.

80. Barry Commoner interview in *Mother Earth News,* March-April 1990, 123.

81. Borelli, "Environmentalism at the Crossroads," 29.

82. Boucher, "Earth Love," 36.

83. See Steinhart, "Bridging the Gap"; Commoner interview in *Mother Earth News;* Franklin, "Earth Day Message."

84. See Hays, *Beauty, Health and Permanence;* and Paehlke, *Environmentalism.*

8. THE ROLE OF CHURCHES IN POLITICAL MOBILIZATION: THE PRESIDENTIAL CAMPAIGNS OF JESSE JACKSON AND PAT ROBERTSON

Allen D. Hertzke

The religious community has a long history of involvement in American politics. Abolition, civil rights, Prohibition, censorship, opposition to abortion, and many other causes have had deep, church-based roots. On occasion, religion has entered presidential politics but rarely so directly as in the 1988 candidacies of Jesse Jackson and Pat Robertson.

In this chapter, Allen Hertzke compares the efforts of Jackson and Robertson in mobilizing their religion-based coalitions as they sought, respectively, the Democratic and Republican presidential nominations.

Hertzke argues that neither candidate can be understood apart from his ties to a core religious constituency—the black church for Jackson, the charismatic community for Robertson. Although both men have powerful public personas, Hertzke focuses on their relationship with the organized elements of their religious bases: the individual congregations and the networks within and among these institutions.

More broadly, Hertzke argues that "the tightly knit church communities . . . by their existence challenge the individualistic assumptions that drive the broader society." He places the Jackson and Robertson efforts in the context of William Jennings Bryan's populism and a general "critique of elites whose greed, materialism, and libertarian immorality undermined the economic well-being and moral fiber of common folk." Group politics operates in any number of ways, and Hertzke reminds us that we should look for the impact of interests in nonobvious contexts.

In the 1988 presidential campaign each political party experienced the challenge of an insurgent Baptist minister who exploited church networks and charismatic religious appeals to galvanize followers. Although neither Jesse Jackson nor Pat Robertson won nomination, their crusades infused national politics with the populist discontent of two distinct communities and unleashed forces that will continue to influence politics in the 1990s. This chapter examines the ways in which church networks facilitated the mobilization of blacks and moral traditionalists, groups that feel passionately that their grievances are not being addressed through conventional interest group action. It is based on two years of field research, including extensive interviewing of campaign officials and delegates, as well as attendance at the two national political conventions.[1]

While not meant to equate the moral claims of Jackson and Robertson, this study is based on the view that unique insights might be gained by looking at the two movements together. There was, indeed, a common thread in the sense of crisis experienced in the respective communities. Among Republicans, it was Robertson supporters who expressed discontent, who felt their way of life was threatened by collapsing moral codes and secular trends—in contrast to the business elites and country club types who had little to complain about during the Reagan-Bush years. Indeed, compared to the "feel good," "morning in America" themes popular among Republicans in the 1980s, Robertson's campaign media painted a darker picture of America, a place where children were victimized by pornographers, misled in undisciplined schools, and manipulated by greedy marketers of glitz, lust, and sloth. Similarly, in the Democratic coalition the singular crisis experienced in the black community set African-Americans apart. Struggling economically and socially with the legacy of slavery, segregation, and racism, blacks saw the advances of the 1960s and 1970s stall dramatically in the 1980s. Black leaders were contending with rising unemployment, births out of wedlock, drug abuse, crime, truancy, and ignorance, yet they saw complacency, or worse, as the response of white America. Many black activists felt taken for granted by the Democratic party, whose other constituencies seemed to have it pretty good in comparison. The question was: What political avenues are available to redress these grievances? Apparently, a number of leaders and followers concluded that conditions were ripe for presidential mobilization as a means of registering discontent.

In the annals of political mobilization, nothing quite compares with the demands of a presidential campaign. Vast amounts of money must be raised quickly, thousands of volunteers enlisted, grass-roots organizations built in fifty states (each with different election rules), and literally millions of voters reached with a message. But if the task is daunting, the glamour and excitement of presidential politics catalyze people in powerful ways. Many people enlisted in the campaign remain active in politics; stung by the political bug, they join state organizations, run for local office, donate to national lobbies, and become an organized cadre for future presidential elections. This pattern is especially true if the constituencies are distinct and the campaigns become social movements, as Jackson's and Robertson's clearly did. In both cases the insurgent organizations continued to pursue political objectives beyond the nomination. Having galvanized the black electorate, Jackson continued to maneuver within the

Democratic party, demanding respect, raising issues, and attempting to build his so-called Rainbow Coalition into a long-term force. Robertson's minions, similarly, concentrated on taking over state and local party organizations, shaping the Republican platform, and preparing for state-by-state lobby battles over abortion, secularization in the public schools, and the like.

Facilitating the efforts of the insurgents was the porous structure of the party system in America. As a legacy of progressive reforms, American political parties, unlike their counterparts in Europe, are highly regulated to enable participation by average party voters and not just party elites.[2] At the presidential level this "plebiscitary" system reduces the role of party officials and creates the opportunity for so-called outsider candidates to penetrate the relatively porous parties and their caucuses and primaries with mobilized followers. Thus, the parties experience intense internal struggles as newcomers vie for influence, especially during presidential nominations when such mobilization is potentially far-reaching. While most of the literature on party reform focuses on the Democratic party, the Republican party (or GOP) is not immune to the kind of internal strife associated with party factionalism, especially with the emergence of conservative evangelical Christians as a feisty new constituency in the Republican coalition.

What sets the 1988 campaign apart is the extent to which churches became the focus of organizational efforts, challenging scholars to reexamine their assumptions about our supposedly secular contemporary society. To be sure, churches have been at the center of a number of political movements in American history. From the abolitionists of the early nineteenth century, to the crusade against alcohol in the late nineteenth and early twentieth centuries, to the civil rights struggle of the 1960s, churches provided the leadership, the organizational base, and often the funds for political battles. But until recently, contemporary political scientists had not taken notice of the potential in our own time for political mobilization through church networks, in part because it had been theorized that religion would wane with advancing modernity.

Religion in America, however, has proven remarkably durable, in spite of trends toward secularization elsewhere. To a much greater extent than other Western industrial nations, America is a churchgoing land, with some 70 percent of all citizens church members.[3] Indeed, far more people belong to a church or synagogue than any other private association, union, or group, making religion a key point of entry to the collective society. Of course, the religious commitment may be tepid and the likelihood of an intense following dim in churches that serve little more than social purposes, yet there are some tightly knit churches whose members seem willing to sacrifice for the faith. Different though they are in a number of respects, predominant black congregations and conservative Pentecostal churches share one thing in common: they are profoundly central to the lives of their members. As ministers steeped in religious traditions and rooted in church communities, Jackson and Robertson understood this fact and sought to capitalize on it for political ends. Neither leader can be understood, consequently, apart from his connection to a religious tradition. Thus, a comparison of the Jackson and Robertson campaigns should help us understand the power, and the limits, of church-based political mobilization.

Jesse Jackson and the Black Church

No other national black leader can match the galvanizing effect achieved by Jesse Louis Jackson, with his intimate knowledge of the black church, his mastery of religious imagery, and his charisma arising from his prophetic approach to politics. Throughout the 1980s he dominated black politics, and, in spite of the emergence of new black leaders, he continues to be a major player. He is recognized around the world. To understand the power of the Reverend Jackson, one must appreciate that he is a product of the distinctive religious heritage of blacks in America.

It is an ironic legacy of slavery and Jim Crow that the black church emerged from the Civil War as the one institution "owned and operated" by the blacks themselves,[4] a fact that profoundly shaped the civil rights revolution in the 1960s. For a century before the civil rights movement the all-black congregation (primarily Baptist or Methodist but decidedly evangelical) was the social center, the refuge, and the place where messages of comfort for the afflicted and judgment for oppressors could be heard. Tremendously diverse, black churches nonetheless produced a unique religious heritage, a blending of pietistic enthusiasm and prophetic witness. If America was the new Israel for the Puritans, it was Pharaoh's Egypt for many American blacks. Thus, biblical themes of liberation and the promised land possessed special poignancy and power in black churches. The centrality of the black minister flowed in part from his economic independence from the white power structure and in part from his dynamic oratorical powers, a legacy of the evangelical heritage of the black experience. The combination of these factors has produced a faith so salient among American blacks that, when asked how important religion was to them on a scale of one to ten, their mean response of over nine surpassed that of every other group Gallup has surveyed around the world.[5]

The political potential of this tightly knit community structure was only realized intermittently before the civil rights movement, but the black church, often conservative and cautious before the revolution, would never be the same afterward. It is now the most highly politicized sector of religious America. Black ministers endorse candidates from the pulpit (something even highly political fundamentalist ministers usually avoid), mobilize voter registration drives, raise money, and solicit volunteers for campaigns. Thus, while Democratic presidential nominee Walter Mondale complained about the mixing of religion and politics in 1984 (in reference to the Religious Right), 29 percent of those voting for him in Alabama (most of them black) had been urged to do so by their preachers versus 9 percent of those voting for Reagan hearing similar appeals.[6] It goes without saying that any political consultant would covet the formidable national network of churches led by some 40,000 black ministers, many (if not most) of whom campaigned actively in behalf of Jackson in 1988, serving as local and state coordinators, delegation leaders, and fund-raisers.

This analysis is not meant to minimize the importance of racial solidarity, even anger, in the black community as the critical source of support for Jackson. But even popular candidates cannot survive without strategic resources.[7] Followers must be mobilized, potential voters activated, forums scheduled, campaign workers recruited, and supporters solicited for donations of time and money. These tasks were done largely through the network of black congregations.[8] Failure to appreciate this dimension of the black experience, however, resulted in egregiously distorted analyses of the campaign, such as when a *New York Times* editorial pronounced, ex cathedra, that religion was irrelevant to Jackson's triumph on Super Tuesday.[9]

The black church figured heavily in Jackson's initial calculations about a run for president in 1984 and his early strategy. Ignited by the election of black mayor Harold Washington in Chicago but still smarting from Ronald Reagan's presidential victory in 1980, Jackson and black leaders around the country began discussing in 1983 the potential impact of a black candidate for president. Black registration was still low in the South and elsewhere, but an increase of 25 percent could reverse the predictable outcome of an election in eight states, they reasoned. So Jackson crisscrossed the South in the summer of 1983, preaching of poverty and oppression from pulpits and employing religious imagery in his registration drive. "Nails in our flesh" was his reference to violations of the 1965 Voting Rights Act; these violations, he argued, kept blacks from exercising their right of political participation. Other black leaders were wary of Jackson, but those who embraced his candidacy were buoyed by the thought of mobilizing the black church: "The word went out that savvy black political operatives

... would assist the Jackson effort and that 40,000 black churches could raise $250 each for what some Jackson aides insisted could be a campaign war chest of $10 million." [10]

Black churches served as the launching pad for the 1984 campaign. Speaking before the Holiness Church in Tyler, Texas, for example, Jackson quipped that although Mondale might have Big Labor, "We have Big Church." [11] And that was not far from the truth. The Reverend T. J. Jemison, president of the 7 million-member National Baptist Convention USA, roared his approval of Jackson at a convention of Baptist ministers: "I don't know if I speak for all Baptists, but I speak for so many, the number I don't speak for don't matter. . . . We are behind him [Jackson] in numbers, in spirit, and we are behind him in sugar [money]." [12]

Four years later, as Jackson moved into his second campaign, he built upon lessons learned in the first. The fund-raising techniques employed in 1988, for example, were patented in 1984 and typically involved the hard sell in congregations. Collection plates were passed with a variation on the alter call ("Come forward now!"), often to provide Jackson's plane fare to his next stop. [13] Given Jackson's flair for capturing free media coverage, the campaign's main task was collecting enough money for a plane to keep Jackson in the air, according to Jerry Austin, Jackson's 1988 campaign manager. [14] As the 1988 campaign gathered momentum, money did begin to flow in from direct mail solicitation, [15] but the churches had sustained Jackson in the critical early stages when other candidates were falling by the wayside.

In both 1984 and 1988 Jackson's campaign events often resembled religious revivals, with choirs and amens and with a sermon by Jackson filled with themes of crucifixion, resurrection, Jesus, and the manger. [16] One journalist even argued that the black churches sustained Jackson psychologically, particularly in 1984 when Louis Farrakhan and "Hymietown" [17] turned things sour:

> Jackson would turn to the black church more and more as the primaries continued. . . . The black church—the traditional haven since slave days, where raids and boycotts and marches were planned and wounds were bound and the dead were mourned— would become Jackson's haven too, the source of some of his best crowds, the bulk of his money, many of his votes. [18]

Even though the second campaign attempted to reach beyond Jackson's core constituency, the churches remained the key forums, as the 1988 news stories confirmed when they described various Jackson campaign events: "campaigning before cheering audiences at Baptist churches in Newark," "a highly emotional address to the Shorter African Method-

ist Episcopal Church," "a speech from the pulpit of the Ward African
Methodist Episcopal Church," "a tumultuous rally at the Pentecostal
Church of Christ," and so it went.

In an effort to broaden his base, Jackson hired Ohio political
consultant Jerry Austin, a Jew from Brooklyn, to serve as his campaign
manager. As a shrewd strategist, Austin affirmed the importance of the
black church, even stressing the need to understand its diverse
denominations. When the Jackson organizers moved into a state, they
began with the churches. Even in as improbable a place as Iowa the
black churches figured in the strategic calculations of the Jackson
campaign. "There are," Austin remarked, with the consultant's eye to
precise detail, "one-hundred-twenty-three black churches in Iowa." [19]
Whether at state campaign headquarters or at the convention, the
leadership ranks of the Jackson organization swelled with ministers, a
fact confirmed by others in Jackson's Rainbow Coalition. As a mayor
and delegate to the Democratic National Convention from California
put it, "I wasn't used to the idea of starting a meeting with a prayer,
but the Jackson meetings always start with a prayer—the Reverends
are in charge." [20]

The strategic nature of black church networks also was confirmed
by a key member of the national organization for Massachusetts
governor Michael Dukakis, who was vying Jackson for the Democratic
nomination. Todd Watkins, constituency coordinator for Dukakis and
a black, compared the black parishes to old-time precinct organizations.
The Michigan caucuses, for example, placed a premium on strong local
organization, Watkins noted, because the 600 district boundaries
recently had been redrawn and the process was confusing. Jackson's
smashing victory there was a direct result of the church-based organization, in which an approach similar to Robertson's was employed:

> The parish is an ideal unit for [political] organization, it's the same
> as a precinct. They [the Jackson supporters] would have a pre-
> caucus coffee at the neighborhood church, in a comfortable sur-
> rounding, and pass out stickers for Jackson. They would create
> strong peer pressure not to back down. Then they would bring a
> bus and the minister, the "Shepherd," would lead them to the
> caucus site.[21]

Early endorsements of Jackson by prominent ministers and associations, moreover, preempted organizing efforts by other candidates. As
Watkins observed, "In Ohio we wanted to do outreach but the churches
endorsed Jackson early. They shut us out. We wanted to have a
meeting with a black state representative, but he wouldn't even meet
with us." [22]

The church basis of Jackson's support was also very much in evidence at the Democratic National Convention. In interviews, black Jackson delegates stressed the importance of their churches in the campaign, and each told specific stories about church-centered fund-raising efforts, endorsements by prominent ministers and church associations, and campaign mobilization through local parishes. Indeed, while these black Jackson delegates stressed the church as the prime institution through which they gained entry to the system, nonblack delegates for Dukakis, Tennessee senator Albert Gore, and even Jackson, emphasized ties to unions, party organizations, educational associations, and interest groups. Thus, for many blacks the church is precinct and interest group rolled into one.

When the campaign reached out beyond Jackson's natural constituency, Jackson found enthusiastic audiences on college campuses and at high schools, at farm meetings, and in state legislatures. He even earned the improbable endorsement of the Iowa Teamsters Union. In reaching out to white voters Jackson also employed the church and "prophetic" rhetoric. As Austin noted, "He speaks frequently at white churches. In fact, he raised money in a white church in Iowa." [23] Jackson eventually got 12.5 percent of the white vote in all the primaries (which was a third of his total vote), no mean accomplishment. Part of his appeal grew out of a populist denunciation of the growing inequality in income and wealth in the nation, a theme that echoes throughout American history. In the shadow of American political leader and orator William Jennings Bryan, Jackson received a standing ovation from the Nebraska legislature with his populist blending of contemporary concerns with Old Testament prophesy:

> If there must be a fight, let that fight be at a plant gate that closed without notice. Let that fight be against farm foreclosures. Let that fight be at the drug exchange. Let that fight be at the missile silos. Then we will be known as the generation that did justice and had mercy and walked in the way of God. [24]

In analyzing the Jackson phenomenon, of course, one must not discount the extraordinary gifts and energy of the man former president Richard Nixon called one of the best campaigners of the twentieth century, nor the importance of black anger, hope, pride, and solidarity, nor the affinity of white liberals for Jackson's economic and foreign policy messages. But it has been shown here that the black churches provided the lion's share of strategic resources and moral support to the campaign, especially in its early stages when those resources were most needed, allowing Jackson to do what he does so well.

Jackson, in summary, successfully exploited the church resources available in the black community. In 1984 his campaign contributed to an energized black electorate, which was decisive in returning Democratic control to the Senate in 1986. In 1988 he received 6.7 million votes (29 percent of the total cast), including 92 percent of the black vote. This effort earned him some 1,200 delegates to the Democratic convention, a force that bought Jackson slots on the Democratic National Committee for his backers and concessions on the platform. In an era of chic investment bankers and leveraged buyouts, Jesse Jackson strove to represent the voiceless and dispossessed. In his 1988 Democratic convention speech, he pleaded with the nation not to forget those who clean the bedpans and wash the toilets, who "catch the early bus" but cannot afford health insurance. His campaign pushed particular concerns—South Africa, the black underclass, the homeless, the growing gap between rich and poor—to prominence on the national scene. Moreover, Jackson's most lasting influence may be that he elevated the drug issue to the forefront of the national Democratic agenda. Once viewed as "soft" on drug use, Democrats, led by Jackson's long-term and passionate involvement, seized the issue and now criticize President George Bush as insufficiently committed. Helping to intensify national concern about drug abuse, indeed, may be Jackson's lasting legacy.

Churches as Strategic Resources: Robertson

As host of the 700 Club, one of the most popular religious programs on television, Pat Robertson cultivated a constituency for years, blending upscale technology with faith-healing Pentecostal practices to create what scholars term a *parachurch.* To understand both Robertson's appeal, as well as its limits, one must appreciate the place of charismatic churches within the broader evangelical world.

During the nineteenth century when the Protestant faith dominated American culture, most believers adhered to evangelical tenets: an orthodox Christian doctrine, an emphasis on personal conversion, and a passionate commitment to the Great Commission to evangelize the world. By the turn of the century, however, the advance of science and its application to biblical criticism had split Protestant America into theological liberals who embraced modernity and traditionalists who clung to the fundamentals of the faith. Among the traditionalists was a distinct group of Pentecostals, who emphasized the "gifts of the Holy Spirit," emotional worship, and faith healing. Many adherents formed local independent churches, but some banded together in new denominations, such as the rapidly growing Assemblies of God, founded in 1914. For people who found modern life shallow and mainstream churches too compromising, the Pentecostal religion was a refuge. Indeed, as social and political changes rocked American society in the

1960s and 1970s, Pentecostal churches experienced dramatic growth, blending with a more contemporary charismatic renewal movement that spilled over into the liberal mainline churches and became popular among Catholics as well. As a protest against "rationalist" modernity, such paranormal practices as glossolalia ("speaking in tongues") separated the faithful from the broader culture.[25] Morally puritanical, fervently religious, devoted to traditional values and thus threatened by a perceived libertine popular culture, Pentecostals felt misunderstood or ignored by media moguls and political leaders. Yet their numbers swelled, and by 1988 they were ripe for political mobilization.

Pat Robertson, the son of a wealthy U.S. senator from Virginia, experienced a religious conversion that placed him in the heart of the charismatic fold. He abandoned a traditional career in law and instead purchased a defunct television station that served as the forerunner of the nation's first Christian television network, CBN. Unlike the Reverend Jerry Falwell, who as an old-time fundamentalist eschews "Pentecostal excesses," Robertson brought the "gifts of the Holy Spirit" into prime time, cultivating a large and loyal following. As one of the pioneers of religious broadcasting, Robertson honed the fund-raising techniques needed to keep paid television ministries afloat, developing a formidable list of followers in the process. In 1986 the Christian Broadcast Network reached 16 million households a month, and in one year the 700 Club logged 4 million prayer calls to volunteers manning telephone banks.[26]

Robertson's key resource, his identification with an ardent religious movement ripe for political mobilization, also severely limited his attempt to broaden his appeal beyond charismatic Christians. Journalists and political cartoonists stressed the "peculiar" practices of his faith throughout the campaign, even as Robertson sought to cast himself more broadly as a businessman and broadcaster. As seasoned political reporter Jack Germond observed, "Most journalists think he is a nut ... [and] every bio piece will include the fact that he claims to cure hemorrhoids with prayer." [27] Yet what secular journalists did not understand is that many fundamentalists and evangelicals are also skeptical, even hostile, toward numerous Pentecostal practices. Robertson, consequently, found his attempt to broaden his political base to include conservative religionists of all theological stripes fraught with obstacles. In the Bible Belt, for example, Robertson failed to gain substantial support from Southern Baptists, owing in part to theological differences but also in part to the popularity of President Reagan (and by association Vice President George Bush) with that constituency.[28]

Still, Robertson's following was formidable, intensely devoted, and dispersed throughout the country. His campaign staff capitalized on that constituency in their attempt to penetrate the Republican party. The early organizational effort to secure names on endorsing petitions was almost entirely church-based, according to campaign manager Marc Nuttle. In addition, the highly successful fund-raising effort was conducted using lists that included many ministers, evangelical associations, and, of course, contributors to the 700 Club. Remarkably, Robertson's campaign raised some $30 million in contributions and matching federal funds, more than any other candidate except George Bush, who raised slightly more.[29] This fact alone illustrates the strategic resources available to Robertson, a man who had neither held an elective political post nor run for political office before. Finally, through churches and networks of religious individuals, Robertson built a formidable network of state organizations[30] that continue to battle traditional Republicans for control of the GOP.[31]

The organizational clout of Robertson's parachurch galvanized followers to overrun party meetings and caucuses, causing apoplexy among Republican party regulars. Robertson's early success in the first stage of delegate selection in Michigan stunned the party veterans and sent the party into a year-long struggle complete with shoving matches, rump conventions, and court challenges. He went on to dominate the Hawaii caucuses, to win in Alaska, Nevada, and Washington, and to do respectably in Iowa and Minnesota. All told, he won slightly over a million votes or 9 percent of the total votes cast. Moreover, even in primary states where Robertson was defeated by Bush, Robertson supporters packed party caucuses to elect delegates, draft platform statements, and control party machinery. In a number of states—including Arizona, Georgia, Louisiana, North Carolina, Oklahoma, Oregon, South Carolina, Texas, and Virginia—they flooded party meetings, igniting fierce clashes, even fisticuffs, with Republican regulars.[32] As a result, many Robertson loyalists were elected to state party slots, and a good number ran for local offices.

Observers of the Robertson caucus campaign have corroborated the centrality of churches as bases of organization. For example, syndicated columnist Jack Germond made these observations:

> Evangelicals are not united, but the church is the glue for the Robertson campaign. At the Florida state convention their participation was impressive. Almost everyone I talked to—45 to 50 people—had reenrolled as Republicans and paid $50 apiece to attend. They are a homogeneous group—united, disciplined.[33]

This infusion of new people into the Republican party—at least at the organizational level—was evident during the campaign. In Iowa the Robertson caucus attendees were largely newcomers, often mobilized by friends from their churches; over half of those interviewed were 700 Club viewers. Many of them had met as a group for prayer before attending the caucus. Some were right-to-life Catholics, but most were from evangelical and Pentecostal backgrounds. Culturally, these new-comers viewed themselves as distinct from the Bush and Dole[34] mainline Republicans, a fact epitomized by a young, pro-life woman who had served as a precinct captain for Robertson. Exuding the excitement of a neophyte, she described how she had packed over half of the caucus with Robertson people, "whereas all Bush and Dole had were a few older men!" [35] She had organized the precinct drive through her church, the First Federated Open Bible Church in Des Moines, which she said was one of twenty such charismatic churches headquar-tered in Iowa.

The cultural distinctiveness of this new group of Republican activists was evident throughout the campaign. Robertson supporters were fervently religious and deeply concerned about families, schools, and moral decay. Comporting least with the stereotype of "elite Republicans," some even wore bluejeans to party conventions. Surveys revealed that many Robertson supporters fit the Democratic profile: blue-collar and female.[36] Among those attending a postelection recep-tion for Robertson in Oklahoma were a janitor, a truck driver, and the owner of a car stereo shop. A major organizational challenge in some states, therefore, was getting Democrats to change their registration to Republican before various deadlines, an effort that was not always welcomed by longtime GOP regulars. Jack Germond observed the same phenomenon and analyzed it this way: "In the South the Bush supporters really are Country Club people, but the Robertson people are a notch below. Church is so important to them. There is a cultural gulf between them and the Country Club types. . . . The new registra-tions are mostly Robertson people." [37]

The key to Robertson's success in mobilizing new activists was the organizational base of a network of large charismatic churches. One of the keenest observers of this phenomenon was a top Bush strategist assigned to court the evangelical constituency and, ultimately, to blunt Robertson. Doug Wead, now special assistant to the president for public liaison, described how the Bush organization monitored Robert-son's efforts and discovered ways to check them. Combining sophisti-cated polling and tracking techniques with "spies" in Robertson's office, Wead's staff discovered that the Robertson organization capital-ized on his popularity with charismatics, many of whom belonged to huge "superchurches," congregations with 5,000 or more members. "His base was the Assemblies of God," noted Wead, "but they weren't aware of it." Given the small turnout at caucuses and even some primaries, these superchurches presented formidable potential. Added Wead, "The pastor of a superchurch is, or could be, the equivalent of a county chairman. In some communities there are five churches, any one of which could take over the party organization." Yet whereas Jackson could openly court the membership of the black churches, Robertson had to work more quietly to exploit this potential, owing to the suspicion of worldly politics among many conservative believers. "Robertson had a hard thing to do," noted Wead. "He had to slowly build a cadre within the church, which could then get the pastor to go along—let them use the church building, place announcements in the church bulletins." The Robertson effort would start slowly, almost imperceptibly; then as the large churches were finally "captured," the campaign would mushroom. "Robertson's pattern was to double [in voter support] in the last week and then double again on the weekend before the vote. They did it four times."[38]

Robertson's defeat of Bush in the Iowa caucuses was a humiliating loss, but the Bush organization, with enormous resources of its own, gained vital information on how to blunt Robertson in the future. Wead discovered that having a Bush supporter in one of these superchurches could inoculate it against Robertson mobilization. When the Robertson cadre attempted to coopt the pastor to allow a table with campaign literature or notices of meetings in church bulletins, all it took was one Bush backer to request the same for his organization and the church was effectively neutralized. Thus, when campaign manager Lee Atwater desperately called upon Wead to develop a plan in the South to blunt Robertson, Wead had his strategy. Employing an army of paid staff and volunteers, Wead identified 215 superchurches in the South that would serve as the organizational base for Robertson. The Bush organization then identified a Bush supporter in each church, designating that person as coordinator and providing instructions on how to check the Robertson impact. They would "schmooze" pastors too, not to gain the support of the members, but just to neutralize Robertson's effort.[39] Bush's popularity with other evangelicals, especially Southern Baptists, would then be enough to ensure him victory. This strategy, coupled with Robertson's untimely misstatements and the aftershocks of scandals among televangelists, succeeded in blunting Robertson's delegate hunt. Ironically, then, Robertson's early success shocked the Bush organization into developing a church strategy of its own. Thus, Doug Wead spoke of churches as he would precincts, recounting that "we took out [neutralized] the First Assembly," and that "the Dole churches stayed with Dole, and the Bush churches went to Dole and Robertson."[40]

One impact of the Robertson infusion was to solidify the national influence of the Religious Right on the Republican platform. More dramatically, the Robertson forces succeeded in dominating the GOP platform in a number of states. In Arizona, for example, they joined with followers of ousted governor Evan Mecham to declare America a "Christian Nation," a move that proved terribly embarrassing. In Oklahoma the platform was a model of Christian Right concerns, illustrating the degree of alienation felt by moral traditionalists. It called for a human life amendment, the closing of "bars, bathhouses, and bookstores where sexual activity occurs," aggressive AIDS testing, enforcement of obscenity laws, opposition to surrogate motherhood, support for the husband as head of the household, opposition to redefinition of the family to include homosexual marriage, and enactment of laws that affirm "Judeo-Christian values rather than humanistic philosophy." Many of the concerns focused on education, where conservative parents felt most under siege. The detailed education proposals included:

- support for tuition tax credits and educational vouchers;
- endorsement of the teaching of the basics, including the "traditional cultural heritage of our country";
- opposition to any "involvement of the NEA in the public school system concerning educational policy" because the "National Educational Association is a teachers-educators union that advocates sex education, ERA passage, abortion, sex clinics, nuclear freeze, a humanistic curriculum, and opposes traditional value systems";
- daily recitation of the pledge of allegiance;
- opposition to "the current advocacy of Secular Humanism in any form in the public schools because it is a violation of the First Amendment";
- revision of textbook adoption procedures to be more responsive to local parents;
- opposition to "utilization of mind-altering techniques for public school students";
- opposition to state-mandated sex education in the public schools;
- insistence that AIDS education emphasize that "sexual abstinence outside of marriage and fidelity within marriage with a non-infected spouse are the only truly safe ways to avoid the sexual transmission of AIDS";
- opposition to the teaching of values education, death education, and situation ethics;
- opposition to the "New Age Movement philosophy, including re-incarnation, mystical powers, Satan worship, etc., as introduced in the textbooks of our education system"; and

• opposition to school-based health clinics that undermine parental values by dispensing birth control to students and conducting abortion counseling.

With his withering critique of culture cut adrift from its moral and religious moorings, Robertson dramatically voiced the angst of cultural traditionalists. Indeed, his supporters were far more concerned about "moral values" than other Republicans.[41] He hammered away at the theme of moral decay: the family under siege, the erosion of standards in education, the effects of rampant individualism and greed in business, the immorality of mortgaging our children's future on debt and current consumption. Rebuking fellow Republicans who had forgotten that pursuit of private gain must be restrained by moral compass, he exposed the contradiction within conservative ranks between economic libertarianism and cultural stability. No friend to feminist groups, Robertson ironically found his strongest support among women, causing Democratic consultant Ann Lewis to conclude: "Pat Robertson was talking about the issues women find important, issues like our children's future, a better educational system, and pressure on today's families." [42] His cross-cutting message thus resonated with those who found the "liberation" of modern society often less than liberating.

Reaction and Response

How well did the respective political parties accommodate the galvanized factions within their ranks? Robertson forces provoked intense intraparty fighting at the state level but were skillfully incorporated into the Republican coalition in the national presidential campaign. The reverse was true for the Jackson people, who were assimilated with few overt struggles at the state level but provoked tension with the party's presidential nominee.

Let us look at how the national campaign staffs and nominees dealt with the insurgent challenges. Although Democratic candidate Michael Dukakis made token appeals to the black community, he largely conceded the black vote to Jackson in the primaries. Then after securing the nomination, Dukakis seemed incapable of comprehending that Jackson viewed himself in unconventional terms, as did his followers. Through excruciatingly poor coordination, the Dukakis staff failed to inform Jackson of Texas senator Lloyd Bentsen's selection as the vice-presidential nominee. Jackson, to his great irritation, learned of the decision as he was swamped by reporters on arrival at Washington's National Airport. This seemingly cavalier treatment of Jackson was profoundly insulting to his followers. Black leaders spoke angrily of "the phone call that was never made." Jackson continued to press Dukakis for "respect," but Dukakis did not know how to respond and retain his own stature. Trying to be conciliatory, Dukakis welcomed Jackson as a key "player" on the "team." But he went on to say that "every team has to have a quarterback—that's the nominee—you can't have two quarterbacks," [43] unaware that Jackson, as a gifted college athlete, had been a direct victim of the prejudice that "blacks can't be quarterbacks." The cultural gulf between Dukakis and Jackson manifested itself in tense negotiations at the Democratic convention. With the "party hanging by a thread in Atlanta," [44] Jackson, Dukakis, and top aides tried to find some accommodation. Under intense pressure from the mercurial Jackson, Dukakis agreed to provide him with a plane and a prominent role in the campaign and conceded an enhanced future role for the reverend in the Democratic party. But Dukakis failed to develop a coherent strategy for dealing with the Jackson forces in the general election, and public tensions erupted over where Jackson would campaign. This maladroit handling of Jackson apparently lessened the enthusiasm of blacks for the Democratic ticket. After a dramatic surge in black participation in 1984, black voting slipped in 1988, to the detriment of the Democratic party. Moreover, Dukakis failed to seize the populist economic themes of Jackson's message that might have energized Democratic voters.[45]

On the Republican side there was considerable disagreement early in the Bush campaign about how to deal with the evangelical constituency. Some underestimated its diversity, equating the lack of broad support for the Falwells and Robertsons as reason to ignore the feisty traditionalists. Others argued that the GOP could not snub the more than one-third of the population that were "born again," noting that many of those believers were Democrats who supported Reagan. The Bush campaign, it turned out, was big and diverse enough to pursue simultaneous, even contradictory, strategies. Thus, in contrast to the Dukakis failure, Bush lieutenants anticipated the Robertson effort, monitored its growth, designed strategies to blunt its impact, and coopted its potential supporters. According to an internal campaign document, in June 1985 Bush staff "predicted that Pat Robertson would be a candidate for the Presidency and further, that evangelicals would successfully take control of the Republican party structure in many counties, congressional districts, and states across the country." [46] The evangelicals would be energized because "theirs was the unfinished agenda." Secular conservatives got what they wanted out of Reagan, but what did the cultural conservatives really get but lip service from the Great Communicator?

A quiet but thorough effort began in 1985 to arrange for Bush meetings with key evangelical leaders, appearances on Christian television programs, and feature stories in evangelical publications. Doug Wead, evangelical Bush aide, even wrote a puff biography on Bush's life and faith for Christian bookstores. Between 1985 and 1988 Bush was photographed with almost 1,000 evangelical leaders. Remarkably, by 1987 information was filtering into the campaign that Bush was the second choice of Robertson supporters. According to Wead, "Robertson was bringing his own people to the process and the people he was bringing were predisposed to support us if we would only go after them." Thus, in a November 1987 memo Wead wrote: "It's time for us to play the evangelical card seriously. It's time for us to take off our gloves and go after the evangelical vote." [47]

In a way, Robertson's early success proved a blessing to the Bush organization because it shocked key Bush operatives into a recognition that they could not snub the born-again constituency. As Doug Wead put it, "The evangelicals are a contradiction to [Bush campaign manager Lee] Atwater. His vision of Republicans is a yuppie thing." But after Iowa, Wead's credibility rose, and he was given free reign to implement the evangelical strategy.[48] This aggressive effort led to a robust born-again vote for the vice president in the primaries and, subsequently, in the general election.

What the Bush people discovered, thanks in part to Robertson, was that they could court the evangelical vote in ways that did not undercut their support among other key voting blocks. Moreover, they learned through experiments with focus groups[49] that themes articulated by Robertson[50] in the primaries—for example, the pledge of allegiance and the American Civil Liberties Union attack on religion— were devastating when aimed at Dukakis, and not just among evangelicals. In the general election Bush got 80 percent of the evangelical vote[51] that included many culturally conservative Democrats. Thus, Bush not only blunted Robertson by courting the born-again vote in the primaries but also benefited tremendously from his cultivation of that constituency in the general election.

After the election, however, tensions increased in the fragile GOP coalition. In wake of the *Webster* decision on abortion,[52] notable Republican candidates backed away from their previous pro-life commitments. Evangelical leaders in turn increasingly complained about being used by the GOP with little to show for their support. Charging that out of "thousands" of Bush's presidential appointments, only three were associated with the evangelical movement, Pat Robertson even intimated that he could support Lloyd Bentsen for president in 1992.[53] Thus, the infusion of this culturally distinct group within the Republican coalition remains fraught with potential snares.

Churches, Political Mobilization,
and Populist Discontent

Consider for a moment the remarkable blending of "sacred and profane" that occurred on Easter Sunday 1988. The campaign had brought Robertson and Jackson to Denver on the eve of the Colorado caucuses, where they simultaneously addressed enthusiastic metro congregations, weaving Easter themes into their remarks. Robertson, who received standing ovations at four evangelical churches, compared the despair of the early Christians on Good Friday to Christians in America. He proclaimed, "It looks like the bad guys are winning in this country, but so did it look that way on Good Friday. . . . It looked as if Satan had beaten Jesus on that day." [54] According to Robertson, just as Jesus rose from the dead, so would moral Americans eventually prevail. For Jackson too there was an Easter message reflecting the political signs of the times. Before an unusual combined service of prominent white and black churches, an emotional Jackson "compared the good Friday Crucifixion to the onset of the Reagan administration, but promised an Easter-like political resurrection for the nation's downtrodden." Later at Our Lady of Guadalupe, a predominately Hispanic church, Jackson compared President Reagan to Pontius Pilate:

> Pilate was in power; Pilate had credentials, but he couldn't make a decision. He said, "I think Jesus is innocent, but he might be guilty. . . . I think he's right, but the crowds say he's wrong. So let me wash my hands." We don't need no more handwashing. We need leaders who will stand in a moment of crisis.[55]

Clearly the presidential campaign brought simmering forces in American society to the surface, challenging conventional politicians to respond. Thus, more than routine interest group action, presidential campaigns sometimes serve as barometers of American society, registering the frustration of particular constituencies. Buoyed by his support in the churches, Jackson capitalized on the sense of crisis in the black community to alter the political configuration in the Democratic party. Similarly, Robertson mobilized religious conservatives threatened by cultural change to confront the GOP establishment. But why in 1988? Why this simultaneous challenge to elites on the Right and the Left?

The answer lies in part in powerful modern forces that appear uniquely disruptive to the economically vulnerable and the morally traditional. In the 1980s many black workers, dependent upon industrial jobs and with little capital to cushion them, were ill-positioned to respond easily to the high-tech revolution of "perpetual innovation" in the global marketplace.[56] This economic plight deepened the cultural crises of out-of-wedlock pregnancies and drug abuse, which left many young blacks further behind in economic competition.[57] Jackson's indictment of multinational corporations reflected the threat posed to the vulnerable and unprepared by a dynamic marketplace increasingly ascendant in the world. By the same token, the free market also acts as a powerful engine of the libertarian change so disturbing to cultural traditionalists. In other words, the free enterprise system which was so eloquently extolled by Reagan, uproots people, undermines traditional culture and morals, and promises secular pleasure, wealth, and power.[58] In America, the most liberal and individualist of all nations, these market forces are exceedingly powerful. After all, what do we export so well as the seductive promises of our mass entertainment, our advertising, and, that most uniquely unwholesome product of U.S. capitalism, our rock video?

It is not surprising then that the critique of modernity would come from tightly knit church communities, which by their existence challenge the individualistic assumptions that drive the broader society. Thus, both Jackson's economic prophesy and Robertson's moral jeremiad can be seen as communitarian challenges to a libertarian emphasis on the self above family, community, or tradition. The question remains: To what extent can politics ameliorate problems that arise out of the very nature of economic and cultural trends? The answer: Perhaps only to a limited extent, which means that the sources of discontent will remain to pique elite complacency for some time to come.

One way to understand Robertson and Jackson therefore is as expressions of American populism. In the late nineteenth century rapid economic and social change produced a movement that spread through the prairie states like a wind-swept fire. Adopting the populist mantle, William Jennings Bryan seized the presidential nomination of the Democratic party in 1896 and twice again thereafter. Bryan denounced capitalists who exploited the poor, while, with equal vigor, he castigated demon rum and the doctrine of evolution. Weaving biblical themes into his speeches, Bryan could sound like Marx one minute and a pietist preacher the next, but the common thread was a critique of elites whose greed, materialism, and libertarian immorality undermined the economic well-being and moral fiber of common folk.[59] This blending of moral traditionalism with economic radicalism was not uncommon in the American past, but in contemporary politics that populist heritage is split; each side of the political spectrum must contend with discontents in its ranks. When Jesse Jackson champions the dispossessed and afflicts the comfortable; and when Pat Robertson trumpets moral renewal and chastises cultural elites for flouting traditional values, what we hear, perhaps, are echoes down through American history, echoes of discontent.

Notes

1. This research is based on what Fenno has called the participation observation method. See Richard F. Fenno, Jr., *Home Style: House Members in Their Districts* (Boston: Little, Brown, 1978). In 1988 I traveled to the Iowa caucuses, attended both the Democratic and Republican conventions, and was invited to a fund-raising event for Pat Robertson shortly after the election. In 1989 I attended the Oklahoma Republican convention, conducted interviews during the summer with political insiders in Washington, D.C., and attended the Democratic National Committee meeting in the fall. I also interviewed the national campaign managers for Jackson and Robertson, as well as regional and state lieutenants, national and state party leaders, convention delegates, caucus attendees, top campaign officials for Republican nominee George Bush and Democratic nominee Michael Dukakis, members of Congress, White House officials, and national journalists.
2. See Leon Epstein, *Political Parties in the American Mold* (Madison: University of Wisconsin Press, 1986).
3. See George Gallup, Jr., "Religion in America," *Gallup Report,* 259 (April 1987): 37.
4. See Robert Booth Fowler, *Religion and Politics in America* (Metuchen, N.J.: Scarecrow, 1984); and A. James Reichley, *Religion in American Public Life* (Washington, D.C.: Brookings Institution, 1985).
5. Gallup, "Religion in America."
6. Reichley, *Religion,* 284.
7. See Stephen J. Wayne, *The Road to the White House: The Politics of Presidential Elections,* 3d ed. (New York: St. Martin's, 1987); and Nelson Polsby and Aaron Wildavsky, *Presidential Elections: Contemporary Strategies of American Electoral Politics,* 7th ed. (New York: Free Press, 1988).
8. This fact is confirmed by scholars both sympathetic and critical of the Jackson effort. See especially Adolph Reed, Jr., *The Jesse Jackson Phenomenon* (New Haven, Conn.: Yale University Press, 1986); Roger D. Hatch, *Beyond Opportunity: Jesse Jackson's Vision for America* (Philadelphia: Fortress Press, 1988); Bob Faw and Nancy Skelton, *Thunder in America: The Improbable Presidential Campaign of Jesse Jackson* (Austin: Texas Monthly Press, 1986); and Lucius Barker and Ronald Walters, *Jesse Jackson's 1984 Presidential Campaign* (Urbana: University of Illinois Press, 1988).
9. *New York Times,* March 8, 1988. This date was dubbed Super Tuesday because twenty states held primaries or caucuses to select presidential delegates, making it the richest delegate harvest in the long presidential campaign.
10. Faw and Skelton, *Thunder in America.*
11. Ibid., 35.
12. Ibid.

13. Gail Sheehy, "Power or Glory?" *Vanity Fair,* January 1988.
14. Statement by Jerry Austin on *Frontline,* "Running with Jesse," a PBS special hosted by Judy Woodruff, February 7, 1989.
15. According to the Federal Election Commission, Jackson's 1988 campaign raised more than $19 million, a huge increase over his 1984 effort.
16. Interview with author; Faw and Skelton, *Thunder in America;* and Sheehy, "Power or Glory?"
17. Jesse Jackson was criticized severely in 1984 for his association with the militant Black Muslim leader Louis Farrakhan, and many commentators took Jackson to task for not repudiating more forcefully Farrakhan's anti-Semitic statements. Jackson's highly publicized slur against Jews (when he referred to New York City as "Hymietown") deepened the rift between his movement and Jewish Democrats.
18. Faw and Skelton, *Thunder in America,* 122.
19. Jerry Austin, interview with author, Iowa, February 1988.
20. Interview with author, Democratic National Convention, Atlanta, July 1988.
21. Todd Watkins, interview with author, Democratic National Convention, Atlanta, July 1988.
22. Ibid.
23. Interview with author, February 1988.
24. *Washington Post Weekly Edition,* March 2, 1987.
25. See Margaret M. Poloma, *Assemblies of God at the Crossroads: Charisma and Institutional Dilemmas* (Knoxville: University of Tennessee Press, 1989).
26. "Gospel TV: Religion, Politics and Money," *Time,* February 17, 1986.
27. Jack Germond, interview with author, Des Moines, Iowa, February 1988.
28. James L. Guth, "A New Turn for the Christian Right? Robertson's Support from the Southern Baptist Clergy" (Paper presented at the annual meeting of the Midwest Political Science Association, Chicago, 1989).
29. Federal Election Commission Report, August 1988.
30. Bill Brock, campaign manager of Kansas senator Robert Dole, said that Robertson "has perhaps the most powerful political machine in America." *U.S. News and World Report,* February 22, 1988, 14.
31. See Rob Gurwitt, "The Christian Right Has Gained Political Power. Now What Does It Do?" *Governing: The States and Localities,* October 1989.
32. This list is based on interviews, as well as on reports in *Congressional Quarterly Weekly Report,* May 14, 1988, 1267-1273; and in Gurwitt, *Governing.*
33. Germond interview.
34. Kansas senator Robert Dole, who, along with Bush, Robertson, and others, was seeking the Republican presidential nomination.
35. Interview with author, Des Moines, Iowa, February 1988.

36. As reported in *U.S. News and World Report,* February 22, 1988.

37. Germond interview.

38. Doug Wead, special assistant to the president, interview with author, Washington, D.C., June 1989.

39. Ibid.

40. Ibid.

41. For example, 70 percent of Robertson's caucus supporters in Iowa listed "moral values" as a key concern, as opposed to only 17 percent of the other Republican participants. See *New York Times,* February 10, 1988, 15.

42. *Ms.,* May 1988, 77.

43. Jack Germond and Jules Witcover, *Whose Broad Stripes and Bright Stars: The Trivial Pursuit of the Presidency* (New York: Warner Books, 1989), 348.

44. Ron Brown, as cited in ibid.

45. Garry Wills, "The Power Populist," *Time,* November 21, 1988.

46. Doug Wead, "The Vice-President and Evangelicals in the General Election," internal Bush campaign document, April 15, 1988.

47. Ibid.

48. Wead interview.

49. Top Bush strategists assembled focus groups of average Democrats supporting Dukakis and found that such issues as the pledge of allegiance and the ACLU were extremely damaging. See Paul Taylor and David Broder, "Early Volley of Bush's Exceeds Expectations," *Washington Post,* October 28, 1988, 1.

50. Radio spots for Pat Robertson in Iowa featured the pledge of allegiance and an attack on the ACLU's protection of pornography and hostility to public religion.

51. *The New York Times-CBS Poll,* November 10, 1988.

52. The Supreme Court, in the case of *Webster v. Reproductive Health Services,* increased the latitude of states to restrict abortion, thus forcing many elected officials to clarify their positions on the controversial issue.

53. "For Conservatives, Breaking Up Is Hard to Do," *U.S. News and World Report,* February 5, 1990.

54. *Denver Post,* April 4, 1988.

55. Ibid.

56. Don Kash, *Perpetual Innovation* (New York: Basic Books, 1990).

57. Leon Dash paints a disturbing portrait of self-destructive behavior in a Washington, D.C., ghetto in: *When Children Want Children: The Urban Crisis of Teenage Childbearing* (New York: Morrow, 1989).

58. Daniel Bell, *The Cultural Contradictions of Capitalism* (New York: Basic Books, 1976).

59. Paolo Coletta, *William Jennings Bryan,* 3 vols. (Lincoln: University of Nebraska Press, 1964, vol. 1, and 1969, vols. 2-3. See also, Willard Smith, *The Social and Religious Thought of William Jennings Bryan* (Lawrence, Kan.: Coronado Press, 1975).

9. PACS IN THE POLITICAL PROCESS

M. Margaret Conway

Observers of American political life would be hard pressed to name a feature of contemporary electoral politics over the past decade that has attracted more attention and aroused more emotion than the campaign spending of political action committees (PACs). By the late 1980s nearly 4,200 registered PACs existed at the federal level, and in the 1987-1988 election cycle these PACs provided 40 percent of the campaign funds received by House candidates and 22 percent of Senate candidates' receipts. The potential impact of such spending on electoral outcomes and public policy decisions is a matter of widespread debate. Unquestionably, PACs represent a key weapon in many (but not all) interest groups' arsenals of influence.

In this chapter political scientist Margaret Conway surveys the rise of PACs as potent political forces and assesses their effects upon electoral and legislative politics. Particular attention is given to PAC contribution strategies and the conditions and circumstances that may maximize PAC influence. She couples an exploration of the variety of criticisms directed toward PAC politics with an evaluation of the various reforms that have been suggested to limit PAC influence. Conway concludes that one problem of the possible reforms is that none address the "imbalance in the representation of interests through PACs," particularly the rapid growth in the number of business-related PACs compared to their labor-based counterparts. In her view, despite the hostility among reformers and the press toward PACs, these groups are not likely to be abolished and their role in the political process will continue, as will the many controversies over their activities.

In the less than two decades since federal laws and Supreme Court decisions conveyed legitimacy on political action committees, their numbers have increased by 600 percent, growing from 608 in 1974 to 4,178 in 1989 (see Table 9-1). While the rate of growth in the number of PACs declined during the 1980s (and their absolute numbers even declined from 1988 to 1989), their role in the funding of congressional elections remained significant. During the 1987-1988 election cycle, PACs provided 40 percent of the funds received by House candidates and 22 percent of Senate candidates' receipts.[1]

Many questions about the role of PACs in American politics are

Table 9-1 Number of Political Action Committees, 1974-1989

Type of PAC	12/74	11/75 [a]	5/76 [b]	12/76	12/78	12/80	12/82	12/84	12/86	12/88	12/89
Corporate	89	139	294	433	785	1,206	1,469	1,682	1,744	1,816	1,796
Labor	201	226	246	224	217	297	380	394	384	354	349
Trade/Membership/Health	318	357	452	489	453	576	649	698	745	786	777
Nonconnected	—	—	—	—	162	374	723	1,053	1,077	1,115	1,060
Cooperative	—	—	—	—	12	42	47	52	56	59	59
Corporation without stock	—	—	—	—	24	56	103	130	151	138	137
Total	608	722	992	1,146	1,653	2,551	3,371	4,009	4,157	4,268	4,178

SOURCE: Federal Election Commission press release, January 17, 1990.

[a] On November 24, 1975, the Federal Election Commission issued Advisory Opinion 1975-23 or the so-called SunPAC opinion.
[b] On May 11, 1976, the president signed the Federal Election Campaign Act Amendments of 1976, P.L. 94-283.

addressed in this chapter, including: What laws govern the activities of political action committees? Have these laws been effective in achieving their intended aims? What has been the role of PACs in financing congressional campaigns? What types of candidates are favored and what types are disadvantaged by the existing laws? How do PACs make decisions about which candidates should receive PAC contributions and how much to give? What strategies govern contribution decisions by PACs? Do the internal needs of the organization giving the money influence patterns of PAC contributions to congressional candidates?

Two types of political action committees operate at the federal level: independent and affiliated. Independent PACs are officially independent of any existing organization and usually focus on a particular issue or advocate a particular ideology. Affiliated PACs are created by existing organizations such as labor unions, corporations, cooperatives, or trade and professional associations. They serve as a separate, segregated fund to collect money from people affiliated with the organization for contribution to candidates' political campaigns or for use as independent expenditures for or against a particular candidate.

Federal Law and the Growth of PACs

Political action committees are governed primarily by the Federal Election Campaign Act of 1971 (FECA) and amendments enacted to it in 1974, 1976, and 1979, as well as the Revenue Act of 1971. Also important are regulations and advisory opinions issued by the Federal Election Commission (FEC) which administers and enforces federal campaign finance laws, as well as several court decisions interpreting federal laws.

To limit the influence of any one group or individual in the funding of campaigns for federal office, individuals and most organizations are restricted in the amount of money that they can give directly to a candidate in any one year. The current limits are $1,000 per election to a candidate for federal office, $20,000 per year to the national political party committees, and $5,000 per election to a campaign committee. No individual may contribute more than $25,000 to candidates for federal office in any one year. Federal campaign finance laws, however, give a distinct advantage to multicandidate committees—those contributing to five or more candidates for federal office—whether they are independent or affiliated. A multicandidate committee may contribute as much money as it is able to raise, yet it is restricted to giving no more than $5,000 per candidate in each election. That permits a PAC to give a candidate up to $5,000 for a primary election and $5,000 for a general election contest. There is no limit on how much a political action committee may spend in independent expenditures in behalf of a candidate as long as it does not coordinate its campaign efforts in any way with the candidate, representatives of the candidate, or the candidate's campaign committee. Because PACs are able to raise and funnel large amounts to campaigns for federal office, their numbers have grown; public concern about their influence on members of Congress has grown as well.

The 1974 amendments to the Federal Election Campaign Act permitted government contractors to establish political action committees, thus greatly expanding the universe of businesses and labor unions eligible to create PACs. The decision by the Federal Election Commission in April 1975 to permit corporations and labor unions to use their treasury funds to create political action committees and to administer their activities, including solicitation of funds from employees and stockholders, facilitated the establishment and operation of political action committees.[2] Authorization of the use of payroll deductions to channel funds to PACs also stimulated the creation and continuing operations of PACs.

Supreme Court decisions as well played a major role in stimulating the creation of additional PACs. In *Buckley v. Valeo,* the Supreme Court in January 1976 indicated that the 1974 FECA amendments did not limit the number of local or regional PACs that unions or corporations and their subsidiaries could establish.[3] That decision also clarified the right of PACs to make independent expenditures (those not authorized by nor coordinated with a candidate's campaign) on behalf of a candidate. In 1976 further amendments to FECA restricted labor union and corporation PAC contributions to one $5,000 contribution per election, regardless of the number of PACs created by a corporation's divisions or subsidiaries or a labor union's locals. The process of clarifying what is permissible continues, with the Federal Election Commission and other interested parties proposing amendments to existing laws and a number of advisory opinions being issued by the FEC.

While political action committees had existed prior to 1974, their numbers were limited, most often among labor unions. Between 1974 and 1989 the number of labor union PACs increased by 83 percent, while the number of corporate PACs increased by 1,900 percent (see Table 9-1). Thus, the first notable effect of changed laws and the FEC's interpretation of the laws was the explosive growth in the number of corporate PACs. Although the number of labor union and corporate PACs has increased significantly, most do not raise and contribute large amounts of money. During the 1987-1988 campaign cycle, only thirty-seven corporate PACs raised more than $350,000 each, but only fourteen contributed to candidates that much from funds raised. Thirty-nine labor union PACs raised $350,000 or more, and twenty-eight contributed at least $350,000 to candidates. More than fifty nonconnected PACs raised $350,000 or more, but only six contributed that much to candidates. Finally, forty-seven trade/membership/health PACs raised at least $350,000, but less than half (twenty-one) contributed at least that much.[4]

After clarification of the laws, other types of PACs were created. The most prominent was the independent or nonconnected PAC. Its numbers increased from 110 in 1977 to 1,060 in 1989 (see Table 9-1).

Affiliated PACs obtain funds through donations for use for political purposes made by individuals associated with the group. Corporations and labor unions are not allowed to make direct campaign contributions from their treasuries, but treasury funds may be used to establish and administer a PAC and to communicate with people associated with the organization—such as corporate employees or shareholders and their families or labor union members and their families—for voter registration and get-out-the-vote drives.

Scholars, journalists, and many political leaders have expressed increasing concern about the role of political action committees in federal campaign funding. PACs may have enormous influence, affecting who is viewed as a viable candidate, the outcomes of elections, access to the policy-making process, and the content of policy. Because PACs have become a major source of campaign funds for congressional candidates, an inability to obtain PAC support may mean a candidate cannot afford to run an effective campaign. If elected, the successful candidate must be ever mindful of campaign funding sources, both past and future. The escalating costs of congressional and senatorial campaigns force incumbent members of Congress to be watchful of how policy positions taken and votes cast on legislation may affect future fund-raising.

Not all aid from PACs, however, is always welcome. The entry of independent PACs into a contest may be unwelcome, even by the candidate the PACs favor. Moreover, a backlash may develop against independent PACs, particularly those that engage in negative campaigning, and that backlash can extend to the candidate supported by the independent PACs. Some candidates believe that identification with a particular PAC's issue positions, the negative campaign tactics often used by independent PACs, or the fact that a PAC is based outside the constituency hurts rather than helps the candidate's chances for electoral success.

PAC Decision Making

A number of variables influence PAC decision making on campaign contributions. These include the goals of the organization, the expectations of contributors to the PAC, the official positions within the organization of those making the decisions, the strategic premises employed by the PAC, and the PAC's competitive position versus those of other organizations.[5]

An organization may follow a "maintaining strategy," simply seeking to continue access to those members of Congress to whom the sponsoring organization already has access. Or, it may follow an "expanding strategy," attempting to gain access to additional representatives or senators who would not normally be attuned to the PAC's interests because of the limited presence of the represented interest within the member's electoral constituency. The results of the limited amount of research done on this topic suggest that PACs generally emphasize a maintaining strategy, with only a third of the contributions representing an expanding strategy.[6] PACs also tend to be more responsive to the needs of vulnerable representatives and senators who have befriended the PAC's interests.[7]

PAC decision-making patterns vary with the structure of the PAC. If the PAC has staff based in Washington, that staff tends to play a greater role in deciding to whom to contribute and how much to contribute. Contributions are also more likely to occur through the mechanism of a Washington-based fund-raising event.[8] PACs in which substantial funds are raised by local affiliates tend to follow the locals' more parochial concerns. That may not be the most rational allocation strategy to pursue, however. Rationality would require that the PAC allocate funds either to strengthen or broaden access or to replace opponents, but parochialism may require that an already supportive member of Congress receive substantial amounts of locally raised funds.[9] The degree of parochialism appears to vary by type of PAC interest—for example, defense interest PACs are more locally oriented than labor interest PACs.[10]

Partisanship and ideology also may influence PAC decision making—for example, defense PACs tend to be less ideological in their contribution decisions than labor, oil, and auto PACs.[11] Business PACs vary in the extent to which they pursue a partisan support strategy; usually this is associated with the vulnerability of a political party's incumbents. When political tides appear to be favoring Republicans, they may contribute more to Republican challengers than when the political climate is less favorable to that party.

Incumbents' voting records on key votes may be a major factor as well in influencing contribution decisions. An incumbent, for example, who voted against legislation the PAC considered of vital importance would be highly unlikely to receive a campaign contribution. One study of PACs affiliated with Fortune 500 companies found voting records on key legislation to be the second most frequently cited criterium used in making contribution decisions (the most frequently cited was the candidate's attitudes toward business).[12]

Some PACs also must be concerned about competition for supporters, and that concern influences contribution patterns. Contributions that would leave the PAC open to criticism sufficiently severe to cost it future support from donors must be avoided. This is a particular problem for nonconnected PACs that raise funds through mass mail solicitations.[13]

Another factor that influences patterns of PAC contributions is concern about relative influence with key holders of power. If other PACs give to a member of Congress and PAC X does not, will that have an impact on relative access? While some PACs act as though it would, others may pursue a different strategy, gaining the member's attention by giving to his or her challenger. The member of Congress will therefore become more attentive to gain support from the PAC. The effectiveness of that strategy, however, is limited by the extent to which the PAC's preferred policy outcomes conflict with the strength of a contrary ideology held by the member of Congress or the intensity of support for a different policy position present in that member's constituency.

Role of PACs in Campaign Finance

PAC receipts, expenditures, and contributions to congressional candidates have increased significantly since the early 1970s. PAC receipts grew from $19.2 million in 1972 to $369 million in 1988, while PAC expenditures increased from $19 million to $349 million.[14] PAC contributions to congressional candidates increased from $8.5 million for the 1972 elections to $147 million for the 1988 elections. Congressional candidates' dependence on PAC contributions increased by approximately 25 percent between 1982 and 1988.[15]

The changing technology of campaigns stimulates candidates' perceived needs for PAC funds. Extensive use of professional campaign management firms, surveys, television advertising, and the other requirements of modern campaigns have greatly increased campaign costs. Total spending in contests for the Senate increased by 568 percent between 1974 and 1988, with Senate candidates spending a total of $189 million in 1988 compared with $28 million in the 1973-1974 election cycle. Candidates for the House of Representatives spent $221 million in 1987-1988, compared with $44 million in 1973-1974. The average campaign cost for a House incumbent seeking reelection in 1988 was $378,000, while the average campaign cost for Senate incumbents was almost $4 million.[16] In 1974 no candidate for the House spent more than $500,000 in a campaign, but in 1988, 140 House candidates spent more than that.[17]

The dependence on PAC funds to meet the large and ever-increasing costs of campaigns for Congress varies greatly by legislative chamber, incumbency status, and party. In 1988 Democratic House incumbents received 52 percent of their total campaign receipts from PACs, while Republican incumbents in the House obtained 39 percent of their funds from that source. Challengers and candidates for open seats received less, with, for example, Republican challengers receiving 10 percent of their funds from PACs and Democratic challengers receiving 32 percent. Senate candidates are less dependent on PAC money; in 1988 Democratic incumbents obtained 29 percent of their funds from PACS, and Republican incumbents received 26 percent from that source. Challengers and open seat candidates in both parties in the Senate received even less from PACs; neither averaged more than 16 percent.[18]

If candidates obtained a greater share of their funds from other sources, public concern about the role of PACs in American politics would probably lessen. The federal campaign finance laws, however, limit how much political parties may contribute to congressional candidates and spend on their behalf. While those limits are not met in all contests, they may be met in open seat contests or in Senate contests, especially by the Republican campaign finance committees. Permitting parties to give more to their candidates and changing the campaign finance laws to permit citizens to give more to political parties would encourage reduced dependence on PAC funding.

To overcome the limits on party funding of congressional campaigns contained within the federal laws, two practices have developed whose effects can only be estimated. In the first practice the political party organizations guide individual or PAC contributions to particular candidates, and especially to those whom the parties believe have a good chance of winning if adequate funding were available. The second practice is to guide money—particularly money that may not be given under federal law but is permissible in some states, such as campaign contributions from corporate treasury monies—to state political party organizations to be used for various campaign purposes. The estimated value of these funds in the 1988 election was $30 million. These contributions can be used, of course, for a variety of campaign activities that promote the presidential ticket as well as congressional candidates.

In the 1987-1988 election cycle 65.4 percent of PAC contributions went to candidates for the House of Representatives.[19] Senate campaigns are much more expensive than House contests, and the $5,000 per election restriction limits the impact of PAC contributions on Senate contests. Generally, only a finite number of PACs are interested in any one contest, and most PACs do not give to any one candidate the maximum amount of money allowed under the law. Among the factors considered by PACs when determining whether and how much to give are the nature of the state or district and the interests of the PAC within that constituency and, for incumbents, committee assignments, past voting patterns, and help previously provided by the candidate to the PAC in support of its interests. Affiliated PACs tend to be associated with a particular business, industry, or other economic or social entity and may focus on contests in states where the sponsoring interest group is particularly strong. Independent PACs have tended to focus more on Senate than on House contests, particularly in making independent expenditures.

Some members of Congress have established their own PACs. Leadership PACs have been created by party leaders within each chamber, and those who have presidential ambitions have formed PACs as well. These member PACs are used not only to fund research on public issues, speaking trips, and other support-building activity among the general public, but also to make campaign contributions to other candidates for Congress. Contributing to other congressional candidates builds support for the attainment and maintenance of formal positions of power within Congress and may accumulate support for a future presidential campaign. Candidate PACs have been used by former representative Jack Kemp, R-N.Y.; Sen. Robert Dole, R-Kan.; and Sen. Edward Kennedy, D-Mass. Candidate PACs also have been used by eventually nominated presidential candidates such as Ronald Reagan, Walter Mondale, and George Bush.

Strategies: Access and Replacement

Two types of strategies are used by PACs to obtain results from their contributions. One emphasizes contributing to obtain access to members of Congress who are positioned to be most helpful in advancing the policy interests of the PAC. The other focuses on electing people to Congress who will be more helpful to the PAC—that is, the goal is to replace members who are not supportive of the PAC's interests or ideology and to elect people to open seats who are viewed as supportive of the PAC's policy objectives.

The access strategy utilizes contributions to obtain access to members who can be of particular help to the PAC in obtaining its legislative goals. The consequence of this strategy is a disproportionate allocation of funds to incumbents. Those members serving on legislative committees whose subject matter jurisdiction includes areas of interest to the PAC are favored in PAC allocations. Also of importance are members who influence budgets for policies relevant to the PAC or who serve on major procedural committees such as the House Rules Committee. PACs also contribute to leaders of the House and Senate whose influence extends over the entire range of legislative policy. PACs are quite aware of a congressional member's voting record on legislation of interest to them, and many PACs make an effort to reward friends in Congress with campaign contributions.

Many kinds of PACs appear to pursue an access strategy; indeed, incumbent support is the strategy generally pursued by most types of PACs.[20] In the 1987-1988 election cycle, 92 percent of corporate contributions went to incumbents. The percentage given to incumbents in the past, however, has varied with the situation, with corporate PACs giving to challengers when the electoral tides indicate that incumbents who have been less supportive of corporate interests may be vulnerable. Thus in 1980, 57 percent of corporate contributions went to incumbents, and 28 percent were given to Republican challengers to incumbent Democrats and to open seat candidates.[21] Other types of business PACs are also highly likely to support incumbents. In contrast, labor union PACs tend to be highly supportive both of incumbent Democrats and of Democratic open seat and challenger candidates. When Democratic incumbents are more vulnerable, a greater share of labor PAC funds goes to incumbents.

The second strategy of trying to replace members of Congress whose ideology and voting records do not coincide with those preferred by the PAC is more likely to be pursued by nonconnected PACs. The proportion of their contributions going to challengers and open seat candidates ranged from 72 percent in 1978 to 33 percent in 1988.[22] Incumbents who are perceived as unlikely to be defeated usually have only limited amounts directed against them.

Sometimes, however, other criteria are involved in targeting. In 1982 Sen. Paul Sarbanes, D-Md., was selected by the National Conservative Political Action Committee (NCPAC) to serve as an object lesson to other members of Congress. NCPAC assumed that other senators and representatives would see the ads run against Sarbanes on the Washington, D.C.-area television stations. The implied threat was that those whose voting records were not sufficiently in accord with NCPAC's preferences also would be the target of negative advertising campaigns. The negative advertising campaign against Sarbanes was not successful, however, and, indeed, the ads were withdrawn before the general election campaign.[23] While not effective in the Sarbanes campaign, other independent expenditure efforts have been perceived as successful. In 1984, for example, more than $1.1 million was spent to influence Illinois voters to cast their votes against Sen. Charles Percy, R-Ill., who lost his reelection bid by 1 percent of the vote.[24] Independent expenditures also can be important in electing candidates; for example, Sen. Phil Gramm, R-Texas, benefited from more than $500,000 spent on his behalf in the 1984 Senate contest.[25]

Although nonconnected PACs ranked first in the amount of funds collected in 1987-1988, raising $97.4 million, they contributed only 20.8 percent of that amount to candidates. In contrast, corporate PACs contributed 58.3 percent of the $96.4 million they collected, and labor PACs contributed 46.7 percent of the $75 million they raised.[26] Nonconnected PACs find it necessary to spend far more to raise money than do affiliated PACs, who have the support of their sponsoring organizations. Nonconnected PACs also allocate more money for direct expenditures in support of or opposition to particular candidates. In 1987-1988, for example, they spent 16 percent of funds raised on expenditures for or against candidates, with three-fourths of that allotted to the presidential campaign.[27]

Partisan Allocation of PAC Contributions

In 1988 Democratic candidates as a group received 62 percent of campaign contributions made by PACs. The division of PAC money between the two parties' candidates, however, differed greatly by PAC, with 47 percent of corporate PAC contributions and 92 percent of labor union PAC contributions going to Democrats. Corporate PACs largely pursued an access strategy, allocating 90 percent of their contributions to incumbents; trade, membership, and health PACs pursued a similar course of action, granting 82 percent of their contributions to incumbents. Labor split its contributions differently; 67 percent to incumbents, 19 percent to challengers, and 13 percent to open seat candidates. Nonconnected PACs also divided their contributions, giving 64 percent to incumbents, 18 percent to challengers, and 16 percent to open seat candidates. In terms of actual amounts, Democratic Senate candidates received more from PACs than did Republicans ($28 million versus $23 million). Democratic House candidates received substantially more from PACs than did Republicans ($68 million versus $35 million).[28]

PACs and the Policy Process

One way in which PACs affect policy is by influencing who wins House and Senate elections. PAC contributions can affect electoral outcomes in several ways. The first is to help incumbents by inciting reluctance among highly qualified potential candidates to enter the contest. Large sums of money in the incumbent's campaign coffers will intimidate many potential candidates and, in effect, act as a preemptive strike against potential candidates. The potential challenger, knowing the incumbent starts with a significant advantage in name recognition and usually with a favorable image with the voters, often concludes that the chance of defeating the incumbent is quite small and thus does not enter the contest.

Large accumulations of campaign funds also permit early campaigning by the incumbent. The objective is to discourage potential opposition, or, if opposition does develop, to control the issue agenda of the campaign. Other goals of early spending include further increasing the incumbent's fund-raising and enhancing the popularity of potentially weak incumbents.[29]

After the campaign has begun, do challengers and incumbents benefit equally from campaign expenditures? One point of view is that the challenger benefits more, as higher levels of funding enable the challenger to establish name recognition and create awareness of his or her candidacy. Thus, substantial benefit accrues from initial expenditures. As more potential voters become aware of the challenger, however, the effectiveness of expenditures decreases.[30] Whether incumbents, who already have greater name recognition, benefit as much as challengers from their expenditures is the subject of considerable debate among scholars.[31] Incumbents may through their expenditures increase turnout, or they may prevent loss of support among those previously committed to them. Those incumbents who spend the most may be the most vulnerable, or they may be aiming for "overkill" to discourage future opposition or to gain public acclaim which will help them seek another office such as the governor's office, a U.S. Senate seat, or even the presidency.

The effectiveness of the challenger's expenditures may depend on whether political trends are favorable or unfavorable to the challenger's party.[32] If the challenger is a Democrat and noncandidate factors that influence congressional election outcomes—such as the level of approval of presidential job performance and economic conditions—favor the Republicans, the challenger's expenditures will buy less support than if these noncandidate factors were less favorable to the opposition.

In addition to influencing electoral outcomes, PAC contributions can influence public policy in other ways. For most PACs a primary objective of campaign contributions is to gain access to the member of Congress in order to present policy views and have them heard in the legislative setting. When an issue is not one of primary concern to a senator's or representative's constituency and not in conflict with a strongly held party position or the member's ideology, the recipient of campaign contributions from a particular source may be willing to vote in support of that interest group's issue position.

Do campaign contributions generally influence legislative outcomes? Unfortunately, insufficient research exists to permit a definitive answer to the question. Studies that examined the relationship between campaign contributions and legislative roll-call votes reached conflicting conclusions. Some concluded that PAC money affects recipients' support in roll-call votes for legislation. Studies supporting this conclusion analyzed votes on minimum wage legislation;[33] the B-1 bomber;[34] the debt limit, the windfall profits tax, and wage and price controls;[35] trucking deregulation;[36] and legislation of interest to doctors and to auto dealers.[37] A study examining the effects of labor's contributions on both general issues and urban issues concluded that their contributions had a significant impact on five of nine issues relating to urban problems and five of eight general issues, but business contributions were significant in only one issue conflict of each type.[38] Other research confirmed the influence of contributions in support for labor's preferred legislation.[39] Still other research, however, suggested that campaign contributions were not important on roll-call votes on such issues as the Chrysler Corporation's loan guarantee and the windfall profits tax[40] and dairy price supports.[41] One study examined a number of PACs and congressional voting behavior over an eight-year period and concluded that contributions rarely are related to congressional voting patterns. When they are, contributions are a surrogate for other support for the member from the interest group.[42] In summary, the evidence on the importance of PAC contributions in influencing congressional voting behavior is conflicting, and obviously further research on this topic is needed.

Campaign contributions may be given to those who were supportive in the past rather than in an effort to gain future roll-call support. Furthermore, the most important effects of campaign contributions may not be on roll-call votes but on the various earlier stages of the legislative process such as the introduction and sponsorship of bills, the behind-the-scenes negotiations on legislative provisions, the drafting and proposing of amendments, and the markup of bills in subcommittees and committees.

Finally, factors such as constituency interests and ideology and party ties may determine whether campaign contributions influence legislative outcomes. If the issue is important to a significant part of the constituency, for example, constituency interests will likely prevail over PAC policy preferences. Thus, PAC money and the interest group concerns it represents may prevail only on less visible issues where the influences of party, ideology, or constituency are not important.

Criticisms of Interest Group Activity in Campaign Finance

The increased role of PACs since the early 1970s in funding campaigns for Congress has generated substantial criticism. Certainly PAC funding plays a role in who is elected to Congress, even if the evidence about the impact of PAC contributions on roll-call voting is mixed and the research is too limited to draw firm conclusions about its influence on other stages of the congressional decision-making process.

Organization simplifies the representation of interests in a large and complex society, and PACs are one manifestation of the organized representation of interests. Criticism of the campaign finance system, however, has resulted in a number of suggestions for changes in federal law. One issue underlying the suggested changes is whether the total amount of PAC money a candidate may receive should be limited. Proponents argue that such a limitation will limit PAC influence; opponents point out that limiting PAC contributions will make it more difficult for nonincumbents to seek office.

Two ways to overcome this problem are (1) to permit individuals to make larger contributions to candidates and to political parties and (2) to permit political parties both to give more to candidates of the party and to spend more on behalf of party candidates. Generally, the Democrats have opposed these suggestions as being more likely to favor Republicans, who could both raise more money from larger contributions and have more money to give to the party's candidates.

Another criticism of PACs is that they weaken the role of the individual citizen in politics. This criticism is based on the disparity between the amount an individual may contribute ($1,000) and the amount a PAC may contribute ($5,000). To increase the role of individuals the limit on individual contributions could be increased or the limit on PAC contributions reduced. Increasing the maximum an individual may give, however, increases the influence of those more affluent.

Another proposal is to encourage more individuals to give small contributions by permitting them to write off part of the contribution as a deduction from gross income in figuring income taxes or as a deduction from taxes owed. Some proposals would permit the deduction only for contributions to candidates or parties within the state the contributor resides.

Yet another idea is to reduce dependence on PAC money by suggesting limits on the amounts that candidates may spend in their campaigns. Those who accepted the limits would receive partial campaign funding from a government-funded campaign fund. If a candidate accepted the limits but the opponent did not, the candidate would receive more from the fund. But finding the money for such a fund in a very tight federal budget and convincing candidates to limit voluntarily how much they spend are highly unlikely in the present political climate. Other suggestions include establishing firm limits on how much may be spent on congressional campaigns (thereby benefiting the better-known incumbent and disadvantaging lesser-known challengers) and financing campaigns with public funds (again probably benefiting incumbents).

President George Bush proposed a number of campaign finance reforms to Congress in 1989. These included abolishing most types of PACs, retaining only nonconnected PACs (all PACs would, in effect, become nonconnected), increasing how much political parties may spend on behalf of candidates, prohibiting leadership PACs from transferring funds to the campaign committees of other members, permitting each congressional candidate to take only $75,000 from PACs, and establishing voluntary limits on how much a candidate may raise ($200,000 for the primary and $200,000 for the general election) with the candidate in return receiving discounted television and radio time and postage costs. Bundling of funds by PACs also would be prohibited, and fuller disclosure of the sponsorship of independent expenditure campaigns would be required.[43] A number of other reform proposals were being considered by Congress as well, as the nation entered its third century.

A potential problem that the proposals do not address is the imbalance in the representation of interests through PACs. For example, the rapid increase in the number of business-related PACs and the considerable potential for their future growth, compared to the much more limited potential for the growth of labor-related PACs, suggests that an imbalance in this kind of access/influence mechanism between these two types of interests exists and could become much larger. While it could be argued that business PAC activities are merely formalizing that which occurred previously—free services, for example—the amounts being contributed to candidates are larger than in earlier elections. Of course, it also can be pointed out that labor PACs do much more than contribute money; they are very active in the mobilization of other types of resources as well. Other types of interests—those less affluent—are not represented through money-based mechanisms of representation such as PACs.

In summary, the politics of PACs and PAC reform in the funding of campaigns for Congress present many problems. PACs are here and

are not likely to be abolished, and their role in the political process will
continue, as will the controversies about their role.

Notes

1. Federal Election Commission press release, February 24, 1989.
2. See Edwin Epstein, "The Emergence of Political Action Committees," in
   Political Finance, ed. Herbert Alexander (Beverly Hills, Calif.: Sage
   Publications, 1979), 159-179.
3. *Buckley v. Valeo*, 424 U.S. 1 (1976).
4. Federal Election Commission press release, April 9, 1989.
5. Theodore J. Eismeier and Philip H. Pollock III, "An Organizational
   Analysis of Political Action Committees," *Political Behavior* 7 (1985):
   192-216.
6. John R. Wright, "PAC Contributions, Lobbying, and Representation,"
   Journal of Politics 51 (August 1989): 713-729.
7. J. David Gopoian, "What Makes PACs Tick? An Analysis of the
   Allocation Patterns of Economic Interest Groups," *American Journal of
   Political Science* 28 (May 1984): 259-281.
8. Larry J. Sabato, *PAC Power: Inside the World of Political Action
   Committees* (New York: Norton, 1985), 42-43.
9. John R. Wright, "PACs, Contributions, and Roll Calls: An Organizational Perspective," *American Political Science Review* 79 (June 1985):
   400-414.
10. Gopoian, "What Makes PACs Tick?" 279.
11. Ibid., 271.
12. Ann B. Matasar, *Corporate PACs and Federal Campaign Financing
    Laws* (New York: Quorum Books, 1986), Table 13, 58.
13. Eismeier and Pollock, "Organizational Analysis," 207-208.
14. Federal Election Commission press release, April 9, 1989.
15. Computed from Table 13.10 in Norman J. Ornstein, Thomas E. Mann,
    and Michael J. Malbin, *Vital Statistics on Congress 1989-1990* (Wash-
    ington, D.C.: American Enterprise Institute, 1990), 88-92.
16. Ibid., Table 3.1, 71.
17. Ibid., Table 3.3, 74.
18. Ibid., Table 3.10, 88-92.
19. Computed from data contained in the Federal Election Commission press
    release, April 9, 1989.
20. Frank J. Sorauf, *Money in American Politics* (Glenview, Ill.: Scott,
    Foresman, 1988), 103.
21. Federal Election Commission press release, March 2, 1982.
22. Federal Election Commission press release, May 10, 1979.
23. Polls conducted by the *Baltimore Sun* indicated that the proportion of the
    public approving of Senator Sarbanes's job performance remained station-
    ary, while the proportion disapproving increased from 20 percent to 29

percent between October 1981 and February 1982. During that period several NCPAC ads critical of Sarbanes's performance were shown on television stations broadcasting to Maryland residents. See Karen Hosler, "Voter Shifts Favor Hughes, Hurt Sabanes," *Baltimore Sun,* February 22, 1982, A1.

24. Federal Election Commission press release, October 4, 1985.
25. Ibid.
26. Computed from data in the Federal Election Commission press release, April 9, 1989, 7.
27. Federal Election Commission press releases, February 24, 1989, and April 9, 1989.
28. Computed from data in the Federal Election Commission press release, April 9, 1989, 4-5.
29. Paul West, " 'Early Media' Push '86 Campaign on the Air," *Baltimore Sun,* December 12, 1985, 1A.
30. See Gary C. Jacobson, "Money and Votes Reconsidered: Congressional Elections, 1972-1982," *Public Choice* 47 (1985): 43-46; and Jacobson, "The Effects of Campaign Spending in House Elections: New Evidence for Old Arguments," *American Journal of Political Science* 34 (May 1990): 334-362.
31. See Donald P. Green and Jonathan S. Krasno, "Salvation for the Spendthrift Incumbent: Re-estimating the Effects of Campaign Spending in House Elections," *American Journal of Political Science* 32 (1988): 884-907; Jacobson's response in "Effects of Campaign Spending"; and Green and Krasno's response in "Rebuttal to Jacobson's 'New Evidence for Old Arguments,' " *American Journal of Political Science* 34 (May 1990): 363-374.
32. Gary C. Jacobson, "Strategic Politicians and the Dynamics of U.S. House Elections, 1946-1986," *American Journal of Political Science* 83 (September 1989): 773-794.
33. Jonathan I. Silberman and Garey C. Durden, "Determining Legislative Preferences on Minimum Wage: An Economic Approach," *Journal of Political Economy* 94 (1986): 317-329.
34. Henry W. Chappel, Jr., "Campaign Contributions and Congressional Voting: A Simultaneous Probit-Tobit Model," *Review of Economics and Statistics* (February 1982): 77-83.
35. James B. Kau and Paul H. Rubin, *Congressmen, Constituents, and Contributors: Determinants of Roll Call Votes* (Boston: Martinus Nijhoff, 1982), Table 7.5, 96-97.
36. John P. Frendreis and Richard W. Waterman, "PAC Contributions and Legislative Behavior: Senate Voting on Trucking Deregulation," *Social Science Quarterly* 66 (June 1985): 401-412.
37. K. F. Brown, "Campaign Contributions and Congressional Voting" (Paper presented at the annual meeting of the American Political Science Association, Chicago, September 1-4, 1983).
38. Kau and Rubin, *Congressmen, Constituents, and Contributors.*

39. Gregory M. Saltzman, "Congressional Voting on Labor Issues: The Role of PACs," *Industrial and Labor Relations Review* 40 (January 1987): 163-179.
40. Diana M. Evans, "PAC Contributions and Roll-call Voting: Conditional Power," in *Interest Group Politics*, 2d ed., ed. Allan J. Cigler and Burdett A. Loomis (Washington, D.C.: CQ Press, 1986), 114-132.
41. W. P. Welch, "Campaign Contributions and House Voting: Milk Money and Dairy Price Supports," *Western Political Quarterly* 35 (December 1982): 478-495.
42. Janet M. Grenzke, "PACs and the Congressional Supermarket: The Currency Is Complex," *American Journal of Political Science* 33 (February 1989): 1-24.
43. "Major Legislative Plans Compared," *Congressional Quarterly Weekly Report,* July 29, 1989, 1919-1923.

10. PACS AND PARTIES IN AMERICAN POLITICS

Frank J. Sorauf

The escalating campaign finance role of political action committees (PACs) in the aftermath of the 1974 revision of the Federal Election Campaign Act (FECA) has raised a variety of questions about the relationship between American political parties and interest groups. The explosion in PAC numbers and expenditures has been viewed by some as contributing to the decline of political parties, to the extent that organized interests have become major sources of candidate funding and have undertaken certain party-like activities such as registering new voters and holding candidate forums or events.

In this chapter political scientist Frank Sorauf contends that the growth of PACs is less invidious than has been suggested by some. He concludes that the rise of PACs has in no way contributed to the decline of the political parties, which was well under way before the rise of the PAC phenomenon.

The relationship between parties and PACs is very complex: part competitive, part cooperative, and part accommodating. PACs and political parties compete at the level of mobilizing the political influence and resources of millions of Americans, with parties attracting the more involved and committed individuals and PACs involving people with lower levels of political attachment. PACs have not had great success in such party-like activities as registering and mobilizing voters, and they "remain specialized channelers of cash to candidates and a far cry from the electoral organizations represented by political parties." In the current era, according to Sorauf, both the PACs and the parties remain subservient to the candidates, especially incumbents.

Without being explicit or self-conscious about it, American political parties and interest groups struck a historic bargain in the twentieth century. The parties dominated the politics of the electoral processes; the groups dominated the politics of policy making. One chose candidates and organized campaigns; the other lobbied and made representations. It was a division of labor that seemed orderly and particularly well suited to the skills and assets of each kind of political organization. And so the parties and the groups grew up with the American democracy, both nourishing it and being shaped by it.

To be sure, the division was never complete. Even the classically electoral American parties had a role in policy making, and some interest groups, especially labor, began early on to recruit candidates for office and participate in their campaigns. But it is probably fair to say that the first major challenge to the division of effort—the first real crossing of the line—came with the rapid growth in the 1970s of those now-famous group vehicles, political action committees. As campaigns for American public office began to absorb greater and greater sums of cash, the PACs, specialists in collecting and transferring campaign funds to candidates, seized the opportunity of an organizational lifetime.

By entering the electoral realm of the political parties, the PACs began with the parties one of the closest, most complex set of relationships in recent American politics between two types of political organizations. In part competitive and in part cooperative, these relationships clarify the strengths and special roles of both the parties and the PACs. They also underscore their special and particular weaknesses.

The Rise and Challenge of the PACs

PAC growth after the revision of the Federal Election Campaign Act (FECA) in 1974 was unprecedented. By the end of 1974, 608 PACs had registered with the Federal Election Commission (FEC); by the end of 1989 the count was 4,178, after reaching a record high of 4,268 a year earlier. More significant, perhaps, PAC contributions to candidates for Congress rose from $22.6 million in 1976, the first election covered by FECA, to $147.9 million in the 1988 campaigns, or more than a sixfold increase. In 1976 PAC contributions accounted for 19.6 percent of the money raised by all candidates for Congress; by 1988 that share had risen to 31 percent.

In a narrow and specific sense the PAC explosion resulted from the FECA of 1974. In an effort to end the flow of dollars from wealthy individuals, Congress set $1,000 limits on individual contributions to a candidate in an election but pegged the limit at $5,000 for multicandidate committees giving to a minimum of five federal candidates. (Effectively, the limits are $2,000 and $10,000 per two-year election cycle, since the primary and general election are considered separate elections.) Moreover, Congress placed a single annual limit of $25,000 on individual contributions to federal campaigns while placing no aggregate limit on multimember committees.[1] The incentives to organized giving were obvious. Furthermore, the FECA made clear for the first time that groups could in fact legally create such PACs to collect and contribute political money. Later clarification by the Federal Election Commission also established that a PAC's sponsoring group—

a corporation, membership association, or labor union, for example—could pay the PAC's administrative and overhead expenses.[2]

In a much broader sense, the growth of PACs reflects all the changes well under way in American electoral politics before the 1970s. The two major American parties had begun to lose their effectiveness. By the 1970s they had far less say in the choosing of candidates for office and in the campaigns those candidates ran. Moreover, voters tended increasingly to vote for candidates rather than parties and to split tickets to do so. A more selective electorate wanted to pick among candidates and issue positions rather than vote loyally, even blindly, for a party ticket. Thus, the party organizations of the cities and counties across the land began to be understaffed and underused. Freed from these enfeebled parties, candidates could run their own campaigns and hire their own campaign apparatus and expertise. But all of that took cash rather than the volunteered activities the parties had specialized in. Therefore, as candidates became the new impresarios of their own campaigns, cash costs rose sharply and the candidates had to pay the bills themselves. Inevitably the candidates began to cultivate the contributors who would provide the cash.[3]

In no sense then did the rise of PACs contribute to the decline of the political parties. It is true that PACs had been present in American politics from the 1940s—indeed, the first one, the Political Action Committee of the Congress of Industrial Organizations (CIO) in 1943, gave its name to the genre—but they entered campaign politics in a big way only in the 1970s, well after the onset of party decline. The fortunes of the PACs and political parties intersected in the 1970s both because of the decline of the parties and because of the transformation of American campaigning. New campaign media—television reached 9 percent of the American households in 1950 but 87 percent by 1960—combined with new expertise in polling and the art of campaigning to reshape the face of campaigns. PACs were superbly designed for the uses of newly autonomous candidates in the new campaign politics. The political parties of that time were not.

One may certainly argue that the flourishing PACs pushed the parties a bit on their downward decline. But it is also the case that they increasingly forced the parties to adapt in ways that have slowed or even broken that decline, for in the classic American way, the parties by the 1980s began to conclude that "if you can't beat em, join 'em."

In a flurry of adaptation in the 1970s and 1980s the Democrats and Republicans retooled for the new campaign politics. In the 1970s William Brock, chairman of the Republican National Committee (RNC), began to move the RNC into computer-based solicitations of contributions and into the new arts and skills of media-based campaigning. The Democrats lagged, but in the early 1980s the Democratic National Committee (DNC) began in a serious way to follow the Republican lead in raising funds for candidates and in providing them with the new skills and technologies. The result was the creation of national party organs that served the candidates in a quasi-commercial relationship, making the parties themselves, in the words of one scholar, "service-vendor-broker" parties.[4] In short, the parties conceded the ascendancy of the candidates and began to vie with the PACs to assist them.

Thus, the PACs and political parties entered a period of complex relationships in the 1980s, one of mixed competition and cooperation. On one level, of course, there was the great national competition for domination of electoral politics, and assessing the competition depended on what one counted. PACs clearly accounted for a far greater share of the cash receipts of congressional candidates than did party committees—in 1988 the difference was 31 percent to 1 percent. But the parties can spend "on behalf of" candidates in a way that PACs cannot, and in 1988 those party expenditures totaled almost five times the sum of direct party contributions to candidates for Congress.[5] Furthermore, the parties provided the candidates with reasonably priced campaign services and expertise, and they also advertised and organized on behalf of the party as a party and on behalf of the party's whole ticket of candidates. If the measure is cash alone, the PACs have a substantial lead; if one includes these party-like activities of the political parties, the balance between PACs and parties is much closer to parity.

PACs and political parties compete at another level: mobilizing the political influence and resources of millions of Americans. This mobilization is what political scientists have in mind when they refer to such organizations as PACs and parties as aggregators, intermediaries, or forgers of linkages. They bind millions of individuals together in the organized pursuit of political influence. By the most modest standards PACs now draw on the cash resources of more than 10 million donors.[6] Although in 1987-1988 both national political parties together raised only $182.2 million compared with the $384.5 million all PACs raised, the parties can mobilize Americans for a far broader range of activities, volunteering their time and skills in addition to their cash contributions. Some of the PAC donors are also active in a political party, but it is only logical that the two kinds of organizations compete for scarce individual commitments. The competition is softened somewhat, however, by the PACs and parties finding their own separate niches in that competitive market. The parties attract the more involved and committed individuals, the PACs the individuals with lower levels of interest in and commitment to politics.[7]

A look at specific PACs and specific parties reveals relationships of cooperation and accommodation mixed with those of competition. Labor PACs traditionally have had a different relationship with the Democratic party than with the Republican party, as have corporate PACs. Moreover, the PAC-party relationship varies according to whether the party one is speaking of is the DNC or RNC or whether one is referring to the party campaign committees in the two houses of Congress.[8]

PACs as Supporters of Partisans

Of the 4,268 PACs in existence at the end of 1988, 3,287 had contributed to that year's congressional elections. Behind the decisions to contribute—and the decisions about whom to contribute to—lay a tangle of complicated, even contradictory, goals and strategies. Scholars have identified the chief ones, and, although the terms may differ,[9] they fall into three broad categories:

1. *Partisan/ideological:* the goals of ideas and issues (the purposive ones) that may be expressed by supporting the candidates of a sympathetic party or by supporting specific candidates who pass some test of "rightness" on issues or ideology.
2. *Access/legislative:* the goals of pragmatic dealing with legislators in which the PAC gives to candidates because, should they win, they can admit the PAC to places of power in the legislature.
3. *Organizational/local:* PAC attempts to respond to special and intraorganizational goals by supporting the favored candidates of donors, by supporting local members of Congress, or by responding to demands that it show a record of supporting winners.

Because very few PACs can afford to pursue one of this set of goals to the exclusion of others, it is in the skill and finesse with which the PAC mixes strategies that it maintains credibility with its donors and its parent while having some broader political impact on policy making.

In their contributions to congressional candidates, therefore, PACs assume two rather different positions vis-à-vis the candidates of the two parties. In some instances (the first category above) they make contributions to candidates *because* of their party affiliation. If they find that the Republican party, for example, takes positions they like on issues of importance to them—whether it is one issue or an extensive conservative or business-oriented ideology—they support its candidates to support the party and to maximize its chance of becoming the majority party in one or both houses of Congress. PACs' pursuits of the second and third categories above, however, cut across parties. They do not really support parties *qua* parties; they support the parties of their chosen candidates because all candidates happen to have party ties. Separating the reasons for so-called party support is at the heart of the issue of PAC partisanship.

Understanding PAC contribution patterns begins with the single most important fact about them: they are going increasingly to incumbent members of Congress running for reelection. Only 60.4 percent of all PAC contributions to House candidates in 1978 went to incumbents, but that percentage had risen to 80.5 in 1988. The jump in support for Senate incumbents within the same period went from 48 percent to 66.8 percent. Obviously, the percentages of PAC monies going to challengers and open seat candidates dropped comparably in that period. By 1988 they were 10 percent and 9.5 percent, respectively, in races for the House. Thus, PACs had come to favor incumbents over challengers by a ratio of eight to one in House campaigns.

What accounts for the increasing diversion of PAC contributions to incumbents? Ultimately, PACs give money for the same reasons that most individuals do: to influence policy making in government whether by electing like-minded people to office or by persuading those already in office. The tactic of electing like-minded people works only if the candidates supported have a chance of winning office. Increasingly, however, only incumbent candidates win elections, leaving little competition and little choice in congressional elections. In 1988, 85.2 percent of Senate incumbents and 98.5 percent of House incumbents won reelection. Moreover, their margins of victory expanded; 88.5 percent of the 435 House races in 1988 were won by more than 60 percent of the votes cast; the comparable percentage in 1980 was 72.9. Why? Incumbents build enormous advantages in name recognition and political support by reason of all the advantages of incumbency, and they parlay those advantages into expectations of reelection and, consequently, into very ample campaign funds.

Growing incumbent power therefore has discouraged PAC strategies other than that of cultivating or maintaining legislative access. No group of PACs better illustrates the resulting dilemmas than the PACs of corporations (Table 10-1). Given the apprehensions that many if not most American corporations have about the Democratic party, it is initially surprising to see their high level of support for Democratic incumbents. Surely it is a sign of the powerful pull of the strategies of legislative pragmatism and access. But their true Republican orientation is revealed in the use of their money in open seat races where there is no incumbent to pressure them into the pragmatic strategies. Indeed, that disparity in the partisan contribution patterns of corporate PACs

Table 10-1 PAC Contributions to Democrats and Republicans among House Incumbents, Challengers, and Open Seat Candidates: 1988 (millions of dollars)

Type of PAC	Incumbents		Challengers		Open Seat	
	Dem.	Rep.	Dem.	Rep.	Dem.	Rep.
Corporate	15.7	13.5	.3	1.0	.6	1.3
Labor	16.7	1.9	5.2	.1	3.2	.1
Membership	14.6	10.4	1.0	.6	1.2	1.3
Nonconnected	4.9	2.5	1.5	.7	1.1	.8

SOURCE: Federal Election Commission.

NOTE: These four categories of PACs are those for which the Federal Election Commission aggregates data. The "Corporate" and "Labor" categories are self-evident groupings of the PAC parent organizations. "Membership" PACs are those of associations; FEC calls them "Trade/Membership/Health" PACs. "Nonconnected" PACs do not have sponsoring parent organizations. FEC also reports data on two other kinds of PACs: those of cooperatives and those of corporations without stock. These two types of PACs, however, accounted for less than 4 percent of PAC contributions to congressional candidates in 1988.

has been a matter of contention among them, the more ideological or partisan corporate PACs charging the others with excessive pragmatism or cowardice in rushing to support the Democratic incumbents.

At the other extreme is the overwhelmingly Democratic giving pattern of the labor PACs (Table 10-1). They are, of course, about as ideologically homogeneous as the PACs of corporations.[10] In their case, however, the course of pragmatism and the course of ideology are more congruent. Were the Republicans to control the House by the same margin that Democrats do today, and were their control to seem as unassailable as the Democrats' control does today, the labor PACs might well experience the same problems corporate PACs faced in the 1980s but probably not as severe. For one thing, labor PACs are more homogeneous in their interests than corporate PACs; moreover, they have a longer history of involvement in electoral politics and its risks and long-term strategies, especially those involved in supporting challengers running against incumbents.

Powerful incumbents therefore shape PAC strategies and thereby skew the partisan patterns of their contributions. Democrats as a group do very well under the status quo. In 1988, for example, Democrats running for the Senate raised $28.3 million from PACs; the Republicans raised $23.4 million. In the House campaigns for that year PACs gave $68.6 million to Democratic candidates and $35.6 million to Republicans. In fact, as the Democratic majority became more en-

Figure 10-1 PAC Support for House Democratic Candidates, 1980-1988

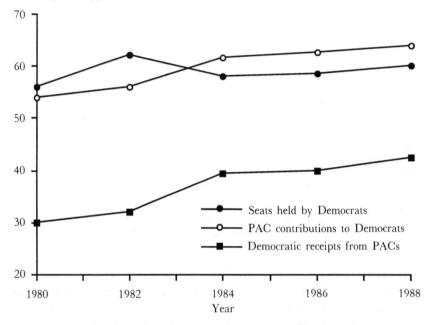

Percentage of support

Seats held by Democrats
PAC contributions to Democrats
Democratic receipts from PACs

Year

trenched in the House and as its campaign committee became more aggressive in fund-raising, Democrats got a progressively larger share of PAC contributions to House candidates, and PAC contributions began to account for a rising share of their receipts (Figure 10-1). Thus, of all PAC money contributed to congressional candidates in 1980 and 1982 Democrats received 54.4 percent and 56.1 percent, respectively; by 1988 their share was 65.7 percent.

   In addition to contributions to candidates, PACs can affect the outcome of elections through so-called independent expenditures. These expenditures—on newspaper ads, billboards, or direct mailings, for example—are made in a campaign without the cooperation or prior knowledge of the candidate. Such spending may be either in support of or opposition (negative spending) to a candidate. Spending in support of Democratic candidates and in opposition to Republican candidates produces a pro-Democratic total. The reverse calculation produces a pro-Republican figure. In their independent spending in 1988 PACs supported Democrats to the tune of $2.5 million; they spent $4.5 million to support the Republican cause. It was the only Republican edge in 1988 PAC spending.

Regardless of how much PAC giving is motivated by a desire to support a political party and how much giving supports a party more or less unintentionally, the result is that PACs heavily support the candidates of the incumbent majority party—the Democrats. Moreover, as the power of incumbents to secure reelection and to raise campaign money grows, the edge of the Democrats increases. If one adds all PAC contributions to all PAC independent spending for candidates for both houses of Congress, in 1988 the Democrats benefited from a $99.3 million PAC outlay. The Republicans reaped support of $63.6 million. (The totals in 1980 were virtually even, Democrats at $30.9 million and Republicans at $29.5 million.) Such are the advantages of being the majority party. Democratic control of the two houses of Congress makes access to Democrats more advantageous than to Republicans; moreover, their majority status means they have the larger number of incumbent candidates for reelection.

The relationship between PAC contributions and Democratic control of the Congress is not easy to untangle. In House races PACs give money to Democrats not to help them win but because they think the Democrats *will* win. Their contributions to incumbents may help a few of them in electoral trouble fend off challengers, either within their own party or in the other party, but, fundamentally, money flows to House incumbents, and especially to the incumbent majority party, because they seem certain to win reelection. Members do leave the House because of death or retirement, of course, but increasingly their successors come from the party of the previous incumbent. Challengers to the incumbents running for reelection increasingly find it hard to raise campaign funds, for individual contributors as well as PACs tend to give to incumbents. Party committees continue to act as substantial supporters of challengers, largely as a part of broader or long-term strategies designed, for example, to maximize votes for a whole ticket or to groom a candidate for a later race. Nonparty contributors, however, will not or cannot assume the high risk of supporting what are at best long-shot candidates.

Competitiveness in Senate campaigns, however, is in better shape. Although 85.2 percent of senatorial incumbents won reelection in 1988, that percentage is well below the 98.5 percent in the House. And in the 1988 Senate races only 54.5 percent of the winners won with more than 60 percent of the general election vote as opposed to 88.5 percent in the House. PACs respond with lower levels of support for incumbents: 66.8 percent in Senate races in 1988 versus 80.5 percent in House campaigns. In fact, almost 16 percent of PAC funds spent in Senate races in 1988 went to challengers; the comparable figure for House challengers was 10 percent. But, then, Senate candidates depend much less on PACs than do House candidates—22.9 percent of their receipts come from PACs versus 36.7 percent for House candidates. Thus, while the greater competitiveness of Senate elections would seem to open more electoral opportunities for PACs, those opportunities are diminished by the lesser role PACs play in Senate campaigns.

PACs and the Party Organizations

Given the partisan nature of American elections, PACs have no alternative to helping the candidates of a political party. They are not forced, however, to contribute directly to political party committees. And, historically, they have not done so with great generosity. Over the decade of the 1980s PAC contributions to the national and congressional campaign committees of the Democratic and Republican parties rose within the modest range of $3-$10 million (Table 10-2). Both the rate of growth and the magnitude of the sums were greater within the Democratic party. More telling, surely, are the relative importance of the PAC contributions. In 1988 PAC funds accounted for only 2.8 percent of the total receipts of the DNC but 18.5 and 21 percent, respectively, of the Democratic committees in the Senate and House. PACs accounted for only 1.1, 1.1, and 2.2 percent, respectively, of the receipts of the same three Republican committees. Political parties, surprisingly and perhaps ironically, raise a far greater share of their money from individual contributors; they have been able to make direct solicitation work, but most candidates, especially those for the House, have not.

Embedded in the data of Table 10-2 is another unmistakable trend: the faster rate of growth of PAC contributions to the parties' legislative campaign committees than to their national committees. The signs of a strategy of legislative pragmatism reappear. Indeed, a look at the contributory behavior of the main types of PACs (Table 10-3) reveals a pattern not unlike that for their contributions to candidates for Congress (Table 10-1).

The two committees of each political party in Congress (that is, the NRSC and NRCC, DSCC and DCCC) are in effect the campaign committees of the congressional incumbents of each party. While the incumbents individually pursue their own goals in campaign finance, their respective campaign committees pursue their collective interests. The overriding collective interest, of course, is in maximizing the number of seats held by the party. In return for support, the legislative party offers sympathy and access for the contributor's cause. Thus, corporate PACs contribute substantial sums to Democratic committees in the House and Senate, just as they contribute to Democratic candidates, but at the national committee level they direct their

Table 10-2 PAC Contributions to National Party Committees, 1980-1988 (millions of dollars)

Committees	1980	1982	1984	1986	1988
Democratic committees					
National (DNC)	1.16	1.03	1.44	1.26	1.49
Senate (DSCC)	.10	.97	1.78	2.37	3.02
House (DCCC)	.29	.80	1.47	1.94	2.62
Total	1.55	2.80	4.69	5.57	7.13
Republican committees					
National (RNC)	.47	.41	.67	.37	1.01
Senate (NRSC)	.21	.49	.38	.71	.73
House (NRCC)	.14	.16	.24	.39	.75
Total	.82	1.06	1.29	1.47	2.49

SOURCE: Federal Election Commission.

NOTE: DNC—Democratic National Committee; DSCC—Democratic Senatorial Campaign Committee; DCCC—Democratic Congressional Campaign Committee; RNC—Republican National Committee; NRSC—National Republican Senatorial Committee; NRCC—National Republican Congressional Committee.

contributions to the Republican National Committee rather than its Democratic counterpart. Labor PACs, freed of the conflict between partisan and pragmatic goals, support Democratic committees heavily across the board. The politically diverse nonconnected and membership PACs move in too many directions to bear generalization. Again, being the majority party in the Congress works to the Democrats' enormous advantage.

Direct transactions between PAC and party are public because the FECA requires full reporting. Far more indirect, even fugitive, are the cooperative, even collaborative, relationships between PAC and party. Two major examples are party attempts to direct PAC contributions to its worthiest candidates and to channel PAC contributions to legal recipients in so-called soft money contributions. In both cases the party acts as a broker, an intermediary, or a cue-giver to PACs, and because the party is neither the giver nor the spender of the money, its activities do not have to be reported to the FEC. The clearest picture of such activities is a mosaic of journalistic tidbits.

The story of the political parties as cue-givers for PAC contributions begins with the parties' constantly intense political nature. Their political information and sophistication usually outstrip those of PACs, a fact that many PACs freely acknowledge. Those PACs that place a high priority on partisan/ideological strategies often take cues from the political parties about the worthiness of challenger and open seat

Table 10-3 Contributions to National Party Committees by Four Main Types of PAC, 1988

Type of PAC	RNC	NRSC	NRCC	DNC	DSCC	DCCC
Corporate	$ 561,200	$307,680	$242,000	$ 176,452	$1,121,550	$ 962,875
Labor	61,050	10,951	25,000	775,050	831,800	676,702
Nonconnected	55,300	29,952	39,150	92,785	250,709	232,384
Membership	254,700	345,223	416,000	342,375	645,814	614,552
Other	76,800	34,350	25,000	100,600	171,500	133,750
Total	1,009,050	728,156	747,150	1,487,262	3,021,373	2,620,263

SOURCE: Federal Election Commission.

NOTE: "Other" includes the PACs of cooperatives and corporations without stock.

candidates, sometimes even of incumbents in a close race. The party committees in the Congress in particular have PAC liaison officials who mediate the contacts between the PACs and the candidates and who also preside over periodic "meat markets" at which supplicant candidates are paraded before a roomful of PAC managers. Party committees may go even a step further to stage fund-raising events for the chosen few among their hopefuls and provide the star attractions at the events.

Party channeling of PAC money also may take a second route—that of soft money. Generically, soft money is money contributed to candidates or parties in less-regulated state or local venues, but whose contribution would have been illegal had it been given under federal law. If, for example, a PAC has contributed the maximum $10,000 to a candidate for the Senate, a party committee may suggest that it give additional money to the candidate's party in the state for party building or voter registration drives or for campaigning for the entire party ticket. Or, if the PAC has reached the statutory limit in contributions to a national party committee, a contribution to a state party or state candidates may free that national committee from the need to transfer the funds itself.

It is as difficult to put dollar values on such forms of mobilizing and cue-giving as it is easy to tally up the sums of direct PAC contributions to parties or candidates. The first case—cue-giving about candidates—is, nevertheless, the more valuable. Not only does it raise money for the party's candidates, but it also raises it efficiently and rationally. The party can mobilize PACs behind the candidates most likely to win and thus serve its goal of maximizing party seats in Congress. Decisions made by PACs on their own—and perhaps influenced by poor information and a PAC's conflicting goals—often work at cross purposes with the political party's goal.

PAC contributions to the flow of soft money, are not of major importance for a number of reasons. The greatest sums of soft money flow in presidential campaigns, and most PACs are not active in presidential politics. The major soft money contributors to state parties via national party brokering are individuals who have reached the $25,000 annual limit in contributions to federal campaigns, followed by corporations and trade unions whose direct contributions are outlawed under federal law.[11]

Trends, Changes, and Adaptations

As the number of PACs and their contributions began to rise so steeply in the late 1970s, it seemed very possible that PACs would develop into potent electoral organizations. One kind of PAC already had gone down that road; labor PACs had been registering voters, endorsing candidates, organizing campaigns or campaign events, and turning out the voters on election day for some years. In the optimistic years around 1980 other PACs began, however cautiously, similar political party-like electoral activities: registration of new voters, candidate events or forums, and even a few attempts to get voters to the polls.[12] Those tentative beginnings never led to much, and most PACs today—always with the exception of labor PACs—remain specialized channelers of cash to candidates and a far cry from the electoral organizations that political parties are.

More surprising than their failure to become party-like, however, was the failure of PACs to develop, even within their limited role, as funders of campaigns. Initially, observers speculated that as PACs matured and became politically sophisticated they would become more "rational" and risk-taking in their electoral activities—that is, they would pursue an issue, a program, or an ideology in ways that maximized the electoral effect of their contributions. To state the point differently, they seemed poised to focus on influencing elections by reducing their aid to safe or hopeless candidates and by setting issue criteria for the candidates they supported. But in the 1980s the PACs collectively failed to "develop" in this way. On the one hand, the rising power of incumbents and their ability to stimulate PAC contributions worked against it. Pressures within the PACs worked against it as well; they never got away from the intraorganizational need to support winners, to placate the political preferences of donors, and to support local officeholders and candidates.

In short, with the exception of labor PACs, PACs remain focused on the single electoral purpose of getting resources (largely cash) to candidates for their campaigns, especially candidates likely to win public office. Moreover, they do so increasingly without observing the two desiderata of an electoral strategy intended to elect the largest number of like-minded candidates: supporting only candidates of similar views and intervening only in races close enough to be affected by new financial support.

Indeed, the contrast between labor PACs and all other PACs makes all of that abundantly clear (see Table 10-4). Labor PACs are more centralized than the other PACs, and they have more funds and make larger average contributions. They also are more closely allied with one political party and less tied to incumbents and the strategy of legislative access. Labor PACs are embedded in a broader and older social, economic, and political movement, one in which political risk-taking is an old tradition and in which overt politicality and Democratic allegiance have become almost a way of life. Other PACs come

Table 10-4   Comparison of Labor PACs and Other PACs, 1988

	Labor PACs	*Other PACs*
Average expenditures	$184,717	$65,477
Average contribution to:		
House incumbents	2,067	1,002
Senate incumbents	3,441	1,889
Percent of all contributions		
to House/Senate candidates:		
House incumbents	68.4	84.5
Senate incumbents	54.0	69.0
House Democrats	92.4	56.3
Senate Democrats	91.5	41.2

SOURCE: Federal Election Commission.

from different political traditions. Their parent organizations exist for far more limited purposes than the labor movement, and their donors give them cash to allocate in carefully constrained ways. Neither their parent organizations nor their donors have authorized them to mount a political movement.

On the other side of the relationship, the political parties have shown a surprising capacity to adapt to the new electoral politics. They have embraced the new cash politics, raising sums of money by direct mail solicitations that were unthought of as recently as 1978 or 1980. The more affluent Republican national-level committees—the RNC, NRSC, and NRCC—spent $15.2 million in direct contributions to or "on behalf of" spending for congressional candidates in 1980. By 1988 that total had risen to $29 million. For the three Democratic committees—the DNC, DSCC, and DCCC—in those same two years the totals were $3 million and $11.2 million, respectively. At the same time the committees of both parties began to develop skills in all of the new campaign arts and sell them to their candidates, usually at prices below those of the "private sector." [13]

In one more key advantage over the PACs in electoral politics, the political parties, although unable to match the sheer sums PACs spend in congressional races, can spend their lesser sums more efficiently for electoral purposes—that is, they can concentrate it on the candidates who need it most. Thus, in the 1980s, as the PACs increasingly supported incumbents regardless of the closeness of their approaching election or indeed whether they had opposition of any kind, the party committees increasingly supported challengers and open seat candidates. In fact, in the 1988 House campaigns—in which more than 80 percent of PAC contributions went to incumbents—only 45.1 percent of DCCC money and 34.7 percent of NRCC money went to incumbent candidates. Moreover, party committees more frequently are applying a "need" test to the incumbents they do help. Making those distinctions thus permits the parties to affect more election outcomes per $100,000 spent than the PACs.

Having reduced their commitments to shaping electoral outcomes, PACs have turned increasingly to legislative strategies that will produce access to Congress, especially to assist the lobbying strategies of their parent organizations. Evaluating their success in the pursuit of legislative influence depends on one's standards of success. PACs have achieved some measure of access—that is, the opportunity to make a case or try to persuade (the foot in the legislative door, in other words)—but the far harder question is whether they do in fact persuade and whether they have gotten some control over policy making in return for their diminished electoral role. It is a matter of great public debate and massive public fears ("the best Congress money can buy"), and here one can only note that political scientists find that money affects congressional votes much less than many journalists and public interest groups believe.[14]

The political parties too have developed a legislative strategy: to maximize their numbers in legislatures in order to secure and keep legislative power. They are seeking to satisfy the collective interests of their incumbent partisans in the legislature. Most of their incumbents seeking reelection can find their own campaign resources, and the party committees in all of their activities look out chiefly for the weakest of them and for their challengers and open seat candidates. Thus far, however, the parties have not been applying policy tests—no tests of party orthodoxy or of support for the party platform, the party leadership, or (in one case) the party's president. If the party committees were ever to use their new financial edge for such policy purposes, we would indeed have a new era both in party evolution and in campaign finance.[15]

Both PACs and the political parties have in their separate ways adjusted to the greater power of incumbents to win reelection and to mobilize their parties' campaign committees in Congress to pursue their collective interests. By contrast, PACs and parties have not had to adjust to changes in the regulatory context of campaign finance. The Federal Election Campaign Act has stood without major amendment since 1976. Although there were some changes in the late 1970s, they largely involved spending by state party committees in federal elections and touched the PAC-party relationship only tangentially. There were no statutory changes of any importance in the 1980s and none thus far in the 1990s.[16] In all of the reform proposals still bandied about, PAC contributions remain a major hostage in the partisan warfare over reform. Proposals abound to cut the $5,000 limit on PAC contributions, to put limits on the sums that candidates may accept from PACs, to prohibit PAC contributions to political parties, even to legislate some or most PACs out of existence. Leaving aside whether such proposals would pass constitutional muster, they would all probably work against either labor PACs, the Democratic party, or both. And they are recognized as doing so. The nature of any alteration in PAC-party relationships thus becomes a part of the politics of reform in the strange world of campaign finance in which the regulators also are some of the regulated.

Conclusion

PACs and political parties met in the 1980s on the field of electoral politics. The outcome was not what one might have expected. The parties had improved their position during the decade, adapting to the new electoral politics by developing new fund-raising capacities and by embracing the new arts and crafts of campaigning. In doing so both the Democrats and the Republicans became somewhat different kinds of political parties: more centralized as party organizations, with their national committees finding it much easier than their state and local committees to raise campaign cash. Both too became more professional and bureaucratized, as well as more dependent on skilled technicians and less on volunteers and old-style party leadership. The shift was particularly wrenching for the Democrats, for it meant compromises with the vision of a mass-based, participatory, issue-centered party that had animated them in the early 1970s.

As for PACs in the 1980s, they grew steadily in number until the end of 1984 when there were 4,009, but they increased to only 4,178 over the next five years. Between the congressional elections of 1984 and those of 1988 their total contributions rose from $111.5 million to $155.8 million; increases in inflation, however, meant that the $155.8 million had a value of only $136.8 in 1984 dollars. Even more important perhaps, most PACs—again with the conspicuous exception of labor PACs—never really expanded the scope of their operations beyond contributing cash to candidates, and even within that circumscribed task, they failed to achieve efficient use of those contributions for electoral goals. In fact, encouraged by the ever more aggressive fund-raising of incumbents and their ease of reelection, PACs found it easy to abandon electoral goals and strategies for those of legislative access.

Indeed, it now becomes clear that *PAC* or *political action committee* is a very capacious term that hides a great deal of organizational diversity. At one pole are the complex, party-like electoral organizations that one sees most clearly in the PACs of the large, international labor unions. (Individual PACs of this kind also are "buried" in those aggregate categories of corporate, membership, and nonconnected PACs.) At the other end of the continuum are the PACs that function much more narrowly as devices for raising money from individuals and channeling it to campaigns for public office.

This latter kind of PAC—the form of the majority of PACs—is a simple political organization with obvious limits. Its parent organization makes it politically cautious and pragmatic if for no other reason than it must serve the parent's public relations policy and its interests in political lobbying and representation.[17] Its donors also have limited political goals; they are attracted to the PAC largely because it is promoting a specific interest rather than a platform or ideology. Those donors also choose a limited political act—the giving of money—in which they delegate to fund managers, the political choices among strategies and worthy candidates, much as one does in giving money to the United Way. They have, after all, chosen to give money to a PAC rather than a political party. Given the limited political commitments of both parents and donors, PACs follow a low-risk political strategy of cultivating legislative ties and supporting candidates certain or almost certain to win. In short, the majority of PACs are poorly designed for the greater risks of a more purely electoral strategy in which one supports like-thinking candidates in a race with an uncertain outcome.

In all of this, however, both the PACs and the parties remain subservient to the candidates, especially incumbent candidates. Electoral politics at the congressional level is overwhelmingly candidate centered, and there is plenty of reason to believe that the candidates also increasingly dominate campaigns in the states and localities. Thus, when we speak of political organizations such as PACs and parties mobilizing voters behind candidates for office, we misspeak somewhat. Increasingly it is the candidates themselves who are bringing together these voters. To be sure, they do so with resources and expertise provided by PACs and parties. But, for now, the candidates accept PAC money and the various forms of party support without surrendering much of their autonomy in the campaign. The candidates still control far more of the the strategies and issue agendas in the campaigns than do the PACs or parties.

Since the 1970s PACs and party committees thus have engaged in a spirited competition in American electoral politics. The PAC movement brought group politics to American election campaigns in a massive way in the 1970s and 1980s, but after more than a decade it seems clear that they and the groups that sponsor them are in fact better suited to the legislative strategies they have always pursued. The political parties, despite their reduced influence in American politics, remain the preeminent political organizations of electoral politics. But the parties and the PACs have fought their battle over electoral turf without challenging the primacy of the candidates themselves. The fact that the candidates, especially the incumbents, have been spared even a cursory challenge probably best testifies to the grip they have on American electoral politics.

Notes

The author is indebted to his research assistant, James Audette, for his help in preparing this chapter.

1. Federal statutes do not use the term *political action committee*. The closest approximation is the multicandidate committee mentioned in the statutes. So-called PACs must be multicandidate committees to qualify for the contribution limit of $5,000 per candidate per election. In a more general sense, PACs are really the residual category of political committees left after the statutes have defined political party committees and the official campaign committees of candidates.

2. FEC Advisory Opinion 1975-23 (December 3, 1975), the so-called SunPAC opinion. The FECA had incorporated into federal law, however, the prohibition against sponsoring groups transferring any of their assets to their PACs for direct political use. The PAC was to be, in the words of the statute, a "separate, segregated fund" that itself would raise all of the money it would spend for political purposes.

3. This decline of parties and the rise of PACs is discussed at greater length in Frank J. Sorauf, "Parties and Political Action Committees in American Politics," in *When Parties Fail: Emerging Alternative Organizations,* ed. Kay Lawson and Peter H. Merkl (Princeton, N.J.: Princeton University Press, 1988), 282-306.

4. Stephen E. Frantzich, *Political Parties in the Technological Age* (New York: Longman, 1989).

5. Party expenditures "on behalf of" candidates may be made with the full knowledge and cooperation of the candidates benefiting from them. They also are called coordinated expenditures. Still other sources refer to them as 441 (a)(d) expenditures after the appropriate section in the U.S. Code.

6. For a discussion of deducing the number of contributors in the early 1980s, see Frank J. Sorauf, "Political Action Committees in American Politics: An Overview," in *What Price PACs?* (New York: Twentieth Century Fund, 1984), 81-82.

7. Frank J. Sorauf, "Who's in Charge? Accountability in Political Action

Committees," *Political Science Quarterly*, 99 (Winter 1984-85): 591-614. It is important to note, however, that while donors to PACs are less involved in politics than party activists, they are still much more informed and involved than the American adult population generally.

8. The four party campaign committees are: Democratic Senatorial Campaign Committee (DSCC), National Republican Senatorial Committee (NRSC), Democratic Congressional Campaign Committee (DCCC), and National Republican Congressional Committee (NRCC).

9. For examples of analyses of PAC contribution strategies, see, inter alia, Theodore J. Eismeier and Philip H. Pollock III, *Business, Money, and the Rise of Corporate PACs in American Elections* (New York: Quorum Books, 1988); and J. David Gopoian, "What Makes PACs Tick? An Analysis of the Allocation Patterns of Economic Interest Groups," *American Journal of Political Science* 28 (May 1984): 259-281.

10. The other two categories in Table 10-1—Membership and Non-connected—are, in contrast, very heterogeneous. Their aggregate data conceals a great deal of varied behavior by individual PACs.

11. Scholars have been slow to deal systematically with soft money, and journalists, less fearful of entering a conceptual and data thicket, have had very mixed success. For a perceptive and rigorous journalistic account of soft money in 1988, see Charles R. Babcock, "$100 Million in Campaign Donations Belie Notion of Federal Limits," *Washington Post,* November 8, 1988.

12. See, for example, Edwin M. Epstein, "Business and Labor under the Federal Election Campaign Act of 1971," in *Parties, Interest Groups, and Campaign Finance Laws,* ed. Michael J. Malbin (Washington, D.C.: American Enterprise Institute, 1980), 107-151.

13. For a discussion of the new campaign activities of the national party committees, see Paul S. Herrnson, *Party Campaigning in the 1980s* (Cambridge, Mass.: Harvard University Press, 1988).

14. The cliché about "the best Congress money can buy" has become the title of a book by Philip M. Stern expounding that point of view (New York: Pantheon Books, 1988). For a more restrained point of view, see Janet M. Grenzke, "PACs and the Congressional Supermarket: The Currency Is Complex," *American Journal of Political Science* 33 (February 1989): 1-24; and John R. Wright, "PACs, Contributions, and Roll Calls: An Organizational Perspective," *American Political Science Review* 79 (May 1985): 400-414.

15. The application of some programmatic test in using party funds in campaigns might, if successful and sustained, usher in something like the classic and elusive "responsible" political parties in which mandated legislators carry out the party program to which they pledged themselves in the campaign.

16. This statement is true as of September 23, 1990. Both the House and the Senate passed reform bills earlier in 1990, but no conference committee had yet tried to reconcile their substantial differences. The president has

threatened to veto an outcome resembling either bill.

17. A number of studies have suggested that when the parent's Washington representative plays a role in the decisions of the PAC, the PAC is more apt to pursue the pragmatic goals of legislative access. See, for example, Edward Handler and John R. Mulkern, *Business in Politics: Campaign Strategies of Corporate Political Action Committees* (Lexington, Mass.: Lexington Books, 1982).

11. INTEREST GROUPS AND ABORTION POLITICS IN THE POST-*WEBSTER* ERA

Alissa Rubin

Abortion politics has produced some of the bitterest confrontations between interests over the past twenty years. Neither pro-choice nor pro-life advocates have been willing or able to find much middle ground on abortion-related issues, which have been hotly contested across all branches of government and at both the state and national levels. In 1989 the Supreme Court opened the door to increased state regulation of abortion with its decision in *Webster v. Reproductive Health Services.* This set off a series of debates in many states.

In this chapter political reporter Alissa Rubin assesses the post-*Webster* strategies of pro-choice and pro-life groups. Although most of their activity was oriented toward the states, much of the direction came from the national level. Pro-choice groups effectively anticipated the *Webster* ruling and reacted quickly to the threats to abortion rights. Pro-life organizations had more trouble building coalitions, but they devised a powerful "model law" strategy, which provided state legislatures with a laundry list of possible abortion restrictions. In the 1990s abortion politics promises to remain on the front burner of almost every state legislature, especially if the Court ultimately overturns its 1973 ruling in *Roe v. Wade,* which legalized abortion.

Idaho's Abortion Bill Vetoed: Possible Challenge to *Roe v. Wade* Ends
—San Jose *Mercury News,* March 31, 1990

Front pages across the country blazed with news from Idaho on March 31, 1990. But it is rare that legislative news makes front page headlines outside of state capitals and rarer still that it makes news in other states.

In the wake of the Supreme Court's 1989 decision in *Webster v. Reproductive Health Services,* the news from Idaho was indeed momentous. Had the Idaho bill become law, it would have been the most restrictive abortion law in the country, outlawing at least 95 percent of abortions in that state. If upheld by the Supreme Court, it would have overturned the Court's 1973 *Roe v. Wade* decision making abortion legal.

Idaho's moment in the national spotlight—replete with symbolic gestures such as calls to boycott Idaho potatoes if the bill became law and round-the-clock vigils by pro-choice groups—was but one of scores of abortion-related political and legislative actions that occurred in the months after *Webster*. These events included the election of two pro-choice governors (New Jersey's James Florio and Virginia's Douglas Wilder), dozens of attempts and some successes at passing state legislation limiting abortion, massive rallies in Washington, and the withdrawal of corporate support from Planned Parenthood. These efforts were influenced, and in some cases completely orchestrated, by numerous interest groups on both sides of the abortion issue.

Pro-life interests had demonstrated a great ability to affect electoral politics and engage in direct action to reduce the number of abortions.[1] Indeed, Marjorie Hershey has argued that by the mid-1980s much of the pro-life movement had turned away from "politics as usual" and had shifted toward private actions that would reduce the number of abortions performed.[2] This trend reached its acme in the late 1980s with the confrontational tactics of Randall Terry's Operation Rescue, which sought to force the abortion issue by physically blocking the entrances to abortion clinics.

With the Court's ruling upholding Missouri's restrictions on abortion in *Webster*, pro-life groups once again oriented many of their actions toward the legislative process—but at the state, not the national, level. Ironically, it was the pro-choice interests that had anticipated the *Webster* decision, and they were better organized and better prepared to react to its implications.

To understand the role of interest groups in the post-*Webster* era, it is necessary to look first at the status of the abortion issue in America in 1989. After setting the scene, this chapter will address three related issues: (1) how the pro-choice and pro-life groups organized to cope with the abortion issue in 1989-1990, (2) their strategies, and (3) their key successes and failures. It is difficult, however, to make any generalizations about who holds the upper hand in abortion politics; the politics of personal morality is often idiosyncratic, unpredictable, and reliant on how individuals react to powerful societal and political symbols. Indeed, it was individual politicians, governors, gubernatorial candidates, and legislators, with their reading of public opinion, who ultimately determined how the abortion issue was framed and whether restrictive laws were put in place. At the same time, the pro-choice and pro-life groups fought hard, both in the national media and in state after state, to frame the abortion issue as well and to seek the legislative results that *Webster* made possible.

It is worth noting that there is a continuing debate about the labels assigned to groups on both sides of the abortion issue. Over the years the media has dropped the labels chosen by the groups to coin its own. The groups prefer *pro-choice* and *pro-life,* each of which has positive connotations. These terms are used throughout this chapter because they are generally understood to refer to the supporters and opponents of legal abortion, respectively.

The term *pro-life,* however, has been attacked by pro-choice groups, because it implies that those on the opposite side are "anti-life." Pro-choice groups underscore that many of those who oppose legal abortion support the death penalty and are disingenuous when they describe themselves as "pro-life." Conversely, groups that oppose legal abortion dislike the term *antiabortion* because they say the prefix "anti-" is pejorative.

Among the terms used by the mass media in 1989-1990 were: *pro-choice, pro-life, abortion rights supporters, antiabortion activists, pro-abortion,* and *antiabortion.* By mid-1989 the Associated Press and many newspapers had changed their official style to "antiabortion activists" and "abortion rights supporters."

Webster v. Reproductive Health Services

During the last few years of the Reagan presidency, abortion politics had quieted. The lobby for the Human Life Amendment was at a low ebb, and by 1989 it was virtually out of money. Ironically, just as the mainstream pro-life movement appeared to be fading from view, the Reagan legacy of Supreme Court appointments began to yield victories for antiabortion activists.

For the public, the watershed came on July 3, 1989, when the Supreme Court handed down its 5-4 *Webster* opinion that demonstrated a significant shift from its 1973 *Roe v. Wade* decision. *Roe* had established that a woman's right of privacy included the choice of abortion. According to *Roe,* a woman has a constitutional right to terminate a pregnancy until a fetus can survive outside its mother's womb. For all practical purposes, viability was considered to begin after the sixth month of pregnancy.

In the *Webster* case a majority of the justices opined that states could limit the circumstances under which an abortion would be permitted. The Court would not say what kinds of restrictions they ultimately might uphold, but the justices ratified the limits on abortion passed by the Missouri legislature several years earlier. They included:

- The general statement that "the life of each human being begins at conception." This raises the question of whether an abortion is a murder.
- A prohibition against public employees performing or assisting in

abortions except to save the life of the mother. This meant that doctors who worked for federal, state, or local hospitals could not perform abortions.

- A prohibition on the use of public facilities, including state and local hospitals, for abortions.
- A prohibition on the use of public funding for pregnancy counseling if one of the alternatives was abortion.
- The requirement that before doctors perform an abortion, they test to see if the fetus could live outside the mother's womb.

Until the *Webster* case was decided, the public had paid only modest attention to the abortion issue in recent years. In some elections, most notably the 1980 Senate contests, pro-life groups had effectively organized multi-state, grass-roots efforts to defeat several incumbents.[3] But abortion had served only sporadically as a cutting issue in the late 1980s. Groups at either end of the abortion spectrum militated about it, but in congressional and other campaigns politicians might or might not talk about it.

In the wake of the *Webster* decision it was impossible for candidates—especially at the state legislative level—to run a campaign without stating in excruciating detail under what circumstances they would limit or allow abortions. *Webster* had placed abortion squarely in the middle of the American political agenda; interest groups scrambled to frame the issue to their best advantage.

Pro-choice Politics: Organizational Anticipation

Two crucial differences between the approaches used by the pro-choice and pro-life groups in 1989 revolved around when and how they organized their reactions to *Webster*. The pro-choice groups began planning for the possibility of a Court decision limiting abortion at least six months earlier than the pro-life groups, and they worked as a coalition, with specific groups taking responsibility for particular elements—legal, political, educational—of their overall campaign. In addition, the pro-choice organizations effectively coordinated their national media relations and overall strategies; they were able, on a limited basis, to translate those strategies into cogent state-level tactics and actions.

The pro-choice forces were battered, however, after Democrat Michael Dukakis's crushing defeat in the 1988 presidential race. Because they had known that Republican candidate George Bush was adamantly opposed to abortion, they had tried, unsuccessfully, to persuade Dukakis to use the abortion issue in his campaign. Despite a general sense of diffusion and defeat, a small group of pro-choice activists, many of whom had been involved in the women's movement in the late 1960s, continued to meet sporadically in Washington to discuss the status of abortion.

The day after Bush's inauguration the Justice Department announced it was planning to seek a reversal of *Roe v. Wade.* According to several pro-choice activists, that announcement moved them to action. A few days later a small group of executive directors from different pro-choice groups met in Washington. Although they did not realize it at the time, these activists later observed that the meeting was the beginning of a massive effort to focus national attention on abortion and to persuade both politicians and voters that it should remain legal and widely available.

That meeting included, among others, representatives of the National Organization of Women (NOW), National Abortion Rights Action League (NARAL), American Civil Liberties Union (ACLU), and Planned Parenthood. Over the next eighteen months they would define their roles, with each group taking responsibility for a portion of the endeavor. NARAL, which had always identified itself as the political arm of the pro-choice movement, focused even more intensely on electing lawmakers who supported its positions. The ACLU took on its traditional role of legal arm, accepting responsibility for preventing restrictive abortion laws from going into effect and challenging ones already in place. Planned Parenthood developed a massive public education campaign and underwent a corporate reorganization so that it could become a political lobby as well as an educational one. NOW became the feminist, activist wing, organizing the sometimes strident and highly visible Clinic Defense Task Force, which guarded abortion clinics from antiabortion activists who tried to stop women from entering.

As with many coordinated efforts, the pro-choice coalition began with only a few participants. The initial meeting, observed former NOW activist Kathy Bonk in 1990, included "just a handful of us . . . [but] if that [coalition] met today, we wouldn't fit in the room." [4] Bonk subsequently became coordinator of the pro-choice groups' media relations.

Frank Sussman, the ACLU lawyer from Missouri who was representing Reproductive Health Services (the abortion clinic targeted in the *Webster* case), remarked, "I don't know how many more years we're going to be able to win in the courts. We've got to build a grass-roots movement and motivate millions of Americans." Sussman's suggestion crystallized the thoughts of many of the activists who had been through the metamorphosis of women's issues into a women's movement. Ironically, the motif they played on was Ronald Reagan's.

Instead of telling America about the "moral majority," they sought to convince politicians and the public that there was a silent, pro-choice majority.

After that first meeting the core group expanded to include a cluster of lawyers and public relations experts who have continued to meet regularly to coordinate pro-choice strategy. The group jointly hired the Communications Consortium, a Washington-based public relations group, to coordinate their media effort. While each of the groups maintained extensive media offices, they used the Communications Consortium to let each other know what they were doing. Thus, pro-choice advocates had not only the Communications Consortium focusing their message but also an array of groups with sophisticated public relations operations, each of whom reinforced the overall message in producing their own publicity.

The pro-choice activists set two goals for themselves. First, they wanted to focus the abortion discussion on the "choice" of who makes the decision to go ahead with a pregnancy: the pregnant woman or the government. Second, using the classic strategy of losers in governmental arenas, they sought to broaden the scope of the conflict to include a wide variety of Americans.[5] "We had to persuade people, politicians, that it wasn't just okay to be pro-choice. That lots and lots of people were pro-choice and that it was politically smart to be pro-choice," said Bonk.

Three months before the Supreme Court handed down the *Webster* ruling, pro-choice activists staged a march in Washington to focus national attention on the issue. Calling the event the "March for Women's Lives," they worked to elevate abortion from the realm of single-issue politics to a movement. To do this, they had to turn the public's attention away from uncomfortable thoughts of abortion and toward those most American ideas—freedom and free choice. The march organizers marshaled one of the largest crowds—upward of 300,000 people went to Washington—since the Vietnam War and the civil rights battles of the 1960s. They even brought in Hollywood stars and television personalities, including the usual Hollywood social issue activists Jane Fonda and Meryl Streep. But there also was Glenn Close, Leonard Nimoy of "Star Trek" fame, and dozens of others. The march slogan, versions of which were used in subsequent election campaigns, was "Who Decides, You or Them?"

In addition to the march, which wound from the Mall to the Supreme Court, there was a three-day series of events. The *Washington Post* carried the schedule in its weekend section, and some news organizations assigned several reporters to cover it. The pro-choice strategy seemed to be working—pro-choicers garnered substantial publicity and demonstrated to Washington politicians that those who supported a woman's right to abortion could mobilize a large number of supporters.

A year later, in 1990, when pro-life groups held their own Washington rally, they had few events scheduled other than the rally itself, and the most prominent celebrity on hand was Cardinal John O'Connor, hardly a Hollywood personality. The other pro-life events that took place were organized primarily by Operation Rescue, but they were not publicized by the march organizers. Most news organizations assigned just one reporter to cover the rally and provided only a single day of coverage, in contrast to the two or three days of stories that the pro-choice forces got out of their march.

In sum, the *Webster* decision, if not totally anticipated by pro-choice forces, came as no surprise. Instead, the coalition was ready to broaden the scope of the abortion debate, reframing it in terms of choice and freedom, not in terms of murder or moral litmus tests.

The Pro-life Lobby Reorganizes

It was only in June 1989, less than a month before the Supreme Court's *Webster* decision was announced, that the National Right to Life Committee hired a new press secretary and began the media work that the pro-choice groups had been doing for the preceding six months. A year later the pro-life forces would still be trying to convince the media that the central issue was abortion, not choice.

Beyond being behind in their public relations strategy, each major national pro-life group worked out its own program in the months after *Webster*. Among these groups there was little of the coordination that had developed among pro-choice organizations, which meant that they had neither the financial strength nor the public relations presence that pro-choice advocates had.

Despite those apparent handicaps, the pro-life activists had one clear advantage over pro-choice groups: a true grass-roots organization. In the year after *Webster*, that organization made the difference in the pro-lifers' ability to elect pro-life candidates and promote the passage of legislation limiting abortion, often in spite of well-financed opposition from pro-choice groups.

The pro-life groups can be loosely divided into two types: (1) those that work in the political or legislative arena, and (2) those that advocate direct action, such as blocking the entrances to clinics, to stop abortion. Both varieties of organization depend heavily on grass-roots activism from deeply committed supporters.[6]

The depth of such grass-roots organization is best exemplified by the National Right to Life Committee, the leading pro-life group.

Although its professional staff has grown in recent years (to fifty paid staffers in its Washington office), it remains a largely volunteer organization that combines the roles of political organizer, legislative agenda setter, educator, and legal challenger. Although it added a lawyer and several other staffers in the year after *Webster,* its most dramatic expansion was in its volunteer ranks.

Within a few weeks of the *Webster* decision, the National Right to Life office was inundated with calls from around the country from people who wanted to know how they could help. "At first there was a big high and people were really energized," said Scott Fishbein, who organizes National Right to Life chapters in the South and Midwest. "Then they realized that in *Webster* we did not really win very much, abortion was still legal, but they saw it could be a state issue." In some states, including Mississippi, Kansas, and Arkansas, the number of chapters grew exponentially. Even a highly organized state like South Dakota, where there were already forty chapters, added five new ones. As of 1990 there were more than 3,000 chapters nationwide. There may be one or several chapters in a county and more than a hundred in a state; Minnesota, for example, has 150 chapters.

Each chapter publishes a newsletter, seeks permission to teach sex education classes in the schools as a counterpoint to the Planned Parenthood classes offered by many school systems, sets up telephone trees, circulates petitions in local churches to identify pro-life voters, and, in concert with other chapters, sometimes hires a lobbying staff to work in the state capital. The telephone tree has been an especially useful political tool for pro-lifers because it costs little and relies on members who are at home—many pro-lifers are women who work part time or are homemakers. Telephone trees allow a National Right to Life staffer to call two people in a state, report that a bill of interest is on the Senate floor, and obtain a large, almost immediate response. The two state contacts each call four people, who in turn call four people, until every member has received a phone call. This kind of telephone campaign can easily give legislators the sense that their districts are overwhelmingly pro-life.

The local chapters elect state officials—one for each state senatorial district or congressional district, depending on the organization's strength in a given state—and each state elects a representative to the National Right to Life board. "There is only one such pyramid in America," said J. C. Willke, president of the National Right to Life Committee. At the very least, there is no counterpart on the pro-choice side.

Willke's Right to Life group differs from the rest of the pro-life movement in that it does not take a religious position and focuses strictly on abortion. The group is also nonpartisan. Although pro-life stands often are considered Republican, that generality is deceptive because it ignores the strong pro-life orientation of many blue-collar voters, predominantly Catholic, who in the 1960s supported John Kennedy and Lyndon Johnson and hardly would be considered mainstream Republicans. Willke likes to point out that in several states National Right to Life has backed Democrats. In 1990, for example, it helped Rep. Romano Mazzoli, an incumbent Democrat from Louisville, Kentucky, win a difficult three-way primary fight.

National Right to Life takes no stand on birth control or other reproductive health issues. It does oppose euthanasia and infanticide, but the latter is never a political issue. Thus, for all practical purposes it is a single-issue organization. This is particularly important in the abortion debate because, contrary to common belief, many people oppose abortion while supporting family planning and birth control. If National Right to Life were to take a position condemning birth control, it might lose a significant portion of its backing, especially younger people who grew up generally accepting the idea of contraception. Conversely, if it took a stand supporting birth control, it would surely lose a large number of Catholics and charismatic Protestants who believe that abstention from sex is the only acceptable form of birth control.

Willke is also open about National Right to Life's reluctance to work with other pro-life groups, especially at the national level. The reason for the reluctance is twofold: first, most other groups dilute the antiabortion message by talking about such issues as birth control, and, second, abortion battles are often fought on a local level. Local chapters must have confidence that they can decide whether to work locally with other pro-life groups. Willke argues that if the national office subsumed that role, it would deprive local chapters of an important aspect of their power. Still, the pro-life groups do cooperate in a general way and talk when they are working on a specific event such as the 1990 Rally for Life.

Operation Rescue, however, is an exception; it is the only pro-life group that National Right to Life refuses to work with at any level. Job applicants at National Right to Life are questioned when they are hired about whether they feel a need to be involved in rescues, which could mean getting arrested. If they do, no job. "There is a perception that Right to Life opposes rescue," said Willke. "We don't oppose it at all, but ... there is such a thing as RICO statutes, and those RICO statutes, which are aimed at racketeering, have been used against rescue people. If we were in any way connected to the rescue groups, our whole organization could be paralyzed." [7]

In addition to National Right to Life, four other groups played significant roles in the post-*Webster* politics of 1989-1990: Operation Rescue, Christian Action Council, American Life League, and Focus on the Family.

Operation Rescue is the best known of the direct action groups. Its opposition to abortion is expressed in "rescues," in which members physically block the entrance to abortion clinics. Some rescue operations involve filling doorjambs and keyholes with glue or honey to stop women from entering. Other rescues have involved members chaining themselves together and then tying the chain to some part of the clinic building. Increasingly, these rescues have ended with mass arrests by police. Although Operation Rescue was fined nearly half a million dollars in 1989—a decision upheld by the U.S. Supreme Court in May 1990—and throughout the year had at least 200 members in jail at any one time, it maintained its ability to grab local and, occasionally, national headlines. And, despite the breakup of its national corporation due to the RICO threat, the group has reconstituted itself as a number of local entities and pursued its rescue strategy.

The Christian Action Council, headquartered near Washington, D.C., in Falls Church, Virginia, has no counterpart on the pro-choice side, but it resembles the National Right to Life Committee in that it relies on a national network of locally organized chapters. As its name suggests, it is a religious group—Protestant and Evangelical—and most of its money and local work goes into running approximately 400 pregnancy counseling clinics.

The American Life League and Focus on the Family were less central to abortion politics in 1989-1990, but they helped form a broader agenda by lobbying on an array of "family issues" that included abortion, obscenity, and other so-called decency issues.

Post-*Webster* Strategies: An Overview

Legislative politics dominated the strategy of pro-life groups after the *Webster* decision was handed down. In contrast, the strategy of the pro-choice organizations was to persist in what they had been doing since early 1989: keeping the public's attention on the abortion issue as a question of choice. They accomplished this goal in the widely publicized 1989 New Jersey and Virginia gubernatorial campaigns; at the same time, they had to marshal their forces to oppose the legislative efforts of pro-life groups to restrict abortion. Moreover, by mid-1990, both groups were heavily involved in state and national elections.

Both groups have drawn extensively on survey research in framing their respective messages. In the wake of the *Webster* ruling, newspapers and television networks commissioned poll after poll in an attempt to discover where the American public stood on abortion. What the polls showed both before and after *Webster* was a deep ambivalence in America about the morality of terminating unwanted pregnancies. Data from a series of surveys made it clear that Americans were both antiabortion and pro-choice. People felt abortion was wrong, but they did not want women to be forced to bear unwanted children. A majority of Americans—63 percent—thought that a woman and her doctor should be allowed to make the abortion decision. Nevertheless, 62 percent considered abortion to be murder, and a majority (52 percent) felt it should be made less readily available.[8] There is no sure-fire way for politicians to translate these ambiguous stands into a campaign position. Nor can they easily frame them as legislation. In addition, because most politicians are uncomfortable dealing with issues of sexuality in public, the interest groups' interpretation of the polls was particularly important.

For the most part, pro-choice and pro-life groups simply publicized the results that best suited their positions and ignored the inherent contradictions. Still, pro-choice groups did give ground on the issue of requiring parental consent for abortion; more than two-thirds (68 percent) of Americans felt that parents should be involved in their minor daughters' abortion decisions.[9]

Pro-choice Strategies: Just Say No (To Restrictions on Abortion)

In the first six months after the *Webster* decision pro-choice activists experienced a string of political victories. NARAL became deeply involved in the Virginia gubernatorial race that pitted Democrat Douglas Wilder, who was running on a pro-choice platform, against Republican Marshall Coleman. The ads that NARAL ran on television and in newspapers showed a picture of Marshall Coleman with the words "Vote No" bannered across it. Underneath it said: "Marshall Coleman . . . Your Television Ads Won't Fool Virginians: He'll return the law to the days when performing an abortion was a crime for which the sentence was three to 10 years in the Virginia State Penitentiary—even in cases of rape and incest." [10]

Wilder won election as Virginia's first black governor by fewer than 7,000 votes, a margin so thin that pro-choice activists avoid talking about it in-depth, even though they clearly can take a great deal of credit.

In the New Jersey gubernatorial race a pro-choice Democrat, Rep. James Florio, was able to make an issue of his opponent's ambiguous abortion stand. Republican candidate James Courter had a voting record that made it unclear exactly where he stood on the issue. Florio thus pointed to his own pro-choice record and assured voters that they could count on him to keep abortion legal.

At about the same time, in the fall of 1989, Florida's Republican governor, Robert Martinez, called a special session in which he hoped the legislature would pass stringent laws restricting access to legal abortion. But the session ended in embarrassment for the governor with every one of his proposals trounced by the legislature. And in Michigan pro-choice activists lost in the legislature as a one-parent consent bill was passed, but Gov. James Blanchard vetoed the measure.

Still, there are many avenues to policy change. The strength of pro-life activists in Michigan was such that they were able to muster more than 300,000 signatures to place the parental consent issue on the 1990 ballot.

For pro-choice activists, the 1990 legislative battles were less than overwhelming victories, even though they were successful in defeating most efforts to limit access to abortion. For the first time they saw the expense and difficulty of waging simultaneous abortion battles in dozens of states at once. In several crucial states they lacked grass-roots organizations altogether. Their supporters, many of whom earn almost twice as much money as pro-life backers, are more likely to send a check than circulate petitions. Several activists said they saw impending problems with always being the ones to oppose limits on abortion, when Americans, for the most part, are uncomfortable with the frequency of abortions. Within the pro-choice ranks there is a deep division about where and whether to compromise and allow some limits on abortion. "There is division on our side about what we're for," said Bonk. "We're all pretty clear about what we're against, but our side has not yet come to grips with what kinds of laws or positions we want." In Connecticut, where pro-choice legislation codifying a woman's right to have an abortion was passed, there is still disagreement about what the law should be for women under eighteen.

Pro-choice activists have agreed that they want to see the *Roe* decision codified. Thus, they drafted a bill that is being sponsored by about 100 members of Congress that would create a statute explicitly sanctioning abortion in the first three months of pregnancy and allowing it, at the discretion of a woman and her doctor, in the second three months. The bill, called the Freedom of Choice Act, is unlikely to pass either chamber within the foreseeable future.

Pro-life Strategy: The Road to Idaho (and Beyond)

The National Right to Life's legislative strategy was conceived after its lawyers analyzed the *Webster* decision in detail. Because several of the justices had written their own opinions, National Right to Life attorneys were able to determine where each justice stood on the issue of legal abortion. The only wild card was Justice Sandra Day

O'Connor. In her opinion she wrote that there was no reason "at this time" to consider overturning *Roe,* but she agreed that a state could set some limits on abortion.[11] She did not specify what limits would be acceptable.

National Right to Life undertook the task of establishing where O'Connor stood. The group's lawyers drafted eight model statutes that limited the circumstances under which abortion could be performed. The goal was to obtain passage of each statute in at least one state, with the ultimate aim of overturning *Roe.*[12] If this could not be achieved, National Right to Life hoped to limit drastically the number of legal abortions. The model laws were brought to the attention of state legislators either by National Right to Life members or by lobbyists who learned about the laws at a meeting for pro-life legislators and activists held in Washington in late September 1989.

It is a tribute to the strength of National Right to Life's grass-roots organization that, despite the massive media and lobbying campaigns by pro-choice groups, six of those eight statutes were passed in various states and one became law in Guam, a U.S. territory. Virtually every state that had a legislative session in 1990 considered at least one of the model laws. Four states—Minnesota, Idaho, Louisiana, and Alabama—attempted to pass laws that would ban almost all abortions. The first three states have a history of passing laws restricting abortion, and they have on the books many types of laws restricting abortion that have been enjoined in court. In short, National Right to Life was reasonably successful at setting the legislative agenda in a host of states. Not only did the group help place items on this agenda, but it also defined, often precisely, the alternatives that were considered.[13]

In Pennsylvania, the only state where several strict limits on abortion were passed and signed into law by the governor, the lobbying was intense on both sides, especially by pro-life groups. Several legislators who were considered swing votes said that in the two or three weeks before the abortion bill came to the floor, they spent six to eight hours a day with lobbyists from one set of groups or the other. Even friends and neighbors lobbied them on the issue, and their mail filled shopping carts. In Pennsylvania some of the most concentrated lobbying came from the Catholic church, the largest denomination in the state. It is especially influential in the state's conservative rural areas and smaller cities where there is a strong Catholic, Democratic, working-class tradition. Pennsylvania passed laws requiring that spouses be informed before an abortion, that a woman wait twenty-four hours between first discussing abortion with her doctor and having the procedure, and that a woman sign an informed consent clause detailing the abortion procedure. Although National Right to Life may eschew religious affiliations, it was well served in this instance by its coalition of convenience with the Catholic church.

Holding the Pennsylvania pro-life movement together was Republican state representative Stephen Freind, who served as the key entrepreneur in building support for the legislation in the statehouse. Conversely, in other states key legislators were those who used legislative procedures to bury antiabortion proposals. In any case, groups must work with legislators and, in certain circumstances, governors.

Idaho was the only state where a bill banning abortion as a means of birth control—legislation that has the effect of prohibiting 90 percent of abortions—made it to the floor of both legislative chambers. Pro-life activists attributed some of their success in Idaho to the willingness of the Mormon and Catholic churches to forge a coalition. In other states there had been divisions between religious factions in the pro-life camp. The bill probably also won support because pro-choice activists had done little to organize opposition to the bills in Idaho.[14] There is no NARAL organization in the state and few Planned Parenthood offices.

Finally Idaho's governor, Democrat Cecil Andrus, considered himself pro-life. Given the state's remote location, the national news media paid little attention until the bill reached the governor.

At that point the pro-choice forces swung into high gear. University students suddenly began vigils, and they hauled sacks of Idaho potatoes to the steps of the state capitol as a symbol of the boycott they said would ensue if the governor signed the bill.[15] Pro-choice Democratic governors personally telephoned Andrus to urge him to veto the bill. In fact, telephone lines to the governor's office were jammed by phone calls during the three weeks intervening between the bill's clearance of its first legislative hurdle in the House and Andrus's veto. Much of the phone calling and mail was triggered by pro-choice activists who put out special alerts to members. Andrus decided to veto the bill the day after the legislative session ended to avoid the possibility of an override.

Andrus said he killed the bill because he was worried that it was written in such a way that even women who became pregnant as a result of rape or incest would be forced to have the child. The bill would have allowed women to have an abortion if they were raped, but only if they reported it within seven days, an unrealistically small amount of time according to rape crisis experts. The incest exception in the bill would only allow an abortion if the woman were under 18.

"What do we do in a circumstance in which a 12-year-old girl becomes pregnant as a result of incest?" asked Andrus. "If, for whatever reason, she does not or cannot report the identity of the perpetrator to the authorities, she will violate the law if she or her family cause the pregnancy to be terminated. This law would demand that this 12-year-old girl who has already been the victim of an unspeakable act, compound her tragedy."

The frame of Andrus's argument, a hypothetical example of an extreme situation, is one used routinely by pro-choice lobbyists when they try to persuade legislators to veto legislation restricting access to abortion.

As long as there was little national attention on the Idaho abortion debate, pro-life forces had little difficulty dominating it. But when the national media, on their own and at the behest of the pro-choice movement, focused a great deal of attention on the state, the nature of the issue changed to one of state autonomy—from the influence of special interests. In addition, the proposed Idaho statute came to symbolize the threat posed to *Roe* by antiabortion legislation. When the scope of the conflict was broadened, the pro-choice forces were able to bring national opinion to bear on Andrus in terms of both the abortion issue and the question of state autonomy.

Pro-life activists did not have to contend with such tactics in Guam. Indeed, while the nation's eyes were on Idaho, little attention was paid to Guam, a distant, predominantly Catholic island territory. Guam's assembly almost unanimously voted to ban abortion except to save the life of the mother, an even more stringent law than the one proposed in Idaho. The legislation in Guam, if upheld, would mean that a woman would have to fly more than a thousand miles to Hawaii if she wanted to obtain an abortion.

In a very different kind of victory, but one that pro-life activists believe was one of their most significant, the Christian Action Council (CAC) persuaded the American Telephone and Telegraph Company (AT&T) to withdraw its $50,000 annual corporate donation from Planned Parenthood. CAC coordinated a letter-writing campaign and threatened to bring to a vote at the company's annual meeting a resolution banning donations to organizations that supported abortion. Customers, suppliers, employees, and shareholders were persuaded to write letters. In March 1990 AT&T's president, Robert Allen, withdrew the company's financial support. It had given money annually to Planned Parenthood for twelve years and was the group's largest corporate donor.

Abortion and Group Politics

In the wake of *Webster* the abortion issue lies on the political horizon like a storm cloud. No politician ventures into the field without formidable gear: polls, media consultants, and carefully worded position statements on when life begins and whether abortion should be legal. If 1989-1990 is any measure, millions of dollars will be spent by pro-choice and pro-life activists on persuading voters to accept their respective views on the issue. But politicians, like other Americans, are uncomfortable applying the strictures of law to this matter of morality and will move gingerly to set legal restraints.

In 1990 the U.S. Supreme Court, however, moved one step closer to ratifying a wide variety of restrictions on abortion. In two cases that dealt with access to abortion, the Court ruled that it was legal to require women under eighteen to notify or obtain the consent of at least one parent. The Court also ruled that it was permissible to enforce a forty-eight-hour waiting period between the time a woman under eighteen first sought an abortion and the time the physician performed it.

The Court, with Justice Sandra Day O'Connor providing the swing vote in a 5-4 decision, rejected, however, a two-parent notification law that lacked a so-called judicial bypass (that is, women have the option of notifying a judge in lieu of their parents.) Still, with the retirement of liberal justice William Brennan in July 1990, the Court appeared poised to overturn *Roe v. Wade,* an action that would open a whole new chapter in the politics of abortion.

Moreover, as long as the spotlight remains on abortion, the number of unwanted pregnancies, the root of the problem, will continue to grow. Activists on both sides agree that if there is any common ground between them, it is to stop unwanted pregnancies. But with the intense and emotional conflict over abortion, this area of agreement remains in the background and generally off the political agenda.

Notes

1. Among others, see Marjorie Randon Hershey and Darrell West, "Single-Issue Politics: Prolife Groups and the 1980 Senate Campaign," in *Interest Group Politics,* 1st ed., ed. Allan J. Cigler and Burdett A. Loomis (Washington, D.C.: CQ Press, 1983), 31-59; and Hershey, "Direct Action and the Abortion Issue: The Political Participation of Single-issue Groups," in *Interest Group Politics,* 2d ed., ed., Cigler and Loomis (Washington, D.C.: CQ Press, 1986), 27-45.
2. Hershey, "Direct Action and the Abortion Issue," 42.
3. Hershey and West, "Single-Issue Politics," 43ff.
4. Unless otherwise noted, this and other quotations in this chapter come

from interviews conducted during April, May, and June 1990 by the author with pro-choice and pro-life officials.

5. See E. E. Schattschneider, *The Semi-Sovereign People* (New York: Holt, Rinehart and Winston, 1960).

6. For other examples of grass-roots organizing, often originating at the national level, see Burdett A. Loomis, "A New Era: Groups and the Grass Roots," in Cigler and Loomis, *Interest Group Politics,* 1st ed. 169-191.

7. J. C. Willke, president, National Right to Life Committee, interview with author, April 17, 1990, Washington, D.C. The Racketeer Influenced and Corrupt Organizations (RICO) Act was designed to help government prosecutors break up organized crime's control of businesses ranging from gambling to frozen pizza production. It allows prosecutors to dismantle the corporate parent companies that handle the assets of criminal organizations. RICO statutes were used in 1989 to break up Operation Rescue by prohibiting it from funding the local operations of Operation Rescue with money collected by the national organization.

8. Survey by CBS News/*New York Times,* January 12-15, 1989.

9. Survey by the Analysis Group, January 1990, for Emily's List, a Democratic group that recruits and offers financial support to women candidates for office.

10. From a campaign poster widely disseminated to Washington news organizations and used on local television during the last two months of the 1989 Virginia gubernatorial campaign.

11. *Webster v. Reproductive Health Services.*

12. Model laws include: prohibiting abortion except to save the life of the mother and in cases of incest or fetal deformity; requiring a husband's permission; requiring a twenty-four-hour waiting period between the time a woman first sees the doctor who will perform the abortion and the operation; informing women of what an abortion does and what the alternatives are; and requiring parental involvement in the abortion decision when the pregnant woman is under eighteen (or sixteen).

13. See John W. Kingdon, *Agendas, Alternatives, and Public Policy* (Boston: Little, Brown, 1984) for an extended discussion of the distinctions between agenda items and policy alternatives.

14. Likewise, Alabama pro-life forces encountered very little organized opposition.

15. The potato boycott became a symbol that caught the fancy of legislators in other states. In Kansas, for example, a group of pro-choice women state legislators dumped 100 pounds of potatoes on the desk of an active pro-life colleague.

12. LOBBYING THE COMMITTEE: INTEREST GROUPS AND THE HOUSE PUBLIC WORKS AND TRANSPORTATION COMMITTEE

Diana M. Evans

How do interest groups get what they want? For all the discussion of political action committees (PACs) and electoral politics, most interest groups concentrate largely on lobbying specific participants in the policy-making process. But apart from some case studies and a handful of large-scale research efforts, we do not know all that much about how groups affect public policy. As Diana Evans notes, the entire question of legislative success has not been addressed systematically. In large part, this acknowledges the difficulty of the endeavor and the fact that success is rarely complete.

In this chapter Evans scrutinizes the lobbying process in one committee on one key piece of legislation. She focuses on how satisfied the lobbying groups were with various elements of their influence strategies. This is not, to be sure, a direct measure of influence. It has the virtue, however, of allowing the groups to assess their own efforts—but for an outside scholar, not an internal audience for whom they might well inflate their impact.

As in other chapters in this volume, most notably Browne's work on policy niches (Chapter 16), Evans discovers that interest groups are most effective when they do not have to compete with other groups. At first glance this seems a very simple, even simplistic, finding, but what could be more effective than presenting a unified front to decision makers? Evans also adds to the debate over the effectiveness of PAC contributions. While not discounting their potential, she notes that other forms of lobbying lead to greater levels of satisfaction among the interests she surveyed. PAC politicking may be an important part of groups' efforts, but it is not one that is viewed with equanimity by those involved in the lobbying efforts. Rather, lobbyists seek inside, nonconflictual methods for achieving their objectives.

In 1987, by the barest of margins, the Senate overrode President Ronald Reagan's veto of H.R. 2, the reauthorization of the nation's highway and urban mass transit programs. It did so only after Terry Sanford, the freshman senator from North Carolina, changed his vote following heavy pressure from his fellow Democrats and many others. Five months earlier, at the end of the 100th Congress, essentially the same bill died for that session in the House-Senate conference committee that had struggled unsuccessfully for weeks to resolve the conflicts between the two houses.

Interest groups were actively, and at the end very publicly, involved in the effort to pass the highway bill. Following the unsuccessful 1986 House-Senate conference on the bill, for example, Associated General Contractors (AGC), a large, wealthy, and reputedly powerful group, placed ads in *USA Today* charging Congress with "trust abuse" and "taxation without transportation" for not reauthorizing the federal highway program, which is paid for by the Highway Trust Fund, the repository for receipts from the federal gas tax.[1]

Policy Making and the Scope of the Conflict

That kind of highly visible lobbying on conflict-ridden legislation is familiar to any observer of American politics. On contentious legislation, lobbying strategy often produces free media attention and, like the AGC campaign for the highway bill, may include both use of the paid media to activate the unorganized public and, occasionally, mass public demonstrations of support or opposition. These are so-called outside lobbying techniques, designed by interest groups to influence members of Congress indirectly through their constituents. Lobbyists increasingly have used outside techniques to supplement the more traditional lobbying methods, which in contrast, include testimony at subcommittee hearings, campaign contributions, and meetings in which lobbyists present their cases to members of Congress and their staffs.[2] These techniques are part of a so-called inside strategy with which a group attempts to influence members of Congress directly.

When do groups use an inside strategy exclusively? Such a strategy is best when there is little conflict on a bill. In that situation groups simply try to communicate their needs to members of Congress and their staffs, working to be sure their wishes are included in legislation. Such a quiet, relatively peaceful process is characteristic of distributive legislation, in which discrete benefits such as special tax breaks or new bridges are given out to particular interest groups or constituencies. When distributive legislation is under consideration in committee, it is usually a simple matter to expand the total pool of benefits to satisfy potential opponents who may feel that they are not getting their fair share. The general public, which ultimately pays for these benefits through higher taxes, user fees, or prices in the marketplace, is normally organized less effectively than the beneficiaries and thus may not even know until it is too late, if ever, what is being considered or what the impact of the legislation will be.[3]

Outside techniques are often used to supplement inside strategies but in a different kind of legislative environment. Because they are more expensive and time-consuming for the lobbying office to organize, and because used at the wrong time they can backfire, outside strategies usually are reserved for situations in which the group faces opposition from Congress, the administration, or other powerful groups. When a bill is conflictual, those on the disadvantaged side have an incentive to bring in outsiders as allies, thus attempting to shift the balance of forces to their own side. The conflict then tends to escalate until all those from the broader public who can be engaged are engaged.

As this description implies, however, conflict produces an inherently volatile, unstable situation in which it is difficult for either side to control the outcome. Interest groups prefer a quiet process of bill writing, characterized by behind-the-scenes negotiation and compromise whenever the political situation is harmonious enough to allow it. Thus, shrewd political strategists attempt to limit the scope of conflict when they initially are in an advantaged position, keeping all negotiations restricted to private meetings among privileged insiders. In this way, potential points of conflict are less likely to be revealed to those who might be equally interested but less effectively organized, and the well-organized are then most likely to get what they want.[4] Because inside techniques are less likely to get out of control and generally produce more predictable results, lobbyists use them predominantly. Thus, inside strategies characterize the normal legislative process.

The history of the 1987 highway bill suggests that the highway and transit reauthorization process itself was racked by highly visible conflict. The 1986 conference was very conflictual, but in its early stages in the House of Representatives, the bill was drafted in an atmosphere of considerably greater harmony and compromise between the House committee that wrote the early version and the interest groups that supported it. Thus, the legislative situation was conducive to a quiet inside strategy for highway and mass transit interest groups in which conflicts normally were dealt with privately among House and interest group negotiators. As a result, most of the bill's provisions were shielded effectively from public view, as they never became matters of contention. It was a legislative environment that offered prospects for a high degree of success for interested individuals and groups.[5]

When this quiet insider strategy involves campaign contributions from political action committees to members of Congress, it arouses the suspicion of informed observers of Congress, including journalists, reformist interest groups such as Common Cause, and the general public, who at least until 1980 increasingly believed that "government is pretty much run by a few big interests looking out for themselves."[6] Yet by its very nature such lobbying is difficult to observe firsthand, and critics are left to rely on possibly misleading correlations between visible indicators—such as campaign contributions and the voting records of members of Congress—as a basis for inferences about what went on behind closed doors.[7]

Although it is impossible to say that nothing untoward goes on behind those doors, we can examine more closely than usual how the interest groups concerned with the federal highway aid and urban mass transit reauthorization used inside lobbying techniques. This chapter focuses on the highway and transit groups' approach to the friendliest and most influential of the committees with which they had to deal, the House Public Works and Transportation Committee, and evaluates their success. Because most of their lobbying was private, I conducted in-depth interviews with almost all the key lobbyists on the bill, during which I asked them what they wanted, who opposed them, what they got, and how they went about trying to get it. While some of them may have omitted some events, there was remarkable consistency across all of the interviews about the techniques lobbyists used and considerable detail about how they used them. The interviews also revealed how the lobbyists organized themselves for action in a legislative environment we cannot observe directly, one that is usually given less attention than highly contentious situations in which outside strategies make the process more visible. But as the inside strategy characterizes the normal, everyday process of legislation, it deserves close attention.

The Bill

The purpose of the Surface Transportation and Uniform Relocation Assistance Act of 1987 (designated H.R. 3129 in the 99th Congress and H.R. 2 in the 100th when it finally became law) was to extend the authorization of federal aid to highway, highway safety, and urban mass transit programs from 1987 to 1991. Fifty-three interest organizations were represented in testimony before the Surface Transportation Subcommittee of the House Public Works and Transportation Committee in three days of hearings held in 1985. Of those fifty-three interests, twenty-three had testified in hearings on previous reauthorizations of the thirty-year-old highway program. Those twenty-three groups can be considered core groups—that is, those most likely to maintain an ongoing, friendly relationship with the committee and its staff, reflecting their central and continuing interest in the highway and transit program. They include such organizations as the American Association of State Highway and Transportation Officials, the American Road and Transportation Builders Association, and the Amalgamated Transit Union.[8]

These groups enjoyed complete consensus on one goal: they wanted funding for existing programs continued at least at current, but preferably at increased, levels.[9] In the subcommittee hearings the interest groups agreed, among other things, that the interstate highway system should be completed by 1991, that Congress should provide money to rebuild deteriorating highways and bridges, and that the gas tax, which funds highway construction, should not be phased out when the interstate system is complete.

Lobbyists made many requests of the subcommittee. To be precise, the eighteen organizations examined here made ninety-eight distinct policy requests, the majority of which were unopposed by other groups.[10] Many of the requests were minor relative to the overall national importance of program reauthorization but were critical to the group making the request. The American Trucking Associations (ATA), for example, wanted permission to use triple trailers in the West. The American Bus Association (ABA) asked Congress to prohibit public mass transit companies from competing with private interstate bus lines on interstate bus charters. And public transit forces wanted a continuation of operating subsidies.

Although the interest groups agreed on the broad outlines of the program, they disagreed on about 25 percent of the issues that they brought to the subcommittee, reflecting uneasy relations among some groups that had inherently conflicting interests. For example, the requests of the ATA for triple trailers and of the ABA for regulatory protection from competition from urban public transit systems were opposed by other groups. There were also conflicts over management-labor issues and affirmative action. Contractors, for example, wanted Congress to abolish federal requirements that workers be paid the prevailing wage in their areas and that a fixed percentage of subcontracts go to minority-owned businesses (so-called minority set-asides). Labor and minority contractors, not surprisingly, wanted to preserve those requirements.

As these examples suggest, interest groups were pulled in two strategic directions. On the one hand, each wanted to maximize its own "take" from the program. On the other hand, they all wanted to minimize the atmosphere of controversy around the reauthorization to avoid expanding the conflict and possibly attracting new actors hoping to exploit it for their own ends. Such an eventuality would endanger existing areas of consensus, which on this bill greatly outnumbered the points of contention. Thus, beyond their testimony in hearings, these groups had to decide how hard and how publicly to fight for the divisive issues and how much energy to devote to maintaining an overall consensus that would help to carry the reauthorization to enactment. The key element in the development and maintenance of a minimum level of consensus is the formation of a coalition. These groups' coalitional styles emerged from overall policy consensus and their habitual interactions with each other.

Coalition Politics

Interest group coalitions in Washington are ubiquitous. Lobbyists spend a good deal of time talking not just to public officials and their staffs but also to each other. On any given piece of legislation groups seek to maximize their chances of success by working whenever possible with like-minded colleagues from other organizations, thus increasing the total resources available to them and the credibility of their efforts. One study of Washington lobbyists showed that 90 percent of the organizations surveyed participated in coalitions and found themselves doing so increasingly since the 1970s. Although groups may work together repeatedly on a number of bills, coalitions on each bill tend to be ad hoc marriages of convenience without a separate staff or formal organizational structure. Participants may enter or leave the coalition as their interests dictate.[11]

Among transportation groups the coalitions were fairly stable but informal and ad hoc. On this bill, as several lobbyists said, there was little actual coordination of lobbying effort, yet groups shared information with each other and some attempted to arrive at a common strategy. In fact, there were several active informal coalitions. State and local government interest groups worked together, as did the highway builders, highway users, and transportation labor unions, respectively. There were alliances among these sectors as well—for example, the unions worked with local government groups. The American Association of State Highway and Transportation Officials moved between sectors, working with both the road builders and government groups. But because groups even in the same sector had different policy priorities, cooperation tended to be high when it came to sharing information but low or nonexistent when public policy disagreements arose.

Information sharing was eased by the fact that, as several lobbyists commented, the transportation community is a small group in which "everybody knows everybody." Representatives of all of the sectors often could be found at meetings at which lobbyists shared news and information about their own goals and strategies. In this process some of the larger, wealthier groups tended to take the lead, conducting big research projects and sharing the information with other groups, who then used it in their own lobbying.

However universal coalitions may be, one lobbyist had a different perspective on the informal coalitions that worked on the highway and transit bill. A representative of one of the largest and wealthiest groups in the transportation community, this lobbyist criticized coalitions as a drag on the process. In his view time was of the essence on the bill because the highway program was about to expire and "we didn't have time to be checking with other coalition members" on strategy. He was annoyed by the informational meetings that were so common: "Coalition meetings just end up being gripe sessions about individual provisions. Ninety-five percent of the people are there to get information from the other five percent." Because his organization was one of the 5 percent he found the meetings less useful than did other groups.

Another large association had a more favorable view of coalitions. Its resources in its own sector were comparable to those of the group just discussed, but it embraced the lead role which it achieved by its ability to conduct research and disseminate its results. "One of our primary functions," said a lobbyist for this group, "was to keep the coalition together. We worked on the specifics and the coalition gave [the effort] legitimacy." Other groups in the same sector confirmed that they took statistics for their testimony from this lead group, although they differed with it over some policy positions.

But cooperation was only one side of the story. On some issues there were conflicts both between and within sectors, as described earlier. To counteract the potentially damaging effects of intergroup conflict, some of the larger groups worked continually to draw attention to the larger issues of program reauthorization. As one lobbyist said, "The highway lobby isn't nearly as monolithic as everybody thinks it is. The bills are so complex, and everyone is interested in their own issues; they don't care about the whole bill." Thus, in each of the broad interest group sectors, except perhaps for labor, at least one group tried to keep the other groups focused on passing the bill with or without each policy detail they wanted, because without the bill no one would get anything.

Only a few big groups played the peacemaker role, however, and they were groups whose members had a stake in many parts of the bill and for whom no one provision was of overriding importance. Nevertheless, all of these groups presented a united front to the committee when they could. Individual groups often publicly endorsed positions that had low priority for them but were important to others in the coalition. But when they disagreed among themselves on high-priority issues, they took their differences to the committee and lobbied individually for their own positions.

The coalitions and their members thus largely worked side by side, as much as possible following a policy of mutual noninterference, with each group and sector seeking primarily to maximize its piece of the pie. Individually, groups lobbied for their high-priority items but at the same time emphasized in public testimony areas of agreement with other groups. As a result of following this inside strategy, disagreement on some measures did not fracture the underlying consensus in the transportation community on the desirability of passing the bill. One of the leaders of the highway coalition said that, in the end, when the legislation was genuinely at risk, coalition members pulled back on their particular issues in the interest of "getting a bill." Before that stage, however, individual group lobbying was critical.

Lobbying

The interest groups that lobbied on H.R. 3129 used the major recognized techniques for influencing the content of legislation. They testified in subcommittee hearings; contacted members of the House committee and subcommittee, especially the leaders; and had meetings with committee and subcommittee staff. A few prodded their own group members to lobby their members of Congress on the committee, and half of the groups made campaign contributions.[12]

In their efforts to influence the content and ensure the passage of the bill in the House, the interest groups concentrated most heavily on the Public Works and Transportation Committee. Heavy lobbying of the committee of jurisdiction is a time-honored strategy for two reasons. First, specialized committees determine the content of the legislation debated on the floor. Second, members of Congress seek appointment to committees that promise to enhance their reelection chances, that have jurisdiction over their policy interests, or that give them influence in the House. Very often their policy interests and their constituents' desires are intertwined. Thus, committees tend to be composed of members who, for constituency reasons or because they have a background and interest in the issues, support the programs within their jurisdictions and are therefore sympathetic to the wishes of the interest groups that make up the committees' organized clientele. The House Public Works and Transportation Committee is just such a committee.[13] Members of the full committee and the Surface Transportation Subcommittee give the highway and mass transit programs their bipartisan support and thus tend to work cooperatively with the organized interests who support program authorization bills after they are reported from committee. On this bill, then, committee members were not averse to entertaining the special requests of those interest groups.

Testifying in Hearings

At the committee level of deliberation the most visible (though not necessarily the most effective) means of influencing the content of legislation is testifying in committee or subcommittee hearings.

Through testimony, groups seek to establish minimal credentials as players in the legislative process and demonstrate to their own constituents that they are doing their job. Although most of the major groups that wanted something in the highway bill testified, only those that lacked resources or for whom the bill was not central to their interests restricted their lobbying to testimony. Of the groups considered here, only two limited their lobbying in this way. One did so because it had "only two-thirds of a legislative person who was also involved in state and local issues." The other appeared to limit its lobbying in this way because it had only one lobbyist, who appeared surprisingly naive about the requirements of effective lobbying. He said, for example, that he "let" members of his association contact their members of Congress without making any attempt to persuade them to do so. Another lobbyist who had lobbied against this man on a particular issue said that he came to the hearing poorly prepared, with incorrect numbers. These two lobbyists were clearly the exception, however. For the rest, testifying was secondary to their attempts to influence more directly those who wrote the bill, the top leaders of the committee and subcommittee and their staffs.

Committee hearings serve a number of functions. Besides allowing groups to satisfy their own constituents that they are working for their interests, they also legitimate the final outcome by allowing those affected by a proposal to take part in the legislative process. Moreover, they permit committee members to "feed" selected lobbyists questions that will elicit the program justifications that the committee wants for the public record. What they usually do not do is persuade committee members of the lobbyists' positions. For that, a more private setting is necessary in which lobbyists meet one on one with committee members and staff to discuss their high-priority concerns.

Negotiations with Members and Staff

Of the remaining techniques for influencing the content of the bill, meetings between lobbyists and committee members and their staffs were critical, as together members and staff wrote the bill. Among committee members, the leaders counted most: James Howard, D-N.J., the committee chairman; Gene Snyder, R-Ky., the ranking minority member; Glenn Anderson, D-Calif., the subcommittee chairman; and Bud Shuster, R-Pa., the ranking minority member of the subcommittee. These members, widely known as the "Big Four," ironed out the details of the legislation in private meetings with their staffs. To a large degree, the Big Four bought the support of other members of the committee and the House for their favored positions with special interest provisions and with the distribution of demonstration projects to members' districts.[14] As one committee staff member said of the committee chairman, "It was the source of his power to be able to dispense those favors."

Thus, most of the lobbyists interviewed described an efficient deployment of their resources: they concentrated on the Big Four. Only two of the largest groups spent much time trying to influence the committee's rank and file members. One of those groups had seven lobbyists on Capitol Hill at all times as the eyes, ears, and voice of the organization. They not only talked with members and staff, participated in hearings, and attended markups but also sat in the gallery of the House for visibility with members on the floor. More typical of the interest groups active on this bill, however, were organizations with three or fewer lobbyists who concentrated on those who actually made policy.

At least as fundamental to success as seeing the Big Four, however, was meeting with committee and subcommittee staffs. A lobbyist for one of the large highway user groups said that he always went to the staff first. If he went to the members first, "the staff resent[ed] it" and might have sabotaged the group's request. Only after obtaining the staff's agreement on a provision did he contact the committee's leaders; "if they sign on then, you've got it." The majority of the lobbyists interviewed considered lobbying staff a key part of their strategy and agreed that the bill was essentially written by them in a bipartisan manner. One lobbyist stressed the bipartisanship of the committee and its staff. When she went to the majority staff with a request, they always asked if she had checked with the minority staff as well and expected her to do so if she had not.

Although these lobbyists viewed negotiating with staff as critical, there was yet a higher level of access achieved by several of the groups, two of them state and local government interest groups. In one of these cases the committee staff asked the group to research, write, and disseminate to all members of Congress a report on the effects on each state of delaying program reauthorization, which, of course, it was delighted to do. In the other case the lobbyists said, "The staff came to us to help rewrite the bill," asking especially for advice on how to move funds more quickly from the Reagan era Department of Transportation to pay for transit projects. When the staff approaches an interest group asking for information, the group knows that it has achieved a high degree of access and legitimacy with policy makers, with potential payoff in the future.

Maintaining access to staff requires continual effort between bills. A staff member to one of the Big Four said that part of the secret of one group's continued success is that "they're always around even when nothing is going on. They just drop in from time to time to say hello and cultivate good relations." This too can benefit the group later when the committee is considering legislation.

PAC Contributions

Previous studies of how political action committee contributions affect congressional decision making present a cloudy picture. Some studies have found strong effects, indicating that members who receive PAC contributions are subsequently more likely to vote for measures that the contributor favors. More commonly, however, studies have found that when they are significant at all, PAC contributions are less important than other determinants of members roll-call voting, such as party and ideology.[15]

Not surprisingly, among lobbyists no one admits to trying to buy the votes of members of Congress with their PAC contributions. Rather, they say that they are trying to ensure access to policy makers, and they think the contributions help. Consequently, because most policy is made in committees and access there is most critical, PACs typically concentrate their contributions on members of the committees that have jurisdiction over their interests.[16]

Of the eighteen groups studied here, eight had PACs that contributed to members of the House Public Works and Transportation Committee in the 1984 election, which immediately preceded the committee's consideration of the highway and mass transit bill.[17] PAC contributions to committee members from these groups ranged from a low of $2,500 from the National School Transportation Association to a maximum of $54,600 from Associated General Contractors, with average total contributions of $26,622. Given the leader-centered modus operandi of this committee, one should expect to see disproportionately large contributions to the Big Four, and that is the case. With the sole exception of the Associated Builders and Contractors (ABC), which only directed 2 percent ($250) of their contributions to the leaders, all of these groups gave more than 30 percent of their total committee contributions to the Big Four, with a disproportionate share of that going to the full committee chair. Two groups gave 70 percent or more to the Big Four.[18] Although some of the lobbyists believed that PAC contributions were necessary to get committee members to talk to them, it should be noted that the six state and local government groups had no PACs, yet most had little trouble gaining access to committee staff. Indeed, the committee worked especially closely with lobbyists for at least two of these groups. Because these groups represent members' states and localities and thus have a connection to members' constituents, campaign contributions from them are less important. In contrast, the private interest groups, two-thirds of which contributed to committee members, evidently felt that they had something to gain from their PAC money, even if it was only a form of access insurance. As one committee staff member said, the large amount of money spent by some groups on campaign contributions and honoraria "gets people's attention."

Grass-Roots Lobbying

Direct lobbying of members of Congress by an interest group's own members has become an important part of the lobbying repertoire of many organizations. In their study of 175 interest group representatives, Kay Schlozman and John Tierney found that 80 percent of the organizations they surveyed had influential constituents make contact with their representatives and senators; almost all the trade associations used this technique.[19] In a study of representatives' voting decisions before the legalization of PACs, John Kingdon found that interest groups could not hope for influence with members of Congress unless they had a connection with members' constituencies, in part because in the absence of a district connection, groups had no negative sanctions to use against representatives who did not go along with their wishes.[20] It is unclear whether PAC contributions from outside the district have changed that.

Fewer than half of the highway and transit groups utilized this outside technique, however. Those that did used methods that ran the gamut from letters written from the district to "fly-ins" of influential group members to Washington. Half of these groups concentrated their efforts on members of the committee, while the rest found that unnecessary. They reserved their grass-roots efforts for later, more contentious stages of the process.

Among grass-roots lobbying techniques, the one that requires the least effort of group members is telephoning their representative's office or writing a letter. Nevertheless, several lobbyists indicated that it was not easy to motivate people to do even that, as group members tended to take the long-established highway and transit programs for granted. In some cases it took the presidential veto to awaken their members to action. One group set up a "hot line" during conference committee deliberations. The lobbyist changed the tape at least once daily, using it to update members (and other groups) on the progress of negotiations. Earlier in the process, when the time element was less critical, he sent periodic legislative alerts to his own group members. But motivating them was so difficult that he sometimes had to travel to the local members and virtually beg them to become active. For this group, as for others, only the threat of imminent failure was sufficient to move its members to action.

In other cases, however, groups had more luck energizing their membership. One had a program of pairing at least one of their influential members from each congressional district with his or her member of Congress. Those influential constituents already were committed to voluntary activism; it thus was easy to motivate them to make a telephone call or meet with the representative at home or in Washington.

One of the large industry groups lobbied six to eight state delegations at a time by flying in influential members of the association from those states, briefing them in the Washington office, and sending them to the Hill to lobby their respective delegations. The visits ended with a reception or dinner for the targeted members of Congress.

Because organizing grass-roots efforts requires considerable expenditure of the Washington office's resources, interest groups tend to reserve this kind of effort for the problematic stages of the legislative process. A number of the lobbyists who were active on this bill said that because the committee and subcommittee were sympathetic to their concerns, grass-roots lobbying at the committee stage was unnecessary. One said that members of Congress "hate it when you call in the dogs," as he referred to constituent lobbying. Moreover, he felt that if a group asked its members to lobby too often, it risked getting a reputation with its own members for crying wolf. For both reasons, he used this technique judiciously, reserving it for the House-Senate conference and the expected veto override effort.

During the unsuccessful 1986 House-Senate conference and the 1987 override campaign, however, this interest group went all out with its grass-roots effort. Late in the conference they gave their members data on how failure to reauthorize the program would affect each state, urging them to write their members of Congress to outline specifically how their (the group members') own businesses would be affected. The group also asked its members to contact their own suppliers, insurers, and financial services groups to tell them how failure to pass the bill would affect them, urging *them* to contact their members of Congress as well. In its final report to its members after the Senate override, this group said that thousands of their members "contacted their congressional delegations in person, by phone, and by telegram . . . and repeatedly." It is no wonder that members of Congress hate it when they call in the dogs.

In the end, fewer than one-quarter of these groups used grass-roots lobbying on the committee; the remaining one-quarter that used this technique did so later in the process and then only when they faced serious congressional opposition. As the lobbyists indicated, grass-roots lobbying is costly. On this bill it was also unnecessary for

Table 12-1   Satisfaction with Committee Action on Interest Group
Requests by Conflict over Requests (percent)

Degree of satisfaction with committee action	Group request nonconflictual	Group request conflictual
Fully satisfied	71	43
Partially satisfied	5	16
Dissatisfied	24	41
	100%	100%
	N=125	N=44

most groups to use this outside strategy with its attendant costs and
risks.

Lobbying and Legislative Success

One of the most critical questions about lobbying techniques is:
What works and what does not? That question has not been addressed
systematically in the literature on lobbying, and it cannot be answered
definitively here, as the results of this case study of lobbying on a single
bill are not generalizable to other legislation. Nevertheless, the interviews of the highway and transit lobbyists allowed an analysis of the
relationship between lobbying techniques and interest group satisfaction with this bill.

Tables 12-1 and 12-2 reveal the results of this analysis by
indicating the overall percentages of interest group policy requests that
the House committee satisfied or did not satisfy. That variable was
measured by asking lobbyists how satisfied they were with the
committee's decision on each of the policy requests that the group made
in hearings on the reauthorization bill. They also were asked whether
there was conflict with other interest groups or governmental actors
over that request and how they lobbied the committee.

According to Table 12-1, when groups were in conflict with other
groups over their policy positions they were much less likely to get what
they wanted from the Public Works and Transportation Committee.
This indicates, first, that the committee made clear choices among
groups, disappointing some and pleasing others when the groups could
not agree (and sometimes even when they did agree). Thus, the groups'
failure to reach a consensus on their issue positions was risky, as the
committee did not always craft a policy compromise that pleased
everyone.

Table 12-2 shows that when there was consensus on the issues, it

Table 12-2 Satisfaction with Committee Action on Interest Group Requests by Lobbying Technique and Conflict over Requests (percent)

Group satisfaction with committee action	Group request nonconflictual		Group request conflictual	
	Committee staff not lobbied	Committee staff lobbied	Committee staff not lobbied	Committee staff lobbied
Satisfied [a]	70	78	44	68
Dissatisfied	30	22	56	32
	N=27	N=98	N=16	N=28
	Committee members not lobbied	Committee members lobbied	Committee members not lobbied	Committee members lobbied
Satisfied	75	77	53	63
Dissatisfied	25	23	47	37
	N=72	N=53	N=17	N=27
	Group members asked to lobby	Group members not asked to lobby	Group members asked to lobby	Group members not asked to lobby
Satisfied	73	83	64	53
Dissatisfied	27	17	36	47
	N=90	N=35	N=25	N=19

[a] The partially satisfied and fully satisfied categories were combined here, as the percentage of responses in the partially satisfied categories was small, and collapsing them simplified these tables.

hardly mattered what lobbying technique a group used. Success rates hovered around 75 percent regardless of technique. And on nearly three-quarters of all policy requests there was no conflict. But when there was conflict, lobbying the committee staff made the biggest difference for a group. Groups that lobbied staff on conflictual proposals were much more successful than those that did not. Groups that lobbied members had an advantage over those that did not, but the net advantage was less than that for groups that lobbied staff. By contrast, as suggested earlier, grass-roots lobbying did not pay off for those groups that did it in conflictual situations.

More refined analysis is called for, however, partly because some groups used two or three of the lobbying techniques. Multivariate statistical analysis of the highway and transit groups' satisfaction with the committee's actions on their policy requests (an analysis that included additional variables) also indicated that lobbying committee staff produced the highest degree of satisfaction and that conflict was detrimental to success. Contrary to popular opinion, making PAC contributions either to the Big Four or to the committee's rank and file members had little effect on groups' success rates. PAC contributions may ease access, but, as we have seen, state and local groups, which do not have PACs, also have access to the committee and relatively high success rates on their policy requests.[21]

Summary

During the House Public Works and Transportation Committee's consideration of the Surface Transportation and Relocation Assistance Act of 1987, there was broad general agreement among committee and interest group actors alike that the highway and urban mass transit programs should be continued, as members of Congress and the groups in question benefited from those programs. Because of this agreement the particulars of the bill were worked out within the committee in mostly private negotiations among top committee members, staff, and, at times, lobbyists. As we would expect under these legislative circumstances, lobbyists confined themselves at this stage mostly to an inside strategy in their dealings with the committee, making a point of publicly stressing areas of agreement among groups while at the same time exposing disagreements that they could not resolve among themselves.

Finally, although the committee bill satisfied the majority of interest group requests, Table 12-1 in particular shows that the committee was hardly the pawn of the interest groups that lobbied it. There were numerous points on which the committee simply refused the requests of interest groups, not even attempting to work out compromises that would satisfy everyone. Facing as they did a hostile president, these groups needed the support of the committee at least as much as the committee needed them. Thus, the inside lobbying techniques that they used offered the additional advantage of minimizing any public perception of discord in the transportation community, which might have been used by other actors to undermine the bill at later stages in the legislative process.

Notes

1. *USA Today,* November 10, 1986.
2. Jeffrey M. Berry, *The Interest Group Society,* 2d ed. (Glenview, Ill.: Scott, Foresman, 1989), 102-116, 231-233; Berry, *Lobbying for the People: The Political Behavior of Public Interest Groups* (Princeton, N.J.: Princeton University Press, 1977), 212-252; and Kay L. Schlozman and John T. Tierney, *Organized Interests and American Democracy* (New York: Harper and Row, 1986), 289-317.
3. Randall B. Ripley and Grace A. Franklin, *Congress, the Bureaucracy, and Public Policy,* 4th ed. (Chicago: Dorsey, 1987); Michael T. Hayes, *Lobbyists and Legislators* (New Brunswick, N.J.: Rutgers University Press, 1981); and Mancur Olson, *The Logic of Collective Action* (Cambridge, Mass.: Harvard University Press, 1965).
4. For a full elaboration of this argument, see E. E. Schattschneider, *The Semi-Sovereign People* (New York: Holt, Rinehart, and Winston, 1960). See also, Olson, *The Logic of Collective Action;* and Hayes, *Lobbyists and Legislators.*
5. The bill did reauthorize programs in which funds were distributed by formula to every state in the country and from which virtually every citizen would benefit. But it also contained many benefits for individual districts and particular interest groups. This chapter concentrates on lobbying for the latter.
6. Elizabeth Drew, *Politics and Money: The New Road to Corruption* (New York: MacMillan, 1983); Brooks Jackson, *Honest Graft: Big Money and the American Political Process* (New York: Knopf, 1988); and Harold W. Stanley and Richard G. Niemi, *Vital Statistics on American Politics* (Washington, D.C.: CQ Press, 1988), 138.
7. If, for example, a Democrat who represents a blue-collar district receives a $5,000 contribution from a labor PAC and then votes as that union wishes, is it because of the contribution or because of the member's constituency? The latter is at least as plausible an explanation for the vote as the former, yet popular accounts sometime fail to control for such influences.
8. In 1987 and 1989, I interviewed top lobbyists for eighteen of the twenty-three core groups and key staff members of the House Public Works and

Transportation Committee. In addition to the groups named, I also interviewed lobbyists from Associated Builders and Contractors, American Correctional Association, American Public Transit Association, American Bus Association, American Traffic Safety Services Association, American Trucking Associations, Associated General Contractors, Association of American Railroads, Highway Users Federation, League of American Wheelmen, National Association of Counties, National Association of Regional Councils, National League of Cities, National School Transportation Association, and Transport Workers Union.

 9. Information on interest group preferences came from the transcript of the hearings: House Committee on Public Works and Transportation, *Extension of the Nation's Highway, Highway Safety, and Public Transit Programs,* Hearings before the Subcommittee on Surface Transportation, 99th Cong. 1st sess. (Washington, D.C.: U.S. Government Printing Office, 1985). Additionally, transcripts of subcommittee and full committee markups were made available by the committee for use in this study.

10. Pursuing a strategy of mutual noninterference, interest groups deliberately seek to occupy narrow "issue niches" where they are unlikely to provoke opposition from other groups in their policy system. See William P. Browne, "Organized Interests and Their Issue Niches: A Search for Pluralism in a Policy Domain," *Journal of Politics* 52 (May 1990): 477-509.

11. Berry, *Interest Group Society,* 165-172; and Schlozman and Tierney, *Organized Interests,* 278-281.

12. For other examples, see David B. Truman, *The Governmental Process,* 2d ed. (New York: Knopf, 1971), 352-394; and Berry, *Interest Group Society.*

13. Kenneth A. Shepsle, *The Giant Jigsaw Puzzle* (Chicago: University of Chicago, 1978), 63-93 and 231-261; Richard F. Fenno, Jr., *Congressmen in Committees* (Glenview, Ill.: Scott, Foresman, 1973); and Steven S. Smith and Christopher J. Deering, *Committees in Congress* (Washington, D.C.: CQ Press, 1984), 108.

14. Burt Solomon, "Staff at Work," *National Journal,* May 16, 1987, 1174-1176.

15. Studies that show a strong impact for PAC contributions include: James B. Kau, Donald Keenan, and Paul H. Rubin, "A General Equilibrium Model of Congressional Voting," *Quarterly Journal of Economics* 97 (May 1982): 271-293; and Allen Wilhite and John Theilmann, "Labor PAC Contributions and Labor Legislation: A Simultaneous Logit Approach," *Public Choice* 53 (1987): 267-276. Studies that have found little or no PAC impact on roll-call voting include: Janet M. Grenzke, "PACs and the Congressional Supermarket: The Currency Is Complex," *American Journal of Political Science,* 33 (February 1989): 1-24; Frank Wayman, "Arms Control and Strategic Arms Voting in the U.S. Senate: Patterns of Change, 1967-1983," *Journal of Conflict Resolution* 29:225-251; and John R. Wright, "PACs, Contributions, and Roll Calls: An

Organizational Perspective," *American Political Science Review* 79 (June 1985): 400-414. Other studies show that the effects depend on the circumstances under which the bill is considered; see Diana M. Evans, "PAC Contributions and Roll-call Voting: Conditional Power," in *Interest Group Politics,* 2d ed., ed. Allan J. Cigler and Burdett A. Loomis (Washington, D.C.: CQ Press, 1986), 114-132; and Jean Reith Schroedel, "Campaign Contributions and Legislative Outcomes," *Western Political Quarterly* 40:371-389. Studies of the impact of PAC contributions on committees include: Richard L. Hall and Frank Wayman, "Buying Time: Rational PACs and the Mobilization of Bias in Congressional Committees" (Paper presented at the annual meeting of the Midwest Political Science Association, Chicago, 1989); Diana M. Evans, "Policy Making in the Concrete Triangle: Interest Group Demands and Committee Responses on Highway Legislation" (Paper presented at the annual meeting of the American Political Science Association, Atlanta, 1989); and John R. Wright, "Contributions, Lobbying and Committee Voting in the U.S. House of Representatives" (Paper presented at the annual meeting of the American Political Science Association, Washington, D.C., 1988).

16. See, for example, Diana M. Evans, "Oil PACs and Aggressive Contribution Strategies," *Journal of Politics* 50 (November 1988): 1047-1056; and J. David Gopoian, "What Makes PACs Tick? An Analysis of the Allocation Patterns of Economic Interest Groups," *American Journal of Political Science* 28 (May 1984): 259-281.

17. The groups with PACs were Associated General Contractors, American Road and Transportation Builders Association, American Trucking Associations, Amalgamated Transit Union, Transport Workers Union, National School Transportation Association, Associated Builders and Contractors, and American Bus Association.

18. For what it is worth, the group that only gave 2 percent of its contributions to the leaders, ABC, had been repeatedly rebuffed on its top priority, repeal of the requirement that workers be paid the locally prevailing wage. None of these contribution figures include honoraria, the fees that interest groups pay to members of Congress, especially those on key committees, for speaking engagements. Such engagements may amount to little more than a chat over breakfast at the group's Washington office, for which members may be paid $1,000. There is some indication that increasingly groups are paying honoraria to top staff members as well, including one of the top staff members of this committee, who was fired by an apparently chagrined chairman after the *Washington Post* revealed the staffer's acceptance of the fees. See Charles R. Babcock, "Toiling in the Capitol's Vineyards Is Not without Its Rewards," *Washington Post,* October 6, 1989; and Babcock, "Committee Aide's Tenure Ends Abruptly after Fee Disclosures," *Washington Post,* November 1, 1989.

19. Schlozman and Tierney, *Organized Interests,* 293.

20. John W. Kingdon, *Congressmen's Voting Decisions* (New York: Harper and Row, 1973), 143-144.
21. Diana Evans, "Policy Making in the Concrete Triangle: Interest Group Demands and Committee Responses on Highway Legislation" (Paper presented at the annual meeting of the American Political Science Association, Atlanta, 1989).

13. OPENING DOORS FOR KINDRED SOULS: THE WHITE HOUSE OFFICE OF PUBLIC LIAISON

Joseph A. Pika

When we think of interest group involvement in politics, what most often comes to mind are electoral initiatives such as campaign contributions or legislative lobbying. Increasingly, however, groups have focused their attention on the executive branch, which has reciprocated by becoming most accommodating to a host of interests.

In this article Joseph Pika details how the Office of Public Liaison has developed into an integral part of the White House bureaucracy. Adopting a historical perspective, he illustrates how public liaison was born at the advent of the modern presidency, with FDR, and how it has become more and more institutionalized over virtually all subsequent administrations. Beginning with the representation of various population groupings (African-Americans, Jews, Catholics, labor, and so forth), public liaison has expanded to cover numerous issues, such as trade, arts, and education.

Pika notes the formalization of public liaison in the Ford administration; indeed, "public liaison has become a feature expected of the modern White House, evolving in much the same way as relations with the press and Congress although not accorded the same prominence." Given its relatively low position on the White House totem pole, the Office of Public Liaison may serve symbolic purposes as much as substantive ones. Regardless, interests cannot afford to ignore the White House, nor can the president and the White House staff fail to attend to a wide array of interests and population groupings. As in most relationships between groups and elected officials, all involve a desire to reduce the levels of uncertainty inherent in political life. The Office of Public Liaison offers one more opportunity to accomplish this goal—at 1600 Pennsylvania Avenue.

Interest groups have never been shy about knocking on the White House door, but until the administration of Franklin Roosevelt, there was not much point in doing so. Presidents, assisted by a skeleton staff of clerks and messengers, performed a modest role in the budget process, cautiously set forth only limited legislative proposals, and exercised little discretion. In today's White House things are dramatically different. Annual presidential proposals on the budget and the economy set the agenda for Washington, even if, as happened so often during the Reagan years, they signal intransigence rather than programmatic initiatives. Full-time White House staffs attempt to coordinate foreign and domestic policy, resolve intra-administration differences, and impose the president's imprint on executive branch actions. Trade policy, environmental protection, and science policy, three areas subject to intense lobbying, are the concerns of specialized staffs housed in the Executive Office of the President.[1] Thus, much of what occurs in the modern White House warrants the attention of groups that seek to shape presidential proposals to advance or protect their interests.

Today's White House also is organized to provide most visitors with a warm welcome from a familiar face. Since the administration of Gerald Ford, each president has established and maintained a specialized White House staff to oversee contacts with interest groups, thereby formalizing a practice that can be traced back to FDR. Assignments in the Office of Public Liaison (OPL) are made on the basis of both constituency and function: aides work with demographically identifiable populations (women, senior citizens, Jews, blacks, Catholics, etc.) or economic and employment groupings (labor, trade associations, consumers, teachers, veterans, etc.). Staff members responsible for overseeing relations frequently share the demographic characteristics or organizational affiliations of the groups with whom they work. Thus, they can both provide a sympathetic ear to group concerns and sell the White House position. Such aides become identified as "resident" staff members, recruited for their contacts and understanding of organized communities.

Not all interest group contacts with the White House can be channeled through OPL, but the unit represents an attempt to provide systematic attention to politically significant actors. Liaison specialists have engaged, in varying degrees, in four principal activities: congressional lobbying, policy making, campaigning, and casework. As the president's policy-making responsibilities have increased, the need to win congressional support has become greater. One response was development of a White House staff for legislative liaison, but efforts to sell the president's program also are enhanced by enlisting the aid of groups sympathetic to administration objectives. Public liaison has become the major vehicle for pursuing cooperative lobbying. Wooing group support for the administration's governing coalition is no less important than maintaining the support of groups who were part of its electoral coalition, and the White House is usually interested in finding ways to attract those groups whose allegiance to the opposition is marginal. To build these coalitions, an administration must be willing to embrace the group's legislative or policy goals, and OPL often has sought to inject such political realities into White House policy making.

As part of the effort to demonstrate responsiveness, White House aides also undertake casework for their charges, running interference with bureaucratic agencies, arranging meetings with White House decision makers, or arguing the case internally.

American presidents also need open lines of communication and a capacity to understand the means and motives of collective action. In the United States more than in many other political systems, interest groups enjoy tremendous freedom to pursue their goals through private actions. When presidents seek to encourage or discourage group strategies, the OPL often serves as the administration's guide to the nuances of personality and intra-organizational competition that characterize the vast array of interests.

Public Liaison in the Bush Administration

In its modern guise, public liaison is part of a conscious, coordinated White House effort to build public support for the president's policies and programs. In the Bush administration OPL is one of four staffs housed within the larger Office of Communications. Within that grouping, the Office of Public Affairs and Media Relations coordinates publications and informational efforts throughout the government and works with regional and local media other than the White House press corps. The Office of Public Liaison provides interest group representatives with access to White House policy makers and organizes briefings on relevant policy initiatives to generate outside support. There also are specialized staffs for research and for speechwriting.

Although the staff assigned to work with interest groups currently does not enjoy the prominence of the staffs working with Congress and the Washington press corps, it remains part of the White House structure that has evolved over time to manage presidential relations with outside centers of power. At the outset of the Bush administration in 1989, fifteen professional staff members worked in OPL, overseeing a staggering array of subject area assignments (sometimes referred to as "portfolios" by earlier administrations). Aides generally mixed policy area assignments with the more traditional constituency group liaison (see Table 13-1). Among the assignments also made in earlier administrations were agriculture, business and trade associations, consumers, and labor. Constituency groups included Jewish organizations, senior citizens, women, blacks, Hispanics, youth, ethnic groupings (Arab-Americans, Asian-Americans, European-Americans), and religious groups (now expanded to include Buddhists, Latter-Day Saints, and evangelicals, in addition to Catholics, Protestants, and Orthodox). As was true in the Reagan administration, a separate aide

Table 13-1 Staff Assignments in White House Office of Public Liaison, Bush Administration, June 1989

Bobbie Kilberg, Deputy Assistant to the President
Agriculture (Scott Sutherland)
Business/Economics (Jeff Vogt, Sutherland)
Child Care/Dependent Care (Joe Watkins, Sarah DeCamp)
Consumers (Vogt, Sutherland)
Domestic Budget/Deficit (Vogt)
Energy (Kathy Jeavons)
Environment (Jeavons)
Health Care (Jeavons, Molly Osborne)
Housing/Enterprise Zones (Osborne)
International Business/Trade (Vogt, Sutherland, Charles Bacarisse)
Jewish Liaison (DeCamp)
Labor/Job Training (Shiree Sanchez, Watkins)
Senior Citizens (DeCamp, Sanchez)
Small Business/Minority Business (Watkins)
Women's Issues (DeCamp, Sanchez)

Sichan Siv, Deputy Assistant to the President
 Domestic Affairs
Arts and Humanities (Jeavons)
Education (Watkins, DeCamp)
Ethics (Jeavons)
Ethnic and Minority Affairs
 Arab-Americans (Vacant)
 Asian-Americans (Bacarisse)
 Black-Americans (Watkins)
 European-Americans (Sutherland, Dan Godzich)
 Hispanic-Americans (Sanchez)
Sports and Youth (Bacarisse, Watkins)

 Foreign Affairs
Captive Nations (Bacarisse)
Defense Issues (Bacarisse)

(Foreign Affairs cont.)
Eastern Europe (Sutherland, Godzich)
European Economic Community (Jeavons)
Freedom Fighters/Regional Conflicts (Vacant)
Foreign Aid (Jeavons)
Human Rights (Watkins)
International Business/Trade (Vogt, Sutherland, Bacarisse)
Latin America/Caribbean (Sanchez)
Middle East (Vacant)
Pacific Rim Nations (Sutherland)
Refugees/Immigrants (Sanchez)
South Africa (Watkins)
Soviet Union (Sutherland)

Doug Wead, Special Assistant to the President
Celebrities (Susan Loud)
Conservatives (Vacant)
Crime/Law Enforcement (Sanchez)
Disabled Americans (Sanchez)
Drug/Alcohol Abuse (Sanchez)
Family Issues (Vacant)
Homeless (Vacant)
Religious Groups
 Buddhists (Siv)
 Catholics (Vogt)
 Evangelicals (Watkins, Godzich)
 Latter-Day Saints (Vacant)
 Orthodox Religions (Vacant)
 Protestants (Watkins)
Veterans (Vacant)

Kilberg, Siv, Wead
Civil Rights (Jeavons)

SOURCE: Documents provided by the White House Office of Public Liaison, June 29, 1989.

was designated to work with conservatives, but the position remained unoccupied halfway through the administration's first year.

In one sense, the dizzying array of assignments may appear absurd—for example, if the White House had sought a single staff member to handle all the portfolios still vacant on June 1, 1989, the job advertisement might have read:

> *Wanted:* Former Maronite Christian converted to Mormonism who has served with distinction in U.S. armed forces despite previous life as a bag person. Must be firmly committed to pro-life movement and freedom fighters everywhere.

Administrations are always looking for just the right person, but this one probably slipped past the talent scouts.

No one person must embody all this experience, of course, but the people who serve in public liaison believe that outside groups look for a liaison person who understands their goals and needs based on shared characteristics and shared experiences. To violate this expectation runs the risk of disruption. For example, when the Carter administration assigned an aide, Landon Butler—who lacked credentials in the union movement—to work with organized labor, labor leaders viewed it as an indication of Carter's insensitivity. Gaining a foothold in the White House has symbolic and potentially important tangible value for interest groups. Access is the first step to wielding influence, and groups can reasonably expect that having a White House contact person is the best way to have an impact on substantive decisions. Groups often develop strong expectations; to the extent that they enjoyed privileged access in the past or perhaps even had the opportunity to approve the White House staff assignment, any perceived slight can be detrimental to future efforts at cooperation. Thus, administrations seek people who will be readily accepted by the most powerful groups in their portfolios. To do otherwise courts unnecessary problems.

The Bush effort in public liaison has its own distinctive features, but it also shares much with the past. To better understand this White House activity, it is necessary to review how it evolved during previous administrations.

From FDR to JFK: Ad Hoc Liaison with Groups

For several decades preceding the Ford administration, presidents drew on their expanded staff resources to designate contacts with critical segments of the population, most often components of the president's electoral coalition. With a few notable exceptions, group liaison was a part-time assignment performed as an adjunct to an aide's principal responsibilities.

Roosevelt

Franklin Roosevelt opened the White House door to interest groups; his successors have kept it ajar. By consulting widely and seeking out the opinions of various figures in private life, FDR used his personal style to facilitate contacts with group representatives. Moreover, the New Deal coalition rested on a carefully woven tapestry of disparate interests whose threads sometimes frayed, thus requiring constant attention. With the provision of additional staff and the onset of war, however, FDR increasingly turned to members of his staff for help in monitoring relations with groups vital to the president's political fortunes or the war effort. Aides were assigned to work with farmers, labor, nationality groups, and Jewish organizations.[2] Jonathan Daniels, a southerner with liberal views on race relations, assembled a team to work with the military services, manpower agencies, and other government departments to minimize the disruptive impact of racial problems on the war effort. But little effort was devoted to changing race relations.[3]

Most liaison activities under FDR were election oriented. David Niles, the White House aide with the widest liaison responsibilities, also was an important election strategist. Thus, the electoral consequences of administration actions were always foremost in his mind.

Truman

Harry Truman retained David Niles as a member of his White House staff and extended his responsibilities. A shadowy figure who was deeply involved in all three of FDR's reelection campaigns, Niles wielded his greatest influence as an advocate for Jewish interests in White House decisions on the partition of Palestine and the independence of Israel.[4] He was the first in a long line of aides to hold the Jewish portfolio in the presidential circle. John Steelman, who had the title of The Assistant to the President, worked with business and labor, particularly during the difficult transition to a peacetime economy when the White House was especially active in seeking to resolve labor-management disputes. Matt Connelly and Harry Vaughn held secondary liaison responsibilities with Catholics and veterans, respectively.

Niles and his deputy, Philleo Nash (also an FDR holdover), developed a liaison operation that was largely outside the main structure of the Truman White House whose activities centered on the special counsel's office.[5] Niles and Nash were heavily involved in the administration's effort to improve race relations; Nash, in fact, credited Niles with originating the term *civil rights*.[6] They also sought to smooth Truman's stormy relations with the most committed New

Dealers, who were critical of his policies, and worked closely with some segments of organized labor. After more than a decade of continuity in the Roosevelt and Truman White Houses, the Niles-Nash collaboration defined group liaison largely in terms of electoral support for the president obtained in exchange for policy decisions favorable to the group in question.

Eisenhower

Dwight Eisenhower's electoral coalition and his approach to the presidency were markedly different. The wartime hero's support did not rest so heavily on a collection of distinctive voting blocs, which made postelection liaison less critical to his future. At the outset of his administration, Eisenhower refused, in the face of pressure, to appoint either a woman or a black to the White House staff to maintain relations with their respective groups.[7]

Despite this reluctance, several "residents" maintained liaison with various interest groups during the Eisenhower presidency. Max Rabb, one of several Jews on the staff, oversaw relations with Jewish groups during the 1952 and 1956 elections and routinely coordinated meetings between the president and group spokespeople. Frederic Fox, corresponding secretary from 1956 to 1961, was a Congregational minister who worked closely with church groups. Jack Anderson worked with farm groups and Earle Chesney with veterans' organizations, but both were involved primarily in congressional relations. In addition to relations with Jewish groups and service as cabinet secretary (his main job), Max Rabb handled liaison with labor and civil rights groups. By 1955, these tasks had become so burdensome that Rabb suggested they deserved full-time attention.[8]

The question of minority representation on the White House staff remained a vexing issue throughout the Eisenhower administration. Campaign literature distributed in 1952 had promised to fulfill a longtime goal of American blacks: "A Republican administration will appoint a Negro to an administrative position in the White House."[9] That promise was fulfilled in July 1955 when E. Frederic Morrow was appointed administrative officer, the first black to serve in a professional White House position. Despite eight years of experience as a field secretary of the National Association for the Advancement of Colored People, however, Morrow was not given responsibility for civil rights matters. His advice was sought and his responsibilities for civil rights correspondence increased after Rabb's departure in 1958, but he was never named the White House assistant for minority affairs. As Morrow's book, diary, and personal papers make clear, his position was difficult. The Negro leadership viewed him as a liaison, a role he also sought to play by mobilizing black voting support during the 1956 election and interpreting black attitudes to the administration. But he lacked the standing needed to have a true impact.[10]

Eisenhower was the first president to consistently utilize group liaison as a means of advancing the administration's legislative program.[11] Robert Gray, who later became president of a major Washington public relations firm, succeeded Rabb as cabinet secretary and headed the grass-roots lobbying effort during Eisenhower's last two years in office. Still, this undertaking remained relatively modest compared to what would come later.[12]

Kennedy

The return of the Democrats to the White House occasioned a restoration of extensive voting bloc ties. Rather than recreating the Niles operation, however, Kennedy aides conducted group liaison on a part-time basis, a practice continued under Lyndon Johnson. For example, among their other duties, Harris Wofford and Lee White were the White House aides responsible for civil rights; they also worked closely with the major leaders of the civil rights movement. Ralph Dungan was concerned primarily with Latin American policy, but he also handled liaison with Catholics. Kennedy aides were assigned to monitor relations with labor unions, Jewish groups, and Protestants; two new portfolios also emerged for relations with academics and the elderly.[13]

Under John Kennedy there were few departures from past techniques of conducting interest group liaison. Organized labor formed a close partnership with the White House in lobbying Congress, much in line with efforts at the end of the Eisenhower years. But more significantly, as violence escalated in the South with confrontations between civil rights leaders and local authorities, a major administration effort was mounted to mobilize national sentiment behind peaceful strategies to achieve reform. In a series of eleven sessions held in the White House from May through July 1963, Kennedy met with a total of 1,558 members of so-called leadership groups. These meetings focused on community leaders who were expected to return to their communities and help organize efforts to defuse racial tension and support concrete attempts to improve minority conditions. The president met with twenty-three governors; thirty civil rights leaders; the seventy members of the Business Council; and larger groups (120-350) of small businessmen (hotel, restaurant, and theater owners), labor leaders, religious leaders, educators, lawyers, and women.

The conferences stretched the resources of the White House to their limits. Departmental personnel helped compile the invitation lists and coordinate many of the details. Because of Attorney General Robert Kennedy's prominent role in civil rights matters, Justice Department aides were heavily involved, although Lee White, the White House counsel, served as the principal coordinator. It was hoped the meetings would serve several purposes: demonstrate the administration's commitment to civil rights; initiate action while legislative efforts were stalled in Congress; enable the White House to seize the initiative, particularly since blacks were becoming increasingly restive and A. Philip Randolph, the prominent black labor leader, had announced plans for the October 1963 March on Washington; and provide a presidential push to establishing a "Negro-white dialogue" between civil rights activists and "representatives of the Southern white power structure." [14]

Subsequent administrations made conferences a routine feature of White House outreach. The Kennedy experience illustrates why such an in-house capacity would be attractive; with the aura of myth and power that surrounds the presidency, few experiences in American life are so likely to influence participants as a visit with the president. The messages communicated in such a setting are likely to take on a special urgency and significance, particularly for less-sophisticated visitors.

Johnson and Nixon: Harbingers of Things to Come

Lyndon Johnson pursued an ambitious strategy of group liaison; during his administration the range of assignments expanded considerably and a subtle mix of roles began to emerge. In conjunction with the emergence of full-time assignments under Nixon, the contemporary structure of group liaison began to take shape.

Johnson

Lyndon Johnson's system of group liaison must be understood in relation to two dimensions: location and purpose. Johnson designated a large number of White House aides to serve as "resident" contacts. Mike Manatos, the principal liaison with the Senate, worked with the Greek community during the Cyprus crisis. Myer Feldman continued to deal with Jewish groups and was later replaced by Harry McPherson, Walt Rostow, and, to a much lesser extent, Ben Wattenberg. Liz Carpenter worked with women, as did Esther Peterson and Betty Furness, both of whom also dealt with consumers. Three Catholics on the staff—Ralph Dungan, Jack Valenti, and Joe Califano—shared work in that area. Eric Goldman, a historian, and John Roche, a political scientist, succeeded Arthur Schlesinger, Jr., in working with academics. Finally, Brooks Hays and Bill Moyers worked with Protestant (especially Baptist) groups, and Hobart Taylor and Clifford Alexander dealt with blacks.

Liaison also was conducted by "nonresidents"—aides who did not share demographic characteristics. Both business and labor received attention from several aides; at least four aides were assigned to work with business, and six staff members shared responsibility for working with labor while also handling their other assignments in congressional relations, policy development, and legal affairs.[15] On another front, Devier Pierson, a polished D.C. lawyer, oversaw contacts with farm and nationality groups in preparation for the 1968 election.[16]

Not every group was encouraged to bring its problems to the White House, nor was Johnson shy about using non-White House aides to help him achieve his purposes. Johnson explicitly chose to avoid becoming too involved in the squabbles of the Hispanic community and located the major administration liaison in the Equal Employment Opportunity Commission (EEOC) rather than in the White House.[17] Similarly, much of the political liaison with blacks was undertaken by an official of the Democratic National Committee.[18] Secretary of Labor Arthur Goldberg provided another avenue to work with the Jewish community, as did private citizens with close political ties to the president such as Abe Fortas, a prominent Washington lawyer and future associate justice of the Supreme Court, and Arthur Krim, head of United Artists and finance chairman of the Democratic National Committee. In short, not every group had a resident counterpart in the White House, nor did Johnson hesitate to use people from inside or outside the executive branch as intermediaries.

It is more difficult to characterize the full extent of the purposes served by these many linkages. Some liaison appointments seem to have been tangible rewards for support or intended to shape substantive decisions, but others seemed primarily symbolic in character. Although Esther Peterson and Betty Furness may genuinely have sought to represent the interests of consumers within the White House, there is little evidence to suggest that the appointments resulted in major policy departures. Much the same might be said of the work with academics, Protestants, and Catholics; it was possibly reassuring to members of these groups to be received by White House personnel and have a contact person for grievances, but the assignments were largely symbolic. At the other extreme, some liaison appointments apparently were regarded as a portion of the spoils derived from political support, a tangible reward for a group's efforts in behalf of the victorious ticket. This viewpoint may partially explain the appointment of black aides to the Johnson staff, a move black spokespeople had sought from Democratic administrations for two decades but had always been denied. Finally, some aides were assigned principally to ensure a community's influence in the shaping of policy. The Jewish liaison, which was especially extensive under Johnson, and the intimate contacts with organized labor may be justly regarded as falling into this category.[19]

It was under Johnson that two other patterns emerged that became increasingly prominent under his successors: (1) expanded White House liaison efforts with the approach of an election campaign, and (2) use of White House liaison to mobilize public support for presidential policies. During 1967 Johnson firmed up White House assignments with a probable eye to a reelection effort. The same pattern surfaced for Nixon, Ford, and Carter; public liaison, in many respects, is a shadow campaign operation, and, to the extent that it becomes a vehicle for projecting favorable presidential images, it represents part of the permanent campaign effort that has become part of the modern White House.

As has been well documented, Johnson was especially sensitive to criticism on Vietnam. White House aides used their connections with organized groups to seek additional public support for the administration's position on the war. John Roche, for example, actively monitored the antiwar movement within the Democratic party and organized presidential meetings with academics in an effort to generate supporters in a community dominated by critics.[20] The White House even encouraged formation of a citizens' group supporting administration policy—the National Committee for Peace with Freedom in Vietnam (also known as the Douglas Committee)—an administration tactic that was expanded significantly under Nixon.[21]

Nixon

Richard Nixon moved public liaison still closer to its current organizational form. Nixon was notoriously uncomfortable in dealing with situations in which he was asked for help or had to do so himself. Thus, it is not surprising that he would have created an institutional framework for conducting public liaison. It was during his final year in office that William Baroody, the first director of OPL under Ford, presented a proposal to Nixon for concentrating group liaison in a specialized White House Office unit. In fact, some steps already had been taken in that direction under Charles Colson, who emerged as a major White House figure during the period 1969-1972. Colson developed a reputation as a specialist in campaign "dirty tricks," but he had joined the administration with the central assignment of generating support for the president's Vietnam policies. As the range of Colson's assignments expanded, he became a major figure in the 1972 electoral campaign, partially responsible for creating a new majority coalition comprised of voters lured away from the New Deal coalition—blue-collar workers, Catholics, and white ethnics. By 1972 Colson's initial staff of four had grown to twenty-three and included several so-called constituency managers responsible for liaison with critical voting blocs, such as the elderly, youth, Jewish organizations, and Hispanics, as well as the groups noted above.

Under Nixon, group liaison was by no means limited to Colson's staff. Civil rights organizations were handled by Bob Brown and Stanley Scott, both blacks. Leonard Garment also dealt with civil rights, but principally he was a contact with Jewish groups and American Indians. Peter Flanigan and his staff specialized in business matters, with Flanigan, a Catholic, also serving as a contact for his coreligionists. Virginia Knauer worked with consumer groups, and Anne Armstrong oversaw liaison with women, youth, and Hispanics. Thus, the Nixon White House replicated, in most respects, the Democrats' attention to discrete segments of the population, often followed Johnson's system of resident assignments, and expanded liaison activity in the days leading up to the 1972 election even more than Johnson had done.

Colson played a pivotal role in the evolution of White House relations with interest groups. His staff, which concentrated full time on the core liaison activities, qualified as the first Office of Public Liaison in every respect but title. Colson's lasting effect, however, was to define the outer limits of acceptable conduct. Although his most questionable activities involved campaign dirty tricks that were not directly related to public liaison, the unit's reputation was damaged. Subsequent administrations, especially Ford's, took care to avoid any semblance of similarity.

Colson joined the White House in the fall of 1969 as an adjunct to the congressional relations effort. Bryce Harlow, a veteran of the Eisenhower White House, sought to replicate the tactics used from 1958 to 1960 in gathering the "outside assistance and outside resources" of friendly groups in confronting a hostile, Democrat-controlled Congress.[22] The first battles focused on winning support for the nomination of G. Harold Carswell to the Supreme Court and for approval of the administration's proposed antiballistic missile (ABM) system. Soon afterward, the focus shifted to thwarting Senate efforts to cut off funding for the Vietnam conflict. Colson became the principal figure in organizing purportedly independent citizens groups that provided support for the administration through newspaper ads and letter-writing campaigns. In reality, the White House (primarily Colson) raised the funds that made such efforts possible, selected the groups' executive directors, designed and wrote copy for the ads, and selected the congressional targets for group lobbying efforts. These activities made the groups virtual White House front organizations.

Colson, a former Marine, adopted an offensive approach to group liaison. The goal was group mobilization, not merely responsiveness. As he explained in a memo to an aide, "We go out and actively seek them, as contrasted to sitting back and waiting for them to come to us with problems." [23] In this vein, Colson organized and chaired the weekly meetings of an ad hoc committee on national security issues. The group first lobbied Congress for approval of the ABM system and then worked to defeat two Senate efforts to curtail the war in Indochina: the Cooper-Church and Hatfield-McGovern amendments. Groups represented on the committee were the American Legion, American Security Council, Veterans of Foreign Wars, Association of the U.S. Army, Naval Reserve Association, Air Force Association, Retired Officers Association, Reserve Officers Association, and the National Rifle Association. White House front groups organized for these efforts were the Citizens to Safeguard America, Tell It to Hanoi, and Americans for Winning the Peace. Group and public pressure was systematically brought to bear on legislators thought to be leaning for or against the administration position or who were up for reelection.

Colson would not have won a popularity contest among his coworkers. He frequently engaged in turf battles with other staff members, a pattern that was attributed to his personality but also reflected the ambiguous position of public liaison in the White House. As Colson explained it,

> It was one of the . . . most painful parts of my job that I overlapped with everybody. . . . The job has an inherent conflict built into it in that people in the White House who were dealing with substance and policy exclusively want to just do that, they want to carry things out the way they see the particular problem. When you inject how the world outside sees it, there is an understandable conflict, and my job had to be at times to be an advocate for a point of view.[24]

As one of the major advocates of a strategy focused on northern rather than southern voters for the 1972 campaign, Colson sought especially to shape administration positions on busing, abortion, and aid to parochial schools to maximize Nixon's appeal to voting groups traditionally part of the New Deal coalition. But, his activities in congressional relations and public relations brought him into conflict with other White House offices primarily charged with these responsibilities.

These internal conflicts, no doubt exacerbated by the personalities involved, chronically afflicted public liaison staffs—for example, State Department officials were no less resentful of David Niles's involvement in shaping Truman's Middle East policy. Colson's experience, an extreme one, illustrates the difficulty of integrating public liaison into the larger White House structure, a problem tackled by each of the four succeeding administrations.

Ford and Carter: Providing Help for Newcomers

Both Gerald Ford and Jimmy Carter assumed office with limited exposure to the major interest groups in American politics. A long congressional career that included more than a decade as a party leader had helped Ford develop contacts with a wide range of groups, but he had never been a candidate for national office. Carter was a stranger to Washington and a newcomer to national politics. Public liaison proved useful for both executives but in quite different ways.

Ford

William Baroody, Colson's successor under Nixon, ultimately succeeded in concentrating and redirecting group liaison under the Ford administration. His reorganization proposals had been considered but never fully adopted by Nixon; Ford found the enhanced public relations aspects of the reformed office especially attractive. From 1974 to 1976 OPL sponsored a series of twenty-four regional conferences around the nation, including nine on proposed plans for consumer representation. Fifteen to twenty organizations were enlisted to cosponsor the sessions in each community. President Ford addressed audiences at eleven of these gatherings and fielded questions at five, which provided opportunities for him to gain much-needed exposure and practice on the campaign trail. Taking the White House on the road also demonstrated that his was an open presidency, anxious to receive public input, in contrast to its predecessor.

Back in Washington the White House staff organized several formats for briefing representatives of business and trade associations. "Theme days" brought together up to 250 participants from relevant interests for discussions in the auditorium of the old Executive Office Building. In the White House, the East Wing family theater housed up to eighty for policy discussions, and the cabinet room was used for briefing groups of eighteen to thirty. The staff sought to take maximum advantage of space availability in scheduling groups to interact with administration officials. Leaders of single groups were brought in for more intimate discussions when it was considered mutually desirable. Demographic constituencies—blacks, women, Hispanics, youth and white ethnics/Catholics—also received the extensive attention that had come to be expected from "residents."

Overall, the Ford OPL operation effected a successful transition from the Nixon years. Public liaison was given a respectable face through operations that were less aggressive and less overtly political. To distinguish themselves from the Colson years, Ford aides consciously suppressed their involvement in the 1976 campaign and made few forays into cooperative lobbying.

Carter

Two distinct phases and two centers of group liaison were evident under Carter, who had entered office with a strong, frequently voiced distrust of self-interested group activity. Carter, like Ford, sought to demonstrate at the outset that the White House door was open. Unfortunately, there seemed to be little systematic thought given to who was invited in. OPL floundered; its initial director resigned after less than two years, and the staff was virtually disbanded. In its place arose a two-pronged approach: one group of relatively senior White House assistants oversaw relations with electorally significant constituencies; a separate staff, operating under the title of public liaison, coordinated its lobbying efforts in behalf of administration programs with the domestic policy and congressional relations staffs as part of the legislative program machinery redesigned by Vice President Walter Mondale. The latter group was headed by Anne Wexler, a Washington insider, who helped to mobilize group support behind presidential objectives.

Wexler's staff members were assigned to work on a limited set of policy issues rather than deal with single, identifiable interest group sectors. They also were asked to involve affected groups in policy development as well as brief them on the administration position. Staff members sought to generate grass-roots support by bringing community leaders into the White House for briefings on programs pending before Congress (such as the SALT II treaty) and frequently asking undecided legislators to suggest invitees. Thus, Carter's staff, like Kennedy's and Ford's, recognized the importance of reaching community leaders; unlike Ford, however, the Democrats more consciously used the White House as a dramatic backdrop.

By its last year in office (just before the election), the Carter administration had completed appointment of a full complement of special assistants to the president to maintain relations with significant constituency groups such as women, blacks, elderly, Hispanics, Jews, labor, white ethnics, and consumers. Several aides were especially well-known figures in their communities. Louis Martin, for example, was brought into the White House to perform many of the same liaison services he had undertaken for Kennedy and Johnson from inside the Democratic National Committee. Nelson Cruikshank was a longtime union specialist in Social Security policy who had become a leader in the senior citizen movement. Esther Peterson had worked with consumers under Johnson and brought a long record of experience in the labor and women's movements with her. The special assistants were quite active in the 1980 campaign, representing Carter at group events and producing an extensive set of newsletters and releases that trumpeted the administration's responsiveness to group needs during the past four years.

Far from being concerned about losing turf, Anne Wexler appreciated being free of the particularized complaints and special pleadings so often vocalized by group spokespeople. Moreover, without firm constituency ties, her staff was less constrained in forming temporary alliances as policy issues required.

In sum, Carter overcame initial doubts about group relations to open still more avenues of access and to mount a more systematic effort to enlist support than any of his predecessors.

Reagan and Bush:
Integration with Communications

Under Ronald Reagan's initial OPL director, Elizabeth Dole, liaison was once again organized as a single White House unit with staff members designated to oversee ties with specific constituencies. Business, labor, Jews, consumers, blacks, women, Hispanics, and the elderly received separate staff assignments. Reagan's staff played an aggressive role in helping gain passage of the administration's 1981 budget and tax proposals by coordinating administration lobbying efforts with the business community.[25] Relations with conservative groups, who also had an assigned contact person in the White House, proved ticklish. Although vocally supportive of the social policy agenda espoused by such groups, the administration did not push these issues aggressively during its first term, resulting in periodic outbursts of criticism.

With Elizabeth Dole's departure, a succession of women held the top post in OPL: Faith Ryan Whittlesey, Linda Chavez, Mari Maseng, and Rebecca Range. Typically, OPL's director has been the highest ranking woman in the White House, a pattern that was also true under Carter. But the unit has gradually declined in significance. When Patrick Buchanan became director of communications, OPL came within the orbit of his staff, where it has remained ever since. Under Buchanan, the office was reorganized by Linda Chavez into three separate divisions: economic issues, domestic issues, and military issues. Interest group residents were housed within these separate clusters.

Ms. Chavez must have been a recruiter's dream candidate for a position in public liaison. An Hispanic whose husband was Jewish, she had become a particular favorite of conservative groups who lobbied hard for her appointment to the post. Upon assuming the job, she acknowledged many of the pressures that typically have plagued members of the staff:

> Having an office of public liaison creates a lot of expectations from constituency groups. . . . A lot of groups would like to think that they have representatives in the White House, . . . [they] want to think you're an Hispanic or a woman and that you speak for that particular ethnic group or gender. I don't believe any individual can do that.[26]

OPL continued to function as part of the administration's public relations efforts throughout Reagan's second term, although it frequently confronted irate groups. Jewish groups, for example, were outraged in 1985 when President Reagan visited a cemetery in Bitburg, West Germany, where Nazi storm troopers had been interred. Despite protests that preceded the president's visit, the stop was not removed from the trip's itinerary, causing a storm of protest among Jewish leaders in the United States.

Group disaffection may not have been isolated during Reagan's second term. Political scientists have hypothesized that a president's support, as reflected in public opinion polls, is affected adversely by an informal "coalition of minorities" that gradually forms among disgruntled groups over the course of an administration's term in office. In short, presidential action or inaction on a range of specific policy issues will alienate some combination of groups, including previous supporters as well as opponents. The cumulative effect of such disgruntlement is a negative impact on popular support for the president.[27] During his final term, Reagan's OPL staff may have operated under unusually adverse conditions. Reagan was the first president since Eisenhower to serve for two full terms, and the staff had to contend with eight years of accumulated dissatisfactions.

Under Bush, OPL remains housed in the communications office. David Demarest, Bush's assistant for communications, gained experience in public and intergovernmental affairs (a euphemism for media and group liaison widely used in the executive branch) during four years in the Office of the U.S. Trade Representative and three years in the Department of Labor before serving as communications director of the 1988 Bush-Quayle campaign. The office also has retained a tripartite organization, with three senior staff members overseeing aides assigned to work with policy issues and constituency relations (see Table 13-1). Two of the three supervisors worked in the 1988 campaign: Bobbie Greene Kilberg was senior adviser to campaign scheduling, and Doug Wead served as deputy director of voter outreach. Sichan Siv, who worked at the United Nations for four years after escaping from Cambodia in 1976, entered the administration after serving as manager of Asia and Pacific programs at the Institute of International Education.

The Bush operation has been low key and has maintained low visibility. As suggested by the senior aides' backgrounds, campaign experience remains closely related to the office's activities, but assignments continue to stress policy responsibilities as well as constituency representation. If past patterns hold true, electoral concerns will become more pronounced in the unit's organization and activity with the approach of 1992. This will be particularly interesting in the Bush case since the president's strategists may seek to increase their support from black and female voters. The structure and operations of OPL during a president's first term are likely to be reasonably accurate indicators of an administration's reelection strategy.

Conclusion

When interest groups have approached the White House over the past fifty years, they have found a very different reception awaiting them than was true during the republic's first century and a half. Modern presidents have found it advantageous, perhaps even necessary, to maintain systematic oversight of relations with organized interests. The relationships often have been mutually beneficial. Groups have approached the White House for help in achieving their goals as the presidency has become a more powerful center for policy initiation and administrative oversight. In turn, presidents have sought to enroll groups as parts of their electoral and governing coalitions and to influence their private conduct as well.

Public liaison has become a feature expected of the modern White House, evolving in much the same way as relations with the press and Congress although not accorded the same prominence. The White House aides now specializing in these liaison tasks are recruited at least in part for their unique skills and personal qualifications. Whereas liaison was once the responsibility of Catholic, Jewish, or labor-affiliated members of the staff, a conscious effort is now made to ensure that women, Hispanics, blacks, and trade associations, among others, will find a kindred soul in the White House, who also can serve as a link with these outside groups when it is needed.

Likewise, group representation in the form of appointments to the

White House staff has become expected, despite the reluctance of some chief executives. Moreover, the range of represented groups has widened considerably, reflecting (albeit imperfectly) the changing composition of groups within American society. Calls to have a woman and a black appointed to professional White House positions could be resisted by Eisenhower, but by the mid-1960s the pressures for representation were inescapable. Similarly, the mobilization of such new constituencies as the elderly, Hispanics, and consumers is reflected in staff composition and assignments.

Internally, public liaison has confronted difficulties in carving out its niche in the White House. Aides combine activities in congressional relations, policy making, campaigning, and public relations-communications, leading them to overlap with other White House assignments. The three most recent administrations (Carter, Reagan, and Bush) have sought to stress the unit's role as a builder of cooperative lobbying coalitions rather than as an advocate of group interests, but the representational nature of staff appointments makes this difficult to avoid. Administrations have created expectations of group advocacy and do not want to lose the credit those activities can garner with supporters, but the pressures also can be dysfunctional.

Is it a good idea to maintain such an extensive liaison capacity in the White House? Critics have contended that representative appointments inflate an already bloated presidential staff and demean the office of president, at least symbolically, by suggesting that the national interest is subordinate to politically expedient special interests.[28] But if we accept the view that presidents must, by necessity, be political animals, it follows that inattention to politically powerful interests would be folly. The important question is how that attentiveness is pursued. There has been considerable variation among administrations, ranging from Colson's aggressive, electorally oriented style under Nixon to Ford's soft-sell. Truman and Johnson were more willing to boost the policy goals held by members of their electoral coalition than was Reagan. Although we are far from knowing whether these relationships are characterized by predictable patterns, it is clear that 1600 Pennsylvania Avenue is now a "must stop" for interest group representatives as well as tourists, and that modern presidents have planned a lavish reception for their visitors.

Notes

The research reported in this chapter was made possible through grants from the University of Delaware Research Foundation, the Lyndon Baines Johnson

Foundation, the Gerald R. Ford Foundation, and the National Endowment for the Humanities.

1. These are the United States Trade Representative, Council on Environmental Quality, and Office of Science and Technology Policy, respectively.
2. Eugene Casey worked with farm groups; Dan Tobin and James Barnes with labor (Sidney Hillman declined the offer of a White House job to work with labor in 1942); and Samuel Rosenman with Jewish groups, despite some personal discomfort. David Niles held responsibilities for labor, nationality groups, and Jewish organizations.
3. Jonathan Daniels, oral history interview, Franklin D. Roosevelt Library, Hyde Park, New York, 29-30. Daniels was assisted by Philleo Nash who remained on as an assistant to David Niles and then became his successor under Truman.
4. Joseph A. Pika, "Interest Groups and the White House under Roosevelt and Truman," *Political Science Quarterly* vol. 102 (Winter 1987-1988): 647-668.
5. For an overview of the Truman staff, see F. Heller, ed., *The Truman White House* (Lawrence, Kan.: Regents Press of Kansas, 1980).
6. Philleo Nash, interview with author, June 27, 1984.
7. For Eisenhower's general attitude on these appointments, see especially the staff note for February 26, 1953, office files, office of staff secretary (Minnich), box 1, misc.-A (1), January-May 1953, Dwight D. Eisenhower Library, Abilene, Kansas.
8. Memo of conversation with Maxwell M. Rabb, secretary to the cabinet, February 25, 1955, office file 72-A-23, box 310, space survey for the presidency, Dwight D. Eisenhower Library.
9. Republican National Committee, "The 1952 Republican Fact Sheet on the Negro," item #42, (E. Frederic) Morrow papers, box 1, Dwight D. Eisenhower Library.
10. Morrow papers in the Eisenhower Library include Morrow's diary, which served as the basis for his book *Black Man in the White House* (New York: Coward-McCann, 1962). Also see the oral history interview with Morrow conducted by Dr. Thomas Soapes on February 23, 1977; available at the Eisenhower Library.
11. The Harry S Truman Library contains evidence of cooperative lobbying, but there is no indication of a conscious, coordinated effort to draw upon group support.
12. Bryce Harlow, interview with author, Washington, D.C., December 2, 1976. These activities are not reflected in the papers of Robert Gray housed at the Eisenhower Library, but that absence is not unusual given the liberal interpretation that once pertained to what constituted personal papers.
13. Ralph Dungan worked with labor, Brooks Hays with Protestants, and Myer Feldman with Jewish groups. Arthur Schlesinger, Jr., became a link with intellectuals as well as the Americans for Democratic Action and

Richard Donahue with the elderly.

14. The conference idea seems to have originated with Louis Martin, vice chairman of the Democratic National Committee. Memo, Martin to the attorney general (Robert F. Kennedy), May 13, 1963, White House central files, box 365A, Lee C. White/Executive HU2/MC, John F. Kennedy Library, Boston, Massachusetts. Other materials can be found in White's staff files.

15. Horace Busby, Jack Valenti, Robert Kintner, and Marvin Watson dealt with business on a variety of matters. Larry O'Brien and Henry Hall Wilson worked closely with labor in congressional lobbying. Joe Califano, Douglass Cater, and Milt Semer held a variety of posts in Johnson's domestic policy process while also working with labor. George Reedy was press secretary and a longtime friend of labor, and Harry McPherson, who also dealt with black and Jewish organizations, rounded out the many labor contacts. On the system of labor liaison, see especially: memo, Robert Kintner to Moyers et al., May 16, 1966, office files of Harry McPherson, box 24, "Labor." Also see memos from the vice president to the president, March 15, 1966, and George Reedy to the president, March 16, 1966, in confidential file, LA, box 60, "Labor-Management Relations," Lyndon B. Johnson Library, Austin, Texas.

16. Michel Cieplinski from the Department of State conducted much of the election liaison with nationality groups.

17. Vicente Ximenes was appointed to the EEOC and served as chairman of an interagency committee on Mexican-American affairs. Ximenes had headed the "Viva Johnson" and "Viva Humphrey" clubs during the 1964 campaign. Johnson explicitly rejected the idea of sponsoring a series of White House conferences on problems confronted by Hispanics. His terse response to an option memo presented to him on December 29, 1966, speaks volumes: "We better get away from this—I don't want any Mexican meetings at all. The more you have the more trouble you have." Memo, Califano to president, December 29, 1966, and note, LBJ to Joe, December 31, 1966, White House central file, EX HU2/MC, box 23, "12/31/66," LBJ Library.

18. Louis Martin, who later served as Jimmy Carter's major liaison with the black community, performed largely identical services for Johnson. Hobart Taylor and Clifford Alexander, however, were black members of the White House staff who also dealt with some civil rights issues.

19. Needless to say, the divisions between these categories are imperfect, and trying to characterize an administration's contacts with any segment of the group universe is difficult.

20. John Roche, a former national chairman of Americans for Democratic Action, also worked to protect LBJ's interests in that group, which represented the liberal wing of the Democratic party. For evidence of his liaison with academics, see memos regarding the meeting he organized on September 26, 1967, with a group of Harvard and Radcliffe faculty who met with the president following sessions with McGeorge Bundy and

Robert McNamara. Appointments file [diary backup], September 26, 1967, box 77, LBJ Library.

21. The White House had discussed such an option since 1966. Roche renewed efforts in May 1967, and the group had been launched by July with former senator Paul Douglas, D-Ill., at its head. See: memos, John P. Roche to president, May 19, 1967, June 15, 1967, June 26, 1967, and July 12, 1967, office files of the president (Territo), box 11, LBJ Library.

22. Charles Colson, exit interview, Nixon Presidential Materials Project, 2.

23. Memo, Colson to Henry Cashen, February 24, 1971, White House special files, staff member and office files of Charles Colson, box 6, "Henry Cashen [2 of 2]," Nixon Presidential Materials Project.

24. Colson exit interview, 11-12.

25. S. Blumenthal, "Whose Side Is Business On, Anyway?" *New York Times Magazine,* October 25, 1981, 29. For a colorful description of White House efforts to mobilize business support, see Bradley H. Patterson, Jr., *The Ring of Power: The White House Staff and Its Expanding Role in Government* (New York: Basic Books, 1988) 209-211.

26. As quoted in the *New York Times,* June 3, 1985, I16.

27. See John E. Mueller, *War, Presidents and Public Opinion* (New York: Wiley, 1973), 205-208.

28. See the discussion by Stephen Hess, *Organizing the Presidency* (Washington, D.C.: Brookings Institution, 1976); and Dick Kirschten, "Accentuating the Differences," *National Journal,* November 15, 1980, 1944.

14. A TOWER OF BABEL ON FOREIGN POLICY?

Eric M. Uslaner

Most studies of interest group politics focus on domestic concerns—highway programs, civil rights, abortion, taxes, and so forth, ad nauseum. As the world shrinks, however, and as post-World War II foreign policy bipartisanship shows signs of breaking down, increasing numbers of organizations and lobbyists have begun to represent foreign and international interests. Indeed, Eric Uslaner notes that many issues have both domestic and international elements, thus becoming "intermestic" concerns.

In this chapter Uslaner describes the growth of interest group activity on foreign policy matters. Of particular interest to him is the great increase in ethnic-based lobbying. Even the American black community, with its traditional emphasis on domestic policy, has been affected greatly by South African initiatives. The 1990 U.S. welcome afforded African National Congress leader Nelson Mandela is only one indication of African-American interest in foreign policy.

After surveying a large number of ethnic groupings, Uslaner focuses on the Israeli and Arab lobbies. The Israeli lobby, broadly defined, surely is the most effective single foreign representation in American politics. The Arab-American lobby, in contrast, has been notably unsuccessful in pressing its concerns. Historically adept at playing the inside game of Washington politics, the Israeli lobby, led by the American Israel Public Affairs Committee (AIPAC), has become increasingly active in electoral campaigns. Although pro-Israel interests have won some significant victories, Uslaner points out the risk in this strategy, to the extent that "the victorious group [could] be viewed with suspicion by the larger public, much as large corporations are."

All in all, more groups are involved in foreign policy lobbying in more ways than at any time in the twentieth century. Whether such activity can be subsumed into regular pluralist politics, or whether there will be a Tower of Babel on foreign policy, remains to be seen.

Interest groups are the stuff of domestic policy making. In foreign policy, we don't generally think of a variety of interests within the United States. Rather, we think of the world as "us" against "them." Especially in international crises, when the stakes are clear and an entire way of life might be threatened, it is critical that the nation speak with one voice, not many. There simply does not seem room for interest groups. The combatants are not lobbyists but heads of state.

Yet interest groups have long been active, if not quite so prominent, in foreign policy, and in recent years group activity has become even more pronounced. How is foreign policy different from domestic policy? Why do we expect less interest group activity? Why has there been more such activity recently? And what does this mean for the conduct of foreign policy?

Foreign Policy and Domestic Policy

What are the key distinctions between foreign and domestic policy making? First, the stakes are much higher in foreign policy. The entire world could be destroyed by nuclear weapons as a result of a decision that might take only minutes to make. Second, foreign policy decisions are often irreversible. Relations between nations change slowly. Domestic policies that are found to be unpopular or that simply do not work can be altered much more easily. Third, relations with foreign nations are not entirely within the control of American policy makers. Both domestic pressures and the attitude of the Chinese government precluded the establishment of diplomatic relations for more than three decades after the United States decided in 1949 not to recognize the Chinese regime. Fourth, foreign policy decisions, particularly in crises, need to be made quickly. During the Cuban missile crisis in 1962, President John F. Kennedy had to set national policy in just a few weeks as the threat of a nuclear confrontation with the Soviet Union loomed. Domestic issues rarely are resolved so rapidly—for example, government provision of medical care to the elderly remained just an interesting proposal on the legislative agenda for more than half a century. Expertise on foreign policy is much more centralized than on domestic policy. The goals of all Americans are posited to be the same: at the very least, the survival of a democratic way of life against a hostile power that is not committed to individual freedoms. If the nation does not speak with a single voice, our adversaries might think that we lack the resolve to defend ourselves.

Finally, foreign policy issues are of less concern to most Americans than domestic policy. Citizens find events in the international arena far more remote than domestic affairs. Many members of Congress thus seek to highlight their role in domestic policy and to play down any interest they have in foreign policy. One member of the Senate Foreign Relations Committee said of his assignment:

> It's a political liability.... You have no constituency. In my reelection campaign last fall, the main thing they used against me

was that because of my interest in foreign relations, I was more interested in what happened to the people of Abyssinia and Afghanistan than in what happened to the good people of my state.[1]

Most Americans are content to let the president make foreign policy, and they give virtually unchallenged support to the chief executive as long as crises do not appear to get out of hand. Congress also generally follows the president's lead, rarely overturning presidential initiatives in foreign policy. Partisan divisions traditionally have not disrupted international affairs the same way they have affected most domestic issues.[2] In this context the capacity for interest groups to affect foreign policy is very limited. If there is a need for the nation to speak with a single voice, the bargaining among interest groups that is the hallmark of domestic politics seems very much out of place in the international arena.

Many Americans may conjure up a diabolical picture of how private interests try to influence international politics for their own advantage, such as the 1970 attempt by International Telephone and Telegraph to rig the election in Chile to prevent the election of a Marxist president. Americans have ambivalent attitudes toward interest groups generally, but a 1988 poll showed that 72 percent of Americans believed that big business had too much influence on American policy, and 47 percent felt similarly about labor.[3] Groups with ties to foreign interests, whether such groups are primarily domestic or foreign, are viewed with particular suspicion.

Interest Groups and Foreign Policy

Because foreign policy is more than crisis politics, there are plenty of opportunities for interest group activity. Many foreign policy issues involve clear-cut economic stakes for Americans. Trade policies are perhaps the best example. A foreign policy issue thereby becomes a domestic politics concern. Because the world has become increasingly interdependent in the past half century, no longer can we say that certain policies are clearly domestic and others are in the realm of foreign policy. Rather, most policies are now "intermestic." [4] As one example, the dramatic increase in oil prices in 1973-1974 (and again in 1979) radically changed our perception of energy policy. Before 1973 energy decisions were made strictly according to the domestic politics of specific fuels. Thereafter our attention shifted to the producing nations. In another example, President Jimmy Carter forbade grain sales to the Soviet Union following that nation's invasion of Afghanistan in 1979. Ronald Reagan then made the unpopular embargo an issue in the 1980 elections and reversed the policy when he became president. In a final example, Americans traditionally have thought of banks as neighborhood bulwarks that were more worthy of confidence than even our governmental institutions.[5] Since the 1980s, however, many banks have faced severe financial problems because of loans to developing nations. Thus, the growing interdependence of the world economy has led new actors—including, of course, interest groups—to participate in foreign policy decision making.

The Vietnam War changed the way Americans react to foreign policy. Protests against the war were widespread, particularly on college campuses. Support of the president's policies was no longer automatic. Various ideological interest groups sprang up to challenge some of the key assumptions behind our involvement in the war. When the war became associated with a Republican president, many congressional Democrats felt free to make the conflict a partisan issue; the post-World War II era of bipartisanship in foreign policy had come to an end. Party conflict was accompanied by interest group activity. Church groups, which played an important role in protesting the Vietnam War, branched out into nuclear disarmament, the conflicts in El Salvador and Nicaragua (some churches gave sanctuary to refugees from these countries), the cessation of apartheid in South Africa, and the establishment of a Palestinian state. Secular organizations formed for each of these policy areas as well, most prominently the nuclear freeze. Groups advocating a more aggressive foreign policy toward the Soviet Union also formed. On energy and agriculture, groups reflecting a dizzying array of complexities made policy making on these intermestic issues very difficult.[6]

The growth of the role of interest groups in foreign policy paralleled the sharp rise in the number of such organizations in domestic policy.[7] One indicator of how important interest groups have become in American society is the number of informal organizations that have formed in the Congress. In 1985 almost 100 such groups were active, and two-thirds had some foreign policy concerns.[8] Foreign policy making often appears more like a Tower of Babel than a clear voice telling friends and adversaries alike where the United States stands. For every group advocating one side of an issue, at least one other is pursuing an alternative course. The Members of Congress for Peace through Law, founded during the Vietnam era to seek an end to the conflict by legislative means, begat the defense-oriented Members of Congress for Peace through Strength. The Ad Hoc Congressional Committee on Irish Affairs presses for an American policy toward Northern Ireland that would be more favorable to the Catholic population; the Friends of Ireland advocates a more conciliatory approach.

Foreign governments have become increasingly active in lobbying the White House and Congress. West Germany, Canada, France, the Arab countries, and especially Japan have mounted extensive efforts to sway American policies, hiring as their lobbyists distinguished Americans who have served in the Cabinet, in the Congress, and even in the vice presidency.[9] Japan alone spent up to $60 million in 1989 on lobbying, four times as much as in 1984. More than 250 Japanese companies, industries, and government agencies have hired lobbyists. In 1987 the Toshiba Corporation mounted a $9 million attempt to block sanctions for illegally selling sophisticated submarine technology to the Soviet Union. The firm enlisted the support of American companies that do business with it: American Telephone and Telegraph, Hewlett-Packard, International Business Machines, Rockwell, and Xerox, among others. Together, these companies pressured members of Congress not to impose sanctions on the Japanese company. Workers at Toshiba plants in the United States even instigated a letter-writing campaign to Congress, and one Texas factory sent 6,500 letters to Capitol Hill in a single week. The Toshiba effort paid handsome dividends when the Congress enacted very weak sanctions on the firm.[10] Similarly Taiwan, which has not had diplomatic relations with the United States since the establishment of American ties with China in 1979, has mounted a lobbying effort on a par with that of Japan so that it can maintain exports to the United States.[11]

Many Americans worry about such lobbying, especially by foreign groups. Some members of Congress, irate at Toshiba, took to the steps of the Capitol to destroy Japanese products with a sledgehammer. The more staid *New York Times* editorialized about former American officials working for other countries: "Rising public revulsion fuels the chance for dramatic action. . . . It's one thing to tolerate lobbying for private businesses, quite another to have a former Secretary of State, say, put his skills and standing at the disposal of foreigners."[12]

It is difficult to determine the scope or the effectiveness of foreign lobbying. Yet not all interest group activity on foreign policy generates such criticism. Some lobbying, especially that by churches and ethnic groups, is considered quite legitimate. In fact, two-thirds of Americans believe it is legitimate for churches to engage in political activity.[13] The United States is a nation of immigrants, and many Americans have strong bonds with the countries of their heritage. Why are some group activities acceptable, while other types are held in disdain? The answer is little different from a distinction made by E. E. Schattschneider between the National Association of Manufacturers (an umbrella organization of major firms) and the American League to Abolish Capital Punishment: "the members of the [latter] obviously do not expect to be hanged." [14]

Thus, while economic interests expect to gain something for themselves from lobbying, neither religious nor ethnic groups do.

Ethnic Groups and Foreign Policy

What do ethnic lobbies seek, how do they go about organizing support in Congress and the executive branch, and how successful are they? Mohammed Ahrari has suggested three conditions for ethnic group success on foreign policy. First, the group must press for a policy in line with American strategic interests. Second, the group must be assimilated into American society, yet retain enough identification with the "old country" to motivate its members to take some political action. Groups that stand outside the mainstream of American life—for example, Arab-Americans, because of the reasons discussed below, and Mexicans, because many are not citizens—cannot mobilize for political action. Yet something more is required: a high level of political activity. In this sense American Jews are almost distinctive in their ability to affect foreign policy. Finally, the more homogeneous a group is, the greater its impact should be—although this condition is less important than the others.[15] Before considering the pro-Israel and pro-Arab lobbies in detail, we turn first to other ethnic lobbies, all of which have considerably less political clout. Why? Who has power and who does not? What makes the pro-Israel lobby distinctive?

Greek- and Turkish-Americans

Greek-Americans generally are considered second in power to the pro-Israel lobby. The American Hellenic Institute Public Affairs Committee (AHIPAC) is consciously modeled after the American Israel Public Affairs Committee; the two groups have often worked together. AHIPAC lobbied successfully for an arms embargo on Turkey after its 1974 invasion of Cyprus and has pressed for a balance in foreign aid between the two states. The 2 million Greek-Americans are very politically active and loyal to the Democratic party. In 1988 they raised more than 15 percent of the early campaign funds of Greek-American presidential candidate Michael Dukakis. In contrast, the Turkish-American community of 180,000 is not well organized. Recently, it employed a Washington public relations firm to lobby the government, but it has no ethnic lobby and maintains a low profile. As one member of Congress stated, "I don't have any Turkish restaurants in my district." [16]

Eastern Europeans

Eastern Europeans have a long history of political activism. Eight million Polish-Americans and almost a million Lithuanians, Latvians, and Estonians live in the United States. Several midwestern states have large concentrations of Eastern Europeans, and both major political parties have recognized the importance of these groups by establishing divisions dealing with their affairs. The bicameral Ad Hoc Congressional Committee on the Baltic States and the Ukraine has seventy-five members. In 1959 Congress proclaimed the third week of July as Captive Nations Week, to be observed until the Soviet Union withdraws from Eastern Europe and the Baltic states.

These ethnic groups have had little impact on foreign policy, however. They are not united among themselves, and many worry that emphasizing their ethnicity will only stir negative emotions among other Americans. Their lobbies are all understaffed and underfunded. They also have pressed the government to sacrifice détente with the Soviet Union, a policy at odds with those of presidents from both political parties. But, especially since the policies of Soviet president Mikhail Gorbachev have led to greater freedom within the Soviet Union and the liberation of Eastern Europe, President George Bush has not wanted to jeopardize this new openness. Thus, although the United States has never accepted Soviet occupation of the Baltic states, it also refused to grant them recognition in 1989 and 1990 when Lithuania, Latvia, and Estonia declared their independence. The ethnic lobbies favored such recognition, but the general public did not. Neither the president nor Congress was willing to take any side of the many ethnic tensions emerging in Eastern Europe, even as the small lobby representing the country's 70,000 Albanian-Americans pressed for a resolution attacking discrimination against Albanians in Yugoslavia.[17]

Hispanics

Almost 20 million Hispanics reside in the United States, but they have little unity. The Cubans are the best organized politically, but they constitute just 5.3 percent of all Hispanics and stand at the opposite end of the political spectrum from most. Like Eastern Europeans, Cubans generally are strongly anti-Communist. They have lobbied successfully against normalization of relations with Fidel Castro's regime and have secured funding for radio and television transmissions from the United States to Cuba. Moreover, they have been very active in Republican politics, especially in Florida.

Most Hispanics are Mexican-Americans (62 percent), Puerto Ricans (12.7 percent), or Central and South Americans (11.5 percent).[18] Each of these groups tends to be poorer, more Democratic, and less active in politics than most Americans. They generally are more concerned with economic issues than with foreign policy questions. Many Mexicans living in the United States are not citizens. Even those who are have ambivalent feelings toward their old country. Many fear that political activity will stir up the anti-Mexican emotions often found in debates on immigration. Until recently, Mexican leaders did not encourage political intervention by Mexican-Americans.[19]

Puerto Ricans are divided on the status of their homeland: Should it remain a commonwealth, or seek statehood, or become independent? A 1985 meeting of the National Congress for Puerto Rican Rights could not reach agreement on the issue of coordinating strategies with other Hispanic groups. Some Puerto Ricans resent other Hispanics because, on average, Puerto Ricans earn less even though they have had American citizenship longer.[20] For such countries as El Salvador and Nicaragua where American policy is more controversial, foreign policy lobbies are dominated by religious organizations (such as the Washington Office on Latin America) with few ties to the indigenous communities. These organizations largely focus on human rights issues. Some have influence on Capitol Hill, but their lobbying activities tend to concentrate more on legislators who already are committed to their causes.[21]

The fragmentation of the diverse Hispanic community limits the unity and effectiveness (especially on foreign policy issues) of the fourteen-member Hispanic Caucus in the House of Representatives.[22] The more affluent Cuban-Americans have had limited success in isolating Castro and none at all in provoking direct confrontation with him, a policy considered too extreme by the American government. Cubans have become politically active, but they are not fully assimilated into American life, nor are they as widespread throughout the nation as Eastern Europeans, Greeks, and particularly Jews. Issues relating to Mexico, Puerto Rico, and Cuba do not attract the attention of most Americans, in contrast to our role in the Middle East.

Blacks

Blacks, like Hispanics, traditionally have been more concerned with domestic economic issues than with foreign policy concerns. Unlike other ethnic groups in the United States, most black Americans cannot trace their roots to a specific country. Until the 1960s black participation in politics was restricted, both by law and by socioeconomic status. Few blacks have served in Congress, especially on the foreign policy committees, or in the Foreign Service. They also have contributed very little money to election campaigns. Electorally, they have had strong ties to the Democratic party, thus cutting off lobbying activities to Republican presidents and legislators.

Black activity on foreign policy heightened over the issue of ending the apartheid system of racial separation in South Africa. The

Congressional Black Caucus and TransAfrica, a lobbying organization with a budget of $400,000 and a membership of 10,000 as of 1982, led the drive to impose sanctions against South Africa. The South African issue in fact united the black community. Whites also strongly opposed the South African regime and, according to public opinion polls, even believed that giving black South Africans freedom was more important than keeping the country as a stable ally.[23] President Ronald Reagan ultimately agreed in 1985 to accept sanctions against the South African government, after being pushed in that direction by the weight of public opinion, a mobilized black community, and a supportive Congress. African-American lobbying paid off on this issue, but the community is still far from united on other foreign policy issues, including the rest of Africa.

Irish and Asians

Irish lobbying efforts have focused not on Ireland but on Northern Ireland. And they have been extremely controversial because of the terrorist activities of the Irish Republican Army (IRA). Two Irish caucuses have been formed in the Congress and two in the larger society. Of the latter, the strongly pro-IRA Irish National Aid Committee was required in 1971 to register as a foreign agent. The Irish National Caucus, with a budget estimated at $500,000 raised from 100 local chapters, is more moderate. These groups have been very effective in places where the Irish population is large, such as New York. There, local politicians feel constrained at least not to criticize the IRA. In other parts of the country, however, the Northern Ireland issue is both too complex and too hot for most decision makers, thus limiting the impact of Irish lobbying.[24]

Given the impressive lobbying efforts of Japan and Taiwan and the size of the Asian population in the United States—for example, 10 percent of California's population—one might expect considerable power from this group. Yet they have not participated in politics in large numbers. Many recent immigrants are preoccupied with economic issues and eschew politics. They came from cultures without democratic traditions, and they have not placed adaptation at the top of their agenda. Older Japanese and other Asians who faced discrimination in earlier periods (especially during World War II) shy away from politics, in contrast to blacks who have used politics to gain civil rights. The Asian-American community, like the Hispanic, is very diverse and the common bonds among the Koreans, Indochinese, Japanese, and Chinese are few.

The Greek, Cuban, and Irish groups are the most active of those considered above. They are well integrated into American society.

Neither activity nor integration is sufficient, however, to ensure power on foreign policy. Successful groups generally support government policies, especially ones that have popular approval. Irish-Americans face the problem that support for the IRA would not only legitimize terrorism but also strike at a traditional ally—one of our closest, Great Britain. What Greeks and Cubans seek, in contrast, conforms with existing American policy and strategic interests as interpreted by many administrations. The United States has never recognized the Turkish invasion of Cyprus nor the Castro regime in Cuba.

Eastern Europeans, however, have pursued policy goals that successive administrations have rejected. The small size of the Latvian, Lithuanian, and Estonian communities has limited their effectiveness, but probably the stridency of their leaders has hurt them even more. Hispanics (other than Cubans) and Asians have a rather different problem; they have no clear agenda and do not mobilize to push any. The Turks, however, have an agenda and have accomplished part of it despite being outnumbered by Greeks. Turkey's status as a member of the North Atlantic Treaty Organization (NATO), indicative of a strong strategic interest, has been key. Blacks traditionally have not mobilized on foreign policy issues. But, despite lower turnout at the polls and little representation in the foreign policy establishment or in political money, blacks were able to mobilize a multi-ethnic coalition on an issue that struck the public conscience. The country's traditional ethnic groups—such as blacks, Jews, Greeks, Poles, and Irish—were socialized into politics by political machines that also mobilized them into political action. But with the passing of such urban machines, it is unclear that newer immigrants such as Hispanics or Asians will develop the same integration and level of political activity in the near future.[25]

Israeli and Arab Lobbies

The best-organized, best-funded, and most successful of the ethnic lobbies, indeed perhaps of all foreign policy lobbies, represents the interests of Israel. Jews, who dominate the pro-Israel lobby, constitute only 2.7 percent of the American population, but they are strongly motivated and highly organized in support of Israel. They seek to provide U.S. financial aid (both economic and military) to Israel and to deny it to those Arab nations in a state of war with Israel. And they have been very successful indeed. Since its inception in 1951, the lobby is believed to have lost on only three key decisions. In 1978 it failed to prevent the sale of F-15 fighter planes to Saudi Arabia and Egypt, and in 1981 and 1986 it could not block arms sales to the Saudis.[26]

Israel receives by far the largest amount of foreign aid from the

United States, more than $3 billion a year. Only Egypt even approaches the Israeli aid figure. In 1985 Israel and the United States signed a free-trade pact that will completely eliminate all tariff barriers between them by 1995. Israel annually benefits from large tax-exempt contributions from the American Jewish community, including some $500 million in direct charitable grants and a similar amount from the sale of Israeli government bonds.[27] No other foreign nation is so favored.

The Israeli lobby comprises one organization devoted entirely to the cause of that country and a wide-ranging network of Jewish groups that provide support. The American Israel Public Affairs Committee (AIPAC), founded in 1951, has a staff of 100, an annual budget of $7.5 million, and 60,000 members. It operates out of offices one block away from Capitol Hill as well as in other major cities.[28] The success of the Israeli lobby has been attributed to its political acumen. According to Sanford Ungar, "In a moment of perceived crisis, it can put a carefully researched, well-documented statement of its views on the desk of every Senator and Congressman and appropriate committee staff within four hours of a decision to do so." [29] With the organization's close ties to many congressional staffers it is well informed about issues affecting Israel on Capitol Hill. Its lobbying connections are so thorough that one observer maintained, "A mystique has grown up around the lobby to the point where it is viewed with admiration, envy, and sometimes, anger." [30] Activists can readily mobilize the network of Jewish organizations across the country to put pro-Israel pressure on members of Congress in their constituencies, even in areas with small Jewish populations. Even though liberals (and Democrats) tend to be somewhat more sympathetic to Israel than conservatives (and Republicans), AIPAC lobbyists are careful to maintain bipartisan support. AIPAC also works with other interest groups, particularly organized labor.[31]

In contrast, the Arab lobbying effort has been singularly unsuccessful. No major Arab organizations were operating at all before 1972, and the Arab presence was not established in Washington until 1978. The largest Arab group, the National Association of Arab Americans (NAAA) claims 13,000 members. The NAAA seeks closer ties between the United States and the Arab world in political, military, and economic arenas. Despite its support for a weakening of the U.S.-Israeli bond and creation of a Palestinian state, it recognizes the right of Israel to exist. NAAA is modeled directly on AIPAC, but with an estimated 1981 budget of $500,000, it commands far fewer resources. Unlike AIPAC, it makes no pretense of being free from the direct influence of its "mother country." The Arab uprising in the West Bank and Gaza that began in 1987 has energized the Arab-American community.

NAAA now maintains a grass-roots network organized by congressional district and patterned directly after AIPAC.[32] A second major Arab organization, the American-Arab Anti-Discrimination Committee, was founded in 1980 on the model of the B'nai B'rith Anti-Defamation League, established some fifty years ago to combat discrimination against Jews. It does not lobby on legislation.

The heart of the difficulty of Arab-American lobbying efforts is found in the existence of another group, the American Lebanese League, which claims 10,000 members and seeks a democratic, pro-Western Lebanon. It represents Christian forces in Lebanon, which have little in common with the Muslims and Druze of that country. Even a past president of the NAAA admits the central hindrance to Arab lobbying in the United States:

> We can't represent the Arabs the way the Jewish lobby can represent Israel. The Israeli government has one policy to state, whereas we couldn't represent "the Arabs" even if we wanted to. They're as different as the Libyans and the Saudis are different, or as divided as the Christian and Moslem Lebanese.[33]

Inter-Arab divisiveness thus accounts for some, but not all, of the difficulties that these lobbying organizations confront.

Public opinion plays a much larger role. For a long time Americans have been much more sympathetic toward Israel than toward the Arabs. Most polls show that Americans favor the Israeli position by better than a three-to-one margin. Occasionally, as during the 1982 Israeli invasion of Lebanon and the 1985 TWA hostage crisis, public support for Israel drops sharply, but it has generally rebounded. Even as the Arab uprising in the Israeli-occupied territories has sapped public support for Israel, there has been no appreciable increase in support for the Arab cause.[34]

The roots of the friendship between the United States and Israel include such factors as (1) a common biblical heritage (most Arabs are Muslim, a religion unfamiliar to most Americans); (2) a shared European value system (most Arabs take their values from Islam, which is often sharply critical of the moral tenor of the West); (3) the democratic nature of Israel's political system (most Arab nations are monarchies or dictatorships); (4) Israel's role as an ally of the United States (most Arab countries are seen either as unreliable friends or as within the Soviet sphere of influence); and (5) the sympathy Americans extend toward Jews as victims (Arabs are portrayed as terrorists or exploiters of the American economy through their oil weapon).[35] The close connection of Arab lobbying efforts to the Middle East does not help to overcome such difficulties.

The smaller Arab-American population, 2-3 million compared with almost 6 million Jews, further limits the political clout of Arab-Americans. Even more critical, however, is the much greater political mobilization of American Jews, particularly in support of Israel. Jews have a very high rate of participation in politics; Arab-Americans have a rather low rate. Jews also are among the most generous campaign contributors in American politics.[36] Furthermore, Arab-Americans own businesses with many Jewish customers and fear they will lose income if they become too politically active.[37] There also are divisions between older, native-born Arab-Americans and more recent immigrants. The latter, including many Palestinian refugees who emigrated in 1948, view the American government as an enemy of Arab interests and prefer confrontational tactics rather than public relations efforts and lobbying.[38]

While Arab groups are divided and have no common frame of reference, American Jews are united behind support of Israel. A 1982 survey of American Jews showed that 94 percent considered themselves either pro-Israel or very pro-Israel. Two-thirds often discussed Israel with friends and, by a three-to-one margin, rejected the notion that support for Israel conflicts with one's attachment to the United States. Three-quarters of American Jews argue that they should not vote for a candidate who is unfriendly to Israel, and a third would be willing to contribute money to political candidates who support Israel.[39] Recently, AIPAC has had to face two sources of opposition. Within the American Jewish community, some leaders have criticized the lobby for being out of step with "the consensus of the organized Jewish community" on the pace of the peace process in the Middle East. Moreover, key politicians, including Reagan defense secretary Frank Carlucci, have charged pro-Israel groups with costing the United States "tens of billions of dollars worth of jobs" when they oppose military sales to Arab countries, while Senate Republican leader Robert Dole from Kansas has called for a reduction in aid to Israel.[40]

The Washington presence of both the Israeli and Arab lobbies also offers a striking contrast. AIPAC is regarded as extremely professional with close ties to legislators from both parties on Capitol Hill. The Arab lobbies are regarded as much more amateurish and too dependent on "hired guns," who are paid large retainers to push the Arab cause. Prominent public figures who have lobbied on behalf of the Arabs include former vice president Spiro Agnew, former secretary of state Edmund Muskie, former budget director Bert Lance, former attorney general Richard Kleindeinst, former treasury secretaries John Connally and William Simon, and former senator J. William Fulbright, D-Ark.[41] Arab groups have found that this approach does not enhance coalition building in Congress.

The few Arab-Americans in Congress do not identify with their cause and do not caucus on Middle Eastern issues.[42] The only Arab-American senator, George Mitchell, a Maine Democrat (and Senate majority leader), is a Lebanese Christian who receives substantial support from pro-Israel political action committees. In contrast, Jewish members of Congress seek out committee assignments that focus on the Middle East. In 1989, 25 percent of the members of the House Foreign Affairs Committee and more than 40 percent of that body's subcommittee on the Middle East were Jewish. Arab-Americans did become more active in 1984 in the campaigns for Democrat Jesse Jackson and for Republican president Ronald Reagan. Jackson argued for a Palestinian homeland and included a former director of NAAA as one of his campaign chairmen. Arab-Americans raised $300,000 in his behalf. Two NAAA leaders reported that in 1984 Arab-Americans were the only ethnic group to provide Republican volunteers in every state for Reagan and that no ethnic group provided more volunteers for the president's reelection campaign than Arab-Americans.[43] Arab-Americans also were highly visible in Jackson's 1988 campaign and unsuccessfully pressed the Democratic party to go on record in favor of a Palestinian state. Still, no leading Democratic candidate other than Jackson has taken up the Palestinian cause, and Israel's supporters often called Reagan the most pro-Israel president since Lyndon Johnson.

Despite the power of the Israeli lobby, it has come under increasing pressure, especially since the Arab uprising in the West Bank and Gaza. When a secretary of defense criticizes the lobby on strategic grounds, when public opinion wavers, when the opposition develops more sophisticated tactics, and when splits develop in the Jewish community, the long-term success of the lobby cannot be assured. Pro-Israel forces determined that a more durable strategy would be to affect the membership of the Congress itself.

The Electoral Connection and Foreign Policy

Most lobbyists concentrate on legislation in Washington, but increasingly they have been shifting their tactics toward the electoral arena. Interest groups use political action committees to channel contributions to candidates for Congress. If a sound presentation does not convince a legislator to accede to one's cause, the argument runs, perhaps a campaign contribution might. Or, indeed, perhaps money given to the legislator's opponent might work even better. At best, a legislator hostile to an interest group might be defeated and replaced by one sympathetic to the lobby's point of view. Almost as acceptable is the fear that might be engendered in the incumbent so that he or she will become more receptive to a group's position.

Former senator Charles Mathias, Jr., R-Md., worried that such tactics might make it difficult for the nation to speak with one voice on foreign policy, observed:

> Factions among us lead the nation toward excessive foreign attachments or animosities. Even if the groups were balanced—if Turkish-Americans equaled Greek-Americans or Arab-Americans equaled Jewish-Americans—the result would not necessarily be a sound, cohesive foreign policy because the national interest is not simply the sum of our special interest and attachments. . . . [E]thnic politics, carried as they often have been to excess, have proven harmful to the national interest.[44]

Mathias and others were concerned about threats of electoral retaliation against members who did not toe the line.

The strategies of pro-Israel groups usually have focused on placing intense constituency pressure on legislators who make either anti-Israel or pro-Arab statements. The most notable efforts occurred in Illinois in 1982 and 1984. Republican representative Paul Findley and Republican senator Charles Percy, who chaired the Senate Foreign Relations Committee, were strong critics of Israel. Jewish sources raised $685,000 to defeat Findley in 1982 and $322,000 to beat Percy two years later. A California donor contributed more than $1 million in "uncoordinated expenditures" against Percy. That same year pro-Israel groups targeted Senator Jesse Helms, R-N.C., an even more strident critic of Israel, who upon reelection dramatically shifted his position on the Middle East.

In 1984 fifty-four pro-Israel political action committees spent more than $4.25 million, considerably more than the U.S. real estate industry, which has the single largest domestic PAC. The scope of the donations was broad: 29 of the 33 Senate races and 154 of the 435 House races received funds. Every state except Utah and Idaho was covered, with particular attention given to races involving members of the committees with Middle East jurisdictions. Almost 80 percent of the contributions went to Democrats.[45] In contrast, Arab-Americans had only three political action committees. One, the Middle East Political Action Committee, reported no money raised or spent as of 1982. The second, Americans for Lebanon Political Action Committee, is related to the Lebanese League. It supports moderate candidates, some of whom are of Arab extraction, but in 1982 gave only $5,500 in total to six campaigns. The NAAA formed a PAC in 1984 that raised just

$70,000 in 1985-1986 compared with almost $4 million by eighty pro-Israel groups. Many candidates refused to accept NAAA contributions.[46]

The imbalance of resources between pro-Israel and pro-Arab groups is not the major reason for concern about the potential for campaign contributions to influence foreign policy. The pro-Israel lobby, after all, had considerably more influence than the pro-Arab lobby long before the former began to contribute heavily to congressional candidates. Rather, the nature of ethnic group, and indeed interest group, participation in foreign policy may well change because of the heavy spending. What should be the role of money in American politics? Is political support to be given to the highest bidder? Even though ethnic lobbies do not stand to benefit financially from a foreign policy that suits their preferences, many Americans are simply so skeptical of the role of money in politics that they will worry that something is not right. Thus, it is conceivable that support for foreign policy initiatives will be seen as open to influence from campaign contributions. It is equally possible that the victorious group will be viewed with suspicion by the larger public, much as large corporations are. The strategy of influencing policy by shaping the membership of Congress thus may backfire. The public and members of Congress may strongly disapprove of winning policy debated by threats. This has happened in some election campaigns in which the New Right has attempted to discredit Democratic incumbents, and there are signs that some Jewish leaders have begun to worry that it might happen to them.

It is even more disturbing that such tactics are used on foreign policy issues. Purely domestic issues traditionally have divided our political parties, while foreign policy has had bipartisan support. A strident electoral campaign by a foreign policy interest group might disrupt this pattern. Jewish groups initially gave far more money to Democratic candidates than to Republicans. Might this endanger support for Israel among Republicans, who have controlled the White House for all but four years since 1968? Pro-Israel groups seem to have recognized this problem. In 1985 and 1986, amidst great conflict over whether pro-Israel groups should become more bipartisan, they gave 60 percent of their contributions to Republicans.[47]

When contributing to ultraconservatives, pro-Israel groups are ignoring many issues about which the New Right and American Jews strongly disagree, especially prayer in public schools. Some observers see this strategy as leading to a situation in which concern for Israel's security will be the only issue for American Jews. This ultimately will make political alliances between members of Congress and pro-Israel forces into little more than contests for campaign contributions (not unlike some domestic political issues) rather than bonds based on long-term philosophical commitments.[48]

As unsettling as this problem is for the Middle East, it is even more widespread and more ominous than it might appear. Because pro-Israel groups do not seek financial rewards for their campaign contributions, they are tolerated, if not by candidates for office, then at least by the general public. A 1988 poll found that a small plurality of Americans did not believe that pro-Israel groups had too much influence on American policy. Respondents were less favorable to pro-contra groups and decidedly less hospitable to labor and big business.[49] Other PACs financed by foreign money, including American subsidiaries of Japanese firms and foreign car dealers, have more direct economic stakes and have used their clout to shape tax law in at least one state. As long as the money is raised exclusively in the United States, such practices are legal.[50] And as such strategies prove effective, they will become more widespread.

The bipartisan nature of our foreign policy is thus threatened by making international politics too much like domestic issues. We can afford to be contentious at home, but the stakes are much greater abroad. Soviet leaders already have complained that negotiating with American presidents is difficult because the latter cannot ensure that agreements reached will be approved by Congress. These problems would only increase if foreign policy issues became important in electoral campaigns marked by heavy expenditures and threats. What the correct policy ought to be becomes less important than which group can yell the loudest, and the volume is affected by the purchasing power of television advertising. Causes that before enjoyed widespread and bipartisan support among the public, such as support for Israel, might become objects of great conflict. The very groups that spawned this effort might ultimately regret such tactics.

Notes

Support of the General Research Board of the University of Maryland at College Park is gratefully acknowledged, as is the assistance of Fred Augustyn, Rodger Payne, and Galen Wilkenson. The comments of Allan Cigler, Burdett Loomis, and George Quester are greatly appreciated as well. Avery gratefully slept through most of it.

1. Richard F. Fenno, Jr., *Congressmen in Committees* (Glenview, Ill.: Scott, Foresman, 1973), 141.
2. See Aage R. Clausen, *How Congressmen Decide* (New York: St. Martin's Press, 1973).

3. Seymour Martin Lipset and William Schneider, *The Confidence Gap* (New York: Macmillan, 1983); and CBS News Poll press release, "The U.S. and Israel," October 23, 1988.

4. Bayless Manning, "The Congress, the Executive, and Intermestic Affairs: Three Proposals," *Foreign Affairs* (January 1977): 306-324.

5. Lipset and Schneider, *The Confidence Gap,* chap. 3.

6. On energy, see Eric M. Uslaner, *Shale Barrel Politics: Energy Politics and Legislative Leadership* (Stanford, Calif.: Stanford University Press, 1989), esp. chaps. 5 and 6; on agriculture, see Barbara Sinclair, *Congressional Realignment* (Austin: University of Texas Press, 1982), chaps. 7 and 8.

7. Jack L. Walker, "The Origins and Maintenance of Interest Groups in America," *American Political Science Review* 77 (June 1983): 390-406.

8. John Spanier and Eric M. Uslaner, *American Foreign Policy Making and the Democratic Dilemmas,* 5th ed. (Belmont, Calif.: Brooks-Cole, 1989), 191.

9. David Osborne, "Lobbying for Japan, Inc.," *New York Times Magazine,* December 4, 1983, 133-139; and Robert Sherrill, review of *The American House of Saud,* by Steven Emerson, *Washington Post Book World,* May 5, 1985, 4.

10. See, among others, Clyde H. Farnsworth, "Japan's Loud Voice in Washington," *New York Times,* December 10, 1989, F1, F6; and Susan Rasky, "Pressured on Trade, Japanese Turn to the Business of Politics," *New York Times,* August 23, 1987, E4.

11. James McGregor, "Taiwan Cultivates America's Support with Lobbying Force the Size of Israel's," *Wall Street Journal,* November 7, 1989, A26.

12. "Lobbying for Foreigners Is Worse," *New York Times,* June 28, 1986, 26.

13. Sixty-four percent uphold the right of religious organizations to endorse candidates and 61 percent support contributions by American Jews to Israel. See Marjorie Hyer, "Tolerance Shows in Voter Poll," *Washington Post,* February 13, 1988, E18.

14. E. E. Schattschneider, *The Semi-Sovereign People* (New York: Holt, Rinehart and Winston, 1960), 26.

15. Mohammed E. Ahrari, "Conclusion," in *Ethnic Groups and U.S. Foreign Policy,* ed. Ahrari, (Westport, Conn.: Greenwood Press, 1987), 155-158.

16. Thomas M. Franck and Edward Weisband, *Foreign Policy by Congress* (New York: Oxford University Press, 1979), 191-193.

17. Z. A. Kruszewski, "The Polish American Congress, East-West Issues, and the Formulation of American Foreign Policy," in Ahrari, *Ethnic Groups and U.S. Foreign Policy,* 83-100; Stephen A. Garret, "Eastern European Ethnic Groups and American Foreign Policy," *Political Science Quarterly* 93 (Summer 1978): 301-323; and NBC News Poll press release #169, April 27, 1990; "The Albanians," *New York Times,* August 24, 1987, A14.

18. Seth Mydans, "TV Unites, and Divides, Hispanic Groups," *New York*

Times, August 27, 1989, E4.

19. Rodolfo O. de la Garza, "U.S. Foreign Policy and the Mexican-American Political Agenda," in Ahrari, *Ethnic Groups and U.S. Foreign Policy,* 101-114; and Robert Reinhold, "Mexico Leaders Look North of the Border," *New York Times,* December 8, 1989, A1, A28.

20. Rodolfo O. de la Garza, "Chicanos and U.S. Foreign Policy: The Future of Chicano-Mexican Relations," *Western Political Quarterly* 23 (December 1980): 571-572; and Jesus Rangel, "Puerto Rican Need Discussed at Home," *New York Times,* June 3, 1985, B18.

21. Bill Keller, "Interest Groups Focus on El Salvador Policy," *Congressional Quarterly Weekly Report,* April 24, 1982, 895-900.

22. David Rampe, "Power Panel in the Making: The Hispanic Caucus," *New York Times,* September 30, 1988, B5.

23. Kenneth Longmyer, "Black American Demands," *Foreign Policy,* Fall 1985, 3-18; Michael Beaubien, "Making Waves in Foreign Policy," *Black Enterprise* (April 1982): 37-42; and David Hoffman, "Americans Back S. Africa's Blacks," *Washington Post,* September 25, 1985.

24. William Glaberson, "Threads of Irish Politics Woven into Mayoral Race," *New York Times,* November 3, 1989, B5; and Robert J. Thompson and Joseph R. Rudolph, "Irish Americans in the American Foreign-Policy-Making Process," in Ahrari, *Ethnic Groups and U.S. Foreign Policy,* 135-154.

25. Sam Roberts, "Political Changes Simmer in New York Melting Pot," *New York Times,* July 22, 1989, 27-28.

26. Franck and Weisband, *Foreign Policy by Congress,* 186; and Ben Bradlee, Jr., "Israel's Lobby," *Boston Globe Magazine,* April 29, 1984, 64.

27. Cheryl A. Rubenberg, "The Middle East Lobbies," *Link* 17 (January-March 1984): 4.

28. Bradlee, "Israel's Lobby"; Bill Keller, "Supporters of Israel, Arabs, Vie for Friends and Influence in Congress, at White House," *Congressional Quarterly Weekly Report,* August 22, 1982, 1523-1530; and Charles Hoffman, "Getting Jews Involved," *Jerusalem Post* (International Edition), October 1, 1988, 8B.

29. Sanford J. Ungar, "Washington: Jewish and Arab Lobbyists," *Atlantic,* March 1978, 10.

30. Bradlee, "Israel's Lobby," 64.

31. Robert H. Trice, "Congress and the Arab-Israeli Conflict: Support for Israel in the U.S. Senate, 1970-1973," *Political Science Quarterly* 92 (Fall 1977): 443-463; and Robert Pear with Richard L. Berke, "Pro-Israel Group Exerts Quiet Might as It Rallies Supporters in Congress," *New York Times,* July 7, 1987, A8.

32. Rubenberg, "Middle East Lobbies"; Keller, "Supporters of Israel"; Steven L. Spiegel, *The Other Arab-Israeli Conflict* (Chicago: University of Chicago Press, 1985), 8; and David J. Saad and G. Neal Lendenmann, "Arab American Grievances," *Foreign Policy,* Fall 1985, 22.

33. Quoted in Spiegel, *Other Arab-Israeli Conflict,* 8.

34. Spanier and Uslaner, *American Foreign Policy Making*, 252-255; and *Washington Post*-ABC News Poll press release, "Middle East Terrorism," April 3, 1989.
35. Keller, "Supporters of Israel," 1523.
36. Edward Tivnan, *The Lobby* (New York: Simon and Schuster, 1987), 55.
37. Keller, "Supporters of Israel," 1528; and Bradlee, "Israel's Lobby," 76.
38. Robert A. Trice, *Interest Groups and the Foreign Policy Process* (Beverly Hills, Calif.: Sage Publications, 1976), 54-55.
39. Leon Hadar, "What Israel Means to U.S. Jewry," *Jerusalem Post* (International Edition), June 19-25, 1982, 11; and Bradlee, "Israel's Lobby," 8.
40. Robert Pear, "Leaders of 3 U.S. Jewish Groups Take Issue with Pro-Israel Lobby," *New York Times*, October 18, 1988, A1, A8; and Molly Moore and David B. Ottaway, "Carlucci Blasts Opponents of U.S. Arms Sales to Arabs," *Washington Post*, October 22, 1988, A1, A18.
41. Sherrill, review of *American House of Saud.*
42. Ungar, "Jewish and Arab Lobbyists," 12.
43. "Arab Americans Take an Increased Political Role," *New York Times*, November 4, 1984, 74; and Saad and Lendenmann, "Arab American Grievances," 22.
44. Charles McC. Mathias, Jr., "Ethnic Groups and Foreign Policy," *Foreign Affairs* 59 (Summer 1981): 981.
45. John J. Fialka and Brook Jackson, "Jewish PACs Emerge as a Powerful Force in U.S. Election Races," *Wall Street Journal*, February 26, 1985, 1, 16; and "Study Finds Pro-Israeli PACs Active in '84 Races," *New York Times*, August 16, 1984, B10.
46. Rubenberg, "Middle East Lobbies," 12; and Ed Zuckerman, "Pro-Israeli PACs: What Role Do They Play?" *PACs and Lobbies*, September 2, 1987, 1, 7-9.
47. Robert Kuttner, "Unholy Alliance," *New Republic*, May 26, 1986, 19-25; and Robert S. Greenberger, "Pro-Israel Lobby Faces Political Tug of War: Conservative Leadership vs. Liberal Constituents," *Wall Street Journal*, December 20, 1988, A16.
48. See Kuttner, "Unholy Alliance"; and Paul Taylor, "Pro-Israel PACs Giving More to GOP," *Washington Post*, November 4, 1985, A1, A11.
49. CBS News Poll press release, "The U.S. and Israel."
50. "As Investments by Foreigners Surge, Their Influence in U.S. Politics Grows," *New York Times*, December 30, 1985; and "Foreign Car Dealers' PAC Is Given a Clean Bill of Health," *New York Times*, September 18, 1989, B6.

15. DYNAMICS OF POLICY SUBSYSTEMS IN AMERICAN POLITICS

James A. Thurber

Political scientists frequently have depicted and analyzed American politics in terms of subsystems that revolve around particular sets of policies. As government has grown in the wake of the New Deal and the Great Society social programs, the erection of an immense defense establishment, and the creation of a maze of regulatory agencies, subsystems have become more complex and variegated. Interest groups have played integral roles in subsystem politics, as they represent nongovernmental interests in continuing relationships with congressional committees and bureaucratic units.

In this chapter, James Thurber distinguishes among various contemporary policy subsystems as he sketches the context in which groups and interests must operate. He differentiates among macropolicy systems, in which major policy issues are decided; dominant systems, in which routine policy making occurs; and micropolicy systems, in which "a relatively hidden elite [attempts] to influence government policy."

Drawing on the work of E. E. Schattschneider, among others, Thurber develops a series of propositions concerning the nature of subsystem politics in which developing policies create new interests and change relationships between interest groups and the government. This allows interests to overcome the constitutional separation of powers as they seek to achieve their policy goals. Thurber's major contribution here is to provide an understanding of the settings in which groups operate and how these contexts are susceptible to change. Groups seek to provide as much certainty as they can in an inherently unstable policy environment. As policies become more numerous and complex, this becomes a never-ending task.

American public policy results primarily from the activities of thousands of actors in hundreds of decision-making systems organized around discrete programs and issues. These decision-making systems operate within the constitutional, electoral, and political party structures of the American political system and, in effect, make it work. Interested individuals, businesses, and groups cluster naturally around the congressional committees and executive branch agencies whose decisions affect them either positively or negatively. An explanation of the organization and behavior of these decision-making systems is essential to understanding American interest group politics and is the purpose of this chapter.

Typology of Policy-Making Systems

It is useful analytically to think of policy-making processes as falling within specific types of systems. One way to think of them is as a decision-making hierarchy ranging from *macropolicy systems* or "high politics" (general policy decisions with major political effects involving broad public interests, visibility, divisiveness, extensive media coverage, and many participants) to *policy subsystems* (ranging in turn from dominant to competitive to disintegrated) to *micropolicy systems* (narrowly focused decision making involving a very small, often-closed group of decision makers).[1] Policy issues may move up or down the decision-making hierarchy from closed micropolitics to subsystems to more open macropolicy-making systems, or they may not move at all. Policy subsystems tend to dominate the political landscape in American public policy making. Table 15-1 outlines the policy-making typology, showing how policy subsystems fit between macro and micropolitics.

Macropolicy Systems

Macropolicy systems, or high politics, make major decisions that may change policies or the power structure surrounding a major policy area. Participants in these systems often are presidents, congressional leaders, the mass media, the general public, the Supreme Court, or the leaders of large broad-based groups in society. The issues considered in macropolicy-making systems might include such major policies as negotiations over final passage of the federal budget, macroeconomic policy, cuts in defense expenditures, or cuts in the capital gains tax. Macropolicy systems also include highly controversial, often emotion-packed issues that are narrowly focused with heavy media coverage and widespread public concern. Examples are the abortion issue, changes in Social Security benefits, or the threat of across-the-board budget cutting through the Gramm-Rudman-Hollings Budget Deficit Reduction Act. The common elements of these issues are: high visibility, extensive news coverage, "gangs" of high-level public officials, divisiveness, potential for extended controversy, and salience in the electoral arena. Macropolicy systems often develop in response to crises arising from an uncontrollable domestic or international social, economic, or political event such as the decline of communism in the Soviet Union and eastern European nations or the Iraqi invasion of Kuwait. The reaction to external major social, economic, and political events often centralizes power, taking control away from policy subsystems. The subsystems appear as obstacles to resolving conflict, but the subsystem experts are

Table 15-1   Typology of Policy-Making Systems

Policy-making system	Visibility of decision	Scope of conflict	Level of conflict	Number of participants
Macro	High	Wide	High	Many
Policy subsystem[a]	Low	Narrow	Low	Few
Micro	"Invisible"	Very narrow	Low and personalized	Few

[a] These are the characteristics of a dominant subsystem, the most common policy subsystem.

relied on for policy options and expertise. Macropolitical decision making brings new and higher-level decision makers into the policy process and produces new policies unobtainable through subsystem decision making.

Often macropolicy-making systems form because an issue could not be resolved at lower levels of government. They evolve from competitive to disintegrated subsystems to macropolitical decision making. Extended controversy, competition, and deadlock often push issues into the White House, onto national television news, and into the living rooms of Americans—that is, into the macropolitical realm. The annual battle over the budget, for example, begins with dominant subsystems considering programs, moves to competitive subsystems attempting to hold on to their "fair share" of federal dollars, then breaks down into disintegrated subsystem politics and into the view of the nation—macropolitical negotiations and high level "summitry."

The transformation from policy subsystems to macropolitics might be an annual process such as consideration of the budget, or it might be dramatic or prolonged. An example of dramatic change was the energy crisis that arose when the Organization of Petroleum Exporting Countries (OPEC) cut off supplies of oil in 1973-1974 and then again on August 2, 1990, when Saddam Hussein, president of Iraq, invaded Kuwait. Before the 1973-1974 oil crisis, oil politics had been controlled by producers of petroleum products, not consumers. The energy crisis, however, pushed energy policy and its many well-organized and closed subsystems out of the congressional subcommittees and administrative agencies and onto television and the front page of newspapers and into national electoral politics. Charles Jones has characterized the dramatic expansion of the oil crisis into macropolitics or "sloppy large hexagons" as follows:

Those cozy little triangles which had come to characterize the development of energy politics had become sloppy large hexagons. Demands by environmentalists and public interest groups to participate in decision making, involvement by leadership at the highest levels in response to crisis, and the international aspects of recent energy problems have all dramatically expanded the energy policy population . . . [so that] the expansion is up, out, and over— *up* in public and private institutional hierarchies (e.g., the involvement of presidents of companies and countries, rather than just low-level bureaucrats, and of congressional party leaders rather than just subcommittees); *out* to groups that declared an interest in energy policies . . . , and *over* to decision making processes in other nations or groups of nations.[2]

During the 1980s the United States had stable and low-priced OPEC oil and subsystem decision making surrounding petroleum policy. The Iraq invasion of Kuwait changed energy policy making in a single day and thrust it back into macropolitics.

A prolonged and incremental transformation of routine politics to macropolitics often results from a single event or from cumulative incidents coupled with a growing public awareness of the gravity of an issue. One of the best examples of a cumulative evolution into macropolitics is the increase in illegal drug use over the past three decades.

Macropolitics can dominate a national policy agenda, the president's energies, and the issues in elections, helping to elect and defeat presidents and members of Congress. Macropolicy systems are not the most common method of making public policy, and the decisions are likely to reflect that. Such decisions have the potential, however, to radically influence political careers and the direction of public policy.

Micropolicy Systems

In micropolicy systems, at the other end of the policy-making spectrum, a relatively hidden elite attempts to influence government policy. The impact of the policy being influenced is often of limited interest to the general public. Micropolicy decision making can focus on areas of such technical complexity that it is removed from the daily living of most Americans and excluded from all but a few of the relevant subsystem actors. Micropolicies seldom appear in election campaign rhetoric; most constituents are unaware or uninterested in them. Micropolicy systems are characterized by limited participation, limited access, and limited communication outside of those decision makers with the inside technical knowledge to understand the issues or those political actors who want a favor and those in government who can grant it. Micropolitical actors measure their success by their ability to control the process and, above all, by their ability to stay out of the news. Micropolitics is often described in the popular media as corrupt, closed, elite decision-making systems linked to vested economic interests. Because of the secrecy, there is potential for abuse but not certainty of it. In the 1980s, the apparent intervention by five U.S. senators in the regulation of the failing Lincoln First Savings and Loan Association and the involvement of members of Congress and their staffs in Department of Defense weapons procurement contracts were two examples of micropolitics or, as some critics call it, micromanagement.

In the wake of the ethics scandals of 1989 with the resignations of House Speaker James Wright, D-Texas, and House Democratic whip Tony Coelho, D-Calif., the media and the American public seemed to think the influence of money and micropolitics was widespread and a major influence on the way decisions are made in Washington. But micropolitical conceptions of policy making detract from a more complex and realistic description of routine federal government decision making: macropolicy systems and policy subsystems. Micropolicy systems obviously have some impact on public policy, but often it is not as lasting and significant an influence as policy subsystems or macropolicy systems, which are more democratic and representative modes of decision making.

Policy Subsystems

The two predominant images of the American policy process are *iron triangles*—relatively closed policy arenas emphasizing stable relations among a limited number of participants—and *issue networks*—fragmented, open, and extraordinarily complex systems not well suited to resolving conflicts or reaching decisions quickly. The iron triangle metaphor, linking executive bureaus and agencies, congressional committees, and interest group clienteles (and also known as power triads or cozy triangles), is used to describe a fixed, closed, autonomous system for making policy. But Hugh Heclo rejected the iron triangle and replaced it with an open issue network, which has disaggregated power and many participants flowing in and out of decision making.[3] Both iron triangles and issue networks are useful metaphors, but they are only part of the picture. A more inclusive term is *policy subsystem*. Talcott Parsons's definition of a social system is helpful in understanding the general nature of a policy subsystem: "A plurality of actors interacting on the basis of a shared symbol system."[4] For policy subsystems, the shared symbol system is the policy of concern to the cluster of subsystem actors. According to Parsons, membership in a system can be further defined by a "criterion of mutual relevance and common fate that stipulates the basis on which members are to take each other into account in their actions." [5] In the same way, subsystem actors will share the fate of the outcome of the policy process surrounding the issue or government program of direct importance to them.

Several political scientists have used the idea of policy subsystems, but few have gone beyond a general conception. J. Leiper Freeman first introduced the idea when he spoke of a "web of relationships in the subsystem." [6] Grant McConnell followed with the comparable term *subgovernment*.[7] Theodore Lowi argued that policy making had been co-opted by status quo interest groups, and he referred to a triad of decision making: "The politics within each system is built upon a triangular trading pattern including the central agency, a congressional committee or subcommittee, and the local district farm committee . . . [so that] each side of the triangle complements and supports the other two." [8]

David Mayhew described policy subsystems from the congressional viewpoint as "Congressmen protect[ing] clientele systems— alliances of agencies, Hill committees, and clienteles—against the incursions of presidents and cabinet secretaries." [9]

Pluralist and interest group theories of politics closely fit the subsystem approach. Pluralists argue that groups make demands on government to foster their legitimate interests and that government has perceived its proper role as the promoter of these interests in society.[10] Pluralists further argue that new policies are enacted, new agencies created (or old ones expanded or reorganized), and new congressional committees or subcommittees added (or jurisdictions expanded) to promote the interest of powerful competing groups in society as groups gain sufficient power to "own" certain "turf" in Congress and the executive branch.[11]

Interest groups gain political power when their policy subsystem receives a "promotion." For example, the elevation to cabinet status of the Veterans Administration under President Ronald Reagan and the proposal to elevate the Environmental Protection Agency to cabinet status under President George Bush were high-level promotions for veterans' groups and environmentalists alike. Similarly, President Jimmy Carter created the U.S. Department of Education during his first year in office after making a public commitment to the National Education Association and other educators during his bid for the Democratic presidential nomination. The broad coalition of elementary, secondary, and higher education interests had sought such a step for at least two decades.[12]

General Characteristics of Policy Subsystems

Policy subsystems can be characterized by networks of actors, their substantive policy domain, and various modes of decision making. They are organized to make focused demands on the political system and to influence specific programs—not to win elections or to form governments. Most public problems of concern to subsystems are addressed without prior consideration in the electoral arena and often with only a cursory nod from presidents, political parties, congressional leaders, or top political appointees in the executive branch. The thousands of clientele-oriented subsystems expressing many points of view form the web of the American public policy dominating the workload of congressional committees and subcommittees, interest groups, and executive branch agencies. Political power in each policy area is wielded by actors who often serve the private interests of their organizations. This has been called *multiple elitism* or *plural elitism,* but such portrayals do not take into account the democratic and open nature of subsystem politics.

Subsystems are decentralized power structures with close informal communications among their participants. Participants are primarily representatives of interest groups, members and staff of congressional committees and subcommittees, bureau and agency personnel in the executive branch, and other policy specialists from universities, state and local government, and the media (see Figure 15-1). Washington lawyers, functioning as lobbyists, also play a key role in the structure of subsystem representation, as well as presidential advisers from the Executive Office of the President. In their various roles, these participants move issues onto the public agenda, develop and pass legislation, make rules and regulations, prepare and pass budgets, administer and implement programs, and evaluate and change them.

The specialized media—professional journals and newsletters associated with specific interest groups or government programs—also frequently play a key role in subsystems and often are the only "windows" to their activities. Television, radio, and the general national news media are usually uninterested and unaware of the day-to-day issues and politics of policy subsystems unless a crisis or scandal occurs surrounding a subsystem's decisions.

Subsystems evolve because of a society's need to divide tasks and promote the development of knowledge. As this natural progression of dividing labor and developing expertise continues, the general electorate frequently is excluded from decision making, especially that related to technical and complex issues. Subsystem actors develop policy expertise and continuing relationships with one another in areas of direct interest

Figure 15-1   The Major Actors in Policy Subsystems

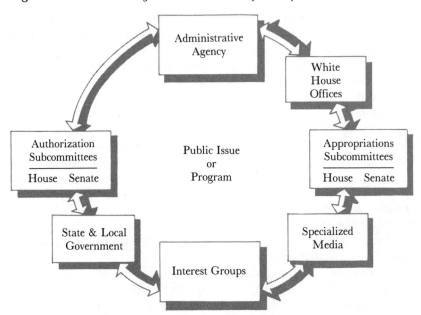

to themselves. Because they understand the issue, they often have considerable independence in the development, implementation, and evaluation of policy under the subsystem's jurisdiction.

Form of Functional Representation

Subsystems are a form of *functional representation*—that is, the representation of societal functions through governmental institutions stems from the division of labor and development of expertise and specialization in society. Functional specialists, or people with expertise and technical competence in an issue or program, dominate the subsystem. These specialists hail from interest groups, academia, Congress, executive agencies, state and local government, think tanks, and the other subsystem organizations.

Functional representation generally has a greater influence on routine policy making than on highly controversial issues, or high politics. Policy enbroiled in controversy attracts the attention and involvement of presidents, congressional leaders, political parties, the media, and the general public, but the political system cannot handle very many highly controversial issues at one time. Most public policy making is routine. Consequently, the functional representation inherent in policy subsystems is more pervasive and influential than the formal and more commonly understood forms of representation based on geographic territory (U.S. Senate) and population (U.S. House of Representatives).

Presidents discover quickly that it is difficult to establish a central core of authority over functional specialists and the policy subsystems. They cannot simply order that something be done and expect it to change. Nor does passage of a law by Congress automatically guarantee its implementation. Power and authority are usually decentralized and housed in policy subsystems around functions in society. Any major public policy arena consists of a complex set of semiautonomous subsystems that are organized around programs or such narrow issues as titles within major legislative acts.

Typology of Subsystems

Although they are the predominant policy-making system in American politics, policy subsystems vary over time and according to the type of policy being considered. Thus, a simple typology may help delineate the dynamic nature of policy making.

Subsystems, like the policy process itself, are dynamic and can vary from dominant to competitive to disintegrated. Table 15-2 outlines the major characteristics of this policy subsystem typology. Although the most "comfortable" state of a policy subsystem is closed, static, and dominant over a particular program, competition and even policy disintegration occurs in any policy area from time to time.

Because subsystems are dynamic, they can range from dominant subsystems—stable, with well-defined jurisdiction, low political visibility, narrow conflict, and few participants—to competitive and disintegrated subsystems—with instability, overlapping or fragmented jurisdictions with many players, and extensive political conflict. The nature of a subsystem is related to the type of policy, issue, and event facing the actors in the subsystem.

Dominant Policy Subsystems

Dominant policy subsystems are relatively stable communications and decision-making clusters with a small number of participants who significantly influence and often control government programs or issues. They are "relatively well-bounded," "differentiated from their environment," and "relatively complex." [13] Within a specific policy area, a few actors tend to be better organized and thus dominate the more passive interests. Dominant policy subsystems are usually structured around such distributive policies as tax deductions for home mortgages, Elementary and Secondary Education Act benefits, federal highway funds, water projects, veterans' benefits, Social Security benefits for

Table 15-2 Typology of Policy Subsystems

Subsystem type	Coalition	Visibility of decision	Specificity of jurisdiction	Scope of conflict	Level of conflict	Number of participants	Access to decision process
Dominant	Stable	Low	Well defined	Narrow	Low	Small	Closed
Competitive	Not stable for short periods	Low	Overlapping and challenged	Moderate	Moderate	Moderate	Open only to those competing
Disintegrated	Not stable	High	Fragmented	Wide	High	Large	Open

retirees, and a variety of other subsidies for business and industry. The flow of information and knowledge follows well-worn and enduring channels among mutually trusted actors sharing common interests and policy preferences. The actors—who include executive branch officials, legislators, business people, lobbyists, representatives of the specialized media, and policy specialists in universities and think tanks—are relatively unknown to the general public. Decisions are made in dominant subsystems without regard for their overall impact on the political system. They are uncoordinated and decentralized.

Dominant subsystems exhibit relatively stable relations because the actors strive to reduce uncertainty, information costs, and the opportunistic behaviors of the subsystem members by creating relatively stable channels of communication and clear-cut norms. The key operating norms of dominant subsystems are cooperation, bargaining, and compromise, and subsystem actors develop methods for working around ideological and partisan lines. There is a high degree of mutually rewarding behavior and a narrow scope of policy conflict, usually at a middle or lower level within government institutions. Dominant subsystems attempt to resist pressure from powerful outside actors such as presidents, high-level executive branch officials, congressional committees that do not have formal jurisdiction over their subsystem issues, and interest groups that are not regular participants in the subsystem; they fight jurisdictional trespassing. Unless the general print and broadcast news media are considered useful to the cause of the subsystem, the key actors try to exclude reporters. In short, dominant subsystems work to thwart challenges to their authority over issues and programs within their jurisdiction, usually with great success.

Although outside challenges to dominant policy subsystems usually do not pose a major threat, when new issues and policy problems are presented, the automatic response is an attempt to control the scope and level of competition, keeping it within the subsystem jurisdiction. Thus, access to the decision process is often closed. Issue resolution occurs among the players within each program network or sector.

Another important norm of dominant policy subsystems is reciprocity. Dominant subsystems help private sector producers through government action, be it new legislation, helpful regulations, or funding programs that the subsystem's clients want.

Dominant subsystems may be organized in well-defined hierarchies with centrally located actors who mediate communications and decision making among actors more peripherally located. Alternatively, they may be structured in a wheel (or at times an "undulating amoeba") of relationships that are more diffuse (see Figure 15-1).

These dominant subsystems lack hierarchy and centralized coordinating actors.

Competitive Policy Subsystems

Competitive policy subsystems are distinguished by the way decisions are made among its players—coalitions of actors are in a constant state of competition. Government actors may have the power to initiate new policies, but this may lead to challenges and conflict. Although the communications network is limited to each competing network of policy actors, the systems are more complex and open than in dominant subsystems. In fact, the political structure of the subsystem may shift dramatically from event to event and issue to issue. National broad-based associations and top government officials often play a mediating role in the conflict between supporters and opponents of a particular policy. Government subsystem actors may even initiate ways to reduce conflict such as setting up negotiated rule making; organizing short-term ad hoc groups of decision makers, such as presidential commissions; or using policy coordinating mechanisms such as the congressional budget committees or budget summits.

Heclo's conception of issue networks fits most closely the description of competitive policy subsystems. The movement of many actors in and out of decision-making networks—described here by Heclo—is a central tendency of competitive subsystems:

> Issues networks . . . comprise a large number of participants with quite variable degrees of mutual commitment or of dependence on others in the environment. . . . Rather than groups united in dominance over a program, no one, as far as one can tell, is in control of the policies and issues.

Relationships among the actors in competitive policy subsystems often are unstable for a short period—that is, until the various factions are structured into competing clusters or there is general agreement among the key actors and the subsystem evolves into a dominant state. Competition can be fleeting or last for years. Competition may evolve through a redefinition of the scope and level of issue conflict among the actors inside an existing subsystem or by attacks from the outside by other actors. In the view of Cigler and Loomis, for example, "increased representation often leads to heightened levels of competition within a given policy subsystem, particularly as budget demands redefine more and more policies as redistributive." [14]

The type of policy considered by a competitive subsystem frequently is defined as redistributive or regulatory. When a redistributive policy conflict cannot be resolved within a single subsystem, other actors and subsystems often join the battle and resort to open conflict. Multiple and sequential referral of legislation is a sign of a competitive subsystem.

Often, when new legislation is needed from competitive subsystems, approval from the larger political system is needed. This creates competition, conflict, and new policy players. Approval is usually forthcoming, however, and the system generally defers to the experts within the policy jurisdiction, but the challenge and heightened visibility create short-term conflict and permeability within and among subsystems. Randall Ripley and Grace Franklin, using the term *competing subgovernments,* have described the competitive subsystems concept:

> [They] ... can develop when an issue area is lodged in the governmental decision-making apparatus in such a way that allows or even promotes the development of institutionalized competition for dominance. The competition may result in the eventual redefinition of jurisdictions so that one subgovernment becomes dominant, or it may result in the competing subgovernments being replaced by some other mode of decision making, or it may simply result in continued sharing of the issue area space, with sufficient adjustments to mute conflict and allow decisions to be made.[15]

Andrew MacFarland designated regulatory negotiation a "power triad." Like the iron triangle, the power triad has three participants, but these actors do not form a tight coalition; instead, they compete.[16] Regulatory negotiation with government actors mediating between two participants in the triad is increasingly common, but it has much more bounded conflict than most competitive decision-making systems. For example, although labor, business, and the government continually battle over regulations to protect the health and safety of American workers, the decision-making system has not designated a static, formal relationship among the three sectors. Occupational health and safety policy is competitive and complex; it includes not only the agency charged with regulating in that area but also other government agencies or departments such as units in the Department of Health and Human Services, congressional committees and subcommittees, the courts, the specialized media, public interest groups, the Office of Management and Budget's Office of Information and Regulatory Affairs, unions, businesses, and a variety of experts from the university and health communities. Competition and decision making is formally organized by the Occupational Safety and Health Administration (OSHA), which is responsible for regulating the health and safety of the workplace for most American laborers. Labor unions, health and safety experts, medical researchers, and workers lobby for a safer workplace, while businesses (those with a private interest in keeping the cost of production as low as possible) and their associations conflict with OSHA and those pushing for more rules to create a safer workplace. The OSHA relationships are a complex, fluctuating subsystem.

Challenges to an existing dominant subsystem are usually short-lived since it is to the advantage of most subsystem actors to keep the costs of competition to a minimum. Above all, the players try to keep final decisions out of the view of the public and the national media. Competition is costly and unpredictable, and widespread publicity about a subsystem battle increases uncertainty. Most subsystem actors want to control the policy outcomes even though they might not win all they desire. Generally, competitive subsystems do not live long, but competition can be institutionalized so that it lasts for years—for example, the conflict between industry and environmentalists over a clean air policy.

A competitive subsystem tends to undermine dominant subsystems and micropolitics but it also tends to remain in a bounded domain. The supporters and opponents of a policy are well known to each other, such as those in the quarrel over the rewrite of the Clean Air Act. Competition often results from external events that have an impact on a subsystem or challenges to an existing subsystem power base. Competition in turn generates new patterns of interaction and eventually a new dominating coalition. Confrontation often erupts over policy jurisdiction or who has the right to decide, and a contest is always held over the substance of a program or policy. Competitive policy subsystems have more participants than dominant subsystems, but numbers are still limited to knowledgeable insiders from two or more subsystems. The general public, congressional leadership, and high-level executive branch personnel can be involved, but they usually are not.

An excellent example of an institutionalized competitive subsystem is the one that experienced intense, sustained conflict between industry and environmentalists over the Clean Air Act in the 101st Congress. The Clean Air Act of 1970 and its amendments in 1977 gave the federal government a role in air pollution abatement and acted almost like a national zoning law. The battle in the 101st Congress pitted industrialists against environmentalists, which in turn put powerful competing pressures on members of Congress. The Clean Air Act has a greater impact on industry than any federal statute except the tax code. Nearly every congressional district has polluting industry targeted by the clean air legislation. Most districts also have well-organized environmentalists pushing for the elimination of toxic emissions.

Industry predicted financial disaster and loss of jobs if the most far-reaching proposals advocated by the environmentalists were written into the draft of the new Clean Air Act in 1990. Environmentalists predicted dire health and environmental consequences from the continuation of acid rain and airborne toxic emissions and the prolonged use of polluting motor fuels. Because most members of Congress try to protect the economic well-being of their districts by protecting jobs, some felt duty-bound to protect petrochemical plants, automobile factories, local utilities, and coal jobs. Others, however, represented districts with serious air pollution and acid rain problems.

In the volatile and highly visible battle over clean air legislation, Republican president George Bush coalesced with such arch Democrats as Sen. Robert Byrd, chairman of the powerful Senate Appropriations Committee, and representative of high-sulfur coal miners and owners in West Virginia, and Rep. John Dingell, chairman of the House Energy and Commerce Committee and representative of the automobile industry, located primarily in Dingell's Michigan district. The two key players representing the pro-environment position were Democratic representative Henry Waxman from Los Angeles, an area with serious air pollution problems (he was also chairman of the Subcommittee on Health and Environment of Dingell's Energy and Commerce Committee), and Senate Democratic majority leader George Mitchell from Maine, a state receiving regular doses of acid rain from the industrial Midwest. For years Congress has been divided into warring camps, with northeasterners and environmentalists on one side and utility and high-sulfur coal interests on the other. Other issues related to the fight over jobs and clean air are acid rain, alternative fuels (ethanol and methanol), acceptable levels of urban smog and carbon monoxide, tailpipe emission standards, requirements to build more efficient and clean fuel automobiles, reductions in chlorofluorocarbons which deplete the stratospheric ozone, and cutbacks in cancer-causing air toxins.

The inability to reconcile the clashing industrial and environmental interests in the rewrite of the Clean Air Act tied up Congress for more than a decade. If most congressional behavior can be explained by the single imperative that members want to be reelected, then it is understandable how this competitive subsystem caused delay and deadlock.[17] Members were buffeted by well-organized, vocal environmental groups and by the polluting industries that had jobs and the economic well-being of the district and state at stake.

Disintegrated Policy Subsystems

Although rare, disintegrated policy subsystems can develop in several ways. Intense, prolonged competition over a policy can push a subsystem into a temporarily disintegrated state and, at times, a macropolitical mode of decision making. The annual battle over the federal budget is an example of this kind of disintegration. Or, repeated losses by a policy subsystem over the jurisdiction of an issue can force the subsystem out of existence. For example, a congressional reorganization like that of the U.S. Senate committee system in 1976-1977 can redefine jurisdiction and break up an old dominant subsystem. Changes in bureaucratic boundaries, such as President Reagan's attack on the Economic Development Administration, can even dissolve an old subsystem for a period of time. The scope of conflict in disintegrated policy subsystems is extensive, often leading to permanent jurisdictional change or to a subsystem's demise. The level of conflict and visibility of policy making are prominent within the executive branch and Congress, forcing issues to the attention of congressional leaders, departmental secretaries, and even presidents, and into the headlines of the mass media. Disintegrated policy subsystems have large numbers of participants at high levels of government and engage the interested public not usually focused on subsystem politics.

Because there is no core of authority over the issues under consideration in disintegrated subsystems, it is difficult or impossible to bring the decision-making process to a quick, rational close. Totally disintegrated policy subsystems allow for policy change by placing an issue at a higher level of decision making in government, by changing the jurisdiction over an issue, or by adding a new set of actors to the subsystems.

An example of the transformation of a dominant subsystem to a disintegrated one is the recent history of the pricing and distribution of refined petroleum products in the United States. Conflict over U.S. oil policy arose quickly in 1973 when the OPEC nations cut off oil exports to the United States, causing shortages in heating oil, gasoline, and jet fuel, and higher prices for all petroleum products. Before the cutoff of foreign oil, there had been a classic closed, dominant policy subsystem over import quotas, oil depletion allowances, pricing and distribution, and other key petroleum public policies. The politics of energy before the 1973-1974 oil crisis was a classic example of subsystem politics dominated by the primary economic interests associated with the exploration, production, and distribution of oil; producer state interests and associations such as the American Petroleum Institute (an association comprised of almost all U.S. petroleum companies); the energy and tax committees of Congress (House Ways and Means and Senate Finance); and the Department of Interior's Division of Oil and Gas (DOG). A key player, Frank Ikard, former president of the American Petroleum Institute (API) and former member of the House Ways and

Means Committee, and his staff had extensive experience in the oil industry and in government. This was a well-established network of influential oil subsystem actors using their expertise and access to pursue narrow economic goals.

The oil subsystem was closed, autonomous, and rarely challenged. It was dominated by tax and oil experts who freely moved information and their careers through a revolving door from private sector to public sector and back. Little public concern was expressed by nonenergy specialists until there was a dramatic change in the nature of the policy conflict caused by the 1973 energy crisis. The old dominant subsystem "controlling" oil policy changed dramatically when Americans quickly discovered the energy crisis in the long lines at gas stations and in increased prices for heating oil, airline tickets, and almost all consumer products. The general population thus entered the world of energy policy, which led to direct challenges and, ultimately, disintegration of the old closed decision-making core of authority over oil policy. It spread to other energy decision-making systems as well. Public opinion quickly (albeit temporarily) turned against the oil corporations. Members of Congress from oil-producing states were challenged by members from non-oil-producing states. Consumer-oriented interest groups were invigorated—and new ones established—to challenge the dominant position of the oil and gas producers and their friends in government over the policy domain. New congressional subcommittees claiming energy jurisdiction proliferated, as well as intense jurisdictional conflicts over the issue. Members and congressional committees wanted to be part of the energy policy-making action because their constituents expected them to have an answer to the energy crisis. In fact, energy policy became part of electoral politics at all levels of government. Finally, a Department of Energy was created.

OPEC's cutoff of oil fractured the hegemony of the dominant oil policy subsystem into dozens of policy positions, making it difficult to set energy policy priorities and legislate an end to the crisis. The old subsystem was faced with intense competition and, ultimately, disintegration, pushing the energy issue eventually into the macropolitical realm.

The increased political competition was all sound and fury; no long-lasting, rational U.S. energy policy was established during the energy crisis. No one dominated the open, dynamic, and complex set of subsystems surrounding energy policy, and the groupings of semiautonomous, dominant subsystems in control of every aspect of energy policy no longer existed. According to Charles Jones, the participation in energy policy "expanded *up* institutional hierarchies, *out* to citizen groups, *over* the other nations, and *across* from one resource subsystem to others." [18]

The disintegrated energy policy systems of the mid-1970s slowly evolved in the 1980s and early 1990s into several dominant subsystems structured around oil, natural gas, nuclear power, hydroelectric power, and other sources of energy. Under the Reagan administration, as other issues pushed energy issues off the macropolitical agenda, the old dominant energy policy subsystem revived and reassembled itself without great fanfare, agreeing on the deregulation of oil pricing and tax expenditures for oil exploration. In short, the post-1973 energy crisis affecting oil producers and consumers thrust the energy issue into turbulence, disintegration, and ultimately into macropolitics from 1973 to 1979. Energy policy making quickly contracted into a world dominated by producer interest groups, congressional subcommittees, and the relevant executive agencies until Saddam Hussein invaded Kuwait creating the Persian Gulf crisis and pushing oil policy to the top of the political agenda again.

Nature of Subsystem Change

Policy subsystems behave like organisms, adapting to new conditions, evolving into new structures, languishing into extinction, and regenerating into new and viable political forces. Subsystems also can be challenged by "outsiders," or new actors, trying to encroach on an established policy territory. Competition can occur between two or more subsystems as well. Competition among subsystems or a disruptive event may expand the interest, conflict, or number of participants in an area and may lead to the temporary disintegration of an existing subsystem or to macropolitics.

Impact of Changing the Scope and Level of Policy Conflict. The power of policy subsystems can be altered by changing the scope of conflict, increasing the level of conflict, changing key personnel, reorganizing jurisdiction over an issue, and using the regulatory processes of administrative agencies and the courts.

The *scope of conflict* and the *level of conflict,* argued E. E. Schattschneider, are the two primary factors influencing the nature of politics and, in this case, the power of policy subsystems.[19] The successful resolution of a policy or issue conflict within a policy subsystem is essential to its survival. If the actors in a subsystem cannot quickly and successfully resolve conflict within their own turf, "outsiders" from other committees, agencies, bureaus, groups, the media, or the general public will take the issue away from them. These new actors in the decision-making system will be able to increase their influence and the probability of a policy change as the amount of internal subsystem conflict increases and becomes uncontrolled. Thus, the primary motivation of the actors in a policy subsystem is to control the *scope* and *level* of conflict associated with the programs and issues within the subsystem's jurisdiction. Subsystems tend to be closed and resistant to externally generated political forces.

Airline Deregulation and Subsystem Change. Although policy subsystems rarely compete for long, a significant policy change is often the result. An example of challenge to a dominant subsystem and a major change in policy is the history of the passage of the Airline Deregulation Act of 1978. For years, airline regulation originated from a dominant subsystem made up of the Civil Aeronautics Board (CAB), the regulated airline industry, airline labor groups, the specialized media covering the airlines, and the congressional aviation subcommittees. From 1938 to the mid-1970s Congress generally followed the lead of the airline industry and the CAB in regulating the routes and rates of air passenger and air freight carriers. In 1975, however, the airline regulation policy subsystem was challenged by Sen. Edward Kennedy, D-Mass., when he held a round of oversight hearings on the CAB through his Senate Judiciary Subcommittee on Antitrust and Monopoly. Those hearings immediately expanded the focus on airline regulation by providing a valuable public forum for those outside the established subsystem, and many expressed displeasure over airline regulation and the CAB. Kennedy also challenged President Gerald Ford to reform airline regulation much sooner and more vigorously than desired. After some prodding, Ford endorsed airline deregulation as a major part of his regulatory reform efforts. He also appointed a new reform-minded chairman to CAB, John Robson, who became a new actor in the subsystem. The result of Kennedy's challenge as an outsider to the commercial aviation subsystem and of Ford's response was a redirection of CAB policy.

During the same period, the new chairman of the Senate Commerce Committee's Subcommittee on Aviation, Sen. Howard W. Cannon, D-Nev., was concerned about Senator Kennedy's challenge to his jurisdiction over airline regulation. The infusion of new players and the competition among Ford, Cannon, and Kennedy over airline deregulation shattered the "holy alliance" of the CAB, airline unions, airline companies, and congressional subcommittees. The issue of airline regulation was highly volatile and competitive for a short time until the major actors compromised and endorsed the reform and a new coalition that favored deregulation was created.

The oscillation between the more dynamic competitive subsystem and a stable dominant subsystem is a common cycle in the American policy-making system. Sometimes, however, there is prolonged and intense competition among actors and subsystems, resulting in a disintegration of well-established lines of communication and patterns of decision making.

Interest Groups and Subsystem Dynamics

The power and influence of interest groups in policy subsystems have increased significantly over the past thirty years, but they have not been all-encompassing. The power of interest groups depends on their resources (such as money, total membership, and the dispersion of members) and their ability to transform those resources (such as leadership and communication) into action toward an objective (such as passage of a law or regulation) without resistance from other actors (such as other groups and government institutions). Resources are of little value if a group cannot transform them into actions that will help it achieve collective goals and gain power within policy subsystems. Powerful interests groups have good leadership, clear objectives, and an effective exchange of services and power between members and leaders. The broader the coalition in a group, the more difficulties leaders face in moving toward the collective goals of the group. The U.S. Chamber of Commerce has much more difficulty moving its membership than does the more narrowly focused National Rifle Association.

If the members feel that the leadership is not delivering what they want—be it higher wages and better benefits for labor union members or more benefits for war veterans—they will not give their association's leaders the power to act on their behalf. Veterans' groups have dominated their subsystem and successfully pushed in 1978 for a new nonservice-connected disability pension program, in 1981 for protection in the overall budget cutting by President Reagan, and in 1988 for cabinet status for the Veterans Administration. During his presidency of the American Federation of Labor-Congress of Industrial Organizations (AFL-CIO), George Meany was able to take strong stands on unpopular issues—such as his personal support for the war in Vietnam—because he had a successful "exchange" with his members; he had delivered high wages, good benefits, and many legislative successes over the years. Delivery of these benefits allowed Meany to pursue a position that was not generally in agreement with the opinions of many rank and file AFL-CIO members.

Even if a group is large, widely dispersed, wealthy, and in agreement on a course of action, its leadership may have little influence on the decision-making system because of resistance from other groups in the policy-making process. For example, the American Medical Association (AMA) and the AFL-CIO have been on opposite sides of the national health insurance policy for more than forty years. Both are large, well-financed, well-run organizations that give large sums of campaign funds to members of Congress, but neither has succeeded in dominating outcomes on this issue. The AFL-CIO's pressure for a national health insurance program has consistently been checked by the AMA.

The probability of an interest group's success—and thus its power—in a subsystem is directly related to the type of subsystem it is in (dominant, competitive, or disintegrated) and its access to other subsystem actors. Interest groups develop close ties with members of Congress and their staffs and the leaders of executive branch agencies. These relationships range from total cooperation by groups of agencies and subcommittees (as in the veterans' benefits policy) to open warfare (as in the clean air policy battle). In interest group subsystem politics, battles are usually among the key subsystem players; there are few permanent friends or enemies. Although often based upon economic interests, the conflicts are usually nonideological and often nonpartisan.

Although campaign contributions can give interest groups access to members of Congress, information, knowledge, and analysis are the primary currencies of interest groups in the policy subsystems. Incrementally and over a long period of time, groups cultivate relationships and trust among members of Congress and agency executives. Campaign contributions, invitations to members of Congress or their staffs to speak to their respective group (for a honorarium or not) or the simple provision of essential, timely information to agencies or members of Congress can help build reciprocal relations in a subsystem. Lobbyists appear before congressional subcommittees and committees, draft legislation to be introduced by friendly members, write floor statements for overworked members, and lobby other members, groups, and agencies for the members who have sponsored bills. In addition, associations play an important role in screening and selecting administration appointees to agencies and commissions. "Capturing" an agency through the power of veto or the final selection of its personnel is the goal of many powerful special-interest groups.

Interest groups, through subsystems, help to bridge our government's separation of powers and federal division between national government and state/local governments. Federal government policy making is made in a wide variety of ways, ranging from fairly open public systems with numerous actors to relatively closed systems with few participants. The location of decision making in government, the scope of an issue, the nature of a policy, and the number of participants, especially interest groups, involved in a decision all have an impact on the characteristics of a policy-making system.[20] The type of policy being considered affects the politics of the decision-making system handling it. Schattschneider put it succinctly: "New policies create new politics."[21]

Yet, circumstances beyond the immediate control of decision makers can upset policy subsystems. Examples of this include the OPEC oil embargo in 1973 (and the 1990 Iraq invasion of Kuwait), the decline of communism in the Soviet Union and Eastern Europe, droughts and floods in the United States, the Exxon *Valdez* oil spill, and the nuclear power plant accident at Three Mile Island. All these events changed the type of policy-making system that routinely handles these energy, foreign policy, water, and environmental policies. Thus, new problems create new policies, which in turn create new politics and new patterns of interest group politics.

Conclusion

How then do we evaluate policy subsystems as a theory and as a way of making political decisions? The concept of policy subsystems is simple but joins a variety of theories about decision making and the American political process. Drawing from the literature on interest groups, sociological network analysis, pluralism, corporatism, power triads, plural elitism, traditional legal-descriptive analysis, behaviorism, rational choice, and policy subsystems can further our knowledge of how the policy-making process works in American politics.

Policy subsystems accurately describe routine policy making, but they are not static, they evolve and adapt to events and changing conditions. Dominant subsystems are the mode of distributive policy making, but redistributive and regulatory policy may range from competitive to disintegrated to macromodes of decision making. Interest groups, be they single issue groups or broadly based public interest groups have adapted to the dynamic nature of subsystem politics. Several basic generalizations may help summarize a model of interest groups and policy subsystem dynamics:

- Government policy making generally is structured around specific programs.
- Interest groups (public and private) organize to put pressure on policy makers in their areas of interest.
- Countervailing groups organize to oppose the interests of existing interest groups.
- Subsystem actors have significant influence over public policy within well-defined jurisdictions.
- Subsystems provide stability for existing equilibriums among interest groups.
- Subsystems provide continual access and opportunity for influence primarily to well-organized interest groups.
- Subsystems are permeable enough to provide some access and

representation to interest groups and individuals that do not dominate
a particular issue area.

- Substantial change in the balance among interest groups served by
  subsystems can be expected to occur primarily through macropolitical
  intervention that modifies the rules and roles operating in the
  systems.[22]
- Subsystem actors generally adopt the norm of reciprocity (government
  actors subsidize interest group actors and interest group actors assist
  government actors).
- The wider the scope of policy conflict, the higher is the level of
  interest group conflict.
- The wider the scope of policy conflict, the less influence interest
  groups and policy subsystems have over policy outcomes.
- The higher the level of conflict, the less influence interest groups and
  policy subsystems have over policy outcomes.

Whether subsystems and interest groups are good or bad is an
issue that goes to the roots of our democracy. The Framers of the
Constitution thought that by providing for elections and by delegating
power to elected representatives they would prevent policy making from
falling into the hands of the "irresponsible" elements in society. In his
Federalist No. 10, James Madison warned of the dangers of "faction," [23] and contemporary critics of American democracy complain of
interest group liberalism, an upper-class bias in pluralism.[24] The
exponential growth in political action committees and campaign
expenditures, the penetration of vested economic interest groups in the
legislative and regulatory process, and the failure of the system to
protect the "public interest" are other common complaints about our
democracy.

Do subsystems contribute to the granting of preferences to a few
favored interest groups, or do they guarantee individual freedom and
check the power of large governmental and economic power bases? The
answer is complex. Subsystems allow for the representation of a wide
variety of interests, but there are no guarantees about fairness of
outcomes in our system. Only guarantees of fairness in the rules of the
decision-making game are given—and those often as a result of
extended political battles.

Notes

1. Charles O. Jones described three types of policy-making systems that
   predominate in American politics—cozy little connections or micropolitics,

cozy little triangles or intermediary politics, and sloppy large hexagons or macropolitics—in *The United States Congress: People, Place, and Policy* (Homewood, Ill.: Dorsey Press, 1982), 362. Also see Emmette S. Redford's useful typology of micropolitics, subsystem or intermediary politics, and macropolitics in *Democracy in the Administrative State* (New York: Oxford University Press, 1969), 84. John W. Kingdon argued that a "visible cluster" made up of such actors as the president and prominent members of Congress has more effect on the policy agenda than a "hidden cluster" that includes specialists in the bureaucracy and professional communities. See *Agendas, Alternatives, and Public Policies* (Boston: Little, Brown, 1984).

2. Jones, *United States Congress,* 353.

3. Hugh Heclo, "Issue Networks and the Executive Establishment," in *The New American Political System,* ed. A. King (Washington, D.C.: American Enterprise Institute, 1978). For an excellent critique of the concepts of iron triangles, issue networks, and corporatism, see A. Grant Jordan, "Iron Triangles, Woolly Corporatism, and Elastic Nets: Images of the Policy Process," *Journal of Public Policy* 1 (February 1981): 95-123.

4. Talcott Parsons, *The Social System* (Glencoe, Ill.: Free Press, 1951), 36.

5. Talcott Parsons, *Politics and Social Structure* (New York: Free Press, 1969), 79. Also see John P. Heinz et al., "Inner Circles or Hollow Cores? Elite Networks in National Policy Systems," *Journal of Politics* 52 (May 1990): 356-390; and Edward O. Laumann and David Knoke, "Policy Networks of the Organizational State: Collective Action in the National Energy and Health Domains," in *Networks of Power: Organizational Actors at the National, Corporate, and Community Levels,* ed. Robert Perrucci and Harry R. Potter (New York: Aldine de Gruyter, 1989).

6. J. Leiper Freeman, *The Political Process* (New York: Random House, 1965).

7. Grant McConnell, *Private Power and American Democracy* (New York: Knopf, 1966). Also see McConnell, "The Public Values of the Private Association," in *Voluntary Associations,* ed. J. Roland Pennock and John W. Chapman (New York: Atherton Press, 1969), 147-160.

8. Theodore J. Lowi, "How Farmers Get What They Want," *Reporter,* May 21, 1964, 35. Also see Lowi, *The End of Liberalism,* 2d ed. (New York: Norton, 1979).

9. David Mayhew, *The Electoral Connection* (New Haven, Conn.: Yale University Press, 1974), 128. Also see Roger Davidson, "Breaking Up Those "Cozy Triangles": An Impossible Dream?" in *Legislative Reform and Public Policy,* ed. S. Welch and J. G. Peters (New York: Praeger, 1977).

10. See the pluralist arguments of Robert A. Dahl, *Who Governs?* (New Haven, Conn.: Yale University Press, 1961); and Nelson W. Polsby, *Community Power and Political Theory* (New Haven, Conn.: Yale University Press, 1963). Also see Dahl, *Dilemmas of Pluralist Democracy: Autonomy vs. Control* (New Haven, Conn.: Yale University Press, 1982).

11. Lowi, *End of Liberalism,* 36-39. For a refutation of this point, see Dahl, *Dilemmas of Pluralist Democracy.*

12. The close relationship between education groups and the Democratic party during the Carter campaign proved helpful in the creation of the Department of Education, but it proved to be a hindrance to the Reagan presidency when it attempted to dismantle the department.

13. These criteria come from Nelson W. Polsby, "The Institutionalization of the U.S. House of Representatives," *American Political Science Review,* 62 (March 1968): 145.

14. Allan J. Cigler and Burdett A. Loomis, "Moving On: Interests, Power, and Politics in the 1980s," *Interest Group Politics,* 2d ed., ed. Cigler and Loomis (Washington, D.C.: CQ Press, 1986), 306.

15. Randall B. Ripley and Grace A. Franklin, *Congress, the Bureaucracy, and Public Policy* (Homewood, Ill.: Dorsey Press, 1980), 93.

16. Andrew S. MacFarland, "Groups without Government: The Politics of Mediation," in Cigler and Loomis, *Interest Group Politics,* 289-302.

17. See Mayhew, *Congress.*

18. Charles O. Jones, "American Politics and the Organization of Energy Decision Making," *Annual Review of Energy* 4 (1979): 105.

19. E. E. Schattschneider, *The Semi-Sovereign People* (New York: Holt, Rinehart and Winston, 1960), chaps. 1 and 4.

20. See Lowi, *End of Liberalism.*

21. Schattschneider, *Semi-Sovereign People.*

22. Mayhew, *Congress.*

23. See Clinton Rossiter (ed.), *The Federalist Papers* (New York: New American Library, 1961).

24. See Lowi, *End of Liberalism.*

16. ISSUE NICHES AND THE LIMITS OF INTEREST GROUP INFLUENCE

William P. Browne

The great increase in the number of Washington-based organized interests spread across many issue areas, coupled with the fragmentation of power inside Congress, has greatly altered the nature of policy making. According to William Browne, one result is that "each policy domain is subject to frequent political change, risk to long-standing policies, uncertainty as to which values count most in deliberations over any issue, and great anxiety among those interests that have long had their way." It might be noted that such a depiction runs headlong into the notion that policy subsystems are necessarily stable.

Under unstable conditions, the "politics of group accommodation" has emerged as "issue niches." Issue niches reflect each organization's narrow policy claims, its identity defined in terms of expertise over these claims, its resource commitment largely to that specific range of identifiable problems, and the provision of numerous services to policy makers— all in a series of actions designed to diminish challenges to its key issue positions. Using the agriculture policy domain as an example, Browne finds that "all the niches, individually and cumulatively, seem to matter in deciding who gets what in agriculture."

Browne's findings challenge the views of those who believe that the proliferation of organized interests in the contemporary era leads to a healthy, pluralistic competition between political interests in the policy process. The politics of interest group accommodation may lead instead to fragmented elite domination within narrow policy areas, which protects the status quo and preserves the essence of most traditional programs. Conflict is minimized rather than heightened, and the broader public interest may not be well served.

This chapter argues against the idea that interest groups are able to mobilize all the resources they can raise to influence a wide range of public policies.[1] It contends instead that interest groups are far more limited in what they can attempt to do in seeking power. Groups are especially limited by how resources of money, time, energy, and skill are consumed within organizations as they wrestle with choices of issues. As a result, policy goals are set with far less frequency than might be expected, and more time is spent restricting than expanding the list of issues to be contested. Organized interests limit and manage conflict with other organized interests as if it were better that controversy be avoided rather than pursued. Thus, some issues, even ones very important to members' wants and needs, fail to be addressed because they appear to be beyond the group's capacity to win.

In the following pages an explanation of the origins of the concept of "issue niches" is followed by the argument that the typical organized interest comes to identify strongly with such a niche as a guide for making choices about what to contest. The issue niche is nothing more than each organization's response to the question: What range of issues should we address? The answer depends on what substantive issues must be lobbied if the group is to retain credibility and legitimacy. Other issues are routinely, if not always, excluded.

Issue Niches and Congressional Change

The issue niche, as a set of issues that an interest group must address, provides a recognizable political identity. This identity in turn enhances and solidifies the complex and necessarily well-balanced political relationships needed to sustain the viability of any organized interest. Quite simply, an identifiable issue niche helps structure the organization both internally and externally, linking the two sets of relationships. Supporters of all kinds—activist members, coalition partners, and public officials—want to know what policy demands to expect from any organized interest in which they invest in a relationship. Structurally, an interest's niche is at least as important as how the group is organized and what internal rules it follows. Those who contribute to the day-to-day management of the organization need a nonarbitrary guide for selecting the most appropriate policy contests. Should they make the wrong choices, the bases for political support at both the grass-roots and policy-making levels are jeopardized.

The changing structural conditions of American government, particularly in Congress, have magnified—even established—the importance of issue niches as a means of communicating group identity. A new congressional equilibrium of power has been evolving just at the time a spiraling number of newly organized interests have formed.[2] Apparently, this is not coincidental. Congress remains the focal point of lobbying attention, if for no other reason than its "open and responsive" nature.[3] But Congress no longer vests power over policy making in the hands of committees and their chairs as was the case through the mid-1960s. Evident today is increased fragmentation with some modest renewed centralization. Fragmentation exists because congressional reforms enhanced the capacity and resources of the individual legislative offices and the subcommittees. In a sense, every legislator now exercises more individual authority than at any point in the history of

Congress. But floor leaders and partisan loyalties have enjoyed some renewed support in dealing with the chaos of fragmentation.[4]

From an interest group perspective, these new conditions have simultaneously created opportunity and anxiety. Public officials wonder who all these interests are and what good they serve. With more numerous centers of congressional power have come greater opportunities for more groups to develop exchanges that bring about useful and instrumental political relationships.[5] For the most part, the new groups have been more narrowly directed organizations with limited policy agendas.[6] Their intense concerns are more easily brought forward and resolved within the confines of subcommittee deliberations or through the advocacy of a single legislator than are a broad array of issues. The advocacy of single legislators is especially likely to occur when geographical representation, as opposed to the jurisdictional representation of the subcommittee system, is at issue. Indeed, any legislator may intervene in any problem when constituency interests from home matter. He or she may even do so for personal reasons of partisan loyalty and affection, even though the political parties have lost institutional control.

This broadening of policy making interest within Congress reduces the predictability of a familiar division of labor among the committees. Likewise, the absence of strong committee chairs reduces the possibility of consistent leadership.[7] Although more points of lobbying access are open, these points also are potentially open to more interests who wish to influence policies from which they were long excluded. Thus, each policy domain is subject to frequent political change, risk to long-standing policies, uncertainty as to which values count most in deliberations over any issue, and great anxiety among those interests that have long had their way.

The benefits of fitting into an issue niche are thus enhanced when conditions are so politically unstable. The more an organization stakes out narrow policy claims, defines its identity in terms of expertise over those claims, fixes its political assets within only that specific range of identifiable problems, and provides a variety of issue-related services to policy makers, the less its key issue positions will be contested and challenged. This produces a politics of interest group accommodation as more and more organizations gain legitimacy inside Washington politics. It is a cautious and largely status quo political strategy. But it works because the set of policies governing a domain appears to be subject to near infinite manipulation, even while preserving the essence of the most traditional programs.

Setting for This Analysis

The research described here examined a single policy domain, agriculture. It was not, however, a narrow case analysis. At one time this domain was a tight alliance of a few interest groups, farm program administrators in the U.S. Department of Agriculture (USDA), and the two agriculture committees of the House and Senate, along with the appropriations subcommittees on agriculture. It was often cited as a classic example of a self-governing iron triangle or subsystem, or as several of these.[8] But this is no longer the case. At the onset of this research project, 215 organizations were identified as active in the wide-ranging related issues that constitute the agriculture policy domain.[9] These groups included farmers, farm suppliers, food industries, textile industries, financial institutions, consumers, environmentalists, the poor, local and state governments, churches, and myriad others. Moreover, research revealed that these diverse interests commonly targeted numerous congressional committees and several federal agencies and departments for their lobbying, even on central issues affecting farm operations.[10] They also regularly lobbied the White House. Clearly, the iron triangle explanation of closed political relationships from which outsiders are excluded does not hold true for the 1990s in agriculture.

In large part these closed political relationships no longer exist because both agriculture and the issues that surround it have become much more complex. Agricultural policy as a set of domain problems no longer equates with farm policy, given the range of interests and numerous contests related to food safety, nutrition, food manufacture and distribution, trade, international competitiveness, international food assistance, environmental safety, welfare of rural residents, and rural economic development. Only the farm sector component of agriculture is small. Less than 2 percent of the population can even nominally be called farmers. Only 11 percent of commercially viable farms receive 90 percent of the financial benefits of federal farm programs. But the collective economic value of agriculture is immense; more than 20 percent of the gross national product is derived from agriculture, and food industries, not farms, contribute over 85 percent of that amount.[11]

For these reasons, a study of the encompassing interests and issues of the agriculture policy domain provides a relatively representative look at American politics. The issue contests are also representative, focusing on redistributive, distributive, regulatory, and self-regulatory policy proposals. Contests over these proposals tend to be relegated to omnibus farm bills, a format that Congress has adopted increasingly to deal with several problems at any one time. Unlike most omnibus legislation though, farm bills are necessarily renewable every four to five years. Other agricultural issues, however, are considered routinely by Congress between farm bills; numerous administrative decisions are left for discretionary judgments by administrators as well. In short, there is nothing so terribly distinct about any of this decision making that would limit seriously its generalization to other domains.[12]

Two studies produced the data used for this analysis. In the first study, interviews were conducted from 1985 to 1986 with 238 lobbyists from 130 organizations active in the agriculture policy domain. Although the interviews were extensive and highly structured, only the responses that refer to issue selection and lobbying follow-up are used in this analysis.[13] Some background information from sixty-eight legislators, legislative staff members, and administrators also is used from that study.

The second study consisted of more loosely structured interviews with forty-two congressional staffers who deal primarily with agricultural issues, as well as forty-six lobbyists and group activists.[14] These 1988-1989 discussions were directed at gaining greater insight into the phenomenon of issue niches.[15] Although I had observed and measured issue niches, did policy participants perceive such niches to be real? [16] My "soaking and poking" among the players convinced me that identifiable and commonly understood issue niches do exist, that policy participants see them as important, and that they are of consequence in allocating power and influence over public policy.[17]

Issue Niches in Operation

First, how were issue niches observed? The concept of issue niches evolved from findings about the agricultural interests surveyed in the first study. The interest politics of the policy domain was broken down into its individual issue contests. An issue selected for contest was considered to be a specifically articulated policy goal, one targeted within discrete government decisions to obtain rulings favorable to the interest's position. As expected, each organized interest focused on only a small number of the many agricultural issues.

That finding was anticipated because the more scholars have refined their reviews of the policy involvement of interest groups, the more they have found balkanized and fragmented attention to the whole of public policy. By nature, most groups pay only partial attention to all that goes on in government. Grant McConnell and Arnold Rose both observed that interest groups in the United States rarely engage the same issues.[18] Two recent, empirically sophisticated analyses focusing on narrower issues offering substantively more common ground found the same thing.[19] Even when researchers posited and observed several interactive networks of decision making, organizations still targeted particularistic issue contests. Most interest groups do not regularly challenge or ally themselves with very many other groups, either on encompassing policy goals central to network politics or on goals that are especially contentious.

An unexpected discovery in the agricultural interest groups study was just how many issues exist in a policy domain. Indeed, the numbers are expanding noticeably. In the 1960s Theodore Lowi identified ten subsystems in agriculture, each of which prospered from its own farm bill provision.[20] By 1985 there were more than 160 major provisions in that farm bill's eighteen titles.[21] The interest groups in the initial survey identified 402 individual issue contests—or 2,764 total demands if allowing for multiple mentions—to which they had given priority for the farm bill or for separate policy action during 1983-1985. Eighty percent of these issues were raised for each of the three years of the analysis. Relating the expected to the unexpected, it appeared that groups ignored much that went on because they continuously had to attend to their own critical issues, which tended to stay on the policy agenda rather than be resolved.

Further unexpected evidence suggested the key assumption of this chapter: there may be more to issue avoidance than limited lobbying resources. Too many policy decisions were being avoided. When respondents were asked whether their group had addressed issues judged (by the USDA policy specialists who assisted with this research) to be in the imputed, or presumed, interest of that specific group from 1980 to 1985,[22] over 80 percent of the groups lobbied on less than 75 percent of the successful issues considered to be in their imputed interest. Fifty percent lobbied on fewer than half of such issues. This evidence confirmed that more needs to be understood about the issue selection of interest groups than the finding that active involvement is simply fragmented and divided.

Two Types of Organized Interests

Two types of organized interests within agriculture were identified as distinctly different in their issue selection. They differed, at first glance, in the number of issues they actually targeted and contested. Twenty-one of the 130 groups were either peak associations or recently formed protest organizations, who gave priority to a broad range of issues. These broad or generalist interests emulated the forms of organization that, almost exclusively, dominated national agricultural interest politics before the 1950s.[23] Of the total number of issue contests raised, these groups were responsible for 1,509, or 55 percent, of them. They averaged nearly twenty-four a year, ranging from a low of twelve to a high of thirty-eight.

The remaining 109 organizations had much narrower agendas. While there were important differences between multipurpose, single-issue, and single-project groups within the narrow range category, these organizations shared one important characteristic:[24] They lobbied actively only on between zero and eight issues a year; the average was fewer than four. Nearly all of these interests organized around a single farm commodity, segment of the food industry, type of product, aspect of the public interest, or some such restricted component of a more generalized concern. (See Table 16-1 for examples of both major types of agricultural interest groups.) Some were business firms that wanted to be represented individually. Most were of a style that, while long organized, became increasingly important in the national politics of agriculture after the mid-1950s. This emergence of narrow interests roughly marked the period during which the farm economy became specialized and industrialized, while a once agrarian society took on predominantly urbanized lifestyles off the farm.[25]

Success of the Two Types

In general, those organizations that defined their active agendas more narrowly were more successful. Over the three-year study period they revealed a greater ability to resolve their constantly changing issue contests—only 74 percent were ongoing for the entire period—than the generalist interests, who saw 85 percent of their issues recurring for each of these years. By itself the percentage difference means little. The narrow interests, however, collectively contested 402 distinct issues, while the generalists, giving far from comprehensive attention to all aspects of agricultural policy, lobbied only eighty-two individual issues. Thus, while narrow interests resolved or newly raised 104 issues, the more traditional organizations resolved or raised anew only twelve.

Legislative, administrative, and lobbyist respondents who were asked to judge 136 group reputations agreed that narrow interests matter most.[26] All 109 of the interests considered instrumental in agricultural policy in the mid-1980s were included in the survey, but, of these, only sixteen were generalists. Ninety-three evidenced a more intense issue concern. The greater number of issues addressed obviously did not enhance an organization's reputation.

Who Represents What?

The evolution of the agricultural lobby clearly has expanded the number of groups that represent a narrow range of issues. Most of the generalist groups were farm organizations, or represented agribusiness; the diverse array of other social and economic interests, including most agribusinesses, restricted their involvement to only a few policy goals. Even the new wave of public—or externality—interests has not attempted to place an environmental or consumer imprimatur on the

Table 16-1 Examples of Agricultural Interest Groups

Narrow interests	*Generalist*
Audubon Society	American Agriculture Movement
Farm Credit Council	American Farm Bureau Federation
Food Research and Action Council	Food Marketing Institute
Industrial Biotechnology Association	National Family Farm Coalition
Institute for Alternative Agriculture	National Farmers Union
National Peanut Growers Group	

whole of agricultural policy. In fact, such groups targeted quite specific agricultural issue contests: environmentalists tended to address safety, and consumers contested issues of nutrition and price.

This intensification of interest meant that most organized interests operated like the farm commodity groups, which reportedly wield the most power in the domain[27]—that is, they framed their issue contests to assign policy benefits only to that segment of the public that specializes, for example, in one commodity, one academic program, one product, or one phrase of the distribution process. Even the externality interests generally did the same. Over three-quarters of externality group demands were made on behalf of specifically designated beneficiaries such as rural residents who lived near farms. While the generalities of clean air and clean water may be at least symbolic goals for these groups, their selection of issue contests led to such ends on a decidedly piece-by-piece basis.

Even the generalist groups tended to adopt the same narrow focus. Only sixteen of the eighty-two total issues addressed by these peak associations and protest groups focused on the wants or needs of two or more types of farmers or agribusinesses. The remainder were issues from the agendas, or within the policy turfs, of the narrower groups in the study. With such limited attention to issues, these generalist farm groups were not using their broad issue structure to integrate policy attention within the domain.

Support and Conflict

The generalist farm groups, however, were quite different from narrower interests in that they encountered more potential for being either partners or adversaries with other domain interests on even these predominantly narrow issues. In this study the generalist groups gave priority to the same positions on sixty-eight of the eighty-two issues on their collective agendas. The narrow interests showed such an overlap on only 36 of their 402 total issues.

Similarly, the generalist groups had competing positions on fifty-one of their eighty-two issues, but the narrow organizations showed such opposition on only 21 of their 402 issues. The tendency of the domain to be one in which active lobbying monopolized rather than shared pieces of policy also is revealed by looking at the number of issues for which only one interest exhibited concern. For 273 of 402 issues, narrowly organized groups encountered no potential allies or adversaries, nor did their choice of these issues bring them into a contested policy decision with other groups to obtain different but noncompeting policy goals. In contrast, one or another generalist group found either allies or adversaries on every issue. Only the broadly based of the two types of organized interest groups acted as a lightening rod for bringing any degree of widespread attention to pending public policy issues. But the impact of these groups was limited greatly by the small number of issues that such interests contested.

Coalitions and Posturing

During the period of the study, this relationship-avoidance behavior also was observed within multi-interest coalitions. The generalist groups were the great coalition players. While they accounted for only 15 percent of the instrumental players in the agricultural policy domain, this type of interest group (sometimes having most of their issue interests outside the domain) held more than 30 percent of the informal memberships in the numerous coalitions that they joined. In contrast, narrow organizations usually restricted their involvement to one such collective enterprise. Fourteen of them claimed to avoid multi-interest coalitions altogether.

Such behavior may suggest that broadly concerned groups address more issues, take greater risks on uncertain positions, and encounter more direct confrontation because they are widely acknowledged leaders within the agricultural policy domain. The fact that most were farm groups might well suggest that, as the traditional forces of domain power, their leadership is expected and others follow it. But that explanation assumes that coalitions are a normal and important part of interest politics and that decisions made in those bodies are highly valued by all participants. That assumption proved flawed.

Only 23 percent of all supporters endorsing coalition positions actually placed the issues around which the coalitions were organized on their own group agendas. In addition, only one-third of coalition participants actively lobbied on issues around which the meetings they attended were organized. While half of these coalition activists were generalist interests, they were not entrusted with any formal or informal responsibility for exercising leadership on those issues that other domain interests determined to be especially vital. Instead, as respondents noted, coalitions were joined for other reasons, such as securing information, making or supporting friends, or appearing more involved in the whole of public policy than is really possible. No participants felt that this posturing was confusing to any important policy makers who, as knowledgeable policy participants, were presumed to understand that a lack of lobbying follow-through indicated minimal interest group concern.

These findings demonstrate the ascendancy of specialization in a public policy universe characterized by both more interests and more issues. These conditions encourage the defining of issue niches as guides for determining what a group might best address. Greater coexistence and political order will result because both group behavior on each issue pending before government and the reaction of most others to that group will be somewhat understandable and predictable. Also, as we shall see later, the new interests emerging within this domain will have less influence on policy because they will in all likelihood be initiating new issues rather than directly challenging established ones. Thus, interest politics within the policy domain is usually about the constrained mobilization of limited amounts of available resources. Lobbyists work mostly to define and keep specific issues as their own rather than to press conflicts or formulate competing policy alternatives.

Explaining Issue Selection: Lobbyists Comment

The findings described above reflect (1) exchange relationships among those involved in interest politics, (2) the high production costs of an interest entering a new issue contest, and (3) the difficulties imposed by the transaction costs of entangling political relationships. This explanation borrows heavily from (1) exchange theorists who argue that interest group members need selective incentives from groups to join,[28] (2) transaction theorists who argue that interest groups gain influence in return for being useful to policy making,[29] and (3) the new institutional economists who argue that the major impediments to serious policy reform are the transaction costs of negotiating settlements.[30] Transaction costs are high for three reasons. First, it is immensely difficult to obtain information about the numerous, complex problems that go into policy decisions. Second, it is likely that many diverse interests will want to participate in policy decisions if the goals of each are negotiated anew. Third, imperfect intelligence will likely result in unforeseen consequences from any new and unproven policy proposal.[31]

These factors combine to produce a cautious, niche-seeking political behavior among organized interests and a related response, as we shall see, by public officials. Old interests, in effect, cling to old issues to limit resource consumption.

At the same time, emerging interests in a domain are generally as conservative and cautious. In challenging old issues directly on any widespread scale, these new interests would have to do far more than simply assume the production costs associated with constructing an organization. To negotiate, they also would have to assume extraordinarily high levels of each of the three transaction costs cited above. Moreover, they would have to do so at a great disadvantage. Their levels of expertise, recognition, and credibility in predicting future policy consequences would be perceived as far lower than those of established groups. New interests know that targeted policy makers, in selecting whom they favor, act with the same cautiousness evidenced by established interests. Public officials slowly abandon old issues in which they too have an investment. New interests, to adjust, avoid those old issues and the entangling policy relationships that sustain them. They concentrate instead on the gradual expansion and accommodation of new issues within the expanding domain in which they hope to carve out a distinct role.

Policy participants agreed with this general interpretation and went on to explain the policy process in compatible terms. Lobbyist respondents made two particularly relevant observations: first, they described the high transaction costs in their organizations as issues were selected; and second, they described each group's need for an enduring and carefully contrived—or high production-cost—policy product.

Organizational Decision Making

Respondents insisted that they practice their own craft from an organizational as opposed to a personal perspective. It was a common complaint of respondents that lobbyists are burdened by the bureaucratic structure of their own organizations. Even consulting lobbyists hired for short-term assignments agreed.

Each lobbyist spoke of endless meetings to decide which issues to address, what positions to take on those issues, how flexible to be on those positions, what actions to take in each alternative event and whom to contact in doing so, and which organizations they should or could use as working allies. All respondents agreed, however, that these decisions could not be made independently on an ad hoc basis. Corporate and mass membership representatives described the need to go beyond their lobbying staff and even the Washington office with their proposals. Consulting lobbyists joked about meeting with other representatives in their own consulting firms to consider whether a likely strategy might negatively affect their image. All described a slow-moving process of deciding what was in a group's interest. Representatives of the Peanut Growers Group, for example, noted that they spent considerably more time agreeing on what they would contest in the 1985 farm bill than they did working to get it.

When asked to explain the seeming irony of such a glacial internal group process in a work environment often romanticized as high-level wheeling and dealing, lobbyists clarified the often-neglected subject of organizational maintenance.[32] Outside observers, they agreed, were far too preoccupied with personality and individual persuasiveness as the keys to group influence.[33] One lobbyist warned against confusing the fast-paced communications vehicle with the slowly determined message.[34] Respondents attributed the influence of even their most successful colleagues to organizational circumstances and internal cooperation, which give rise to what a group can address with credibility. Many mentioned the diminished influence of the American Agricultural Movement (AAM) as an example of a group discredited by policy makers after they observed that the Washington activists were not being straightforward with the grass-roots rank and file.[35] "When members got so many mixed messages about what AAM was all about," said one farm group lobbyist who had worked with AAM, "their influence over policy content was all done." [36]

Lobbyists also explained the benefits of interacting with others in determining strategy, pointing out that the complexity of lobbying an issue had changed along with the complexity of domain politics. The same farm group lobbyist noted that "Farm Bureau staffers no longer know all the relevant circumstances as they did in a simpler period. But collectively their members do." Lobbyists saw themselves as experts on the policy process and well versed in the worldwide dynamics of their own segments of agricultural politics. But they also believed that their groups' members, especially those in leadership positions, provided critical information about what they face in everyday life and their specific expectations about government. Agribusiness lobbyists wanted to know which new product lines and investments to protect, and environmental lobbyists wanted to know which issues would most likely attract certain types of financial supporters.

The process was kept slow for one other reason—lobbyist survival. Because most organizations target so few issues, lobbyists felt that intense issue review was commonly expected by active members or patrons. "They pay the bills and they just want to talk things over," said one agribusiness trade association lobbyist, and others agreed. "I'd be quickly terminated if either I were found to be working for something other than what the board had decided or if I were not working on some part of what I had been assigned."

A factor frequently mentioned as responsible for heightened issue review was the increased prominence of full-service interest group staffs. Publications personnel, research analysts, educational specialists, communications advisers, and consultants perform important organizational services, and they work closely with activist members in doing so. Because the selective benefits these services provide are so highly valued, efforts to promote them often limit the discretion of lobbyists.

Developing a Policy Product

But it is not just this ponderous process of negotiation and information-sharing that helps structure and maintain a group's issue niche. Because of high transaction costs, this give and take could be reason enough for little change in a group's policy direction. Discussions go on between members in whom property rights are vested by existing government policy and lobbyists who understand better how to defend old programs than start new ones.[37] Lobbyists also noted why established groups adhere to identifiable issues over time and why they selected them in the first place: interest groups simply need something recognizable to represent, both to policy makers and for members and patrons. Long-standing policy positions that are severely altered are not recognizable.

A repeated comment emphasized that for effective representation, a product must be easy to sell. Lobbyists spoke of "winnable issues" as more important than the pursuit of maximum rewards for their members.[38] Bad bills, for example, were ones difficult to understand, or they made the organization look greedy. "We have to be seen as fiscally responsible before we can go anywhere in protecting commodity programs," said a feedgrains lobbyist.

In referring to lobbying as "sales," "marketing," "retailing," and "product merchandising," respondents agreed that they sell nothing more than intangible policy ideas, hard products to promote. "The trick," said one consulting lobbyist, "is to take ownership of the essence of one of the policy ideas that go around town. It doesn't matter if it's your idea or not, your association just has to make and keep it important."

Ownership of ideas was well understood; respondents spoke consistently of "my" or "our" issue. Even respondents from groups that addressed a wide range of topics tied group marketing to issue selection. One lobbyist noted "an obvious issue selection tied to the purpose of the Farm Bureau." He explained that its staff wanted high visibility on any issue threatening the production practices of U.S. agriculture. This thread linked the Farm Bureau to actively contested tax, environmental, research, trade, and regulatory issues. A National Family Farm

Coalition activist responded with a nearly identical rationale: "We have to get on any dispute that people see costing us more American farmers." In doing so, he acknowledged, the coalition often acted against its members' real stakes in research and trade. For both organizations, perceptions about the feasibility of their involvement in the issue contest, not analytical information about economic consequences, explained issue selection. An existing group identity clearly mattered in determining who lobbied for what.

Detailed questioning of lobbyists revealed more. When lobbyists spoke of seizing ownership of a policy idea, they were not suggesting only mastery of the factual information needed to prove an issue's worth. They also argued that a successful organization is the vehicle that provides the focus that gets and, more important, keeps a place on the government's policy agenda for each issue.[39]

Groups therefore must lobby to promote an image of what each represents, as well as to advance specific solutions to pending policy problems. When asked how they sold a group's image, lobbyists detailed a two-step process. First, they articulate the general problems that are affecting the organization's clientele, and, second, they demonstrate the broader impact of these problems on society or the economy. For example, dairy products are portrayed as nutritionally beneficial; consumers are shown to be recipients of inexpensive milk products; past policy support is revealed to be responsible for this cheap and plentiful supply; the dairy industry is pictured as habitually on the edge of chaos without that support; and a call for continued government intervention is issued. For the National Wildlife Federation, a peak association with a relatively recent interest in agriculture, this means that its image must say, "We are willing to cross anyone to protect what we can vividly show is a badly damaged and worsening environment."

All this largely symbolic activity consumes a great deal of resources, which are, from that point on, tied to a dairy program, a conservation reserve for fragile land, farm debt protection, or any one of the other conceptual approaches that outlines a general means for solving specific policy problems. The assets of any group are not just fixed on the technical aspects of how to make resulting programs work. More important, they are fixed on the construction of an organizational scenario that explains why a problem exists and what logic needs be applied to it. "Interest groups, for better or for worse, all build their own paradigms," said one policy consultant, "and they have a damned hard time breaking out of them." Once an approach is determined and issues selected, group representatives can keep issues alive by tinkering almost endlessly to make them compatible with changing conditions. In fact, several lobbyists attributed the rise of policy consulting and public affairs firms to farm and agribusiness groups finding increased policy scrutiny. Because of heightened attention, expertise was hired to, in one consultant's words, "freshen up the central issues of agricultural policy."

Most groups thus find it difficult to address many issues at any one time. While more lobbying efforts could be mounted if only external actions consumed resources, both the internal processes of the organization and the workload of developing credibility on new issues are too consuming. This problem is especially severe for organizations that are perceived as outsiders, without domain experience. Until a new interest finds an issue that contributes to ongoing policy making in the domain, it lacks legitimacy with other players. As one environmental lobbyist stated, "You need to come into a new situation talking about one little thing that might work out rather than make a big splash by chasing several big things that won't." All respondents agreed that opposition, conflict over demands, and the resulting likelihood of a policy impasse are what ultimately prevent policy ideas from succeeding in the pursuit of congressional attention.

Judging Issues: Public Officials Comment

Public officials also suggested that development of an identifiable issue niche meet a real need. But the success with which organized interests do so, often through no fault of their own, appears mixed. As part of this study, members of Congress, their staffs, and USDA policy makers provided important insights into which organizations are identifiable, why they are, and how policy information is linked to this recognition.[40]

The most striking point that these officials raised about the expanded universe of agricultural interests was about the confusion it creates. "Who are these guys?" was the often-repeated question.[41] Respondents frequently acknowledged that they had no idea what interested most organizations. And they frequently failed to be accurate in linking specific groups to the issues and policy problems each represented. But they did care, at least in general. Both the legislative and, to a lesser extent, the administrative workplaces housed communication networks that buzzed with a forerunner to Harold Lasswell's essential question of politics: "Who wants what and why?"[42] This question was asked by public officials across the branches of government, frequently to friendly and familiar lobbyists in attempting to grapple with the demands of policy making and the impact of interest groups on the process.

Public officials did not care about all groups, however. The interest groups most recognized and viewed as important were those actively supporting a major issue of a farm bill or other legislative provision on which the respondent worked. These groups were involved in legislative subcommittee or agency planning and markups. In contrast, respondents often did not recognize other organized interests that, for the same provisions, were actively challenging ongoing programs or contesting distinctly different issues. And public officials often failed to see conflict even when organized interests were openly at odds. The high consumer price for sugar and antitrust complaints about dairy cooperatives, for example, did not bring recognition to challengers. Such issues were widely seen, and dismissed by a House Agriculture Committee member, as "not winnable, why fight them, why pay attention?" To him, Congress was already too complicated. Even to federal agency administrators, meaningful conflict between legislators was of consequence, but when interest group controversy had not yet reached Congress, it was perceived to be largely irrelevant.

Organized interests also were well recognized when their members or staff were especially active in a senator's state or a House member's district. USDA officials quickly learned from congressional offices who counted most at the grass-roots. As one USDA official stated, "We get calls. I'm really not always sure why these people are important, but I do know they get to legislators at home on those long weekends."

Legislative staffers felt that the agriculture protest groups such as the American Agriculture Movement and the National Family Farm Coalition, the once-dominant American Farm Bureau Federation and National Farmers Union, and several broadly concerned women's farm groups had the greatest grass-roots recognition in the mid-1980s. All were perceived to be important because they regularly contacted all congressional offices having any stake in agriculture. Thus, these groups gained prominence by talking to so many offices about district problems, and articulating the problems commonly faced by what many respondents saw, mistakenly, as "all of agriculture." Yet, none saw any of these groups as essential to resolving recent issues, and public officials cared little for what those interests actually represented as final policy solutions. Indeed, all were seen as either spread too thin or beset internally by mixed views about policy solutions. As a result, they could not address effective solutions to issue contests. "These people are wall-bangers," noted one Senate committee staffer, "not carpenters."

A majority of congressional staff members portrayed a contrast between the generalist groups and the individual business firms that less frequently request support through grass-roots strategies. Such firms usually lobbied a single legislative office, sometimes two. Cargill, ADM, John Deere, Monsanto, and other agribusiness companies lobbied on, as one legislative assistant carefully phrased it, "small issues with a back-home need." Such issues, that Corn Belt staffer continued, "are usually settled just as [the firms] request because content is noncontroversial, the legislation affects few other offices on the Hill, and because most of these ideas make business sense." The proposals were also deemed credible because they were made by prominent constituents who were local business—and opinion—leaders.

For recognizable groups, public officials had accurate impressions about the issues of interest to each of them. These officials maintained as well that they were rarely surprised by the demands of these known interests. But, even in the face of acknowledged confusion about an expanding universe of interest groups, respondents also felt they were seldom caught off guard or surprised by the demands of new or unknown groups. Why? Because they simply do not listen to a group until its issues are already familiar. Some groups get no meaningful attention because public officials use a highly selective recognition process.

Respondents spoke of a predictable order to the events surrounding the entrance of new issues into domain policy discussions. That order, in which the exigencies of policy problems lead eventually to recognition of an interest group, explains much about why organized interests work hard to establish an image of what they represent. Each apparently needs to define how it can be of service before anyone listens to what the group wants.

The process of recognition, as explained by policy makers, begins when the generalities of a problem in agriculture or rural America are discussed in Congress, USDA, or another administration unit.[43] Problems usually are recognized after being brought forward not by lobbyists but by a public official or an experienced agricultural expert. The media, both nationally and in congressional districts, later comment on any ensuing controversy. In rare instances a threatened interest group might raise some potential policy dilemma posed by that problem. As a consequence of such unfocused discussion, the problem gains some degree of recognition. When that now credible problem eventually is seen to have immediate consequences by someone with a jurisdictional or geographic responsibility for it, a limited search begins for organized interests who have something to say about the issues surrounding the problem.[44] Groups that were pictured as "having command of the situation, really knowing what goes on," as one USDA agency administrator explained, become recognized as legitimate policy participants by at least a few others. Reputations spread slowly but effectively when more policy makers feel compelled to listen. This fixes an interest group's identity and some idea of its potential usefulness among the policy makers most closely involved in the relevant policy deliberations.[45]

These respondents also suggested the prevailing importance of the policy-making services provided by organized interests. Interest groups matter because the policy ideas that they bring to government become useful in ongoing deliberations. To public officials, it was inconsequential whether or not group activity generated initial perceptions of policy problems. An organized interest's potential for influence depends, it seems, on how well or how easily its goals help either clarify the problems or provide the solutions on which policy decisions are based. Organized interests win when the transaction costs of integrating their ideas into policy content are low. Some organizations select issues that bring them influence, others remain burdened by having chosen issues that do not. As we shall conclude, however, even the greatest amount of group influence within agriculture is something necessarily shared. Influence over policy is not just a product of what any single organization does with its own resources from within its own issue niche.

Present Patterns of Domain Power

The findings in this chapter signal a broad shift in interest group influence. No longer are farm groups in charge of the private sector's place in agricultural policy making. Now a variety of interests have demonstrated the credibility of their issues in this very extensive policy domain. The findings also indicate an actual redefinition of influence, or power, within the domain. Agricultural policy exists less because it satisfies the needs of an industrial sector—farming—than because it divides the rewards of public policy activism quite broadly.

The shift in influence and the reasons for it are more readily apparent than the redefinition of power. Because so many organized interests can select issues that service contemporary agricultural policy making, influence is potentially widespread. That potential is realized because the market for policy ideas within the domain is (1) broad in that many desire the products, and (2) highly specific in that those who desire something want rather small pieces of the policy puzzle. Congressional reforms have indeed transformed the market for interest groups, so that numerous interests are encouraged to organize around the narrow issue niches described here.[46]

Legislators of the 1940s and 1950s rubbed elbows with one another, developing great familiarity and norms of behavior in so doing. Without staff and pressed for time, each concentrated on but a few issues. For the rest, they deferred to colleagues. But, as the Legislative Reorganization Act of 1947 propelled staff increases in Congress throughout the 1960s, things changed. Each congressional office became its own enterprise, and committee staffs grew as well.[47] With full staffing came less personal involvement, both on each issue and with colleagues. Staff, however, not only insulated legislators but also made it more feasible for the collective office-as-enterprise to address a broader range of issues, including ones posing purely electoral problems. Any member concerned about agriculture domain policies could appoint a legislative assistant to develop office expertise on any of its expanding issues. Members pursued that option whenever it was felt issues might arise from their committee work or from the home district. Legislators, as a result, were able to get involved in more issues, but less personally, than before. Norms of deferring to committee and colleague judgments, already weakened by less personal interaction, gave way as legislators felt more capable of intervening on issues that previously others would have handled. The conflict between jurisdictional and geographic responsiveness became more real than ever as committees could no longer contain it.

As the committees and their chairs lost further power to the subcommittees through the legislative reforms of the 1970s (especially the Subcommittee Bill of Rights of 1973), geographical balance was less easily accommodated. All this was especially true of agriculture. Agriculture subcommittees were populated by a variety of legislators; some had strong regional commodity concerns, but others had no particular commitment to farm problems. The nutritional problems of the poor, for example, were injected into agriculture committee debates. Whatever policies came out of these committees, in consequence, were less predictable than before. Intricate bargaining between those with diverse visions of the problems faced by U.S. agriculture replaced the will of the chair and regional farm commodity agreements, the two key ingredients once needed in passing a farm bill. Legislative leaders and party advocates felt compelled to use their renewed influence to exercise a say in negotiations. More than anything, the complexity of transacting so many bargains moved agricultural politics from its near sole preoccupation with farming problems to those of that presently broad agenda. The addition of more amendments to farm bills from the floor had a similar effect.

The changing congressional structure and its attendant shift in issues for agriculture meant traumatic times for traditional agricultural interests. They had to learn to provide services to a broader range of congressional participants, some overtly hostile to farm programs. Some interests could not. The peak associations of general farm groups, especially the Farm Bureau and Farmers Union, had fared well with their highly partisan post-World War II identities. Recognized respectively as the Republican and Democratic party voices of American farmers, legislators had long used them in formulating programs that farmers would accept. Even the commodity groups used them through the 1950s and 1960s to negotiate deals between crops. But so much fragmentation in Congress destroyed whatever enthusiasm remained for philosophical debates over comprehensive farm policy. It was hard enough for Congress to negotiate any end product at all. This left the peak associations anachronisms in policy debates, maintained to argue symbolically for farming when it periodically faced unavoidable contests.

Even as symbol bearers, though, the peak associations proved inadequate. As economic times worsened for farming and as farm legislation became harder to pass, farm protests rekindled within the domain.[48] But those groups were only another set of elephantine interests that, while generating considerable grass-roots opposition to Congress, did little to actually service policy making.

The trauma that beset the farm commodity groups was considerably less than that for the general farm groups. Alerted to the declining influence of their broader-based cohorts, representatives of dairy, cotton, and wheat diversified their issue demands to add concerns over disease, research, trade, marketing, and the like to their earlier preoccupation with price supports. As narrow organizations, several commodity groups were nonetheless taking on the multipurpose role that through the 1960s was exclusively played by the general farm organizations.[49] The only major policy adjustment that commodity groups needed was to frame their more numerous issue demands so narrowly that each could be handled in comfortable transactions with a subcommittee or single legislator and resolved without opposition from another.

To minimize conflict on these issues, commodity groups practiced the same form of accommodation and deference that had largely given way among members of the reformed Congress. Issue niches, as limiting guides to group involvement, took on great importance as the keys to identity and recognition. Accommodation meant that commodity groups assisted legislators in developing a rationale for policy decisions and then worked to provide technical detail. These became important services in the new Congress because, while legislative staff played an important office role, they were seldom on the job long enough to develop policy expertise.[50] After group services were performed, Congress was left responsible for passing the bill and for judging which other interests were credible and deserving of some policy recognition.

Commodity groups also learned to adjust their issue demands to the changing, much larger context of agricultural politics. Agribusiness and public interests, in particular, went largely unchallenged by these groups as they gained congressional agenda status. As long as the core of traditional farm programs remained largely intact, conflict with new interests was left to the defensive work of broadly focused groups and, more important, to public officials who were reluctant to foster too much change.

But what made public officials reluctant to see changes in agricultural policy, even when governing responsibilities spread to numerous congressional committees and federal agencies? [51] Why make even a pretext of maintaining a related set of costly domain policies that no longer serve an encompassing social need when such component pieces as farm, food, and environmental issues pass or fail largely because of their own inherent value? The explanation of a shift in influence answers neither question. While many interests now have *individual* influence by identifying and staying in their own issue niche, none can move much of agriculture policy very far. Nor can any of them protect the whole. To gain influence, each group essentially limited its policy options just as the Farm Bureau did when, in another era, it stayed within its philosophically conservative Republican niche to keep favor with midwestern legislators.

To explain both questions, influence within the domain must be seen as redefined as well as shifted. *Collective* influence is as critical as individual influence to explaining trends in agriculture policy. As respondent lobbyists explained, interests within niches still need a broader context in which to place their demands. The symbols referred to in this chapter do matter. Narrow groups find the appropriate imagery in the traditional economic problems of agriculture, even though farmers are not the policy beneficiaries either solely or often at all. For example, an implement manufacturer found a successful "back-home" advocate in Congress during the tax reform debates of 1986 by asking for favorable treatment to survive the devastating effects of the farm debt crisis. The issue, however, was decided as a special allowance for firms using specific accounting practices. Yet, without the harsh critiques of farm protest groups and the chorus of related complaints from general farm and commodity groups, the firm's demand would have found no favor. Omnibus farm bills, farm credit bills, and immigration reform acts passed for the same reason. They provided preferential treatment to an extensive set of policy beneficiaries so that the numerous policy makers who played a part in the deliberations were kept satisfied with the results.

Collective interest group power exists for several related reasons, starting with the sheer number of participating interests. The general farm and protest groups are important for the unique purposes they serve in keeping the symbols of a besieged and combative agriculture prominent. Their proponents among the respondents to this study—who were both public officials and lobbyists from narrow interests—argued that the conflict orientation of these groups lends an urgency to agricultural policy demands that otherwise would be lacking. This is particularly important in mobilizing support from congressional leaders and in neutralizing opposition from the budget-conscious White House. Consulting firms organized around a Republican or Democratic set of agricultural issues add the same sense of encompassing value to final policy transactions with those numerous congressional participants.

The social and economic diversity of the more typical narrow interests also helps bring collective power to agriculture. So too does the fact that the most recognizable organizations have cooperated in unvoiced bargains to get the pieces of legislative puzzles assembled. There are usually few questions about whether a bill in some form or another should pass once it gets to the committees from the subcommittees. Hard decisions as to which interests and constituents matter most, therefore, are not central to congressional actions that involve large numbers of legislators. This was seen again in Congress's reluctance to significantly change or restrict agricultural policy in the 1990 farm bill. Couching so many issues in imagery about farm conditions as well as in servicing the technical problems of legislation also adds to what one House Agriculture Committee member saw as "agriculture's advantageous mystique, its house of cards vision of itself. What we need to know and can't," he continued, "is whether they all fall if we pull one. Does the agricultural economy fall too? So, of course, we don't stop anyone." All the niches, individually and cumulatively, seem to matter in deciding who gets what in agriculture.

Notes

1. This idea is often assumed to be true of lobbies. See David B. Truman's seminal effort, *The Governmental Process: Political Interests and Public Opinion* (New York: Knopf, 1951), especially pages 188-210. Then, for the modern confluence of interests, see the selected comments of Kay Lehman Schlozman and John T. Tierney, *Organized Interests and American Democracy* (New York: Harper and Row, 1986).
2. Kenneth A. Shepsle, "The Changing Textbook Congress," in *Can the Government Govern?* ed. John E. Chubb and Paul E. Peterson (Washington, D.C.: Brookings Institution, 1989), 238-266; and Jeffrey M. Berry, *The Interest Group Society,* 2d ed. (Glenview, Ill.: Scott, Foresman, 1989), 18-20.
3. Schlozman and Tierney, *Organized Interests,* 271-274; and Terry M.

Moe, "The Politics of Bureaucratic Structure," in Chubb and Peterson, *Can the Government Govern?* 281.

4. Roger B. Davidson, "The New Centralization on Capitol Hill," *Review of Politics* 50 (Summer 1989): 345-364; and Steven B. Smith, *Call to Order: Floor Politics in the House and Senate* (Washington, D.C.: Brookings Institution, 1989).

5. Michael T. Hayes, *Lobbyists and Legislators* (New Brunswick, N.J.: Rutgers University Press, 1981), 40-63.

6. William P. Browne, "Policy and Interests: Instability and Change in a Classic Issue Subsystem," in *Interest Group Politics*, 2d ed., ed. Allan J. Cigler and Burdett A. Loomis (Washington, D.C.: CQ Press, 1986), 183-201.

7. John Berg, "Reforming Seniority in the House of Representatives: Did It Make a Difference?" *Policy Studies Journal* 5 (Summer 1977): 437-443.

8. Theodore J. Lowi, *The End of Liberalism: Ideology, Policy, and the Crisis of Public Authority* (New York: Norton, 1969), 101-115; and James L. Guth, "Consumer Organizations and Federal Dairy Policy," *Policy Studies Journal* 6 (Summer 1978): 499-509.

9. See Browne, "Policy and Interests."

10. This research is reported in William P. Browne, *Private Interests, Public Policy, and American Agriculture* (Lawrence, Kan.: University of Kansas Press, 1988); and in his "Organized Interests and Their Issue Niches: A Search for Pluralism in a Policy Domain," *Journal of Politics* 52 (May 1990): 477-509.

11. This data was provided by the Economic Research Service (ERS), U.S. Department of Agriculture (USDA), January 1990. Most reflects 1987 statistics. For an extraordinarily good overview of the complexity of agriculture policy, see David Rapp, *How the U.S. Got into Agriculture and Why It Can't Get Out* (Washington, D.C.: CQ Press 1988).

12. The only thing unique about farm bills is that they are not, as it appears, sunset laws. If allowed to expire, the law would revert to the original enabling legislation, the Agricultural Adjustment Act of 1933. This feature certainly provides an inducement to pass a new bill each cycle.

13. This research was funded by ERS, USDA; the National Center for Food and Agricultural Policy, Resources for the Future; and a research professorship award from Central Michigan University. The methodology for this study is found in Browne, "Organized Interests and Their Issue Niches," 504-506.

14. This follow-up research was funded by ERS, USDA, and the Institute for Social and Behavioral Studies, Central Michigan University. Both awards were for grant development work and preparation of a preliminary report, *How Congress Decides*, USDA cooperator's agreement, Washington, D.C., 1990.

15. Browne, "Organized Interests and Their Issue Niches."

16. They probably do since Paul C. Light saw niches for members of Congress. See "Niches in the System," in *Setting Course: A Congressional*

Management Guide, ed. Ira Chaleff et al. (Washington, D.C.: American University Press, 1988), 49-76.

17. "Soaking and poking" is a phrase inseparably linked to Richard F. Fenno, Jr.

18. Grant McConnell, *Private Power and American Democracy* (New York: Knopf, 1966); and Arnold M. Rose, *The Power Structure: Political Process in American Politics* (London: Oxford University Press, 1967).

19. Edward O. Lauman and David Knoke, *The Organizational State* (Madison, Wis.: University of Wisconsin Press, 1987); and Robert H. Salisbury et al., "Who Works with Whom? Interest Group Alliance and Opposition," *American Political Science Review* 81 (December 1987): 1217-1234.

20. Lowi, *End of Liberalism,* 110.

21. Lewrene H. Glaser, *Provisions of the Food Security Act of 1985* (Washington, D.C.: Economic Research Service, U.S. Department of Agriculture, 1986).

22. Browne, "Organized Interests and Their Issue Niches," 504-506.

23. Harmon Zeigler, *Interest Groups in American Society* (Englewood Cliffs, N.J.: Prentice-Hall, 1962), 163-198; John Mark Hansen, "Choosing Sides: The Development of an Agricultural Policy Network in Congress, 1919-1932," *Studies in American Political Development* 2 (1987): 183-229; and Browne, "Policy and Interests," 190.

24. These distinctions were explored during the preliminary research for the 1985-1986 study. See Browne, "Policy and Interests," 194-196.

25. James T. Bonnen and William P. Browne, "Why Is Agriculture Policy So Difficult to Reform?" in *The Political Economy of U.S. Agriculture: Choices for the 1990s,* ed. Carol S. Kramer (Washington, D.C.: Resources for the Future, 1989), 7-33.

26. Eighteen staff economists with solely analytical responsibilities were asked to judge imputed interest. Another fifty Agriculture Committee and USDA policy makers were asked to judge political influence.

27. Don Paarlberg, *Farm and Food Policy: Issues of the 1980s* (Lincoln, Neb.: University of Nebraska Press, 1980), 44; and Don F. Hadwiger, *The Politics of Agricultural Research* (Lincoln, Neb.: University of Nebraska Press, 1982), 99-102.

28. Mancur Olson, Jr., *The Logic of Collective Action* (Cambridge, Mass.: Harvard University Press, 1965); and Robert H. Salisbury, "An Exchange Theory of Interest Groups," *Midwest Journal of Political Science* 13 (February 1969): 1-32.

29. Raymond A. Bauer, Ithiel de Sola Pool, and Lewis Anthony Dexter, *American Business and Public Policy* (New York: Atherton, 1963); and Hayes, *Lobbyists and Legislators,* 60-63.

30. Oliver E. Williamson, *The Economic Institutions of Capitalism* (New York: Free Press, 1985); and Douglass C. North, "Institutions, Transaction Costs and Economic Growth," *Economic Inquiry* 25 (July 1987): 419-428.

31. Daniel W. Bromley, "Economic Institutions and the Development Problem: History and Prognosis" (Paper presented at the Phase II Social Science Agricultural Agenda Conference, Houston, March 1988).

32. Schlozman and Tierney, *Organized Interests*, 141-142; and William P. Browne, "Organizational Maintenance: The Internal Operation of Interest Groups," *Public Administration Review* 37 (January-February 1977): 48-57.

33. See, as some respondents pointed out, *Beacham's Guide to Key Lobbyists* (Washington, D.C.: Beacham Publishing, 1989).

34. In keeping with Edward C. Banfield, *Political Influence* (New York: Free Press, 1961), Lester W. Milbrath argues that existing influence must be exerted to be felt. Thus, the communications managed by the lobbyists as the link to government becomes meaningful. Because of all those within the organization the lobbyist best understands the "decisional processes of authoritative decision-makers," he or she makes influence real at a level at which others cannot. This respondent, citing Milbrath, felt that to be a somewhat overstated position. See Milbrath, *The Washington Lobbyists* (Chicago: Rand McNally, 1963), 329.

35. Allan J. Cigler, "From Protest Group to Interest Group: The Making of American Agriculture Movement, Inc.," in Cigler and Loomis, *Interest Group Politics*, 46-69.

36. Respondents were first asked to comment and follow up on three questions: "What is required to effectively get your policy demands across?" "How do you go about doing so?" "What affects issue selection?"

37. Respondents to the second set of interviews expressed strong beliefs in the "defensive advantage" that group theorists so often discuss. See Truman, *Governmental Process*, 353-362; and Milbrath, *Washington Lobbyists*, 349-350.

38. Browne, *Private Interests*.

39. These comments parallel the observations made about focusing by John W. Kingdon, *Agendas, Alternatives, and Public Policies* (Boston: Little, Brown, 1984), 99-106.

40. A reputational survey of interest groups was completed by legislative staff as part of this study. Some of those findings support these conclusions about who is important and why. See William P. Browne, "Access and Influence in Agriculture and Rural Affairs: Congressional Staff and Lobbyist Perceptions of Organized Interests," *Rural Sociology* 54 (Fall 1989): 365-381.

41. With apologies to *Butch Cassidy and the Sundance Kid,* but numerous respondents kept repeating that question. It is hoped that things worked out better for them.

42. Harold Lasswell, *Politics: Who Gets What, When, How* (Cleveland: Meridian Books, 1958).

43. The same thing happened when the generalities of the long-neglected problem of agricultural water pollution were finally recognized in both

the Environmental Protection Agency and Congress. New groups had to be identified as knowledgeable.

44. This search is much like the informational scan described by Harold L. Wilensky, *Organizational Intelligence: Knowledge and Policy in Government and Industry* (New York: Basic Books, 1967).

45. Only for a very few issues in which interest groups were small or otherwise lacking in resource commitment did respondents pin the issue niche identity on a single lobbyist rather than the organization.

46. Shepsle, "Changing Textbook Congress," 240-256.

47. Robert H. Salisbury and Kenneth A. Shepsle, "U.S. Congressman as Enterprise," *Legislative Studies Quarterly* 6 (November 1981): 559-576; and Burdett Loomis, *The New American Politician* (New York: Basic Books, 1988).

48. William P. Browne, "Mobilizing and Activating Group Demands: The American Agriculture Movement," *Social Science Quarterly* 64 (March 1983): 19-35.

49. Browne, "Policy and Interests," 193-194.

50. Of the eighty-three legislative staffers who worked for Agriculture Committee members and attended the 1989 Congressional Research Service pre-farm bill seminars, more than 85 percent were appointed to those positions after the 1985 farm bill passed (Larry Hamm, respondent, dairy specialist, Michigan State University).

51. James T. Bonnen, "Observations on the Changing Nature of Agriculture Policy Decision Processes," in *Farmers, Bureaucrats, and Middlemen,* ed. Trudy Huscamp Peterson (Washington, D.C.: Howard University Press, 1980), 309-329.

17. PUTTING INTERESTS BACK INTO INTEREST GROUPS

Robert H. Salisbury

In this provocative chapter Robert Salisbury sharpens our understanding of the concept of "interest." He argues that much of our
difficulty in understanding the role of interest groups in the modern state
stems from failures of conceptualization. His contention is that "it is the
conjunction of private wants and public action that constitutes the interest
of an interest group" and that an organization's status as an interest
group depends on whether or not its values are enmeshed in public
policy. From this perspective interests are not necessarily givens, but
something that often must be discovered by means of monitoring what
government does since they frequently are constructed in the policy
process. One consequence is that private interest representatives must
closely follow government activity to identify relevant policy developments, bring them to the attention of their respective groups, and develop
strategies to deal with policy concerns.

A number of implications flow from Salisbury's conception of
interests. Traditionally, interest groups have been viewed as "aggressive
protagonists," who take the initiative in urging legislators, executives,
and administrators to take actions in specific policy directions. From
Salisbury's perspective, however, much of the activity of group representatives involves reacting to the initiatives of others in an attempt to try
"either to turn those initiatives to their own advantage, to neutralize their
effects, or perhaps only to adapt their organization's actions to fit new
conditions." These more passive roles emphasize the importance of the
policy monitoring work undertaken by many groups and their Washington representatives.

In the first decade of the twentieth century Arthur Bentley said,
"When the groups are adequately stated, everything is stated." [1]
Bentley was trying to fashion a tool, to develop a conceptual orientation
that would enable the observer, whether scholar, journalist (as Bentley
himself had been), or citizen to understand what truly was happening
in the political world. It was advice that was deeply embedded in the
Progressive Era, and it carried an implicit reformist agenda: unmask
the powerful, strip away the ghosts of legalism and abstract philosophy,
and thereby not only know what is "really" happening but have a
much better chance of designing effective strategies of counteraction.

After more than eighty years of discourse and research on the subject of interest groups in American politics, it seems more than ever that Bentley was right, but that the core of his argument—focus on the interests, all else will follow—has seldom been incorporated adequately into our analysis. This chapter presents an interest-based perspective on group politics and policy making. Much of the argument implicitly criticizes the work of others for failing to give sufficient attention to interests, but, like every serious scholar, I could not have arrived at my current intellectual positions without the accomplishments of my peers and predecessors to learn from, argue with, and build upon.

The Dependent Variable

The literature on interest group politics has long been troubled by a basic dilemma. Bentley, David Truman[2] to a large extent, and many others, both in the United States and abroad, have seen in interest group analysis a general (and in Bentley's case sufficient) theoretical orientation toward politics—that is, by conceiving of politics as the clash of interests and establishing empirically the configuration of group pressures at work, one could explain political processes and outcomes quite satisfactorily. Thus, David Easton identified interest group analysis as one of the paradigms of comprehensive political analysis with which his systems orientation had to contend.[3]

Today, group theory is seldom advanced as *the* central theoretical stance for effective analysis of the whole of the political order, but in diverse subfields much of the most interesting scholarship focuses on the impact of group interests on the functioning of governmental institutions and processes. Thus, we have a plethora of studies of group efforts to influence the courts, Congress, national party conventions, and so on. Moreover, although group analysis was once alleged to be a peculiarly American enthusiasm, more recently it has come to play a central role in the study of political systems all over the world. Few would claim that group pressure is the only factor of relevance in shaping the ultimate decisions, but the significance (and potential damage) of interest groups nearly always receives prominent billing.

Another strand of analysis and interpretation of interest group politics has developed alongside the first. Its roots go back at least to Peter Odegard's study of the Anti-Saloon League,[4] and it is of major importance in the work of Truman. But surely it was Mancur Olson who most effectively turned our attention to the study and explanation of interest groups, not primarily as forces affecting the political process but as problematic phenomena whose existence and activities themselves required explanation.[5] Since Olson's work, it has become increasingly clear that any persuasive argument about the impact of interest groups on policy must rest on a plausible theory of interest groups. Group theories of politics and theories of groups, while distinct in purpose and largely so in substance, are highly interdependent. Each may be a legitimate focus of inquiry, but without incorporating results from the other line of work, the inquiry is likely to go astray.

A second point of confusion regarding what to study grows out of the traditional assumption—central to much discussion of America's culture as well as its politics—that interest groups are all voluntary associations. In fact, a wide range of corporate actors, including diverse types of institutions as well as membership groups, can be observed.[6] Moreover, when we map all the pressures brought to bear upon the policy process, we find that we cannot safely ignore any actors, including private individuals, who engage in policy advocacy. They all reflect or articulate interests (as Bentley knew), and it is the total phenomena of interest advocacy that ultimately concern us.

The two words in the term *interest advocacy* present very different problematics. *Advocacy* is reasonably straightforward; it can take many forms and utilize many different media, but there appear to be few intractable ambiguities in its meanings. *Interest,* in contrast, is one of those eternally contested concepts whose usage can carry many quite diverse meanings. There is not room here to explore the disputations over this term; they fill a considerable shelf. Ironically, however, students of interest groups have contributed very little to these discussions and, indeed, seem rarely to have given much sustained critical attention to what the word *interest* might mean. In the remainder of this chapter I argue that an adequate theory of interest group politics must be based on a clear notion of what is meant by interest, of how interests are formed as well as advocated, and of the dynamic impact on interests that results when private actors interact with public officials. I will contend that for the most part, interests are constructed rather than given, that they are continually *emergent* from the political process and are thus both inputs and outcomes, and that much of the task of interest group representatives lies in discovering what their groups' interests are so as to protect and perhaps advance them.

The Concept of Interest

Let us imagine that there are two interest groups, the Northern Widgetinkers Association (NOWA) and the People United for Future Favors (PUFF). Two distinct meanings of *interest* immediately come to mind. One is that members of each group hold certain values they wish to see incorporated into public policy. NOWA may want tariff protection for widgets, for example; PUFF might strive to nationalize the airlines. In turn, however, those policy goals are intended to serve more fundamental values: higher incomes for widget makers and more equitable distribution of airline profits and service for PUFF members. The policy is a means toward the goal, often only one of the relevant methods of advancing its realization. But in using the term *interest* to refer to both means and ends, we introduce one kind of confusion.

Another source of confounded meanings is the frequent interchange of objective and subjective concepts of interest. Two slightly different adjectives might be used to identify objective interests. For example, in speaking about the "real" interests of a political actor, we generally mean that lurking behind the arguments and assertions being advanced are unstated but actually dominant criteria of judgment and action. What is being said is a mask for what is "really" desired. Thus, during the 1940s it often was the case that arguments in behalf of states' rights or unlimited debate in the Senate were essentially a "front" for the defenders of racial segregation. Similarly, an organization urging aid to "anti-Communist" forces in Central America might "really" reflect property interests there threatened by "reformist" regimes.

The other word we employ to modify interest is *true*. Marxists historically have placed great emphasis on what they believe to be the true or objective interests of the workers and have sought to combat the alleged false consciousness that misdirects their political understanding. Thus, it has been said that the failure of workers to realize that their true interests are best served by collective class action leads to working class Toryism and weakness in the labor movement. To be sure, it can be argued that allegations of real or true interests, which by definition are different from those observably articulated in the political arena, are rhetorical devices by which contending parties strive to persuade others that their cause is deserving and ought to be supported. In any case, these apparently minor linguistic modifications of the central concept of interest can introduce further confusion.

Interests, like policies, may be material, symbolic, or any combination thereof. Reductionists may wish to argue that one type of interest (usually symbolic) "really" consists deep down of the other, but such disputes may best be regarded as part of the process of interest conflict rather than essential conceptual matters. There seems to be no reason a priori to insist that some values people hold constitute interests or the basis of interests while others do not. The question is empirical: What in fact do people value sufficiently to engage in political activity (such as participating in voluntary associations or lobbying their members of Congress) to get it? The full range and variety of human motivation are potentially involved, which is one of the reasons that the study of interest groups is so rewarding.

A distinction of real importance must be made, however, between self-interested motivations and those that are not self-interested. Actually, that rather misstates the matter since all motivation must be regarded as self-interested. People want, in some sense, to do everything they do, and they serve their personal values (though not always their true or best interests) with their every act. In the world of political interest groups, however, there is a difference between a group whose actions are directed toward improving the lot of its own members—for example, the widget makers—and one devoted to improving the condition of others. A classic example of the latter would be the National Coalition Against the Death Penalty which is devoted to the elimination of capital punishment—a fate that none of the likely members of such a group could ever realistically anticipate for themselves. They, of course, derive some satisfaction from the effort; otherwise, they would stay home. But there is a difference, nevertheless, not only in motivational basis between what are often called public interest groups and private or special interests but also over their place in the moral economy of the political order. Public interest groups, not being selfish, are regularly applauded by editorialists and academics, while many public officials, noting the absence among such interests of any direct personal stake in the outcome of political conflict, may deride them as "morning glories," or at least give them less credence than they accord to those more directly affected by the issue at hand.

A significant political difference exists then between selfish interests and the others. Is there a fundamental conceptual distinction as well? Probably not. In actual practice a great many self-interested groups assert and believe that what they are after will be good not only for them but also for the nation, even the world. When during his 1953 confirmation hearings to become secretary of defense, former General Motors president Charles Wilson said, "What's good for General Motors is good for the country and vice versa," it was not simply a maladroit expression but a very standard self-justification shared by people of many different persuasions. The observable combinations of selfish and generous motivations are surely enormous in number and range.

At the core of the concept of interest is a particular motivation mix as it is related to government action, past or prospective. For the student of interest groups, the focus of attention is never simply the values or "goods" sought by a group but how those values are expressed in or affected by some action of government, some public decision. The interest may be negative—that is, the prevention of action. Indeed, the underlying value itself may be negative—for example, opposition to social change. The differences in signs are not important. *It is the conjunction of private wants and public action that constitutes the interest of an interest group.*

It follows that a particular organization is very likely to move into and out of the status of interest group depending on whether or not its values are entangled with public policy. No firm or permanent line of demarcation differentiates political interest groups from those that are not political. Interests change, emerge, or are discovered; the actualization of interests is a dynamic process. The implications of this point will be elaborated shortly, but, first, two other points must be made. One is that, given the above definition of interest, the larger the scope of public policy, the more interests there will be. *Why* policy expands may or may not be a consequence of group pressure or of interest group liberalism. Nonetheless, as government expands its activities, more and more people will discover they have been or might be affected. Thus, interests are generated as government grows.

The second point involves whether and to what extent the perception of interests, as defined there, will be followed by the formation of an organized group or by political action undertaken by an existing group. Here we encounter the heart of Mancur Olson's classic argument that rational individuals will not pay their share of the costs of organizing or acting to achieve a collective (that is, public policy) benefit, the pleasures of which, if enacted, cannot be denied them whether or not they contribute to the effort. Various scholars have shown that when people think they might possibly make a critical difference it can help partially to overcome so-called free-riderism.[7] So can the spirit of philanthropy. And, as Olson himself acknowledged, so can face-to-face pressures in small group situations. Still, there surely remains a substantial number of potential groups for which Olson's argument holds and which, therefore, are likely to be far smaller than they would be if all those sharing the same value positions and similarly affected by government action (that is, having the same interests) got together. Selective benefits, as Olson showed, may overcome part of the problem, but substantial free-riderism undoubtedly remains.

Now, however, let us reconsider "the Olson problem" from the perspective provided by the concept of interests used here. How, for example, are we to think about free-riders when the interest in question emerges *after* government action has been taken? Olson said it would not be rational to organize to secure old age pensions, for example. Most senior citizens could be expected to await the policy outcome without saying much or doing anything. But after legislation is passed and a social security system is in place, two things change. One is that "rational ignorance" now helps *sustain* the program, not prevent enactment. Free-riderism now works in favor of the unorganized since most people will not bother to try to repeal an unfavorable law any more than they would work for one to their benefit.

The second change results from the vastly increased awareness of pensioners that they are in fact affected by the policy and vitally so. Each month's social security check reminds them. By no means have all the recipients of Medicare joined the American Association of Retired Persons (AARP) to help maintain the benefit flow, of course, but that organization's growth to some 30 million members surely reflects in part the discovery of policy interests by people who previously had been largely unaware of their possibilities.

It follows from what has been said that interest groups will spend a great deal of their time and effort watching what the government does and monitoring policy developments to see how their group interests might be affected. Indeed, a recent study of lobbying found that monitoring proposed changes in public policy was a substantially more prominent activity of Washington lobbyists than giving formal testimony, arranging for financial contributions, mobilizing grass-roots support, or engaging in litigation.[8] Moreover, when asked to compare the extent to which they reacted to the initiatives of others with the extent to which they tried to secure new programs, lobbyists indicated that reaction to the initiatives of others was substantially more common. Thus, the picture of interest groups as organizations constantly seeking to advance their own policy agendas formulated before coming to Washington is off the mark. Much of what they seek to accomplish only emerges after they are in contact with government officials and discover what is possible and what others are proposing to do.

Interests as Emergent

The usual thinking about interests treats them as givens, defined by a group before entering the political thicket to advance them. Environmentalists know they oppose acid rain and favor wilderness protection. This is where they start; indeed, it is what defines them as environmentalists. These interests are appropriately treated as givens. But consider the position of an oil industry association executive who reads in the *Federal Register* about proposed regulations requiring more detailed flight plans to be filed by noncommercial planes.[9] He realizes that the Freedom of Information Act could be used to force oil companies to divulge to competitors the flight plans of their aircraft looking for oil under the sea. An interest has emerged requiring his best lobbying efforts. Or take the case of a university whose tax-free borrowing for construction will be shut off because the Tax Reform Act of 1986 set an upper limit on how much could be borrowed in this way. Again, a policy interest has emerged that was not there before the tax reform proposals took shape. Although the core values of both the oil companies and the university predate the policy development and are far more stable, those core values do not in fact tell us much about the particular policy issues in which the interaction of private values and public actions generates interests among various groups. And it is around those issues that "interested" political activity centers.

Insofar as interests emerge from the interactions of the political process, it is necessary for the protagonists themselves to observe that process with care so that they can spot emerging concerns in a timely way. Private interest representatives must spend much of their time monitoring what goes on in government so that they can identify relevant policy developments, alert their respective groups, and develop constructive strategies of reaction. Again, we are accustomed to thinking of interest groups as aggressive protagonists, urging policies upon lawmakers or bureaucrats and pushing hard to get things done. But much of what group representatives do is react to the initiatives of others, including government officials and try either to turn those initiatives to their own advantage, to neutralize their effects, or perhaps only to adapt their organization's actions to fit new conditions.

Interests and Policy Domains

Because the most important feature of interest groups is their interests, public policy instruments that, for good or ill, affect group values should be at the analytic center. Yet the most common categorizations of groups do not keep this criterion clearly in mind. The category of business interest groups, for example, tells us almost nothing about the incredible array of particular policy objectives pursued by corporate business actors. The labor category is somewhat more helpful because the array of labor organizations is smaller and more homogeneous in its values. But category labels such as *nonprofit* or *citizens*[10] hardly begin to identify substantive group interests.

If the concept of interest is placed at the center, however, and defined more or less as done here, a reasonably clear basis for meaningful interest group categories can be developed. This classification standard is called a *policy domain*. A policy domain consists of a bounded set of interactions among political actors both in and out of government involving a set of policy determinations. The key term is *bounded,* and its meaning must be derived empirically—that is, whether a system of policy interactions is called Health or Welfare depends on whether one configuration of government units, officials, and interest groups displays more intensive interactions than another within issue boundaries that common usage would recognize as health rather than those we call welfare. Is prenatal care, for example, a matter of health or welfare? Both, in principle, but in terms of federal policy prenatal care is a health program. Food stamps and school lunches are located in the agriculture policy domain, not welfare or education. Different congressional committees and subcommittees, executive agencies, and interest groups can be observed acting on agriculture issues, and so the politics of food stamps are different as a consequence of the issue's location in the agriculture domain rather than in welfare. Within each domain the interactions are far more frequent than occur across domain boundaries. If they are not, and the boundaries are more nominal than descriptive of behavior, the domain's existence must be questioned.

Implicit in the concept of policy domain are several related ideas. One is that different policy questions are carried along somewhat differentiated institutional paths. A housing policy proposal does not go through the same structures of deliberation and decision that an international trade issue would follow. That is obvious enough. What is perhaps equally obvious is that interest groups interested in housing policy—including builders, construction unions, real estate organizations, lenders, groups of local officials, and advocates of increased housing assistance for the poor—will focus their efforts to monitor and to advocate on a particular set of committees and agencies. Moreover, because housing issues have been reasonably prominent matters of national policy, at least since World War II, the interactions among officials and groups concerned will have developed a considerable degree of definition, of boundedness, whereby they are readily demarcated from other policy domains, even those such as welfare or urban renewal with which the housing system of interests has quite close ties.

Both lobbyists and officials tend to work within particular policy domains. In the four domains examined by Nelson et al., three-fourths of the interest group representatives and two-thirds of the officials spent at least 25 percent of their policy work time in their primary domain.[11] In the energy and health fields, the proportion of domain specialists was considerably higher.

It might be supposed that policy domains are permanent establishments, or that this is just another term for iron triangles, or that there are no players among both interest groups and government officials who transcend particular domain boundaries. Each of these points merits argument. The easiest recent example of a policy domain for which boundaries have developed to encompass an array of actors who formerly were separate and largely autonomous is the energy domain. Until the United States felt the joint effects in the 1970s of the startling increases in oil prices—stemming largely from the operations of the Organization of Petroleum Exporting Countries (OPEC)—and the environmentalists' persuasive arguments about the adverse effects of the current patterns of energy usage, the policy concerns of oil, coal, nuclear power, and electric utility regulation were almost entirely separate. Moreover, none of these energy interests was much bothered by environmentalists or ecologists. Different government agencies were involved and the most prominent interest groups overlapped very little. Even natural gas and oil interests were largely separate from one another.

In the course of a decade or so these sets of interests came into ever more frequent contact. A principal consolidating force were the initiatives taken by Presidents Richard Nixon, Gerald Ford, and Jimmy Carter to establish a more centralized federal executive agency. The creation of the Department of Energy in 1977 did not bring all the energy interests under one administrative authority, but it went a considerable distance in that direction. Restructuring of committee jurisdictions in the 1970s left several units of Congress with a piece of the energy action, but there was a much more coordinated focus across the several fuel types than before. Thus, in Congress and the executive branch a policy domain had been established, and early Reagan rhetoric about disbanding the Department of Energy foundered on this new configuration of energy interests.

Policy domains are thus dynamic phenomena. Their shape and substance are affected by institutional changes, as well as changes in the relevant interest group participants. The entry after about 1960 of substantial numbers of citizens groups, emphasizing the adverse externality effects of existing programs of producer subsidies in agriculture and energy altered the contours of those domains in important ways. Moreover, by 1960 the proliferation of specialized commodity groups in agriculture had already so fragmented that domain that it became very difficult to achieve a working majority for any particular policy option.[12] Changes in the structure of domain participation are not the only factor accounting for policy change, of course. Elections often place new personalities with innovative ideas into decision-making positions even though the institutional and group components have remained essentially stable. Developments elsewhere in the world, such as the upheavals in Eastern Europe, also can have a significant impact on the positions some groups take on issues in U.S. politics. The point of this argument is that interest groups can be more effectively assessed by placing them in the specific substantive context of policy determination that attracts their efforts and explains their investment.

Domain-centered analysis is not simply another label for an iron triangle. The iron triangle metaphor rests on the assumption that interest groups and public officials, executive and legislative, essentially agree about what policies to enact and that each component symbiotically serves the others, thus maintaining the triangle. No such assumption lurks behind domain analysis. It predicates that an observable set of actors participates in a bounded arena of action, but they may be hostile to one another as often as not. Intradomain conflict is normal, though not inevitable, politics.

What is to be said of groups or officials who transcend domain boundaries, participating meaningfully in two or more sets of policy interests? First, we expect this to be true of those in positions of political leadership. The White House is likely to be involved in every policy domain of any significance, as is the leadership in Congress. The stronger and more activist the leadership in the White House and Congress is politically, and the more centralized the structure of the institutional authority, the more comprehensively those institutions and their chief occupants will be involved. A weak president or a weak Speaker may prefer to delegate, de jure or de facto, with regard to some policy domains, but it is clear that in recent times more and more policy issues have been brought within and dominated by the central leadership figures and/or their staffs.

Interest groups, however, have tended to move in the opposite direction. The encompassing peak associations such as the U.S. Chamber of Commerce in business and the AFL-CIO in labor take positions on a wide range of issues and are active across more policy domains than most other groups. Yet in nearly every domain both these organizations refrain from active involvement in many issues and do not act at all on some. Their resources, however impressive, are simply inadequate for the tasks of detailed monitoring and timely intervention across all the differentiated policy areas—perhaps two dozen in total— and the full array of institutional components engaged in each—some fifty or more in most policy domains. Other peak associations—for example, the American Farm Bureau Federation or the American Medical Association—find it no longer within their capabilities to participate in every major issue even in their primary domain, much less in others. A few hardy enterprises try at least to take positions across large portions of the total policy space—for example, at one end of the political spectrum Ralph Nader advocates a variety of consumer-oriented positions while at the other end the Heritage Foundation espouses a broad array of conservative positions—and nearly always opposes Nader. Position taking is only one facet of interest group action, however (as it is also in Congress[13]). The larger, more pervasive trend among groups in national politics clearly has been for each to concentrate on specific policy domains and, indeed, to search for a *niche* within that domain, a piece of the policy action of greatest importance to the group which it can perhaps dominate without too much intrusion from others.

Interest Advocacy and the Problem of Bias

What is really meant when it is said that a group "gets involved" in an issue? According to Bentley, our concept of group interest must be closely tied to the actual behavior of the group representatives. We must start with what they do. Several recent studies of group activity completely agreed on one point: groups do a great many things, constrained mainly by their resources, but only some of the activities appear to constitute lobbying, even in the broad sense of that term.[14] As noted earlier, a significant amount of time and energy is devoted to monitoring, tracking, and assessing the activities of government officials and of other groups in the policy domain of concern. Further substantial effort must be devoted to building and maintaining the strength of the interest group organization lest the lobbying effort lose its essential foundation. On average, about one-third of the work time of lobbyists is devoted to the internal affairs of their organizations.[15]

That part of a group's efforts actually devoted to lobbying officials about some policy question takes many different forms. None of those forms of action is authoritative, however. No group can make public policy. It cannot legislate, it cannot execute the laws or promulgate the regulations, and it cannot judge their legality. Interest group spokespeople can only *advocate* a policy action. They can urge that something be done or not done and use many techniques of persuasion. Often the advocacy will succeed; indeed, sometimes success is so swift that it seems as though the group, not the official, had the requisite authority. But however influential interest groups may be, they remain advocates of policy, not decision makers.

The chief importance of this point is its relationship to the problem of bias in the interest group system. Many treatments of interest group politics in the United States and in other industrialized democracies have expressed concern about the alleged bias in the interest group system.[16] Specifically, it is said that corporate business interests far outnumber the lobbyists from organized labor and that citizens groups are seldom a match in numbers or resources for the groups that seek to advance their respective economic self-interests. That much is certainly true, but it does not necessarily follow that business interests or even self-serving groups invariably prevail. The total system of policy advocacy is far broader than the array, vast as it is, of organized interest groups. Every holder of public office—indeed, every candidate for public office—is or may be an advocate of some policy alternatives. Members of Congress do not wait passively for lobbyists to persuade them one way or the other; they too are advocates, as are the more prominent members of the administration, the editorialists and commentators in the mass media, the academic pundits and writers, and a host of other citizens who write letters, attend rallies, argue with each other, and generally make their views known on policy questions of the day.

This total system of advocacy also may incorporate biases of one sort or another. Business interests may well have an advantage there too, as Charles Lindblom[17] and others have suggested. But the question of bias in a policy system cannot be answered simply by assessing the composition of the active interest groups. Many other policy advocates also are at work advocating other interests, and it is at this comprehensive level of interest advocacy that the problem of bias should be addressed.

Putting Substance Back into Process

This chapter has stressed the importance of incorporating their substantive policy interests into any analysis of the groups that press their claims for and against government action. A survey of lobbying tactics and strategies in abstract and general terms tells us very little until the findings are linked to the particular concerns of specific groups. Considered from the other end of the relationship—that is, in terms of the actions of officeholders and the framing of policy choices— the same case can be made. One learns relatively little about which interests are stronger simply from examining political institutions and processes detached from the substantive matters (read: interests) with which they deal.

To some extent we recognize this in ordinary discourse. We regularly differentiate foreign policy making from domestic issues, on the rough-and-ready assumption that the distinction reflects differently structured configurations of interests. We sometimes separate out tax policy, civil rights, and national security, recognizing that different institutional units are involved in each of these policy domains and that the predominant interests are rather sharply differentiated. Clearly implied in such cases is the idea that the special substantive features of these domains must be incorporated into any meaningful analysis of the role of congressional committees, the judicial process, bureaucratic bargaining, agenda control, and so on. Any broadly encompassing theory that is not grounded in the substance of policy interests is likely to go astray.

Implicit in what has been said is the notion that much recent political science, employing the assumptions and techniques of formal or positive theory largely derived from economics, has displayed considerable abstract theoretical virtuosity at the expense of providing relevant explanations of observable political phenomena. It would take us too far afield to develop that argument fully. Nevertheless, it is ultimately the fighting faith that animates the student of interest groups. Without an adequate understanding of the interests involved, an analysis of institution, process, or policy choice will not get it right.

Notes

1. Arthur F. Bentley, *The Process of Government* (Chicago: University of Chicago Press, 1908), 208.
2. David B. Truman, *The Governmental Process* (New York: Knopf, 1951).
3. David Easton, *The Political System* (New York: Knopf, 1953).
4. Peter Odegard, *Pressure Politics: The Story of the Anti-Saloon League* (New York: Columbia University Press, 1928).
5. Mancur Olson, *The Logic of Collective Action* (Cambridge, Mass.: Harvard University Press, 1965).
6. Robert H. Salisbury, "Interest Representation: The Dominance of Institutions," *American Political Science Review* 78 (March 1984): 64-76.
7. Terry M. Moe, *The Organization of Interests* (Chicago: University of Chicago Press, 1980).
8. Robert H. Salisbury et al., "Who Works with Whom? Interest Group Alliances and Opposition," *American Political Science Review* 81 (1987): 1217-1234.
9. Edward O. Laumann and David Knoke, *The Organizational State* (Madison, Wis.: University of Wisconsin Press, 1987).
10. Jack L. Walker, "The Origins and Maintenance of Interest Groups in America," *American Political Science Review* 77 (June 1983): 390-406.
11. Robert L. Nelson et al., "Private Representation in Washington: Surveying the Structure of Influence," *American Bar Foundation Research Journal* (Winter 1987): 141-200.
12. John P. Heinz, "The Political Impasse in Farm Support Legislation," *Yale Law Journal* 71 (April 1962): 952-978; and William P. Browne, *Private Interests, Public Policy, and American Agriculture* (Lawrence, Kan.: University of Kansas Press, 1988).
13. David Mayhew, *Congress: The Electoral Connection* (New Haven, Conn.: Yale University Press, 1974).
14. Kay L. Schlozman and John T. Tierney, *Organized Interests and American Democracy* (New York: Harper and Row, 1985).
15. Nelson et al., "Private Representation in Washington."
16. E. E. Schattschneider, *The Semi-Sovereign People* (New York: Holt, Rinehart and Winston, 1960).
17. Charles E. Lindblom, *Politics and Markets* (New York: Basic Books, 1977).

18. ORGANIZED INTERESTS AND THE SEARCH FOR CERTAINTY

Allan J. Cigler and Burdett A. Loomis

The rapid social and political changes of the past three decades have presented formidable challenges to those assessing how organized interests operate in American politics. The New Deal organizing themes that dominated and framed our political system through the 1960s have given way to an apparently less structured environment, characterized by centrifugal tendencies and a weakened capacity to build lasting coalitions in both the electoral and the policy processes.

The 1960s and 1970s were a reform era in American political life, with an emphasis on openness, participation, and aggressive challenges to politics as usual. Institutional and policy changes were dramatic, as were changes in the composition of the interest group universe, which expanded to include a large number of citizens' groups that encouraged membership without special occupational qualifications. Because nongroup, special interest actors increasingly entered the fray as well, the term *organized interests* may well be more applicable and make more sense today than the term *interest groups*. Many of the new players in the influence process are now such institutions as corporations, churches, state and local governments, hospitals, and think tanks, to say nothing of such "institutionalized personalities" as consumer advocate Ralph Nader, Moral Majority leader Jerry Falwell, Jeremy Ripkin of the Foundation on Economic Trends, and Arthur Simon of Bread for the World. Since the early 1960s, a similar proliferation of organized interests has taken place at the state level (see Chapter 3).

The major focus of political scientists studying organized interests until the early 1980s was on group mobilization and explanations of the tremendous expansion of group activity. Assessments of the impacts of interests were more speculative than empirical.[1]

The mid and late 1980s saw a change in research focus. Although the proliferation of organized interests continued, albeit at a slower rate,[2] the introduction of new federal initiatives came to a virtual standstill under the Reagan administration. Politicians and policy makers sought to digest the systemic changes placed on the table during the turbulent 1960-1980 period. Most interests, old as well as new, found themselves in a highly competitive, atomistic environment, which was both discomforting and threatening. By the latter part of the 1980s the role of interests in this new environment had become a major subject of research interest for political scientists.

Although this volume continues to explore aspects of group mobilization (Chapters 8 and 11), the predominant theme of this third edition of *Interest Group Politics* is the continuing saga of organizational adaptation to changes in the world of influence politics. Much of politics, for all involved, concerns the creation of certainty in inherently uncertain, fluid situations. Organized interests seek certainty in both of their major political realms—within their organization and within the broader political process. As more interests have gained representation since the 1960s and as federal priorities changed dramatically in the 1980s, the search for certainty has become, if anything, more difficult and of greater importance, especially given the high stakes of many policy decisions, ranging from banking deregulation to weapons procurement in a *glasnost* era.

At the organizational level, the continuing imperative of maintenance confronts all political organizations that wish to survive. Central concerns include retaining and expanding memberships, developing stable financial bases, complying with legal regulations, and responding to membership interests and preferences. Paul Johnson (Chapter 2) finds, for example, that even such a powerful political force as the American Federation of Labor-Congress of Industrial Organizations (AFL-CIO) faces a major task in rebuilding its membership in the 1990s as it confronts a declining industrial base and a set of business interests that have learned to make nonunion jobs attractive. He suggests the expansion of benefit packages along the lines of such groups as the American Association of Retired Persons (AARP) as a partial answer to the declining membership dilemma.

Many of the newer groups and movements also face major organizational challenges in a highly competitive environment that may affect how and if they survive. Ronald Shaiko (Chapter 5) argues that various public interest organizations have had difficulty adjusting to the government regulations that affect their abilities to raise funds and to advocate directly for their policy positions. He contends that many such groups have a difficult time translating their substantial resources into policy influence and that without stronger management in the future, their resource bases may be threatened.

Christopher Bosso (Chapter 7) observes that the environmental movement has been involved in a continual organizational evolution and has become more rather than less diversified. He contends that the "intramural competition over policy niches and resources" in the 1990s may see a wave of group mergers as like-minded organizations attempt to maximize their expertise and "clout." For an individual organization such as the American Agriculture Movement (Chapter 4)—which apparently developed the financial resources to survive without a mass membership base—the biggest organizational challenge of the new decade may be adjusting to the aging and attrition of its leadership cadre. A system-challenging group that first came on the scene in the late 1970s, the AAM also faces a challenge to its hard-won role as a watchdog for grass-roots farm interests from the National Family Farm Coalition, a group with a similar policy agenda but with little of the emotional, radical baggage that has handicapped the AAM in the policy process.

The ways in which organizational maintenance questions are addressed have a strong bearing on the representational capacities of organized interests. The mere proliferation of these interests may not lead us closer to the pluralist ideal if the internal operation of groups reflects elite domination. Many of the new groups, particularly in the public interest sector, function as staff organizations, funded by outside patrons or by sponsoring members who furnish funds, but little else, to the organization. Still, as Lawrence Rothenberg's study of how organizational goals are set at Common Cause reveals (Chapter 6), groups can produce internal decision-making arrangements that provide leaders with the discretionary authority necessary to exercise agenda and policy initiatives while remaining accountable to the mass membership. Establishing such accountability is difficult, but it can produce great rewards in strengthening the internal structure of a group like Common Cause, which can lobby effectively at both the state and national levels. More generally, as we enter the 1990s, questions about the internal operation of organized interests should be high on political scientists' research agendas.

Role of Interests in Politics and Policy Making

How and under what circumstances do organized interests make a difference? Increasingly, scholars have sought to understand the impact of organized interests on elections and public policy; a number of articles in this volume contribute to this set of difficult tasks. Perhaps nowhere in political science is impact harder to assess than in judging the role played by organized interests. The controversy over political action committee (PAC) expenditures is an especially good example. Statistical associations between PAC contributions and legislative behavior tell us little about causal relationships. For example, PACs and public officials insist that money ordinarily follows votes rather than determines them. In any event, legislative decisions are usually complex, with an official's constituency, party, ideology, peer influence, and independent judgment all potentially important. Beyond campaign contributions, groups employ myriad influence tactics, including direct and grass-roots lobbying, but it is difficult to assess even generally their separate impacts, although a number of clever efforts have been made.[3]

Overall, however, a look at the PAC phenomenon in 1990, seven years after the publication of the first edition of this volume, does not reveal a political system overrun by PAC politics. The role of money in politics remains a central concern, nevertheless, as the savings and loan (S&L) crisis and the Department of Housing and Urban Development (HUD) scandal give pause for reflection. But PACs represent only one funnel of funds—and a well-reported one at that—to politicians and parties. Indeed, the number of federally active PACs has leveled off and may be declining, and their role in electoral financing is growing at a much slower rate than in the late 1970s and 1980s. Margaret Conway (Chapter 9) continues to worry about the "imbalance" in the representation process due to the growth of business PACs, and Eric Uslaner (Chapter 14) points out the problems associated with PAC spending in the foreign policy process. If Frank Sorauf (Chapter 10) is correct, however, PACs have not overwhelmed the political parties as some experts had predicted in the early 1980s. Rather, parties and their incumbent officeholders often have turned the PAC phenomenon to their own advantage.

Within the policy process, we see a clear need to reconceptualize the role of organized interests to understand their impact in a different political environment. The subgovernment or "iron triangle" model of policy making, in which decisions are negotiated among a limited number of congressional, bureaucratic, and interest group actors, characterized much thinking about the influence process before the Reagan years. The iron triangle model suggests a stable system of policy making largely impervious to information, influence, or accountability from those outside the system, including party leaders or the president. By the late 1970s, however, the context that had encouraged iron triangles to operate in some areas of American politics was breaking up.[4] Congressional fragmentation, budget deficits, and enhanced representation of interests helped to create a much less stable environment. This environment was characterized by a large number of organized interests (including "externality" groups with no direct occupational interest in policy deliberations—for example, environmental organizations), intergroup competitiveness within policy sectors, fewer dominant interests, more openness in the decision-making process, and a willingness among partisan officials, including the president, to attempt intervention even in narrow policy areas (see Chapter 13 by Joseph Pika).[5]

One major research challenge is to evaluate the impact of organized interests in the new policy environment, especially given the diversity of policy arenas in Washington. No scholarly consensus exists on a satisfactory model of the impact of interest groups on policy, although notions such as issue networks and policy communities seem to offer better descriptions of the new policy environment than the subgovernment or iron triangle model.[6] For some scholars the new policy system configurations offer hopeful signs to those worried about excessive interest group impact and reduced open competition among contending interests—conditions that would undermine the bases of pluralism.

A strong case can be made, in fact, that the new environment mitigates against domination by special interests, and that such interests may have less "clout" than previously assumed.[7] Robert Salisbury, in his provocative essay (Chapter 17), argues that organized interests may not be typically the "aggressive protagonists" in the policy process that has become part of conventional wisdom. He argues instead that issues of concern to organized interests tend to emerge in the political process and these interests largely react to the initiatives of others. Thus, groups spend much of their time monitoring the policy process to determine whether or not they have an interest, and often they are unsure where their interest may lie. Salisbury has contended elsewhere that the huge number of special interest players, the increased electoral security of contemporary legislators, their increased staff, the reduced specialization in Congress, and a more centralized, more assertive executive branch, all mitigate against anything like impervious iron triangle politics.[8]

Empirical research carried out by Salisbury and his colleagues in the mid-1980s in four policy areas (agriculture, energy, labor, and health) suggests that domain-based politics is highly conflictual, although the intensity and nature of the conflict varied by domain.[9] They found that only in a very few areas (for example, veterans' affairs within the health policy domain) do organized interests go unchallenged. No longer is it possible for such groups as the American Medical Association and the American Farm Bureau Federation not to face serious, continuing challenges in their policy domains. Despite impressive resources, even those groups assumed to be the most influential do not have the capacity to get involved in all potentially relevant issues, even inside their major policy domains. Research by scholars in a variety of other policy areas, ranging from small marine research grant programs[10] to water resources management[11] to health care and energy[12] supports the generalization that organized interest competition and policy domain openness are now the norm.

Nevertheless, as Diana Evans notes in her essay on lobbying congressional committees (Chapter 12), organized interests have the most potential for influence *when they do not compete with other interests.* As with iron triangle politics, there is a great tendency for lobbyists to seek inside, nonconflictual methods for achieving their objectives. James Thurber's essay (Chapter 15) on the varieties of political subsystems suggests a similar theme: as policies become more numerous and complex in an inherently unstable policy environment, groups are involved in the never-ending task of seeking certainty.

William Browne (Chapter 16) contends that organized interests learn to deal with unstable environments, and what appears to be substantial group competition in a policy sector does not necessarily lead to pluralistic politics. For example, large numbers of interests and government actors, including environmentalists, consumer groups, and the so-called hunger lobby, participate in major agriculture policy issues, such as the farm bills that are constructed every five years; indeed, the policy debates are relatively open and often highly contentious. Not surprisingly, the major farm bills are open to substantial change, which creates great anxiety among those interests that have long dominated agricultural policy making. The stakes are high, and the outcomes have important redistributive implications.[13]

Conversely, much of the day-to-day policy making in the agriculture sector (as well as narrow programs within the main farm bills) involves concentrated benefits for single or small numbers of interests for which the overall costs are small and widely defused. These issues thus draw little or no opposition. Interests have learned to create so-called issue niches by seeking a recognizable identity on narrow, specific issues and by investing political assets in defending their favored positions through the provision of services to policy makers. Over time, groups in the agriculture policy domain have learned to "accommodate" each other on such issues, and potential challengers (such as the consumer or environmentalist groups) do not enter the fray because they do not have the resources or inclination to contest "minor" issues. Browne suggests that many aspects of agriculture politics are characterized by "elite pluralism," a form of fragmented elite domination within narrow policy areas, which serves to protect the status quo and most continuing programs.[14] Other researchers have found similar patterns in other policy sectors, including even the social regulation realm, where business interests, in an effort to reduce uncertainty, appear to be evolving a form of "neocorporatism" that resembles closed subsystems politics.[15]

Interests and the Search for Certainty:
An Organizing Scheme

Writing more than thirty years ago, E. E. Schattschneider argued that within group politics, outcomes depend on what conflicts are joined and what arenas are used to decide the conflicts.[16] In the time since his book *The Semi-Sovereign People* was published, groups have proliferated, many formerly private interests have organized, political parties have grown weaker, and more issues have become the subjects of public debate and government action. Schattschneider offered a meaningful discussion of private and public interests, but such a distinction is much more difficult to make in an era of extended governmental intervention, ranging from environmental awareness to intense contestation over abortion policy and the so-called right to die.

In this volume various authors have drawn on Schattschneider in developing their analyses. In particular, Browne's development of the concept of policy niches makes excellent use of the "scope of the conflict" as a key element of the shape of interest-oriented decision making. Policies also affect widely varying numbers of people and interests. Those that have a broad impact engender distinctly different decision-making patterns than those with more restricted effects.

Schattschneider's basic proposition is that "the outcome of every conflict is determined by the extent to which the audience becomes involved in it. That is, the outcome of all conflict is determined by the scope of the contagion." [17] At the same time, even a very broad scope does not mean that a large number of people or interests will be greatly affected. For example, proposals to outlaw so-called cop-killer bullets with teflon coating affect only a small group of interests, but one of those is the National Rifle Association, which endeavors to portray every prospective limitation on weapons as an attack on the "right to bear arms."

Thus, two distinct breadth dimensions affect how interests approach their political activities: the scope of the conflict and the number of people and interests affected. This can be expressed most simply in a four-cell configuration that outlines four major types of interest group policy-making contexts (see Table 18-1).

Much of what traditionally has been called subsystem or iron triangle politics occurs within the niche and, to an extent, policy community categories. As fragmentation has occurred in many subsystems, there has been movement in one of two directions: (1) toward reducing the scope of conflict and creating small policy niches, or (2) toward competing among many interests in a more open policy community, which remains bounded by technical or information-based

Table 18-1   Scope and Impact of Group-Related Conflict

Number of people and interests affected	Breadth of scope of conflict	
	Narrow	Broad
Few	*Niche* politics (ex.: weapons procurement)	*Symbolic* politics (ex.: flag amendment)
Many	*Policy* community politics (ex.: banking, insurance)	*Public* confrontation politics (ex.: abortion, tax increase)

requirements for effective participation (for example, social welfare and urban mass transit policy areas).

Without question, most groups and interests seek to narrow the scope of conflict. A narrow scope means that relatively high benefits can be obtained at relatively modest cost (see Table 18-2). This is especially true if the number of interested parties remains small and niche politics prevails. Thus, the banking or insurance industry may expend substantial sums to support its lobbyists, but these funds (often in the millions) pale before the stakes (often in the billions) involved.

Conversely, symbolic politics can be extremely expensive, and the ultimate benefits are frequently modest. The struggle over the proposed amendment to ban desecration of the American flag was intense and highly publicized, but the end result would have been a constitutional amendment that would have made illegal a practice that very few individuals engaged in. That did not make the debate any less significant, given its First Amendment implications, but the contest was not primarily about tangible benefits.[18]

Although the bulk of group politics takes place within policy niches or policy communities, it is in the realms of symbolic politics and, especially, public confrontation politics (see Table 18-2) that interests are seen as most active. In the post-*Webster* era, for example, pro-choice and pro-life groups have mounted highly public campaigns in the national press and in state legislatures to press their positions. Indeed, as Alissa Rubin points out (Chapter 11), pro-choice groups have been especially effective in producing a coordinated public relations campaign. Much of public confrontation politics does involve symbolism and emotion, but this category differs from symbolic politics in that the stakes are extremely high. In the case of abortion, they

Table 18-2   Conflict Types and Group Actions

| Type of conflict | Group action characteristics | | | |
	Costs	Stakes	Number of actors	Key tool
Niche	Low to medium	High	Few	Access
Policy community	Medium to high	Low to high	Many	Information
Symbolic	Medium to high	Low	Few organizations	Emotion
Public confrontation	High	High	Many (in coalitions)	Threat/ retribution

revolve around life and control of one's body—central issues for almost all women and many men.

Much of group politics focuses on maneuvers to affect the scope of the conflict and to articulate the numbers of people and interests affected by group-related policies. The evolution of the savings and loan issue is a particularly good example of how interests struggle to define the nature of the problem, thereby producing favorable outcomes.

From the birth of the savings and loan industry until the 1970s, savings and loan interests practiced niche politics that protected their modest interest rate advantages over conventional banks. Their political goals emphasized maintaining the stability of their institutions in a highly regulated environment. Although banking groups objected to the slightly higher interest rates that savings and loans could offer their customers, they did not press too hard because regulations prevented S&Ls from competing directly with banks on most of their services beyond home mortgages.

In the late 1970s, however, inflation reared its ugly head; S&Ls could not compete with the high interest rates offered by money market funds and other financial instruments, and billions of dollars flowed out of the savings institutions. Thus, savings interests lobbied Congress to change the rules under which they operated. Niche politics evolved quickly into policy community politics, in which banking, savings, and other financial interests moved to compete in a deregulated environment. Savings institutions won the right to offer higher interest rates and to make loans that were more profitable (and riskier) than home mortgages. In addition, savings and loan accounts were federally insured to $100,000, up from $40,000, in another move to maintain high levels of savings assets.[19]

Savings and loan actors—groups, institutions, and individual entrepreneurs—then became players within the broader financial policy community, where decision making was much more competitive and significant to increasing numbers of individuals and interests. Still, in the early 1980s the scope of the conflict remained modest, even in the face of early savings and loan scandals in the "oil patch" of Texas and Oklahoma, where declining oil prices led to the failure of an increasing number of financial institutions (see Table 18-3).[20] Even as some reporters and newspapers were beginning to raise questions about the deregulated savings industry, its major interest groups sought to reduce the scope of conflict. In their chronicle of the S&L debacle, Stephen Pizzo et al. noted that "trade groups like the powerful U.S. League of Savings Institutions worked overtime to make sure that the industry's dirty little secret [that there was substantial fraud, aside from misman-agement] never got out." [21] Even when the outlines of problems in the savings industry were taking shape, its lobbying operation functioned effectively in policy community politics. With savings and loans in every congressional district, tremendous pressure was applied. Rep. Charles Schumer, D-N.Y., observed that "the thrifts have a lot of clout, and they lobbied us very heavily. They did a full-court press and very effectively." [22]

Only in the late 1980s did the scope of conflict broaden as the savings and loan "problem" was labeled a full-fledged "disaster" with a possible price tag of $500 billion.[23] At this point, interests far beyond the financial policy community had become involved. Given the budgetary implications of a $100 billion to $500 billion bailout, few interests were not affected by the savings and loan debacle. Moreover, elected officials, especially in Congress, were faced with increasing public dismay over the issue—with its great costs and panoply of illegal and unethical activities.

The savings and loan bailout did briefly enter the public con-frontation arena, but the complex nature of the problem and its potential threat to the economy did not allow for extended public discussion (in contrast to abortion or gun control, which can absorb almost limitless argument). Still, the savings and loan lobby had little luck in affecting policies put in place to "rescue" the industry.

In the wake of the 1989 establishment of the Resolution Trust Corporation, the savings issue proceeded toward the symbolic politics quadrant; the key financial decisions already had been made, and the central political issue remaining was the apportionment of blame. Thus, by 1990 the most visible side of savings and loan politics had

Table 18-3 Evolution of Group Politics on Savings and Loan Policies

Niche politics	*Symbolic politics*
1930s to 1970s	1990-
• Small subgovernment	• S&Ls as electoral issue
• Little competition	• Key policy decisions already made
• Great stability	• Blame apportionment

Policy community politics	*Public confrontation politics*
Most of 1980s to 1990	Mid to late 1980s
• Little stability	• Many actors, many not from policy community
• More actors, most in financial community	• Executive, congressional leaders involved
• Warnings of impending crisis	• Great conflict
• Substantial competition	• Omnibus deal produced (Resolution Trust Corporation)

been reduced to finger pointing and blame assessment, with members of Congress being most vulnerable to charges of favoritism and incompetence. In addition, George Bush's son Neil became embroiled in the scandal because of his position as a director of a failed Denver S&L (Silverado). More than any other event, Neil Bush's involvement personalized the politics of the savings industry, mostly at a symbolic, blame-assessment level. At the same time, the bulk of decision making on savings policy returned to the financial policy community, where the contending interests (banks, savings institutions, governmental regulators, and other financial actors) could work through the endless difficulties of implementing the restructuring of the savings industry.[24]

Conclusion

In tandem with the growth of government in the 1960s and 1970s, organized interests grew more numerous and more active within the increasingly complex American policy-making process.[25] Many new groups formed to deal effectively with what Anthony King labeled in 1978 the "shifting sands of American politics."[26] And, although the Reagan administration failed to reduce the overall size of government, it did continue to change the nature of the policy challenges facing many groups: deregulation, reduced domestic spending, and increased financial responsibilities by the states.

Given the series of large annual budget deficits and the growing national debt, organized interests will continue to seek stability by working to retain existing programs, rather than fighting for new or expanded initiatives. Groups cannot reduce uncertainties just by maintaining program funding, however; federal regulations may impose costs that far outweigh any benefits from continued funding. The 1990 farm bill, for example, sets commodity subsidies at the same levels as the 1985 legislation, but contains conservation and environmental provisions that may well escalate farming costs. In this context, farm groups must contend with other interests inside the agriculture policy community as well as with consumer groups, environmental interests, and administration forces that seek to cut budgets.

The uncertainties within the agriculture sector are mirrored in other areas as well, including transportation, education, and health care. Budget limitations and increased levels of federal intervention (for example, Medicare reimbursement) create uncertainties to which groups must continually adapt. And the search for certainty is often as great inside organizations as it is within the broader policy community. All interests—membership groups (such as the National Rifle Association), private institutions (such as universities), or trade associations (such as the National Association of Manufacturers)—seek certainty, and their endeavors are unceasing. Next year's budget, or a proposed change in regulations, or an external event (for example, higher oil prices) will continually require adjustments. More and more, group resources are spent monitoring a growing set of complex policy environments.

This kind of policy environment affects the organizational maintenance efforts of many groups. The entitlement revolution begun in the 1960s has created high expectations among many people for enhanced governmental benefits, and interest groups have been quick to take credit for such gains. Still, leaders' explanations to group members that losses have been kept to a minimum may be more difficult to sell than claims of credit for program expansion. Although we tend to think of organized interests existing forever—for example, the National Rifle Association, the American Medical Association, or even Common Cause—the fact is that many groups fail.

In the end, the most successful organized interests will respond effectively both to internal demands and external circumstances. In an era of fiscal restraint, however, almost every interest stands to lose something within the policy process. How interest groups contend with this redistributive environment may be a hallmark of interest-based politics in the 1990s.

Notes

1. For a review of the interest group literature before 1975, see Robert H. Salisbury, "Interest Groups," in *Handbook of Political Science,* vol. 4, ed. Fred I. Greenstein and Nelson Polsby (Reading, Mass.: Addison-Wesley, 1975). Also see Allan J. Cigler, "Interest Groups: A Subfield in Search of an Identity," in *Political Science: Looking to the Future,* vol. 4, ed. William Crotty (Evanston, Ill.: Northwestern University Press, forthcoming) for a review of the more recent work dealing with interest group politics.
2. Mark A. Peterson and Jack L. Walker, "Interest Group Responses to Partisan Change: The Impact of the Reagan Administration upon the National Interest Group System," in *Interest Group Politics,* 2d ed., ed. Allan J. Cigler and Burdett A. Loomis (Washington, D.C.: CQ Press, 1986), 162-182.
3. See, for example, John R. Wright, "Contributions, Lobbying and Committee Voting in the U.S. House of Representatives," *American Political Science Review* 84 (June 1990): 417-438.
4. Tom L. Gais, Mark A. Peterson, and Jack L. Walker, "Interest Groups, Iron Triangles, and Representative Institutions in American National Government," *British Journal of Political Science* 14 (April 1984): 161-185.
5. Ibid.
6. See, for example, Hugh Heclo, "Issue Networks and the Executive Establishment," in *The New American Political System,* ed. Anthony King (Washington, D.C.: American Enterprise Institute, 1978), 87-124; and Jeffrey M. Berry, "Subgovernments, Issue Networks and Issue Conflict," in *Remaking American Politics,* ed. Richard M. Harris and Sidney M. Milkis (Boulder, Colo.: Westview Press, 1989), 239-260.
7. Robert H. Salisbury, "The Paradox of Interest Groups in Washington— More Groups, Less Clout," in *The New American Political System,* 2d ed., ed. Anthony King (Washington, D.C.: AEI Press, 1990), 203-229.
8. Ibid., 229.
9. Robert H. Salisbury et al., "Who Works with Whom? Interest Group Alliances and Opposition," *American Political Science Review* 81 (December 1987): 1217-1234.
10. Lauriston R. King and W. Wayne Shannon, "Political Networks in the Policy Process: The Case of the National Sea Grant College Program," *Polity* 19 (1986): 213-231.
11. Daniel McCool, *Command of the Waters* (Berkeley, Calif.: University of California Press, 1989).
12. Edward D. Lauman and David Knoke, *The Organization State* (Madison, Wis.: University of Wisconsin Press, 1987).
13. William P. Browne, *Private Interests, Public Policy, and American Agriculture* (Lawrence, Kan.: University of Kansas Press, 1988).
14. William P. Browne, "Organized Interests and Their Issue Niches: A

Search for Pluralism in a Policy Domain," *Journal of Politics* 52 (May 1990): 477-509.

15. *Neocorporatism* refers to a system by which political conflicts among contending interests are "managed" for efficiency reasons and in an attempt to reduce uncertainty for the participants. Richard Harris, for example, has contended that within parts of the usually contentious social regulation domain, business interests and their public interest opponents, over time, have developed a "certain level of empathy and mutual respect," which has brought the interests "into more or less formal arrangements through which policy conflict can be managed." The style of such politics is collaborative rather than combative. See Harris, "Politicized Management: The Changing Face of Business in American Politics," in Harris and Milkis, *Remaking American Politics,* 261-286.

16. E. E. Schattschneider, *The Semi-Sovereign People* (New York: Holt, Rinehart & Winston: 1960), 2.

17. Ibid.

18. Symbolism in politics remains a complex subject. For illuminating discussions of the tangible and the symbolic, see Murray Edelman, *The Symbolic Uses of Politics* (Urbana, Ill.: University of Illinois Press, 1964); and Edelman, *Political Language* (New York: Academic Press, 1977).

19. For the most complete picture of the savings and loan disaster, see Stephen Pizzo, Mary Fricker, and Paul Muolo, *Inside Job* (New York: McGraw-Hill, 1990).

20. Ibid., 19-20.

21. Ibid., 15.

22. Kathleen Day, "The Decline and Fall of a Powerful Lobby," *Washington Post National Weekly Edition,* August 7-13, 1989, 19.

23. David E. Rosenbaum, "A Financial Disaster with Many Culprits," *New York Times,* June 5, 1990, C1.

24. This bears substantial resemblance to Anthony Downs's notion of an "issue-attention cycle" in agenda setting and policy formulation. See Downs, "Up and Down with Ecology: The Issue-Attention Cycle," *The Public Interest* (Summer 1972): 38-50.

25. Among others, see Kay Schlozman and John Tierney, *Organized Interests and American Democracy* (New York: Harper and Row, 1986).

26. Anthony King, "The American Polity in the Late 1970s: Building Coalitions in the Sand," in Anthony King, ed., *The New American Political System* (Washington, D.C.: American Enterprise Institute, 1978), 371-395.

CONTRIBUTORS

Christopher J. Bosso is an associate professor of political science at Northeastern University. His teaching and research interests include American politics and policy processes, particularly environmental policy making.

William P. Browne is a professor of political science at Central Michigan University. Most of his research has been in agricultural policy or interest groups, including work with the Economic Research Service of the U.S. Department of Agriculture.

Allan J. Cigler is a professor of political science at the University of Kansas. His research and teaching interests include political parties, participation, psychology and politics, and interest groups.

M. Margaret Conway teaches at the University of Florida. She received her Ph.D. from Indiana University in 1965. She has written or coauthored several books focusing on political participation and political parties. She also has published a number of articles in academic journals.

Diana M. Evans is an associate professor of political science at Trinity College. Her research interests include interest groups and congressional committees, as well as congressional-executive interactions in policy making.

Allen D. Hertzke is assistant director of the Carl Albert Congressional Research and Studies Center and assistant professor of political science at the University of Oklahoma. He has a published a book and a number of articles and book chapters on the role of religion in American political life. He is currently writing a book on church-based populist politics.

Ronald J. Hrebenar is a professor of political science at the University of Utah. With Clive S. Thomas, he is coeditor of a series of books on interest group politics in the states. He specializes in interest groups and political party politics.

Paul E. Johnson is an assistant professor of political science at the University of Kansas and is currently a visiting assistant professor of politics at the Yale School of Management. His primary substantive interests include national interest groups and congressional decision making; he has published research articles on these topics in several academic journals. He also is coauthor of a college text on American government.

Burdett A. Loomis is a professor of political science at the University of Kansas. His writing and research deal with political careers, legislatures, and interest groups.

Joseph A. Pika is an associate professor of political science at the University of Delaware. His publications include reviews of presidency research as a field, studies of White House staffing, and analyses of presidential relations with Congress and interest groups. He is currently coauthoring a book on the presidency. He is involved with ongoing projects focusing on White House management and White House relations with interest groups from Roosevelt through Reagan.

Lawrence S. Rothenberg is an assistant professor of political science and public policy at the University of Rochester. His research interests revolve around organized groups and bureaucratic politics. He is currently writing a book on Common Cause and working on another book tracing the politics of transportation regulation.

Alissa Rubin reports on abortion and reproductive health politics for Knight-Ridder Newspaper's Washington bureau. Her interests include politics and moral issues.

Robert H. Salisbury is the Souers Professor of American Government at Washington University. In addition to a large-scale collaborative investigation of interest representation (with Heinz, Laumann, and Nelson), he is writing a book on American pluralism.

Ronald G. Shaiko is an assistant professor of government at American University. His research and teaching interests include interest group politics, congressional representation, and political campaigning. He is currently working on projects that focus on public interest organizational maintenance and representation and on interest group influences on constituent letter writing.

Frank J. Sorauf has taught political science at the University of Minnesota since 1961. He has written about PACs and political parties and has recently written a book about money in elections.

Clive S. Thomas is a professor of political science at the University of Alaska—Southeast at Juneau. He is coeditor with Ronald J. Hrebenar of a series of books on interest group politics in the states. He also has worked as a lobbyist in Alaskan state politics.

James A. Thurber is a professor of government and director of the Center for Congressional and Presidential Studies at American University. He has coauthored a book on congressional management and has published numerous articles on Congress, interest groups, and congressional budgeting.

Eric M. Uslaner is a professor of government and politics at the University of Maryland—College Park. In 1981-1982 he was Fulbright professor of American studies and political science at the Hebrew University, Jerusalem, Israel. His interests focus on Congress, elections, energy policy, and Canadian politics. He is the author or coauthor of four books and more than fifty articles in professional journals.

INDEX